Cease and Desist, An Unwanted Companion

By Abbe de Vere

First published in Great Britain in 2026
by Dragon Publishing / The Royal Dragon Court ®
www.royaldragoncourt.com

ISBN Paperback 978-1-918588-98-9
ISBN Hardback 978-1-918588-99-6

Ebook 978-1-918588-64-4

Library and Cataloguing Data available from the British Library
Cover design, internal layout, and editorial production Dragon Publishing©.

Copyright acknowledgments

Every reasonable effort has been made to identify and acknowledge the copyright holders of quoted material and images. Ancient and pre-1900 sources are treated as public-domain material where applicable. Modern extracts are reproduced only where necessary for fair dealing, quotation, criticism, review, scholarly reference, and evidential comparison.

This work has been prepared by Abbe de Vere, rights holder, editor, publisher, and literary representative of the Nicholas de Vere / Dragon Publishing material under review. The purpose of this book is to examine and critique the use of material connected to my owned and administered works, including The Dragon Legacy, The Dragon Cede, the House of Vere material, and the wider Royal Dragon Court / Dragon Publishing source-field.

This book has been prepared in response to correspondence from the publisher requesting specific examples of the passages, quotations, excerpts, or portions of text forming the basis of my complaint. Any third-party extracts are reproduced only where necessary for criticism, review, quotation, evidential comparison, and formal response.

An additional disclaimer and reservation of rights appears at the back of this book.

A Dragon Publishing Title

Motto:* Vero Nihil Verius — *Nothing Truer Than Truth

Preliminary Copyright and Framework Comparison Review
Prepared by Abbe de Vere, Dragon Publishing

This review does not reproduce Gary Wayne's work as substitute reading material. It uses limited extracts only where necessary to demonstrate overlap, citation-chain reliance, source displacement, and hostile recharacterisation of Nicholas de Vere's Dragon Legacy / Dragon Cede / House of Vere framework

For the benefit of formally recording my concerns, I am preparing this chapter-by-chapter comparison to examine the extent to which Gary Wayne's work appears to rely upon, reproduce, paraphrase, restructure, or otherwise apply the copyrighted work, terminology, genealogical framework, and distinctive presentation of Nicholas de Vere, Laurence Gardner, and related Dragon Publishing material.

This review concerns, in particular, material drawn from or associated with:

The Dragon Legacy by Nicholas de Vere;

The Dragon Cede by Nicholas de Vere and Michael Hunter;

Co Authored works:

The Realm of the Ring Lords; Laurence Gardner

Genesis of the Grail Kings; Laurence Gardner

and other works or passages in which Nicholas de Vere's research, writing, contribution, terminology, genealogy, and framework appear to have been used.

I, Abbe de Vere, am the legal heir and copyright representative of Nicholas de Vere's literary estate. I also hold and administer the Dragon Publishing editions of *The Dragon Legacy* and *The Dragon Cede*, and I assert my rights in relation to the works, editorial material, inherited copyright, and associated Dragon Publishing intellectual property. Along with the owner of

The Royal Dragon Court trademark is registered in the UK and has be en filed with the UK Intellectual Property Office (UKIPO). The trade mark application number is #UK00004277183, and it is currently registered.

The trademark covers various products related to book covers, jackets, and other book related items, as well as educational and entertainment services

CONTENTS

Process, AI-Assisted Review, and Omissions Notice

Disclaimer,

For transparency, I need to state that I have used ChatGPT as a tool for the review process.

In order to carry out this review, I had to upload my own books, along with chapters of Gary Wayne's books, initially only where my father's work and Laurence Gardner's work had been cited. As I also stand from an emotional viewpoint, I had to ensure that my work did not carry any accusations, defamatory wording, or anything that I could not prove.

For this reason, I used a framework to review each page. Where some wording is repeated, this is because each chapter had to ask the same necessary questions: is this fair use, is this hidden citation, is this framework reliance, is this paraphrasing, is this direct citation, and is this material being used in a way that requires further concern?

I have had to purchase both books of Gary Wayne's, which both have over 1,000 pages of content. My main review is on the second book. However, now that I have seen the whole situation, it is clear to me that it is not just the second book that has discrepancies.

Due to further investigation of my own, literally going through some chapters, like looking for a needle in a haystack and trying to be fair, I may have missed some material. On the odd occasion, I have also found nuances where chapters do not cite my father's work directly, but where, in my opinion, through hidden citation, framework reliance, or surrounding context, the work still appears to have been very much in the mind of the author when writing it.

Likewise with the podcast interviews, I have paid for and downloaded certain podcasts, Had to listen to hours of these interviews and copied the transcripts in order to find certain information, admissions by Gary Wayne, and context that is directly associated with my books, my father's work, Laurence Gardner's work, and the wider Dragon Publishing / Royal Dragon Court framework.

I needed a second opinion. A voice of reason at a time when I was bewildered and upset with what I had found. I had to ensure my legal position. This is why I questioned myself several times when writing this book.

Where I have not given citation, this is my own experience, voice, observation, freedom of expression of opinion, and my own account of events.

This is not a flaw, This is integrity and honestly, When I first started this process on the 10th June 2026, I have been up until 3am most nights, working some 17 plus hours a day, Which already is over 25 days straight working on this same investigation, Is over 425 hours of dedication to this book.

Every page has been manually reviewed and edited by me. ChatGPT did not investigate the material independently, formulate the complaint, or determine the conclusions of this review. It acted solely as an editorial, structural, framework and an analytical assistant, helping me organise evidence, maintain consistency throughout the review process, refine language where appropriate, and identify wording that could otherwise become speculative, defamatory, or legally unsupported.

Ultimately, I remain solely responsible for the contents of this publication. Any errors, omissions, or conclusions are my own.

Likewise, any legal opinions, criticism, commentary, or analysis expressed throughout this book are mine alone, As I apply my knowledge and law degree whilst delivering this critique review.

INTRODUCTION

At the beginning of this review, I will set out my own books, *The Dragon Legacy*, *The Dragon Cede*, and the House of Vere material written by my father. I will also include the material that remains available on certain websites with my knowledge, because keeping those pages preserved helps maintain provenance and timestamped evidence. Sites such as Drakenberg Weebly and archived pages through the Wayback Machine assist with this.

The Drakenberg Weebly material was written by Iona Miller on behalf of my father. It was created to ensure that our work would remain available online for research purposes, not so that others could lift it and use it as their own. Iona wanted to pay homage to my father, and at a time when I was being infiltrated by strangers online, she was not only a companion to me but a matriarchal figure who stepped in when I asked her to hold the fort until I was ready.

I will show the Introductions, title pages, and surrounding context to demonstrate that our framework has remained consistent and was already set out from the early 2000s. This predates later claims by others that they have been independently researching the same framework for twenty years. I see through that because it is a pattern I have seen many times, going back to the early copycat websites that appeared when my father first asked me to act as his copyright controller and help him take them down.

After setting out that provenance, I will provide a chapter-by-chapter comparison showing how another person's work has been written using my framework. The book I am reviewing is Gary Waynes Genesis 6 Conspiracy part 2, Published By Deep River Books in 2024. The Core focus of his book are primarily biblical, To see my father's framework in that context stood out to me.

Where the chapters in my provenance are solely my father's written work, I have the right to reproduce relevant material in order to show the extent of the similarity. There is no other practical way to assess the comparison.

I understand the irony of having to quote someone else's book in order to show where they have used my work, but the original copyright and framework belong to my father's estate and to the material I now administer. I am entitled to review, critique, and compare the use of that work in the same way I have been told others are entitled to review and critique mine. In this case, Gary Wayne's publisher has also personally asked me to show the proof, so this review is being prepared in response to that request.

After the chapter comparisons, I will discuss the legal framework, including fair use, fair dealing, good faith, quotation, criticism and review, moral rights, and relevant case law.

My aim for this book is not defamation. I have a legal background in copyright law, I own and administer this space, and I have dealt with this kind of behaviour for many years. My purpose is to show pattens, flaws in responses, educate, to show what is not acceptable in regard to copyright law, I aim to help others who may be experiencing similar issues but do not have the knowledge, confidence, or platform to challenge it.

Too often, legal language is used against people as a way to silence them. People are made to feel as though they cannot respond because someone else claims to know the law better. By setting this out clearly, I want to show that legal words without substance do not decide the matter. If the people involved understood copyright law as well as they claimed, they would have taken the appropriate steps to ensure that their author had not placed them in this position.

I will show the evidence of the citations and the sheer volume of them. I stand by the fact that permission was not granted and still has not been granted. I sent a cease and desist to the publisher, who initially attempted to play the matter down by saying that my father's work had only been used once. It was only when I showed him the extent of the citations that he came back to me on a more grounded and equal level, asking me to show him.

I had already shown him numerous times. However, rather than searching for the material himself, or purchasing my book and checking the material directly, he placed the burden back onto me. He could purchase an eBook copy and find the information himself. He could also look at the many one-star reviews of Gary Wayne's books where other readers have commented that the work appears heavily lifted from my father, Nicholas de Vere, and Laurence Gardner in order to build the framework of his own book. My argument is simple: remove all the citations and framework drawn from my father and Laurence Gardner, and what remains is largely an edited version of the Bible.

The Bible is in the public domain, and everyone has the right to create their own edited versions or interpretations of material where copyright has expired. This happens a lot in the industry with people reusing and editing public domain works.

That is legal n copyright terms when a work is in the public domain.

But my work is not in the public domain.

My work remains protected, and because I have republished it under my own publishing name, Dragon Publishing, it remains protected for the relevant copyright term. If I want to edit it, I can. I own and administer it. No one else does.

That is the law.

The Commandments, Confirmation Bias, and the Responsibility of a Christian Bible Teacher

When a writer presents himself as a Christian Bible author and openly states that his purpose is to push people towards the Bible through his books, his work must be judged by the very biblical standards he invokes. It is not correct for a man to quote Scripture and to claim that his intention is Christian. If his method depends upon cherry-picking, selective genealogy, hostile interpretation, confirmation bias, and the darkening of another family's history, then the moral question becomes unavoidable.

The Ten Commandments and the teachings of Christ do not only apply to ordinary private conduct. They apply to authorship, preaching, scholarship, public claims, and the way one handles another person's name, work, family, and legacy. If Gary Wayne wishes to lead people to the Bible, then his conduct as a writer must also be brought before the Bible.

The commandment "Thou shalt not bear false witness against thy neighbour" is central to this question. False witness is not only a courtroom lie. It is also misrepresentation. The act of presenting another person, family, bloodline, tradition, or body of work in a distorted way. It is selecting only those details that support a hostile argument, while ignoring the context that would make the picture fairer, fuller, and more truthful.

This is particularly serious where Gary Wayne appears to cherry-pick the darker or more sensational aspects of biblical interpretation, mythology, genealogy, and esoteric history in order to force a predetermined conclusion. If an author begins with the desire to push people towards the Bible, and then admits to a form of confirmation bias in the way he frames his material, then a reasonable question arises: is the written work functioning as fair research, or is it functioning as religiously motivated accusation?

Confirmation bias is not the same as evidence. Evidence requires discipline. It requires the willingness to stop where the record stops. It requires the humility to say, "I cannot prove this, therefore I cannot stand by it." Confirmation bias does the opposite. It looks for anything that can be made to fit a conclusion already chosen in advance. That may be useful for selling books, creating drama, or frightening readers towards a religious position, but it is not the same as truth.

This is where my position must be clearly distinguished from the way my family and the Royal Dragon Court have been portrayed. I have never needed to claim descent from the Anunnaki, Enki, Odin, or any other mythological being in order to give my family history meaning. I do not believe I am related to Enki. I do not need to be related to Odin. Where the genealogy reaches the legendary or mythological horizon, I stop. In the case of the Anglo-Saxon royal genealogies, I can work with the historical lines as far as the evidence allows. If a line reaches Alfred the Great, then that is where I remain grounded. If later medieval or royal genealogies attempt to extend themselves into Odin for political, divine kingship, or legitimacy-building purposes, I recognise that as a genealogical and ideological construction. I do not treat it as courtroom evidence.

That distinction matters.

I am not trying to weave myself into the Bible. I am not inventing a biblical connection for status, drama, or spiritual authority. Where there is historical evidence connecting families to the House of David through recorded royal and dynastic lines, that is not the same as forcing oneself into Scripture. That is a matter of historical genealogy. It exists in records, lines, claims, marriages, dynastic traditions, and inherited frameworks that must be examined carefully. I did not ask history to place certain families where it placed them. My responsibility is not to exaggerate it, but to handle it honestly.

This is the difference between evidence and sensationalism.

I fully accept that some of Laurence Gardner's work, some of my father Nicholas de Vere's work, and some of the wider material influenced by writers such as Zecharia Sitchin entered areas that were highly speculative, sensational, or difficult to prove. I don't deny that. But at the same time I don't blindly defend every claim because my father made it. Where I am very different to my father I cannot stand beside every idea because it appeared in a book connected to my family or the Royal Dragon Court. That is not stewardship. That is worship of legacy, and I refuse to do that.

For thirteen years, I have had to sit with that inheritance, separate what can be evidenced from what cannot, and take responsibility for the Royal Dragon Court under my own stewardship. That means I must now treat the Royal Dragon Court as I would treat a courtroom: with evidence, facts, documents, historical context, and standards of proof. If I can't find the truth of a claim, I do not stand by it. I work with finding the evidence. Over the years I have always been very straight forward with my views, when something belongs to mythology, allegory, medieval political theology, or dynastic propaganda, then I say so.

That is not the same method Gary Wayne appears to use.

Gary Wayne seems to select the aspects of the Bible, genealogy, bloodline history, and esoteric tradition that best serve his own Christian argument, while presenting those same materials through a darkened lens, In podcasts its appears that he stands by what he has read in our books as fact and taken every word as literal. In doing so, he risks creating the very distortion the Bible warns against. If he takes from Gardner, from Nicholas de Vere, from older genealogical traditions, from biblical material, and then from secret societies and esoteric history, but then arranges it all to imply evil, deception, or spiritual corruption, the question is not merely whether he cited enough pages. Due to his misunderstanding of an satirical iconoclast that enjoys provocation, the question is whether he bore false witness.

The commandment "Thou shalt not steal" is also relevant. Theft is not only the taking of physical property. A writer may take another man's labour, framework, research, terminology, structure, argument, and spiritual or historical capital. If he then uses that material to elevate his own authority while undermining the people from whom the material came, the moral problem becomes even sharper. He is not simply borrowing. He is harvesting.

There is a further question of covetousness. "Thou shalt not covet" speaks to the desire to possess what belongs to another. In this context, that may include the desire to possess another man's research, a family's mystique, lineage's symbolic capital, or another author's framework, while reshaping it into a hostile Christian narrative. It is one thing to critique a source. It is another to depend upon that source while condemning it.

Christ's warning in Matthew 7 is especially important: "Judge not, that ye be not judged." This does not mean that no one may ever use discernment. It means that hypocritical judgement is spiritually dangerous. Christ asks why a man looks at the mote in his brother's eye while ignoring the beam in his own. If Gary Wayne judges the Royal Dragon Court, the Vere family, Gardner, Nicholas de Vere, or related bloodline material as spiritually suspect, while his own work relies heavily upon those same sources and traditions, then he must first examine the beam in his own eye. In his own words on podcasts he has claimed that he had read exactly what these people said and wrote about it, and cited it word for word, while he is saying this, his posture is defending himself in a way that casts judgement and at the same time some level of ignorance, Almost a naïve, They said it, don't blame me, was the impression I got from his body language.

I was taught never to believe everything you read in books or see on Television, My father time and time again said, Question everything. Gary made his judgement without doing the extra work by questioning further.

Has he fairly represented the material?

Separated fact from speculation?, Acknowledged the full scale of his reliance?

Has he avoided using another family's history as a dark theological prop? Applied the same evidential standards to his own claims that he applies to others?

Those are fair questions.

Christ also warned that a tree is known by its fruit. The fruit of a work matters. If a book claims to lead people towards Scripture, but does so by encouraging suspicion, fear, accusation, and hostile interpretations of other families or traditions, then the fruit must be tested. Does it lead to truth, humility, fairness, and repentance? Or does it lead to spiritual sensationalism and the demonising of others?

This is where the reasonable reader must ask whether Gary Wayne's work is operating as balanced scholarship or as confirmation-driven religious polemic. If he has admitted that his purpose is to move people towards the Bible, then his selection of evidence must be scrutinised. A Christian goal does not sanctify an unfair method. A religious intention does not excuse distortion. A Bible-based conclusion does not become righteous simply because it quotes Scripture.

It is also important to say that my own position is not anti-Bible. Nor is it an attempt to compete with the Bible, But at the same time, you cannot just pick your favourite scriptures and cast aside the ones about job, or the request of sacrifice of Abrahams son. I question these scriptures, I do find it amusing however when a person of this faith preaches but doesn't read all of the scriptures or defends some of these monstrous requests and actions.

I am not trying to insert myself, my family, or the Royal Dragon Court into Scripture for personal elevation. I am passionate about history, genealogy, evidence, and the truth of what was recorded. Where biblical genealogical intersections arise through historical dynastic traditions, they must be examined like any other claim. Where DNA ancestry, family tradition, or maternal lines raise interesting questions, they may be noted, but they do not replace historical proof. They do not give licence to exaggerate. They do not become doctrine.

That is the difference between responsible stewardship and sensational writing.

My father once recognised that some people want to sell books. That statement now carries a painful irony, because some of the very material connected with my father, Gardner, and others was itself sensationalised in ways that I have had to revisit, or in the past distance from. I have always maintained that I would never change the voice of my father and ensure that his material remains the same.

That is precisely why my present approach matters. I am not simply repeating the past, nor am I defending every old claim. I am trying to clean the table, preserve what is true. This is why sometime when I see others present the same work of my fathers but adding misinterpreted layers onto it, I feel that the 13 years of damage control has been diminished and I have to start the process again.

Gary Wayne has the right to believe in the Bible and to critique bloodline traditions. The question is whether he has done so fairly, honestly, and proportionately, with proper regard for the sources, families, and legacies he has used.

The Bible does not point to the House of Vere as evil. It warns against false prophets, false witness, and those who use information selectively in ways that mislead others.

If Scripture, genealogy, and the darkest possible interpretations are cherry-picked and arranged to push readers towards a predetermined Christian conclusion, the work must be questioned. Not because it is Christian, but because Christianity itself demands truth.

A man cannot claim to lead people towards the Bible while acting against the commandments that protect truth, honour, labour, and neighbour. Nor can he use another family's history to support his own ministry, accuse that same family of weaving itself into Scripture, and then call that righteousness.

My father's own words make his position unmistakable. He wrote:

"Sacred Cow. As an iconoclast I have only one use for Sacred Cows: Sacred Burgers in a Bun with Garlic Mayonnaise. In promoting their ignorant, unresearched dogmas and forcing them on others, their ridiculous lies become legitimate targets for those of us who have taken the trouble to delve deeper for the truth. As such, Satan stays in my texts and genealogical tables and if it upsets the precious sensibilities of the mindless religious conformists who cling to their orthodoxy, in their cowardly desperation for spiritual certainty and psychological comfort in a transient and frightening world, then to my mind I have done a good day's work."[1]

This statement is crude, funny, provocative, and deliberately offensive to religious conformity. But it also explains the nature of his work. Nicholas de Vere was not writing as a Christian preacher or to comfort orthodoxy. He was writing as an iconoclast, and his purpose was to attack what he regarded as unresearched dogma, inherited religious fear, and the lazy acceptance of spiritual authority without investigation.

That distinction matters enormously.

Gary Wayne appears to take the presence of figures such as Satan in my father's genealogical material as though this automatically proves darkness, corruption, or evil intent. But my father's own explanation shows something different. He was deliberately refusing to remove difficult, uncomfortable, or religiously offensive names from his texts merely to satisfy orthodox Christian expectations. His position was not devotional Satanism. It was iconoclasm. It was his refusal to sanitise the material for people who, in his view, wanted spiritual certainty without doing the research.

---

[1] De Vere, Nicholas The Dragon Legacy. The Book Tree 2004.

Whether one agrees with my father's tone or not is beside the point. The point is that his work cannot honestly be understood if it is stripped of that iconoclastic context. To take the provocative fragments, remove his stated purpose, and then present those fragments as evidence of evil is not fair scholarship. It is selective framing, Whilst at the same time, I can clearly see how my fathers work offends people of the church, it all boils down to intention, Dad's intention was humour, Whilst it appears that other peoples intentions are to use dads work and make a mockery of it while making money.

This is especially important because I do not treat my father's iconoclasm as a doctrine to be obeyed. I treat it as part of the historical inheritance I have had to examine. My stewardship of the Royal Dragon Court is not based on repeating every provocative statement my father made. It is based on evidence, documents, law, genealogy, and the disciplined separation of fact from speculation. I can recognise that my father used shock, humour, insult, and symbolic provocation without having to turn those methods into my own, Albeit, this is a family trait of ours, All Weirs in my family have a funny sense of humour, I actually started to wonder if we got that from the last laird Logan from whom the book was written about The Laird of Logan; or, Anecdotes and Tales Illustrative of the Wit and Humour of Scotland.

But Gary Wayne's treatment appears to do something else. He seems to preserve the shock value of my father's work where it helps his biblical argument, while ignoring the reason that shock value existed in the first place. My father was attacking religious conformity and sacred cows. Gary Wayne appears to have repackaged The Dragon Legacy as a whole attack, using it as evidence that the material itself is spiritually dangerous. That is not interpretation. That is inversion.

In that sense, Gary Wayne's use of the material becomes deeply defensive and questionable. He is not merely disagreeing with Nicholas de Vere. He appears to be using Nicholas de Vere's iconoclastic language and genealogical provocations as fuel for the very religious dogma my father was challenging. The result is a distortion: the iconoclast is turned into the villain, the provocation is turned into proof, and the refusal to bow to orthodoxy is reframed as evidence of evil.

That is precisely why context matters. A Christian writer cannot honestly cherry-pick the most offensive or uncomfortable elements of another man's work, detach them from the author's stated purpose, and then use them to push readers towards a predetermined biblical conclusion. That is not truth-seeking. That is confirmation bias dressed as discernment.

CAN YOU HANDLE THE TRUTH?

Lastly, I ask this.

If Gary Wayne had done all of his research, and if he had fully understood DNA, genealogy, anthropology, population history, royal descent, cousinship, endogamy, migration, bottlenecked communities and the way human families actually interconnect over time, would he not have reached the same unavoidable conclusion I have reached through my own work in *The Royal Dragon Court: Inbred Britain* and *The Forgotten Royals of the USA*?

We are all related somewhere down the line.

This is the ordinary consequence of human ancestry. Families intermarry. Lines collapse. Cousins marry cousins. Royal houses cross into noble houses. Noble houses cross into common houses. Migrants carry bloodlines across countries and continents. Over centuries, the idea that one family alone can be isolated as the uniquely evil bloodline becomes not only morally dangerous, but genealogically absurd.

So what would Gary Wayne say if the same standard were applied to him?

What would happen if I were to research his genealogy, (not that I would waste my time) and discover that he too descends from the very same line he has spent the last twenty years warning people about? What would he say then? I doubt very much that he would refer to himself as part of the so-called satanic bloodline? Would he appreciate it if his peers turned on him and call himself the bloodline of the Antichrist? Would he apply to himself the same dark language he so freely attaches to my House of Vere?

Or would the rules suddenly change?

This is the danger of theological bloodline accusation. It is easy to demonise another family when one imagines oneself safely outside the genealogy. It is easy to point at the supposed darkness in another person's ancestry when one has not examined the complexity of one's own. But genealogy does not obey religious prejudice. It does not stop at the borders of someone's doctrine, nor does it protect the accuser from the ancestry he assigns to others.

In Some context where Gary Wayne has discussed Good and Evil, I think he has a mild understanding of the fact that my father did not fully separate the two, To Nicholas, he questioned much like I do, How can a god be good but do so much evil, He cannot ask the services of Satan the adversary to do his dirty work and then blame him for the outcome. If a bloodline is evil simply because it intersects with contested biblical, royal, or ancient genealogical traditions, then the accusation eventually turns back upon the accuser. The very net he casts over others may catch his own house.

That is why the argument is so flawed.

I have never claimed that ancestry makes a person holy, divine, superior, cursed, demonic, or evil. Ancestry is evidence of descent, not evidence of moral character. Blood does not make a person righteous. Blood does not make a person wicked. If Gary Wayne truly believes people are known by their fruits, then he cannot honestly condemn a family by bloodline while exempting himself from the same logic.

This is where the phrase "pot, kettle, black" becomes unavoidable.

A man cannot spend twenty years warning others about a bloodline, attach sinister meaning to another family's genealogy, use that accusation to push readers towards his own religious confirmation bias conclusion which he admits in the many podcasts he repeats, and then refuse to face the possibility that he may share the very same human, royal, biblical, or ancient ancestral intersections himself.

If he would not accept that accusation against his own house, he has no moral right to place it upon mine.

This is why the biblical issue returns again to false witness, hypocrisy, and unrighteous judgement. Gary Wayne may be pointing at a family tree without realising that, far enough back, he may be standing on one of its branches.

In my next work, I can and will show how these genealogical traditions connect through Charlemagne, the Carolingians, the Merovingians, and the Davidic line, using evidence rather than fear, invention, or religious theatre. I am not asking to be woven into the Bible. I am not forcing my family into Scripture to claim superiority. I am following the historical and genealogical record where it leads, and where the evidence stops, I stop.

That is the difference between research and confirmation bias.

The Royal Dragon Court under my stewardship does not exist to tell people they are cursed, evil, chosen above others, or bound to some dark prophetic bloodline. It promotes sovereignty. It promotes the divine principle within the self. It promotes the right to create one's own destiny, one's own path, and one's own relationship with God without being controlled by a church built on fear, shame, and spiritual dependency.

If God created humanity in his own image, then the divine is not locked inside a pulpit, a priesthood, a church institution, or a man selling books by frightening people back into obedience. The divine spark is within us. The voice of God does not belong exclusively to those who claim authority over Scripture. A person can be moral, honest, kind, disciplined, courageous, and spiritually awake without needing to recite verses at another person like weapons.

This is where Gary Wayne's argument becomes inverted. He accuses others of weaving themselves into the Bible while he appears to weave other people's genealogies into his own biblical warning system. He claims to push people towards Scripture, yet he does so by darkening bloodlines, selecting frightening fragments, and attaching theological suspicion to families he has not properly understood.

That is not spiritual liberation. That is religious control.

A church or preacher that needs fear in order to guide people is not freeing them. It is binding them. A book that uses genealogy to frighten readers into a religious conclusion is not teaching sovereignty, truth, or moral responsibility. It is using ancestry as a cage.

My position is the opposite. I am very proud of my bloodline, Like my father I promote freedom, providing my fans and followers, friends and family a safe space for spiritual growth.

The message of The Royal Dragon Court is sovereignty, We do not believe we need to be afraid of our blood, ancestry, our names, our parents, our symbols, or our past. We have seen throughout history the persecution of our bloodline and we refute this sort of behaviour to continue, It is not part of god's plan according to the scriptures and likewise, persecution in this days and age is a medieval mindset.

Background Context: Misrepresentation, Sensationalism, and the Re-Anchoring of the Royal Dragon Court

This section is included as background context and provenance, before turning to the specific Gary Wayne comparison

When my father first began writing and publishing his work, the Royal Dragon Court material did not emerge into a quiet or neutral space. From the beginning, it attracted attention, support, argument, misunderstanding, opportunism, and, at times, outright attempts by others to take the work, reshape it, and use it for their own purposes.

My father, Nicholas de Vere, had various early associations with people who were around the Dragon Court material at different stages. Some were friends, collaborators, supporters, website helpers, commentators, publishers, or public-facing figures who helped the work reach a wider audience. Others later became a problem. Names connected to that wider early field include Laurence Gardner, Tracy Twyman, Mark Pinkham, Bill Barkley, Richard Dufton, Other he mentioned in his videos who he lately found out to be not as genuine as he first thought There were others who were either involved in the early public spread of the Dragon Court material, helped with websites or publicity, commented on the work, or later attempted to reshape, claim, commercialise, or distort parts of it.

This is one of the reasons there has always been so much contention around the copyright, public meaning, and ownership of the Dragon Court and Royal Dragon Court material.

My father reconstituted the Royal and Imperial Dragon Court / Royal Dragon Court in 1993, and I have letters and written material to support that history. I have also written about this in my previous books. Yet despite this, various people have tried to come along and build their own versions of Dragon orders, chivalric/ freemason-style orders, "Dragon Court" structures, or similarly named organisations. Some have attempted to sell orders, titles, initiations, or associated spiritual and esoteric claims for large sums of money. Others have written books using titles close to *The Dragon Legacy* in order to catch the same audience and exposure. Some created their own "Dragon" orders or "Royal Dragon" structures around material that, in my view, came directly from my father's work and the field he built.

This is not a new problem. It has been happening for years.

Part of the difficulty is that when my father's work first reached wider audiences, it was not always presented in the way he intended. My father was attempting to move the Dragon material toward an anthropological, historical, genealogical and symbolic argument. He was not simply trying to create a fantasy religion or a sensational alien mythology. He was trying to frame the material through ancestry, bloodline, culture, myth, royal history, anthropology, and older esoteric traditions.

The problem was that some of the people who helped bring his work into the public arena also distorted it.

Tracy Twyman is one of the clearest examples of this early problem. Tracy helped catapult my father's work into the United States arena, and that did give the Dragon Legacy material visibility. However, the difficulty was that Tracy also brought her own sensational framework into it. In my view, she wanted to make the material more extreme, more shocking, and more marketable. She used language around aliens, extraterrestrial beings, demons, occult sensationalism, at the same time she was playing with Ouija boards trying to summon demons, This is exactly the sort of ideas that distorted what my father was trying to explain. (You can understand why someone would want to distance themselves away from this sort of behaviour)

My father was trying to take the material back toward an anthropological stance, especially around human origins, hybridisation, bloodlines, royal ancestry, and older mythic traditions. Tracy's framing pushed parts of the work into a more sensational, conspiratorial, and occult direction. That created long-term confusion.

In my view, Tracy was one of the first major online clout-chasers around the Dragon Legacy field. She had the platform, the audience, and the media instinct to make the work sound more dramatic, but in doing so she distorted much of the original context. She did not simply help publicise the work; she also helped create some of the misunderstandings that I have spent years trying to correct.

This is one of the reasons that when I later republished or reworked parts of my father's material, including *Transylvania to Tunbridge Wells*, I removed certain contextual material connected to Tracy's presentation. I was already dealing with my own publisher issues at the time, and I was trying to regain control of the way my father's work was being presented. I did not want the books to continue carrying framing that had contributed to misinterpretation, sensationalism, and confusion.

After my father died in 2013, the situation became worse.

Almost immediately after his death, I experienced a wave of people online surrounding me, watching me, contacting me, commenting on me, and in some cases behaving in ways that felt frightening and invasive. It reached a point where I had to withdraw from parts of the internet because it no longer felt safe. This is part of my lived experience. I do not have documentation for every message, every fear, every online encounter, or every moment of being watched and overwhelmed. But I know what happened to me, and I know the atmosphere that followed my father's death. Although I will say this that some of these stalker have continued to harass me because they wanted a piece of the Dragon Court pie and are but hurt that they are not in close association with me, so they tend to send me sometime 50 messages, emails and make up over 20 different profiles to attack myself and my co-workers.

One of the most damaging parts of that period was the way certain people who had once been close to my father, or presented as his friends, allowed hostile or defamatory commentary to circulate. Renee Barnett is one example. She had been named in *The Dragon Cede* as a friend of my father. I have since removed her name from later context because of what followed. In my view, it was deeply wrong for someone who had been placed so close to my father's work and memory to allow damaging commentary about him on her radio show after his death.

That was part of where the click baiting began by Tracy Twyman..

From 2013 onwards, the death of Nicholas de Vere became an opportunity for others to speculate, sensationalise, reinterpret, demonise, claim, or build platforms around his name and work. Some people did this through radio shows, podcasts, websites, books, YouTube videos, online orders, or copied material. Some did it through conspiracy, hostile religion. Some did it through fantasy, money. But mainly attention.

I was left dealing with the consequences.

For the last thirteen years, I have worked to re-anchor the Royal Dragon Court away from that misinterpretation and misrepresentation. I have had to deal not only with outsiders attacking the work, but also with "fans" who misunderstood it, exaggerated it, or wanted to use it to create their own fantasy identity. I have had to separate my father's stronger historical and genealogical material from weaker claims, unsupported claims, bad citations, sensational commentary, and the distortions added by others. I have become repulsed by the words, alternative historian, pseudo history as the internet uses guardrails on certain topics, as soon as you get that shiny tin foil hat, your work is diminished, Likewise with dads association with Laurence Gardner, due to the conflated made up titles, association with people who pretended they were royalty and attempted to say they were the King of Scotland, You can understand why any child from these men would want to run for the hills The only credibility there is lies with the fantasist free masonry wanna be's I stand my ground when I say, That you are not a templar or freemason in this modern day era, they only exist for cosplay, pretence and theatre masking, if you didn't go on a crusade or fight battles then your just pretending. Which is why I became emotional when I saw my fathers work misrepresented in Gary Waynes Podcasts and then his book. The way he presented Laurence Gardner over the way he presented my father was awful considering he has used most of my father inspiration, But then calls him the antichrist and evil, The very work Gary discusses concerning Laurence Gardener was my dad's, Nicholas de Vere, How wrong can you get it?

My aim has been to bring the work back into a historically grounded and academically understandable context. We are not Occult nor are we a secret society, I have laughed so many times about this, If it was so secret how does anyone even know about us.

That has meant correcting evidence, improving citations, republishing the books, writing my own works, clarifying the Royal Dragon Court's position, strengthening the historical framework, and making sure that there is less room for fantasists, opportunists, internet scrapers, and unauthorised commentators to take the brand and twist it into something else.

This is also why the trademark and modern legal protection of the Royal Dragon Court matter, I never felt I needed to go to such lengths to brand myself but then when you look at the amount of people who attempt to take it for themselves and change it into a chivalric order, there was no way I was going to be associated with fraud.

The Royal Dragon Court is not an open playground for anyone who wants to attach themselves to Dragon language, sell fake titles, create orders, scrape my work, or rebrand my father's material as their own. My father reconstituted the Court in 1993. I inherited and continued that legacy.

That work now carries both personal and academic weight. I have worked hard to bring my father's work into a more mainstream context, and I have also built my own body of research around it. I know I have done that well because the work is now more widely available, more historically framed, and better understood than it was when I first inherited it.

Robert Sepehr is an example of authorised use. Robert used my work with my permission and with mutual understanding. Whatever money he made from those videos, I regard as his right for the time, effort, production, and presentation he put into them. I hold no malice or regret about that. In fact, I am grateful, because that permission was given and the understanding was mutual. He exposed my work in a way that the publisher had never done before, reaching more than one million combined views for both videos, that is mutually beneficial.

But Robert having permission does not mean everyone else has permission.

It does not give other commentators, digital creators, internet scrapers, podcasters, writers, or commercial opportunists free rein to use and abuse my work at will.

Permission is specific. Consent is specific. Context matters.

This entire background explains why I am so protective of the Royal Dragon Court, *The Dragon Legacy*, *The Dragon Cede*, Dragon Publishing, and my father's literary estate. It is not possessiveness for the sake of it. It is the result of more than twenty years of lived experience, public misrepresentation, online stalking, distortion, opportunism, hostile religious framing, fantasy claims, copyright misuse, and attempts by others to monetise or claim what my father built.

My current work is therefore not only a correction of Gary Wayne or any single author. It is part of a much larger corrective project.

I am making sure that the Royal Dragon Court is no longer left open to misinterpretation, misrepresentation, fantasy orders, false claims, hostile religious reframing, or people attempting to click the copyright out of my brand.

The new way forward must be historically grounded, academically sound, strongly evidenced, and protected.

I have had to deal with many infringements in the past, I should also include my own issues with Mongrel's Cross, because that was another example of the Royal Dragon Court material being used in a way I did not authorise.

They used certain logos and emblems on their album covers, and also used titles connected to my books as their own titles. I understand that they did this because they resonated with the work, but because of the genre of music they were involved in, especially heavy metal, I refuted that association. I could not stand seeing the Royal Dragon Court linked publicly with that image or genre.

I sent my first cease and desist to them in 2018, but it fell on deaf ears. Their management company ignored me. They also ignored Thomas Kelly, who is an ambassador for the Royal Dragon Court under my authority. When Thomas brought the matter back up to me, I decided that was it, and that the matter had to be dealt with once and for all.

In 2025 I sent numerous emails to their record label. Again, many did not appear to get through or were not acted upon. Eventually, in January, the lead member of the band contacted me personally. He apologised and admitted that they had not understood copyright law. He said they had used the material because they loved our work.

As sweet or endearing as that may be, it does not remove the issue of passing off through name and brand association with my work. This is one of the reasons I had the Royal Dragon Court trademarked. I already knew I had this issue before, not only with musicians, but with authors coming to me and asking me to read their books, with an implied expectation that my attention would validate them. It creates a layer where people can then say, "Abbe de Vere has seen this," or "Abbe de Vere thinks this is acceptable." In many cases, I do not accept that.

I have also had other people trying to use my brand name as an association with themselves. In one instance, I pulled someone up on what I would not accept. That person dealt with my grievance humbly, took action to remove her content, and changed the name she had wanted to use. She acknowledged that I was the owner and authority on the Royal Dragon Court. We are still in contact, and I support her efforts online where I can.

That lays down a precedent in the way I work. If someone approaches me properly, respects my position, and corrects the issue, I can move forward with them. If someone wants to use my work or my father's work without permission, or tries to build themselves through my brand, I will not accept it.

A few months ago, someone else contacted me because they wanted to use my father's work. They said they had big plans for writing their own book and asked permission. I said absolutely not. I have had this done to me too many times before. I had seen that his own books were not selling, and that he had placed himself on a very high pedestal. When he realised he was not as famous as he thought, it appeared to me that he had decided to use me as clickbait, as others have done before. That is not happening.

The last major issue I had was with my own publisher, who wanted to hold on to the copyright licence as if it were Gollum's ring. He used phrases such as "ironclad contract," but failed to remember that even contracts can become null and void. I sent him, and the main platform involved, a full legal dossier.

His last move was trying to add audio files to KDP. We had already argued about this because I was not happy with a generic AI voice being used for the voiceover on audible, I had not given him permission to do this, along with not being happy with the lack of efforts for protecting my copyright.

Eventually, in January, after I had given him time to sit with the fact that I would not back down, he came back to me and said that he did not know what I had done, but Amazon was not letting him upload any files because they were saying he was using copyright material.

He admitted where he was wrong and finally decided it was in his best interest to let me take back what was mine.

Over the years I have had many copyright infringements, many reproductions of my books The dragon Legacy and The Dragon Cede, some which hide behind VPN handles and some with embedded virus's attached. The internet Archives also played a part in infringement which it took me more than 2 years to ensure they remove The Dragon Legacy, From this sort of ongoing behaviour it is reasonable why people would think that if its on the internet then its ok, But they are not legally trained in copyright law.

In order for this review to be honest I must admit that infringements started well before I had even noticed Gary Wayne, I had only noticed him last September 2025, The reason being because I make infringement checks on a regular basis, with all due respect he was not made relevant to me until this time. But this is something I have gotten used to People know about us, but I do not know about them. I was having issues with some AI generated material from something called Emspiracy, People would regularly message me with her videos saying she has lifted the framework, As it seems the internet has turned on content farming factories. So, I set out to check you tube and found direct use of my dad's work attached to Gary Wayne.

This is not my first time defending against misuse; I have already had content removed regarding over 30 DMCA takedowns in the past.

So unfortunately, This has now become the major example of how not to behave, what not to do, How I will not accept our work being a cash cow.

This is my boundary

So here we are.

The Original Royal Dragon Court Framework

The Background and provenance

Firstly, I have inserted the inclusion within the Genisis of The Grail Kings by Laurence Gardner. This is the exact historical context and not my words.

ACKNOWLEDGEMENTS

For their invaluable assistance in the compilation of this work, I am indebted to the good offices of the Imperial and Royal Dragon Court and Order (Sarkany Rend 1408), Curia Regis et Ordo Draconis; the President of the European Council of Princes, and the directors of Media Quest International.

My particular gratitude is due to HRH Prince Nicholas de Vere von Drakenberg, and to HRH Prince Michael of Albany, for affording me privileged access to their respective household archives. I am also thankful to my wife, Angela, and son, James, for their enduring tolerance of my time-consuming quest.

Grateful thanks also to Simon Trewin, Susy Behr, Chi-ann Rajah, and all at Sheil Land Associates, together with Broo Doherty, Simon Taylor, Katrina Whone, indexer Valerie Elliston, copy-editor Brenda Updegraff, and those others at Bantam Press who have seen this book through to its publication.

To those many friends and colleagues who have directly aided this project I similarly offer my appreciation, while acknowledgements are individually due to those whose inspired research has been of considerable assistance. In this regard, and for their pioneering scholarship in variously related fields of contemporary study, I am greatly obliged to Chevalier David Wood, Baron Richard von Hymir de Dufton, Chevalier Yuri Stoyanov, and Herbert Kessler.

For their generous support of this undertaking, my special thanks to JZ Knight and all at Ramtha's School of Enlightenment; to Christina Zohs of *The Golden Thread*, and to Duncan Roads, Ruth Parnell and

Note: the final acknowledgement paragraph is cut off at "and" in the image.

FOREWORD

In a genuine attempt to find answers to the problems and pressures of our modern age, many people are today seeking enlightenment from books which purport to convey the hidden mysteries of ancient wisdom. Unfortunately, there are numerous quasi-mystical and pseudo-magical offerings in this regard, and much of their dubious content stems from misconceptions of the root elements of the Draconian scientific tradition. This occurs because researchers, who might well study literature that is readily available in the public domain, do not have access to those archives wherein the original base material is held. They are, furthermore, not remotely connected to the ancient Dragon Court or to any of its related Grail families or institutions.

It pleases me, therefore, to convey to readers the fact that Laurence Gardner writes not as an uninitiated commentator, but as an extremely well-informed member of the time-honoured school upon which he so eloquently reports.

In *Genesis of the Grail Kings*, the author has imparted a good deal of ancient material from the archives of the Imperial and Royal Dragon Court, and has aligned this with a hitherto rarely published classical chronology of events in Old Testament times. The result is a work of scholarly integrity which advances a radically alternative view of history, challenging that which has for too long been foisted upon people by those following a predetermined course of vested interest.

The destiny of any individual depends upon whence they begin their journey and the path they elect, or are obliged, to travel. What pertains to individuals is also pertinent to society as a whole, and the conditions, culture and ultimate achievements of society are marked by the inherent perceptions of its origin and purpose. Such perceptions are generally the result of an authorized education programme, but when this teaching is at odds with the underlying truth, a dichotomy of interests will prevail, and the society will have no attainable goal except that of disunity and ultimate demise.

In this work, Laurence Gardner paves the way for a restitution of our society's true history and for the rightful return of its cultural heritage to the front line of conscious awareness. In view of this, and in recognition of his erudite accomplishment in restoring the Messianic Dragon tradition to its position as the *fons et origo*, I commend this text to all who quest for the eternal Grail.

HRH Prince Nicholas de Vere KGC, KCD
Princeps Draconis, Sovereign Grand Master
and Magister Templi of Sarkany Rend
The Imperial and Royal Dragon Court and Order

Relationship Breakdown with Laurence Gardner

Nicholas de Veres own words the issues that came about with his relationship breakdown with Laurence Gardener and those who attempted to steal dad's work. This is not a case of flogging a dead horse, this is a clear representation of facts and what happened at that time, emotional as it was for my father to be betrayed by a lifelong friend who's estate still gathers royalties for my fathers work, Alas my work is not to impede on the Gardner family, I wish them peace and well, and my actual stance is that they deserve whatever royalties they get over someone like Gary Wayne who's reliance on fair use as a defence where, in my view, the scale, repetition, framework reliance, and hostile recontextualisation go beyond what fair use or fair dealing should reasonably permit.

You will see many lack of citations within this book as it is me writing it as my lived experience, Therefore for certain aspects citation are not require because I have not lifted it from anyone but my own hand,

Extract from 'The Dragon Cede' by Nicholas de Vere.
Page 87 et sub.
Having defended Laurence from David Icke, I must regrettably add, as a cautionary public addendum, my own criticisms, and my reply to his libels of 16th May 2000 onwards. This reply has been a long time coming, and previously I considered any reaction to be beneath my dignity. Now however, such a response, though reluctant,

appears to be absolutely necessary in order to restore my good name, my honour and integrity, and that also of the true Imperial and Royal Dragon Court.

Under Hungarian constitutional law AL royal; or; noble courts or orders are actually banned in Hungary; this is a well-known fact throughout Europe. A Catholic Monseigneur (remember the "Donation of Constantine!") and a nondescript, minor baron, registered "Sarkany Rend" (Ordo Draconis: The Dragon Order?) in the High Courts in Budapest as Gardner asserts, but as nothing more than a social club. Certainly NOT as "The Imperial and Royal Dragon Court."

Laurence Gardner and Michael La Fosse, were dismissed by me from the Vere Dragon Court, so they then STOLE the Imperial and Royal Dragon Court and Sovereignty names from us and hurriedly decamped to this Hungarian Social Club, claiming that I was a fraud and that this Glorified Hungarian Boy Scout Troop they had joined was actually the REAL Dragon Court. However, I had registered the Vere "Imperial and Royal Dragon Court" years before, as a royal and noble organisation, in a British Court of Law. I then passed all the documentation to the Home Office who acknowledged it by bestowing me with Passport documents, within which were included my royal and ambassadorial titles,

dated 12th March 1997. Laurence had inspected these Government documents three years prior to the schism and subsequent libels concerning me.

(See Appendix C, pages 446-7: (The Original Dragon Legacy, Dragon Cede)

H.H. Nicholas the Prince [Furst] de Vere von Drakenberg.... H.E. Nicholas de Vere KGC., KCD.").

The present Hungarian Pseudo-Dragon Order never existed as an "Order" originally, it isn't Hungarian in Origin and despite Laurence's assertions to the contrary, it NEVER was registered as a Court of Nobility or Chivalry in the High Courts in Hungary. It has no legitimate fons honorum and no right to bestow noble rank or title. It is that organisation which is fraudulent, thieving and usurping, not mine. Its original leaders have no bloodline descents or genealogical connections with any of the original 1408

membership, whilst I have numerous. So, on all levels, it is simply an insubstantial, baseless and illegal artifice, embellished largely after the fact by Laurence to cover his

tracks, after his dismissal from the real Imperial and Royal Dragon Court of the House of Vere. Mrs. Angela Gardner told me on 8th October 1999 that she and Laurence were & I quote;

only in the Dragon Tradition for the money. & quote; By that time, I had had enough of him, his literary impertinences, the petty political hubris of his faux prince, and the boorishness of his equally faux and untalented lift-music writer chum. That, and the fact that he plagiarised me repeatedly by failing to credit my research and writing (Realm of the Ring Lords).

Laurence proceeded to libel me in order to keep his gravy train rolling along nicely and cover up the fact that I had very politely kicked him and his awful cronies out of the Court. On May 16th, 2000, he publicly announced that the name on the 1997 passport he had seen was Nicholas Weir and that this name appeared on all my official documents. Not so. (Please see Appendix C, Pages 442 et seq: Proofs of Title and Identity. You can find all of this in the original book The Dragon Cede newly released by Abbe de Vere, Dragon Publishing.

As for he suggests that the name de Vere that I bear is a fraud, that is hilarious, laughable in the extreme and sadly pathetic. There are about 15 different, clearly historically recorded spelling variants for this name, including de Vere, Vere, Weir, Were, Wier, Ver, Uerre, Wer, Vir, Mhaior, Muir, Vor, Fir, Fer and so on.

Whether Laurence likes to admit it or not, he knows full well that my titles are legitimate, as is my genealogy (which he inspected thoroughly and helped to fine tune in research and collation) and both are recognised by governments in their numerous strata, and by those governments' numerous administrative departments. I have published herein the

documentary proofs along with my recognised right of fons honorum. King Sigismund changed his family tree fraudulently in order to be descended from Princess Melusine Vere, a REAL Dragon Royal, and in any event the Society of the

Dragon never was and is NOT Hungarian, it is Angevin French. Like Sigismund I am descended from the House of Luxembourg in numerous lines, I am his descendant cousin on both sides of my family and my right to hold the Dragon Court is legitimate, far more so than that of a bunch of contemporary Magyar arrivistes and a dubious Catholic Priest. Societas Draconis was NEVER founded as a Catholic body, it had no Chapel or Cathedra, no Patron Saint and no Chaplain. It's Inner Spiritual Guide – Ibrahim Eleazar –was a Muslim! Its Sacred day was Friday, the Holy Day of Venus-Lucifer in whose honour members would wear black, hence the modern Gothic and Hollywood association

of vampires with that colour. My Family Seals bore the double Dragon Motif 100 years before Sigismund was even born.

Laurence Gardner knows full well that 12 years ago I confirmed my Imperial and Royal lineage by genetic testing and I do indeed have 127 recorded Imperial, Royal and Noble descents stemming from antiquity. Finally, most of the secret, central genealogical, spiritual and biochemical knowledge he received, he obtained from me and from my family's archives, so the foreword I wrote in Genesis of the Grail Kings concerning his having inside, initiated access to hidden wisdom, was actually only through me. I trust this statement will settle the matter finally. It has not been easy to publish these criticisms of Laurence; I once considered him to be a friend.

In 2002 The Dragon Court went into abeyance and all titles, honours and memberships formerly bestowed were rescinded and annulled. In 2009 the Dragon Court was revised

and re-opened to Family Members, Seneschals and Companions.
Entry to the Inner Family Court is permitted when an application is accompanied with a verifiable royal genealogy and/or a comprehensive genetic profile compiled by FTDNA.
Entry as a Seneschal is at the discretion of Family Members and entry as a Companion is open to all who support the aims of the Dragon Tradition. We do not bestow titles, rather, we recognise the individual's rights to bear such, and we do not charge any monies whatsoever for membership.
As a Scythian, Dragon Family and Court, Yr Llys Y Draig Ymerodrol ac Brenhinol, we adhere to "Yr Cyfraithau Am Anrhydeddei Cymraeg" in all matters concerning heraldry
and honours.

The foregoing excerpt from my Book 'The Dragon Cede' was written in 2005-6. Clearly, if there were any confusion, it is apparent that Dufton et al were kicked out of the IRDC
in 2002, and Johnson (Note this is the same Johnson that still stalks and harasses me Abbe de Vere and Thomas Kelly today)
whom I had never heard of NEVER supplied a verifiable genealogy nor genetic test paper after 2009.
Johnson's genealogy was obtained from a Mr. William King without a bibliography, and therefore Johnson was accepted as a Companion of The Family who would serve as a probationer for a year and a day or until I and the rest of us were satisfied that he was acceptable and a genetic test was forthcoming. He was not and the gene test never turned up, nor did a verifiable genealogy, instead he has now simply copied mine, which appears in full in my Notes Section on Facebook. Unfortunately, I was patently a little too generous with people back then. No matter. Not anymore.

(This was later verified by myself Abbe de Vere and it was a laughable Frankenstein Tree, Unverifiable, no matter what he says)

Who rightfully owns the IRDC?
(Well me now, I have the trademark)

The world-famous Dragon Princess Melusine de Vere (Milouziana An Mhaior) decamped from Caledonia to Anjou in 746, taking her entourage with her as the legitimate Fairy Dragon Court of a universally accepted Elven Witch Queen and Dragon Princess is ubiquitously recorded in European history as such. Subsequently and consequently, some centuries later, the House of Luxembourg and King Sigismund altered their genealogical descent in order to be able to claim Dragon Blood from our Melusine and add legitimacy to their usurpation of The Imperial and Royal Dragon Court of the House of Vere.
Melusine's Vere name in Gaelic is spelled Mhaior. This has corrupted down the ages to become spelled in many variant ways, including Muir and most significantly 'Murray'.
The Murrays are members of the 'Pictish Clan of Mar' of Caledonia, which in modern terms is 'The Pictish Clan of Vere.
We all still bear the Pictish/elven/fairy/ Scythian armorial of the 'three stars argent/or; on either a field or fesse azure'. Domiciled for centuries around The Moray Firth (Murray or Mhaioray or Vere-ay Firth), the Veres - as the Murrays - still own vast swathes of north-eastern Scotland today and bear the name of the Fairy King who first settled there – King Vere – ancestral grandson of Cait, Last King of the Tuadha de Danaan. In Iron Age terms, from 400 bc onwards, the Kingdom of Vere became vast; stretching from Great Eastern Caledonia in the north, to the Western Isles, and beyond the contemporary Scottish Border in the south. It was probably the largest single northern European

kingdom of its age and the Dragon King Vere was the first sovereign high king of Scotland in its unified form.

The name Vere – through adaptation - contemporarily means 'Officer' in Gaelic. This actually is recorded historically as being derived from an earlier Gaelic term meaning 'Keeper of the Knowledge', clearly and distinctly encapsulating the Vere family's role in society as Bhruidhes (Bh = V. Ergo sometimes pron. Breeths or more properly 'Vrees') and Archdruid Kings, the ancient custodians of the history and wisdom of their elven species. Such a state of affairs pertains and is indeed pertinent today. I am still the Hereditary Keeper of the Wisdom of my Vere family, My Dragon race and species, and thereby I still hold the Keys of The Kingdom *(see below).

Two hundred years prior to the birth of Sigismund, our family were already using the Double Dragon Motif as supporters in their heraldry denoting Dragon ancestry in both the patrilinear and matrilinear descents. Following on from this, Richard de Vere, 11th Earl of Oxford became recognised as a Dragon Court Member by Emperor Sigismund when both were installed as Princes of the Order of the Garter at St. George's Chapel in Windsor Castle. We founded the first Dragon Court in Europe in 749 ad. The Luxembourg's misappropriated it, now we have it back again.

In Summary and closure: Instances of the exclusive Vere ownership of the IRDC appear numerously in history. In 749 a.d. it moved from Scotland and was re-established in Anjou

by Melusine de Vere, heiress of the largest kingdom of Albha (Scotland): The Scythian Kingdom of The Calle Daouine or Caledonia. She had previously completed the rites of Chronos/Arachne to become the head of our House, prior to her removal to Gaul. In 1200 a.d., it was still in the hands of Hugo de Vere Earl of Oxford, who displayed the alchemical dragons of the IRDC in his arms appended to which was the Archdruidic Crest of the Blue Boar.

By 1066 the Vere Dukes of Angiers and Anjou had become the Vere Earls of Guisnes in Flanders, following the usurpation and theft of Anjou by the faux "count" Fulk the Red, descendant grandson of a common woodcutter 'Tortulf the woodman of Nide de Merle' (a dhamphyr) and were forced to accompany William the Bastard to England, he having taken our children hostage to ensure our complicity in his crimes of usurpation; the rightful king of England being, neither Harold Godwinsson or Guillaume le Batarde, but Eustache de Vere, count of Boulogne and the elected Atheling of the Witan, who was the husband of the sister of Edward the Confessor.

Consequently the IRDC had returned to these Isles in those days, and by 1640 it had removed again to its original birthplace Scotland in the form of the Royal Dragon Court and it's 13 Covens of the Lallan headed by Major Thomas Weir of Vere, King of Witches and Laird of Kirkton. Following the Covenant Wars and our escape to Ireland to avoid persecution for "witchcraft" in 1670; the senior, premier IRDC contemporarily originates from him and subsequent to the family's homecoming to Scotland in 1840, the IRDC descended directly in the unbroken senior bloodline to me as the eldest surviving scion of the Vere Race. All the time that I and the senior heirs bearing de sanguine, de jure et de facto the Vere name are still alive, no man nor woman may claim to own the IRDC by virtue of any obscure, tenuous, irrelevant blood link to the family in dim and distant centuries past. Simple.

Today the IRDC and The Sovereign Grand Duchy of Drakenberg indivisible are recognised under British and International Law as a corporate entity with its own rights and duties; and it is registered with, and recognised by the British Government as a Corporate 'Membership Organisation', rather than any form of common or garden trading outfit. It is also registered as an NGO within the United Nations and is a member of both their Civil Society Organisation and The U.N. Global Compact.

Within all these registrations I am the recorded, recognised hereditary Prince, the Head of the Grand Duchy and Sovereign of the Imperial and Royal Dragon Court. In none of these International Legal recognitions or registrations are the names of Mr. Charles Dean

Johnson, Mr. Mark Pinkham or Mr. Richard Anthony Dufton mentioned in any sense......not even in passing, and they NEVER WERE. They are simply not IRDC

members and have absolutely no rights or claims whatsoever over The Sovereign Grand Duchy of Drakenberg or the Vere IRDC in any way shape or form.

1) Do any of them own or bear the Original Letters of Recognition and Validation?.........No.

2) Do any of them own or bear the subsequent International Legal Documents of Validation, Recognition or Inclusion?......No.

3) Are any of them even mentioned in any of the aforementioned documents?.....No

4) Do any of them own or possess the Legal Documents on En/Incorporation?.....No.

5) Do any of them own or possess the Seals of En/Incorporation?.......No.

6) Do any of them own or bear the Heraldic Seals of the Grand Duchy of Drakenberg

and/or The Imperial and Royal Dragon Court?.......No.

7) Do any of them own or bear the Traditional Dragon Staff of Office?......No.

Do any of them own or possess the Dragonstone; the gateway Altar Stone of the Dragon Princes upon which kingship is sworn and founded?....No.

9) Do any of them have any documents of recognition or membership of the IRDC from

me or any Vere in the senior (Logan Manor) branch of the family, bearing the
aforementioned seals or impresses?......No.
10) Do any of them have clear and unequivocal documentation from me stating that any of them, singularly or plurally, are designated as my rightful and legitimate (Blood or
Legal) heirs or successors to the Grand Duchy of Drakenberg or the Imperial and Royal Dragon Court?....No.
11) Do any of them have legal recognition as sovereigns of Drakenberg and the IRDC
under International Sovereign Law, as determined and ratified by the European Courts of Cassation which are further ratified and upheld internationally by Constitutional Experts
and Academics?....No.
12) Are any of them recognised as aristocrats, nobles or royalty by ANYONE other than
a dwindling and increasingly disaffected group of misguided, gullible supporters on
Facebook?.....No.
13) Do any of the aforementioned persons have any claims to my property and my sovereignty whatsoever.?...................
No, they don't have a leg to stand on. Not one of them.

After the problems caused by associates in mid to late 2011, I discontinued those associations and closed the IRDC on the 6th of January 2012 and posted the closure publicly. This document now follows:
"NOTICE Given on the 6th January 2012. To all persons whomsoever: All those declaring an official interest in the matters proceeding, may write formally to me by letter to: HI&RH Prince Nicholas Tarnawa de Vere-Sachsenstein von Drakenberg,
Rathdragun Mor, SY23 4BA, United Kingdom.

Personal and unofficial correspondence may be directed to 'His Imperial and Royal Highness Prince Nicholas de Vere' at the email address devere@drakenberg.eu

Unless otherwise directed, all future correspondents whomsoever, will adhere to the prescribed protocols and address me as indicated. Alas, my generosity has led to familiarity, and familiarity has led to contempt it seems. If the accepted protocols are ignored, so too will be any correspondence. On behalf of myself and the Family of the Imperial and Royal House of Tarnawa-de Vere including certain selected adoptees and named cousins, The Sovereign Grand Duchy of Drakenberg therein, The Imperial and Royal Dragon Court, The International Council of Princes, Dragon Heritage and the International Dragon Corporation, I hereby give notice of the following. Henceforth our association with this social facility is terminated. All memberships, formerly enjoyed by individuals, of any of the foregoing institutions, corporations or bodies derived during the sojourn of these corporate entities on the Facebook social networking facility, are herein declared null and void. Whilst we have never given any noble or royal titles but have only ever recognised a persons right to such titles, or have only bestowed title purely as a form of specific job description, such recognitions and all or any executive directorships whatsoever are now rescinded forthwith and in their entirety.

The right to use the de Vere and Drakenberg Titular-Nominatives by others not directly related by blood as a first, second or third cousin of the name, unless otherwise indicated by sealed letter, is also banned. These proscriptions in their entirety shall pertain to all persons unless otherwise indicated by letter. As none have ever received signed and sealed warrants of membership from either myself or my family, this being a legal requirement, no person may consider themselves to have been members of these bodies other than as Companions by verbal consent. The name &; The Imperial and Royal House

of Tarnawa-Vere including certain selected adoptees, The Sovereign Grand Duchy of Drakenberg therein, The Imperial and Royal Dragon Court, The International Council of Princes, Dragon Heritage and the International Dragon Corporation&;, remain the property of myself and the House of Tarnawa -Vere and are registered as such with and under the United Nations, The European Union and the United Kingdoms Companies House, with all legal articles and penalties pertaining. The registration with both the United Nations and the European Union are under my name alone and are not transferable. Unless an individual has specific written authority from me bestowing ownership of any or all parts of these institutions, which no other person actually does, or ever will have, any attempt to obtain the latter by any persons, either on Facebook or elsewhere, will be deemed by the U.N. and the E.U as criminal acts of fraud, and the perpetrators will face Federal Prosecution in the United States and European International Courts. Furthermore, my rights and those of my family by heritable extension concerning my sole irrefutable and unassailable ownership of The Imperial and Royal House of Tarnawa-Vere, The Sovereign Grand Duchy of Drakenberg; therein,; The Imperial and Royal Dragon Court
and The International Council of Princes; singularly or plurally as a titular ;government in exile are recognised, supported and protected by International Sovereign Law.

Consequently, any attempt by any persons whomsoever to wrest ownership of the foregoing by any means is considered by International Sovereign Law to be both illegal and an act of aggression. Whilst it was formerly considered tenable, the cessation of all or any of these foregoing bodies has been suspended. We have returned to our position prior to being placed on Facebook without our knowledge or consent, two years ago. Any persons encountering the use of any of the foregoing names, titles or institutions
associated with myself or my family or company on Facebook may consider such to be fraudulently usurped and perpetrated by individuals

who have been dismissed from these organisations in disgrace. You know who you are. These individuals will be reported to the appropriate authorities and retributive action will be taken in full. Under Flemish Law only those persons having parents who are both noble, may be considered to be noble themselves. Other than myself, as it stands at present, with certain exceptions, no person who was formerly associated with the IRDC on Facebook has any noble blood whatsoever. This is why we did not give out titles.

To continue:

The Letter to Miss [redacted]

"Nicholas de Vere.

Rathdragun Mor,

[redacted]

Friday 9th March 2012.

Dear Miss [redacted],

My attention has been brought to a posting of yours wherein you state that I have been replaced as Head of my own Family Court and Order by Mister Richard Dufton. I regret to have to say that you are disinformed and have been manipulated.

A) In order for Mr. Dufton to have acceded to the Sovereignty of The Imperial and Royal Dragon Court, it would have been necessary under International Sovereign Law for me to have abdicated in his favour. I did not at any point or on any occasion hand over The IRDC to this individual. I am therefore protected by the rulings of the European Courts of Cassation in this regard. Sovereignty can never be passed to another.

B) Mr. Dufton has no legal proof of his baronial title, which he claimed was bestowed upon him by letter by (the disinherited, I later discovered) Prince Paul of Romania, I had asked him on numerous occasions during the 1990's to produce this letter or a legal document supporting his claim to nobility, however he declined to do so.

C) He is not knighted by the British Monarchy and therefore his use of the titular prefix of "sir", as you have cited on his behalf, is constitutionally illegal in the United Kingdom.

D) At the time I knew him his genealogy was incomplete and full of holes. This genealogy in any event claimed only a patrilinear descent from a minor member of the House of Plantagenet some 900 years hence. His mother's genealogy was not available and under nobiliary law, if the mother's descent is unproven or common, the child cannot be deemed to be of noble birth. Further I know of no occasion when Mr. Dufton ever had the resources to be able to afford a significant genetic assay of his claims. The absence of the vital female descent also applies to Mr. Johnson.

During the 1990's Mr. Dufton attempted to persuade me to give him the IRDC (which is impossible) and, having failed on several occasions to wrest it from me by guile, in 2003 he sweet-talked and disinformed the now deceased Mr. Bill Barcklay (the webmaster of **dragoncourt.org**) into allowing him to take the site over. Mr Barcklay, somewhat confused and out of his depth, permitted this and Mr. Dufton published a unilateral claim to ownership of the IRDC and the website. Nonsense. The facts are simple. Mr. Dufton has no claims or rights with regard to my family property; I dismissed him with dishonour and him stripped of any vocational ranks he may have tricked me into allowing him. Mr. Dufton is a liar, a fraud and a manipulator. If indeed he had any rights to the IRDC, why has he done nothing with it in 10 years. If he had, I would have been informed by my people long ago. The only reason he is attempting to hoodwink the public now is because he has been approached by Mr. Charles Johnson, who has also been dismissed having disgraced himself in public on several occasions and proved to be a liability and an embarrassment. In any event, having not had the resources to ever submit a gene test, which is a prerequisite for full membership, Mr. Johnson was only a probationer. The motivation for this alliance, I am reliably informed, is to sell bogus titles, amongst other nefarious pursuits.

Since Christmas 2011 Mr. Johnson and Mr. Dufton have attempted to discredit me on Facebook by claiming that they have evidence that I am "Tom Weir", that I am not a Vere, that I am guilty of fraud regarding Airbus, That I am a member of the Russian Mafia, an international terrorist and arms dealer. Mr. Dufton has claimed to be in contact with MI5/6/Special Branch/CIA and the FBI and has been told by them that I am under investigation. Bunk. I once made a complaint to Special Branch in 1999 because we had been infiltrated by two neo-Nazis, one of whom, Mr. Ralph Harvey, was a long standing friend of Mr. Dufton.

Both individuals were invited to publish their "irrefutable evidence" against me by the 11th January 2012, both failed to do so. I would draw your attention to the Police Report enclosed. A report that Mr. Johnson is fully aware of but seems somewhat foolishly to have forgotten about. This catalogue of blatant falsehoods they have promulgated with some ludicrous notion that by lying through their teeth to all and sundry, they will somehow fulfil their fantasy and take possession of the Dragon Court through the popular support and the vote of "the people".

As far as I and the other participating European royal families are concerned, these two individuals are barking mad opportunists who don't seem to know when they are beaten.

They can both whine and lie all they like, but the IRDC has been a Vere possession for over 1300 years and a Vere possession in the senior line – mine own - it will always .

Miss Lindsay, whatever ridiculous, flimsy argument they invent, I can counter it with evidence to the contrary. We do not see either you or

Messrs. Dufton and Johnson of being any threat whatsoever, there are no threats to either myself individually or to the IRDC as a whole, and never will be from any quarter. Therefore, with no ulterior motive,
I am free to advise you strongly to duck and cover at the very least, or to walk away from this situation with a considerable modicum of haste.
For several reasons Messrs Dufton and Johnson have been reported for fraud and misrepresentation in the United Kingdom.
This is not in relation to their fraudulent nobiliary claims so far. Lastly, I have seen the Dragon Society website and I am appalled. At no point was I ever involved with it in any event, and I know that my dear friend Martin Lunn would turn in his grave to see what has happened to his pet project. Disgusting. I am sorry that you have been misinformed so cavalierly . Thank you for your kind attention. I remain,
Yours sincerely,
Nick de Vere.
cc. ICP
IRDC".
Yet another attempt to discredit me and take my property:

THE WORLD ACCORDING TO DUFTON.
"There is a ridiculous, contrived rumour – simple disinformation for personal gain - doing the rounds at present which states that the current Duke of Norfolk – Miles Stapleton Fitzalan-Howard – is the rightful head of the House of Vere. This is nonsense. Never, at any stage of their family history have the Norfolks ever been known by the Vere name, nor have they ever been heads of this House. They originated with Thomas Brotherton, 1st Earl of Norfolk between 1300 – 1338. At this period in time the House of Vere had already been in existence as a dynasty by name for over One Thousand Seven Hundred Years.

The House is divided into three main branches: Scotland, Ireland and Oxford. By primogeniture the House of Vere of Scotland was senior in rank to that of Oxford, which became extinct with Robert de Vere XXII earl some 400 hundred years hence. From the extinct Scottish Branch the senior lineage devolves to the Irish Branch via Sir William
Vere of Stonebyres Castle in Lanarkshire. His, the senior lineage of the House of Vere in it's entirety, and the subriquet of 'Head of the Imperial and Royal House of Vere' descends to your correspondent, not to the House of Norfolk.
At one point Mr. Dufton attempted to take the IRDC and Drakenberg because he claimed that "He had been contacted by my cousins – The Percys and The Howards – and asked to remove me and take my place as Head of the Dragon Court and Drakenberg". Mr. Dufton doesn't actually know any Percys or Howards, they were never members of the IRDC or Drakenberg, and couldn't give a toss about either institutions. Just another contrived lie, like the rumour aforementioned, geared to his personal advantage. Sorry Mr. Johnson, but the "Baron" von Ersatz has purposefully mislead you The Dukes of Norfolk.
In addition to the title of Duke of Norfolk, the Dukes of Norfolk also hold the hereditary position of Earl Marshal, which has the duty of organizing state occasions such as the state opening of parliament. For the last five centuries, save some periods when it was under attainder, both the Dukedom and the Earl-Marshalship have been in the hands of the Howard family. According to The House of Lords Act 1999, due to his duties as Earl Marshal, Norfolk is one of only two hereditary peers automatically admitted to the House of Lords, without being elected by the general body of hereditary peers (the other being the Lord Great Chamberlain). It is worth noting therefore that as the United Kingdom already has an Earl Marshal, how is it that Dufton claims that honour as being legitimately his. Additionally, the Duke of Norfolk participates in the ceremony of the State Opening of Parliament. He is among the four individuals who precede the monarch, and one of the two of these who

walk always facing the sovereign (thus backwards). As the Earl Marshal, the Duke of Norfolk is head of the College of Arms, through which he regulates all matters connected with armorial bearings and standards, in addition to controlling the arrangements for state functions. He is one of three claimants to the title Chief Butler of England.

The Duke of Norfolk currently hold the following subsidiary titles: * Earl of Arundel (1289) * Earl of Surrey (1483) * Earl of Norfolk (1644) * Baron Beaumont (1309) *

Baron Maltravers (1330) * Baron Fitzalan (1627) * Baron Clun (1627) * Baron Oswaldestre (1627) * Baron Howard of Glossop (1869) All titles are in the Peerage of England, save for the Barony of Howard of Glossop which is in the peerage of the United Kingdom. All descend to heirs male except the Barony of Beaumont, which can pass in the female line. The style Earl of Arundel is used as a courtesy title by the Dukes eldest son, the present one of which is Henry Fitzalan-Howard, Earl of Arundel. The style Lord Maltravers is used as a courtesy title by the eldest son of the Dukes eldest son (the Dukes grandson).

No mention of any claim to either membership or the headship of the House of Vere in any sense, substantive or otherwise.

Any more begrudging, acquisitive fantasies doing the rounds?".

PLEASE.....do your research and come to your own conclusions.[2]

Note on the Source Material

Over the next few pages, I have laid out the contents, s, and framework found within *The Dragon Legacy*, *The Dragon Cede*, and the House of Vere material. This gives the reader a starting point for the review by showing where the information originated and how long this framework has existed.

Some of the provenance goes back to 2004, and some to 2010. I have set it out this way so the reader can see the structure of the work before later comparisons are made. As the review progresses, it will become

[2] See bibliography for full citation Niicholas de Vere Amendments

clear how this same framework is later repackaged and used within Gary Wayne's work, in what I call his False Prophet framework.

One point needs to be understood before reading these extracts. Nicholas had a way of using words in a puzzle-like format, very much like my own style. A title may not always tell the reader exactly what context follows. That was part of my father's humour, and it is something I share with him. Many of our relatives have noted that we both use shock, misdirection, and what I call "puzzle waffle" before eventually getting to the point.

For that reason, the reader should not judge the material by title alone. The context is found in the structure, the argument, the repeated terminology, and the framework that sits beneath the words.

Why I Published *The Sechnaill Kings*

This is also why, in 2026, I published *The Sechnaill Kings: The Original Provenance Manuscript 1995*. I did not publish that manuscript in order to retrospectively create provenance or construct a new version of the Royal Dragon Court's history. I published it because the manuscript already existed and dated from 1995.

Its importance lies precisely in its age.

At a time when I am being required to demonstrate where this material originated, when particular terminology was being used, and whether the Royal Dragon Court framework existed before the later books, websites, podcasts and interpretations discussed throughout this review, an original manuscript from 1995 becomes an important part of the documentary record.

Publishing it made that source available in its own right rather than merely asking readers to accept my statement that I possessed it. It allows the provenance to be examined against the later publication history and helps establish that the Royal Dragon Court material, terminology and associated framework were already being recorded decades before the present dispute.

For that reason, *The Sechnaill Kings* should be understood as a provenance publication. Its publication date is 2026; the manuscript itself is from

1995. Those are two completely different things, and that distinction is essential.

The Royal House of Vere PDF by Nicholas de Vere,

Present by Tracy Twyman on from Dagobert's Revenge Website

"The Beast, the Dragon, the terrible monster, is the disguise of the beloved; the horror to be overcome itself is, or contains, the Reward. Beauty and the Beast must be conjoined. The old tag that a serpent becomes not a Dragon save by devouring another serpent, has an Alchemical sense: These are the two Dragons, male and female: they destroy one another, or one destroys the other and a new and mightier one is born, a fiery wonder: A Phoenix * , a leaping glory, a STAR of dream ascending to the throne of the world. This was the Transmutation, the Great Work of the hidden glory of perfection". Arthur Machen, Fr.GD. (Frater of the Hermetic Order of the Golden Dawn). The mating of Ravens is the rhythmic inhalation and exhalation of the breath of Ravens, one by the other. And in this way are the children of Ravens fashioned. (The Raven is the Phoenix of the Elven Kings). Traditional country folklore (England) * The red and gold tinctures and metals on the field of their heraldic escutcheon, [traditionally symbolizing the plumage of the Phoenix] superimposed by the White Star – literally the falling star of Lucifer – are the Arms of the Vere and reflect their ancient line of descent from Satanael (Gnostic Bogomil) or the Devil. The escutcheon, supported by two dynastic, hermetic Dragons becomes, historically, the Ancient Alchemical Seal of the House. The Phoenix of the Scythians was the Raven. The Raven itself, or rather the double-headed Raven found in

Transylvania, devolved down to the Hittites and from them it was eventually adopted and modified as the double-headed black Eagle of the Holy Roman Empire. Editor's Notes In the following material the reader will find that the genealogical descent is interspersed with blocks of information. These are included to give greater background to the document. In this added information the reader will also find repetitions of the same material. These repetitions are gathered from a wide variety of sources and are included here together to act as corroboration, one source with the other. Published comments concerning the House of Vere Vere-de-Vere stalked into the English vernacular as a playful term meaning the grandest, proudest, most historic, indisputably aristocratic and absolutely creme de la creme of Anglo-'Norman' antiquity. In fiction the expression is used for characters of, or assuming, unquestionable ancient lineage - and with good cause. In the Middle Ages, owing to plagues and battlefield mortality, the average noble dynasty in England lasted not more than three generations. The de Veres, however, managed to maintain a line of twenty earls of Oxford over 561 years*. (*Our note: The senior descents in the male line today reach back One Thousand Three Hundred Years). Lord Thomas Macaulay, Victorian historian supreme calls this family: "The longest and most illustrious line of nobles that England has seen..........the noblest House in Europe". Vero Nihil Verius (nothing truer than truth) is the family motto granted by Queen Elizabeth I. The family crest was already the Blue Boar. The Falling Star of Vere A legend lingers round the acquisition of the de Vere (star) badge. In the version as told by Leland, Aubrey was 'at the Conquest of the Cities of Nicque, of Antioch, and of Hierusalem' and: "In the year of our lord 1098, Corborant, Admiral to the Soudan of Persia was fought with at Antioch and discomforted the Christians. The Night coming on in the Chace of this Bataile, and waxing dark, the

Christianes being four miles from Antioche, God, willing the saufte of the Christianes shewed a white Starre or Molette of fyve Pointes, which to every Manne's Sighte did lighte and arrest upon the standard of Albrey, then shining excessively". The mystic star from this miracle became the de Veres' badge, which they wore on their shields from then onwards - quarterly gules and or, in the first quarter a mullet argent. Later heralds argued that it was merely 'a mullet with a difference' as always used to distinguish a younger son from an elder. Others said that it was not a star at all, but the rowl spur, from the French word mollet, which could have been held up as a pre~arranged sign to muster supporters and was caught in a ray of sunlight. "But for the de Veres the badge was simply "God" pointing out the family's near~deity". From Verily Anderson, 'The Veres of Castle Hedingham'. The House of Vere "The noblest subject in England, and Indeed, as Englishmen loved to say, the noblest subject in Europe, was Aubrey de Vere........who derived his title through an uninterrupted male descent, from a time when the families of Howard and Seymour were still obscure, when the Nevills and Percys enjoyed only a provincial celebrity, and when even the great name of Plantagenet had not yet been heard in England. One chief of the house of de Vere had held high command at Hastings; another had marched, with Godfrey and Tancred, over heaps of slaughtered Moslems, to the sepulchre of Christ. The first Earl of Oxford had been minister of Henry Beauclerc, The third earl had been conspicuous among the lords who extorted the great Charter from JOHN. The seventh earl had fought bravely at Cressy and Poictiers. The thirteenth earl had, through many vicissitudes of fortune, been the chief of the party of the Red Rose and had led the van on the decisive day of Bosworth. The seventeenth earl had shone at the court of Elizabeth I and had won for himself an honourable place among the early masters of English poetry.........". See source profile. Baron Thomas Babbington Macaulay Lord Macaulay of Rothley Temple (1857) Professor Vivian Greene: "The Counts of Anjou: Princes of Anjou" Sir Bernard Burke, Ulster King of Arms, when speaking of the Vere called them singularly and in plural: "The Princely Noble......The Race of Vere" (Extract from 'Vicissitudes of Families', page 424 line 12 and page 426 para 2 line 12). G. E. Cokaynes Complete Peerage Volume X. Page 208 OXFORD II. 2.AUBREY (DE VERE) IV, EARL of OXFORD, hereditary Master Chamberlain of England. 1st s. and h. by 3rd wife, (a) b. 1163 or later. (b) While still a boy he attested his father's charters for Colne Priory (c) and a charter of Ranulf de Mandeville for St. Osyth ; (d) and he witnessed 7 more of his father's charters for Colne (e) and joined him in attesting a number of other charters for that priory (f) and 2 other charters. (g) Early in 1190 he Was with the King in Normandy. (h) He obtained the Bolebec fief with Isabel the heiress, (i) and together they gave a tenement in Wavendon to Woburn Abbey. (j) On 21 Feb. , 1190/I he confirmed his father's foundation of Castle Hedingham Priory, and at the request of his father and rnother gave it his church at Castle Hedingham and the wood at Gosfield; (k) but at Michaelmas in that year he owed 100 marks for what was imposed on his men for burning the nunnery.(l) Within the years I191-9, he witnessed a charter of John, Count of Mortain (afterwards King), for Rouen Cathedral. (m) In Dec. 1194 he suc. his father, and in 1195 as Aubrey de Vere junior, he rendered account for £100 for his relief............ Footnotes (a) Item in comite Alberico Alberici comitis de Ver filio, simile naturae miraculum vidimus. Cum enim pater ejusdem, matre jam Praegnante, filia scilicet Henrici de Essexia, ob ignominiosum patris eventum jam ad divortium modis omni elaborasset, partu prodeunte; quem pater in oculo casuali laesione sustinuit, eadem parte defectus in filio parentavit (Giraldus Cambrensis, OP. cit, p 132). Albericus Comes Oxeneford.

His testibus Alberico filio meo et Herede et Roberto Henrico Filiis meis (Colne Cart., no.42). (b) There is no proof that his parents did not cohabit between 1163 and ii or 1172; for his mother's age cf p.206, note "e." (c) His Testibus Alberico filio meo Radulpho de Ver. Radulpho magistro Alberici (Colne Cart., no.38; cf Idem, no. 45) That Aubrey had a master proves that he was a boy at the time. OXFORD III. 1214. 3. ROBERT (DE VERE), EARL OF OXFORD, Hereditary Master Chamberlain of England, being 3rd but eldest surv. S. of the 1st Earl, by 3rd wife. Footnotes. (1) His afilliation is proved by his attestations to 4 of his father's charters Colne, e.g. "His testibus Albrico filio meo et Roberto fratre ejus" (Colne Q no.46). He has always been described as the 2nd son, but in the 3 charters for Colne Priory................. (2) OXFORD Footnotes. ....which are witnessed both by Robert and by his brother Ralph, his name precedes Robert's (Idem, nos. 36, 41, 85). (a) On the assumption that Robert was the 3rd son; after 1172 if his parents did not resume cohabitation before I 171. He seems to have been with his brother Aubrey in Normandy in Aug. 1197 (Landon, op. cit., pp I20~2I) See Source Profile. 'The Royal Genealogies' Table CCXVI Milo de Vere was Count of Anjou before the emergence of the Plantagenet ancestor Tortulf. In consequence of this fact, The House of Vere are the senior Counts of Anjou. Tabular Section of the above right Milo: Count of Anjou (Page 450 'The Royal Genealogies' The Rev. Dr. James Anderson, D.D., M.A : Milo I de Vere was Count of Anjou, (hence eldest son of Melusine/Milouziana de Scythes /Maelasanu: The Elven, Dragon Princess, neice of the Swan Princess Morgan La Fey de Avallon del Acqs). See Source Profile.

A count of Anjou came back with a new wife, a strange girl of extraordinary beauty but she kept very much to herself. Unusually in so religious an age she was reluctant to attend the Mass. When she did go she always hurried from the church before the consecration of the host. Her husband, who was puzzled by her behaviour, told four knights to keep watch and to try to delay her departure from the church. When she got up to go, one of them trod on the hem of her train. As the priest raised the host to consecrate it she screamed, wrenched herself free, and still shrieking, flew out of the window, taking two of her children with her. It was from the children that she left behind that the counts of Anjou and the Angevin kings of England were said to be descended. (Of the Plantagenet Branch):

The Duchy of Angiers was a Ducal principality in the Comite region of Anjou. In the work of The Rev. Father Sabine Baring-Gould Angiers is referred to as the country where the Scottish, Pictish Princess Melusine eventually became a native after having fled from Avallon. Angiers is now the city of Angers in northern Anjou. As a Ducal principality its rulers constituted a regnant royal house who, in the case of the Vere, were also the Counts of the region in which this 'city state' was situated.

See Source Profile. Vere Princedom Although Merovingian culture was both temperate and surprisingly modern, the monarchs who presided over it were another matter. They (The Sorcerer Kings) were not typical even of rulers of their own age, for the atmosphere of mystery legend, magic and the supernatural, surrounded them, even during their lifetimes. If the customs and economy of the Merovingian world did not differ markedly from others of the period, the aura about the throne and royal bloodline was quite unique. Sons of the Merovingian blood were not 'created' kings.

On the contrary they were automatically regarded as such on the advent of their twelfth birthday. There was no public ceremony of anointment, no coronation of any sort. Power was simply assumed, as by sacred right. But while the king was supreme authority in the realm, he was not obliged - or even expected - to sully his hands with the mundane business of governing. He was essentially a ritualised figure, a priest-king, and his role was not necessarily to do anything, simply to be. The king ruled in short, but did not govern. Even after their conversion to Christianity the Merovingian rulers, like the Patriarchs of the Old Testament, were polygamous. On occasion they enjoyed harems of oriental proportions. Even when the aristocracy, under pressure from the Church, became rigorously monogamous, the monarchy remained exempt. And the Church, curiously enough, seems to have accepted this prerogative without any inordinate protest. According to one modern commentator: Why was it [polygamy] tacitly approved by the Franks themselves? We may here be in the presence of ancient usage of polygamy in a royal family - a family of such rank that its blood could not be ennobled by any match, however advantageous, nor degraded by the blood of slaves ... It was a matter of indifference whether a queen were taken from a royal dynasty or from among courtesans... The fortune of the dynasty rested in its blood and was shared by all who were of that blood. And again, 'it is Just possible that, in the Merovingians, we may have a dynasty of Germanic Heerkonige* derived from an ancient kingly family of the migration period'. Extracted and expanded upon by Henry Lincoln, from 'The Long Haired Kings' by J. M. Wallace-Hadrill; Fellow of Merton College Oxford. * Fritz Kern, Gottesgnadentum und Widerstandrecht (1954).

The House of Vere are descended in numerous lines from the Merovingian dynasty and consequently share in this ancient Germanic Royal Blood Tradition. Prince Milo de Vere - married to Charlemagne's sister - and as Head of the Imperial House and Chief of the Imperial Army, was himself an Imperial Prince. The Descent of the 'Imperial and Royal' House of Vere of Anjou 700 -2000 a.d. Ex libello Genealogiae Comitum Oxoniensium Official de Vere family records Repetit genus á Noe. Deinde á Tideo Graeco. Insuper á Vero nobilis Romano Postremo á Milone comite de Genny, alias Gisney (GUISNES). 760+ AD Milo de Ver: Duke of Aungiers and Duke Leader of Great King Charles house and army (son of Rainfroi: de Ver) - Milo married Bertbelle, sister of Great King Charles Charlemagne. Merovingian descent of the House of Vere. 800+ AD Rouland de Ver (son of Milo and Bertbelle): Held the titles of the "Earl of Palatine", "Earl of Maunce and Bleuys", "Governor of the Marches of Brittany" however, he was killed by warring Pagans at Rumcidevale. 800+ AD Baldwine de Ver: became "Duke of Maunce" after his brother Rouland's death. 800+ AD Milo de Ver II (ii) (son of Milo [i]) Held title of the "Earl of Genney or Gisney or GHISNES" given to him by Charlemagne, he married Avelina the daughter to the "Earl of Nauntes" and they had two sons, Nicasius and Milo(iii). 800+ AD Nicasius (Nicholas/Nissé) de Vere : married Agathe daughter to the "Earl of Champaign" and gave issue to Otho "de Vere" who later became the "Earl of Genney". [Nicasius de Ver Erle of Genney sonne to yong Milo Erle of Genney. This Nicasius had to wyfe Agathe the dowghtar of the Erle of Champain. Of Nicasius cam Otho de Vere Erle of Genney, maried to Constance dowghtar to the Lord of Charters] Underlined excerpt from Stow MSS, British Library, London. 800+ AD Otho de Vere: married Constance daughter to the "Lord of the Charters" and gave issue to Amelius de Ver. Amelius

("Aldolphus") de Vere: Earl of Genny (GHISNES or GUISNES) married 1. Maud de Ponthieu and 2. Helena daughter of Earl Bloys His son by Maud: Gallus/Guillaume (Guy Blanc Barbe) de Vere: Earl of Genny (GHISNES - GUISNES) married Gerbrudis daughter to the Lord Cleremont. (Gallus - Guillaume went with Aubri and the King to England). Descent to Godfroi de Bouillon and the Counts of Boulogne. Manasses de Vere: Earl of Genny married Petronilla daughter of the Earl of Boleine. Their son: Alphonsus (Alberic) I de Vere: Earl of Genney, Count of Ghesnes (Genny, alias Gisney or GHISNES or GUISNES) married Katarine daughter to Arnalde Earl of Flaunders. And was a "Counsellor (earl of the Witan) to Edward the Confessor".

The Vere Earls of Guisnes In the matter of the succession of Robert de Vere to the earldom of Oxford in the reign of Charles I, the title was contested for by Lord Willoughby de Eresby. Several Judges of the day were appointed to guide the Lords in legal matters regarding this succession. Leading them was the Lord Chief Justice of England, Sir Randolph Crew. Robert de Vere won the case and the Crown vouchsafed the earldom of Oxford to him. The summing up speech delivered by the Lord Chief Justice before the House of Peers (The House of Lords) was recorded as part of the judicial process (Sir Bernard Burke) and its comments are therefore part of English Law. On Saturday 1st April 1626 Sir Randolph Crew addressed their Lordships saying: "This great and weighty cause, incomparable to any other that hath happened at any time, requires great deliberation, and solid and mature judgement to determine it, and I wish that all the judges of England had heard it - it being a fit case for all - to the end we all might have given our humble advice to your Lordships herein. Here is represented to your Lordships certamen honoris, and, as I may well say, illustris honoris, illustrious honour. I heard a great peer of this realm, and a learned, say, when he lived there was no king in Christendom had such a subject as Oxford. He came in with the Conqueror, Earl of Guynes; shortly after the Conquest, made Great Chamberlain of England above five hundred years ago, by Henry I., the Conqueror's son, brother to Rufus; by Maud, the Empress, Earl of Oxford; confirmed and approved by Henry II., Alberico comiti, so Earl before.

This great honour, this high and noble dignity hath continued ever since in the remarkable surname of De Vere, by so many ages, descents and generations, as no other kingdom can produce such a peer in one and the self-same name and title.................And yet let the name and dignity of De Vere stand for so long as it pleaseth God" That the Vere were Earls of Guisnes before 1066 is recognised by British law. With thanks to Miss C. Shelton; the House of Lords Archivist, for the primary sources consulted.

1000+ Albery II de Vere: Earl of Genney wed - Beatrice Sister to King William the Conqueror: Vere descent from the Merovingian dynasty. Alberic went with the King to England. He used the motto,"Albri Comes" which some say is "Albery of truth cometh", de -of ; Ver- true. But Comes simply means Count. Albery is also Aubri, Albury, Alberic (in Latin); Alphonsus (in Greek). He built "Hedingham Castle". At the time of the general survey, Alberic de Ver was already noted as a person of ancient and noble descent (Domesday Book). Leland, stated or deduced that the pedigree of this family was from "Noah", Meleager, who slew the Caledonian boar, and Diomedes, who was at the seige of Troy.- N.B. Caesar and Charlemagne. Alberic held a number of lordships in several counties in England and particularly 14 in Essex; where Hedingham was his castle, chief seat and caput or head of his barony.

This Alberic, the second styled Alberico senior, took the habit of a monk; and was buried in the church of Colne priory, which he had founded. Albericus III, Junior, was successor to his father; and became so much in favor with Henry I that the said King made him great "Chamberlain of England", in fee; (click image to enlarge) Patent extracts: "H Rex Anglrorum, &c. Sciatis universi quoniam dedi & concssi Alberico de Ver & hereib, ' suis post eum de me & meis tenend' magistram camerarim ,eamtotius Anglie in feode & hereditate quare volo & firmiter precipio quod ipse & heredes sui eam jure hereditario teneant cim omnibus dignaitatibus & libertatib'& honorisicentitis ad eam pertinentibus, ita bene &libere & honorisice sicat Robertus Malet vel aliquis alius ante vel pst cum inquam melius & nonorisicntius tenuit, cum liberartionibus & hospiciis curie mee que ad ministerium cameratieae pertinent" Test. &c. ....to hold the same, with all the liberties and privileges thereto belonging, as fully and honourably, as Robert Malet (Robert de Vere or Veer had been banished and disinherited), had holden that said office. This Alberic was also justice of all England in that king's reign, but about the 5th of king Stephen, was killed in a popular turmult at London; leaving by Adeline his wife, daughter of Gilbert de Clare, or, according to Collins, in his Extinct Peerage, daughter to Roger de Ivery, three sons; viz. Alberic, n.n canon of St. Osyth, in Essex; Robert lord of Twiwell, in the county of Narthampton; Geffery, who, the 12th Henry II, certified his knight's fee to be nine deveteri seossamento and three de novo, and then resided in Shropshire; and William; (constituted "chancellor of England", by Maud the empress), and Juliana, Hugeot Bigot, earl of Northfolk. Alberic the third, succeeded his father, and was so considerable a person, that Maud, the empress, in order to engage him to her interest, confirmed to him the office of great chamberlain, and all his father's estates, with diver other inheritances, likewise the earldom of Cambridge, if the earldoms of Oxford, Berkshire, Wiltshire, or Doreseshire. all which grants, Maud's son, Henry II, confirmed, and constitutes him Earl of Oxford, with the grant of the third penny of the pleas of the county; a perquisite then belonging to the earls of this kingdom. He died the 6th Richard I. having been twice married: • First, to Eusamia, daughter of Sir William de Cantilupe, by whom he had no issue; • secondly: daughter (api) to Lucia, daughter and heir of William de Abrincis (by his wife, daughter and heir of William de Archis), by whom he had sons. From 'The Itinerary' of the Reverend John Leland 1503 - 1552. Dictionary of National Biography. See Source Profile down below. Aubrey (Alberic or Oberon) III de Vere Had several issue including: Robert de Vere - scion of Odin - the Hooded God Robert de Vere. The historical claimant to the earldom of Cambridge and Huntingdon, heritor of the lands of FitzOoth or Hood. Robert or Robin - a Knight Templar in accordance with his legend - was outlawed by King John and lost all his lands and castles. Robert was the historical Robin Hood, Robin Goodfellow or Puck; see published commentaries to Shakespeare's i.e. Edward de Vere's 'A Midsummer Night's Dream' : Robin Hood or 'Puck's' father Oberon or Alberic (de Vere) the Elf King descended - via Melusine - "from Morgan la Fey and Julius Caesar". Such accords with Vere family genealogy. Essentially a ritualised figure, Robin 'of the Hood' - the Green Stag of the Wildwood - (a variation of the White Hart of Annwn, Elphame or Faery) was an ancient, druidic form of the psychopomp or guide of souls, in a similar manner as the Blue Boar.

The ceremonial office of the Robin Hood became - in late Dark Age and early medieval times - that of God-King of the Witches and representative of the Elven Host in decline, a Dragon Lord of the Grail. Robert's descendant Edward de Vere, 17th Earl of Oxford, continued the role of Robin Hood 'The Stag of the Wildwood' and King of the 'Calle Daouine' in the reign of Good Queen Bess. Major Thomas Weir of Vere - Grail Prince and Dragon Lord - also continued this role, that of the Fairy God of the Witches, in the senior Scottish Branch of the family descending to Nicholas de Vere. Le Joli-Rougés du Templars Aubrey's eldest surviving son: Ralph de Vere, elder brother of Robin Hood. Ralph de Vere, founder of the Veres of Scotland The first Aubrey de Vere on record (in Britain) came to England with William the Conqueror.

He is usually held to be a Norman, though he may have been a Breton; he certainly had strong Connections with Brittany. Before the Conquest he was described as one of the barons of Conan, Count of Brittany, and after the Battle of Hastings he or his son (a second Aubrey) was allotted lands in Essex by the overlord there, who was Alan of Brittany, now called Alan, Count of Richmond in Yorkshire. Like all civil wars, the conflict between the Empress Maud and King Stephen was a very troubling one. It was really a fight between Normans and Flemings for the English throne; and since Stephen's wife was the Flemish Matilda, Countess of Boulogne, those Flemings already in England naturally flocked to her side. For reasons best known to himself Aubrey III de Vere sided with the Normans; he got his reward when the Empress Maud created him Earl of Oxford. It has been said, I think correctly, that before a man could be given an earldom he had to have another honour. Among those who supported Stephen and Matilda against the Normans was Alan Earl of Richmond, and Aubrey III's second son, named Ralf, went against his father and fought for Stephen in the army of his own overlord. The first officially recorded de Vere in Scotland was a Radulfus (or Ralf) who was holding estates in Lanarkshire during the reign of Alexander II. In 1160 Conan, Earl of Richmond, had married Margaret, sister of the King of Scotland, and it seems likely that this may have been the time when his follower, Ralf, was awarded his lands there. We may note that when Aubrey III died, he was succeeded as Earl of Oxford by his first son, Aubrey IV; but when that son died childless the earldom passed to a third son, missing out the second son, Ralf. With thanks to Mrs Beryl Platts, author of 'The Scottish Hazard'. Hereto and in published narratives it is made manifest that the most senior bloodline of the entire Royal House of Vere in Great Britain and Eire descends - not through the Oxford posterity - but through the Scottish Branch extracted from Ralph de Vere, eldest son of Aubrey III Earl of Oxford; and culminating contemporarily in the elder progeny of the Veres of Kildress. The senior Scottish descent of the Vere Earls of Oxford. The Scottish name Weir is derived from the Norman-French de Vere..... Alberic de Vere... accompanied the Conqueror. Ralph or Radalphus de Ver was the first of the name on record in Scotland. As Ralph de Ver he was taken prisoner at Ainwick in July 1174. As Radulphus de Weir, he witnessed a Charter of King William, between 1174 and 1184. and as Radulph de Veir he gave a bovate of land in Sprowston, Roxburgh, to Kelso Abbey. As Radalphus de Vere he witnessed another Charter by King William to the Abbey of Lindores. He also witnessed another undated Charter of King William's to William de Hala, Herd (Errol.) The same, or perhaps a succeeding Radulph de Ver, or de Uer witnessed about 1204 a grant to the Abbey of Arbroath, and before 1214 another Charter by William the Lion.

The Weirs of Lanarkshire claimed to be descended from this Radulph. Richard Wer, Lanark, rendered homage to Edward I in 1296. Between 1398 and 1400 Rothald de Were, Baille of Lesmahagow, had a Charter from Patrick, Abbot of Kelso, of the lands of Blackwood, Mossiygning and. Durgundreston. and in 1497 Abbot Robert granted Rogerhill and Brownhill to Robert Weyr for services rendered.

The English 'Weirs' (however) are descended from a progenitor who dwelt at a weir or fishing dam. One Scottish Weir crest is (was in 1700's) a demi-horse in armour proper, bridled and saddled gules. The motto is Nihil Verius. Source: From Dr. George Black. The descent of the senior Scottish Branch of Vere of Oxford from 'The Surnames of Scotland', New York Public Library Edition. Primary sources in italic. WEIR............As Ralph de Vere he was taken prisoner at Alnwick along with King William the Lion in 1174 (Bain, I, p. 174).He witnessed a charter by King William 'de decimis episcopatus' of Moray between 1174-84 (REM., 2), and as Radulph de Veir or Veyre, within the same period, he gave a bovate of land in Sprowestun, Roxburgh, to the Abbey of Kelso, his brother Robert being one of the witnesses (Kelso, p. 177). The same or perhaps a succeeding Radulph de Ver or de Uer witnessed a little before 1204 a grant to the Abbey of Arbroath (RAA., I, 11) and before 1214 another charter by King William (Panmure II, 126)

DE VERE and WEIR Tartan: Weir (also Hope-Vere) Motto: Vero Nihil Verius (Latin: Nothing Truer than Truth) ......Ralph de Ver, from whom the Weirs of Blackwood, Lanarkshire, claim descent, was captured, with King William I (the Lion), in 1174 whilst besieging the castle of Alnwick in Northumberland. Others of the name held land in Lesmahagow, Lanarkshire, in the fifteenth century. Major Thomas Weir (1599 - 1670) Consort of the Queen of Elphame; was born at Kirkton House, Carluke. As an adult he lived at West Bow (below left) and was burned at the stake in Edinburgh (below right) for Witchcraft, Human Sacrifice (vampirism), Animal Sacrifice, Congress with the "Queen of Hell", Incest with his stepdaughter Elizabeth Bourdon and also with his sister. His sister was hanged the next day for her part in some of his activities. 'Scotland and her Tartans' Alexander Fulton. (Major Thomas Weir was the grandson of William Vere of Stonebyres and Lady Elizabeth Hamilton. His father Thomas married the witch, Lady Jane Somerville. Major Weir was the ancestor of the Tyrone Kildress Branch). 'Of The Fesse' Chapter X. From the Archives of: The Lyon King of Arms of Scotland. The Scottish Clan and Family Encyclopedia (The Armigerous Clans and Families of Scotland)' Hope Vere and Weir Arms (of Blackwood LR 4/94)1 Argent, on a fess Azure, three mollets of the first (Of The Royal Scythian, Pictish Clan Of Mar) Crest (As Oxford) Upon a chapeau Gules furred Ermine a boar standant Azure armed Or. Motto (As Oxford) 'Vero Nihil Verius' (Nothing Truer than Truth) 1. Lyon Roll of Arms. Court of the Lyon King of Arms, Edinburgh. Ralph de Ver was captured along with William the Lion at Alnwick in Northumberland in 1174. He witnessed a charter of his king of lands in the bishopric of Moray sometime between 1174 and 1184. He also donated land to the Abbey of Kelso, and his brother Robert was a witness. The Weirs of Blackwood in Lanarkshire, who (through a female descent) were to become the principal family, claim descent from Ralph de Vere. (The claim is upheld in the Lyon Rolls as evidenced above). Senior descent of the Veres of Oxford in Scotland and Eire continued. Ralfredus ('Baltredus'/Ralph) de Vere - the eldest surviving son and rightful heir of Aubrey III de Vere Earl of Oxford opposed his father in the Flemish war, was disinherited and fled to Scotland with his Liege Lord Conan of Brittany in approx 1165. Conan married the sister of the king and Ralph was given his lands in Lanark. He was a witness to a charter of King William, The Lion of Scotland 1165 - 1214. Ralph and William were captured after beseiging the Castle of Alnwick in Northumbria in 1174. Had a son: Walter Rory de Vere Who had a son: Ralph (Rudolphus) de Vere Confirmed his father's donation to Kelso Monastery. Died at the end of the reign of Alexander II of Scotland 1214 - 1249 Had a son: Thomas de Vere Living in 1266. Witness to a charter of a donation to Kelso Monastery by Hemicus St Clan. Had a son: Richardus de Vere (de Were) Living approx 1294. Laird (Lord or Baron) of Blackwood. Lanarkshire. Mentioned in a donation to Kelso Monastery Had a son: Thomas de Were (de Vere) of Blackwood Proprietor of the lands and Barony of Blackwood, Lanarkshire. Died in the reign of David the Bruce; David II of Scotland 1329 - 1371 Had a son: Brian (Buan) Were of Blackwood Living around 1386, Brian's 6th cousin, Robert De Vere IXth earl of Oxford, Lord of Hedingham, was Marquess of Dublin and Duke and Vice Regent of Ireland. Robert was effectively the Sovereign Prince of Ireland during his lifetime and was permitted by King Richard II to mint coins with his own likeness. Although attainted during his lifetime, after his death King Richard restored Robert's titles in full in memorium and these are now held de jure by the Irish Branch. Brian died in the beginning of the reign of King Robert III of Scotland 1390-1406. Whilst the House of Vere bore heraldically the 'Double Dragon Device' of the Dragon Court of Melusine long before this period - id est circa 1200 a.d. - it is believed academically that it was 200 years afterwards, during the investiture together of Emperor Sigismund and Richard de Vere XIth earl of Oxford into the 'princely degree' of the Knights of the Garter at St.

George's Chapel, Windsor by King Henry IV, that Richard de Vere also received his investiture into the Societas Draconis by Emperor Sigismund.

On the evidence of historical precedent, such an investiture; and the Dragon Name, became heritable. In this regard and by a process of lateral inheritance the Vere Dragon Court includes the degree of 'Sarkany Rend': Societas Draconis. Ancient Alchemical Double Dragon Seal of Vere In Heraldry the Supporters of a shield or escutcheon, to give it its proper name, are derived from the ofttimes preheraldic family badges or totems of the father and mother's Royal and Noble antecedents.

The father's supporter is to the right or dexter of the shield -as it would be held by the combatant- and the mother's supporter is to the left or sinister of the escutcheon. As we can see from the seal above, the Veres are of dragon blood in both the patrilinear and matrilinear descents and are consequently of pure Elven lineage. The Boar crest surmounting the shield is the Blue Boar or La Solitaire, which in ancient Gaelic is the symbol of the Arch-Druid. Brian had a son: Rotaldus Were of Blackwood Received a charter from Patrick, Abbot of Kelso Monastery; dated 1404. He was Baillie of Lesmahagow from 1398 - 1400. Died in the reign of King James II of Scotland 1437 -1460 Had a son: Thomas Were (de Vere) of Blackwood Had a son: Robert Veyr of Blackwood Died soon after receiving a charter of confirmation from Robert, the Abbot of the Monastery of Kelso dated 1474. Had a son: Thomas Weir of Vere of Blackwood Married Lady Aegidia, daughter of John, 3rd Lord Somerville (of the Dragon) in 1483. Acquired vast holdings of land and was patron of St. Mary's Church in Lesmahagow. Died in the beginning of the reign of Queen Mary of Scots in 1542. Plantagenet descent of the House of Vere Thomas had a son: James Weir of Vere, 7th Baron Blackwood Married Lady Euphemia Hamilton, (Merovingian descent) sister of the Duke of Chatelherault, Marquess of Hamilton, 5th Grandson of King Edward III Plantagenet. The Hamiltons were the Heirs Presumptive to the Throne of Scotland during this period. James lived to a great age. He died in 1595. Had sons: 1. James Weir 2. William Vere of Stonebyres who married Elizabeth Hamilton. 3. Robert Weir James married Lady Marriotte Ramsay, daughter of George, Lord Dalhousie. James was an ancestor of the Hope-Veres of Craig Hall. George Ramsay was created Earl of Melrose in 1618 and changed this to the earldom of Dalhousie in 1619. The 9th earl was Governor of Canada, Nova Scotia and New Brunswick. His son was Governor General of India. 1. James had issue: George Weir of Vere who married Margaret Vere of Stonebyres with whom he had one daughter: Marriotte Weir who married: 1st. = Major James Bannatyne (a sept of the Stewarts of Bute). 2nd. = William Lowry by whom she had a Son George who retained his mother's superior Vere name and became Sir George Weir Bt. (descent to Hope-Vere of Blackwood). The Hope-Veres died out in 1974. In the beginning of the 18th century Catherine Weir - daughter of Sir George Weir Bt. - married Charles Hope and changed the spelling of the name Weir back to Vere, not wishing to be continually known by a series of historical spelling mistakes and variations.

The Lord Lyon King of Arms of Scotland acknowledges and records the restoration of the name Vere from its incorrect rendition as 'Weir'. Today the senior families use the affectation 'Weir of Vere' or simply 'de Vere' as the name is correctly accepted and most often historically rendered. (See Burke's extraction below). It is also to be noted that - as recorded in historical dissertations, documents and Wills pertaining thereunto - the Weirs or Veres made it a clause in their inheritance practice that any man marrying a Vere heiress had to change his name in order to enjoy the benefits of his intended spouse's wealth and lands. Furthermore the name Vere was considered to hold seniority and superiority over all other names in Britain and in the case of a female becoming sole heiress, it was not considered fitting that she should take to herself solely her husbands surname, as was usually the practice. In this family - when the occasion arises - the female surname of Vere is either taken by the husband and father to be or occupies the latter position traditionally taken by a husband's surname in other families. 2. William Vere of Stonebyres. See 'Vere of Tyrone' below. (Merovingian descent). 3. Robert Weir of Vere of Craighead, sold or assigned his estate in 1610 and moved to Monaghan Hall in Co.Fermanagh, now renamed Hallcraig House. Robert married the sister of the alchemist Sir David Lindsay, The Lord Lyon King of Arms of Scotland. Robert had sons, the eldest surviving son was: Alexander who married Anne, Daughter of Sir John Dunbar (Graham descent) of Derrygonnelly, Co. Fermanagh. Their eldest son: Alexander married Sarah, daughter of Captain Goodwin and secondly, Elizabeth, daughter of Sir Paul Gore Bt. Their eldest son: Robert Weir of Hallcraig married Anne, daughter of Captain Carleton of Tullymargy Castle. They had a son Captain Alexander Weir of Hallcraig (from whom the Normanised branch of the House of Vere descends to Nicholas de Vere's ducal kinsman – Prince An Mhaior - by Papal Decree HI&RH The Archduke of Argentina) and Captain Noble Weir of Hallcraig who married Catharine Graham (descent from the Grahams of Scotland 1600) and had issue. From Robert various branches descend. ('Burke's Irish Landed Gentry' 1891-1915; 'Burke's Landed gentry' 1974; 'Burke's Peerage, Baronetage and Knightage' 1957; Burke's Dormant and Extinct Peerages). From the senior surviving son - William Vere of Stonebyres by Elizabeth Hamilton - a son Thomas of Kirkton who by the Witch - Lady Jane Somerville - had Major Thomas Weir of Edinburgh: Sorcerer, King of the Witches of the Lallan and Elven Prince Consort to the Queen of Faery or Elphame - or as some say - "The Queen of Hell". The Somerville Badge was the Fiery Dragon surmounting the Pentacle. Major Weir served with his Irish cousins as a Captain Lieutenant in Sir John Hume's Enniskillen regiment in Ulster in 1640 and by family tradition he founded the Tyrone Branch of the family. From Major Weir - who was burnt at the stake at Leith, Edinburgh in 1670 - a son Thomas whose issue decamped to Ireland during the witch craze, from whom John of Kildress whose son Andrew had a daughter - Margaret Weir of Vere of Kildress - who by Archibald Thompson had a son Archibald Weir of Vere. Archibald married Rachael Stewart and had issue. The eldest son Robert Weir of Vere married a Vere cousin - Sarah Graham - and had a son John who moved back to Scotland and married Mary Logan of Logan Manor in Galloway. The Logan families have held their lands in Galloway and the Stranraer Peninsula since the 1100's, whilst others of that name held Restalrig. Accompanying Sir James Douglas, two Logan Knights, Sir Walter and Sir Robert Logan, were killed in Spain whilst taking the heart of Robert the Bruce to the Holy Land for burial. John's eldest son: Thomas Weir of Vere of Lewes married a Gael, Anne Grant Macdonnell of Inverness. They had male issue, the eldest of which died without heirs. The second eldest and surviving son: James Weir of Vere of Lewes who married a Vere-Collison family cousin Natalie Hopgood, daughter of George Collison Hopgood Esquire and Julia Harding of Godalming, granddaughter of Captain George Butcher of the 11th Light Dragoons (Lieutenant Colonel of the Regiment in the field), of Windsor Castle and Osbourne House; Tapetiere to Queen Victoria. Family Colleges: Charterhouse,

Godalming, Surrey UK., and St. Ursula's College. James and Natalie had an only son: Prince Nicholas Thomas Logan Weir of Vere (Nicholas de Vere) Gm.K.T., K.C.D., Knight Templar; Knight of Clan Donnachaidh of Eire; Magister Templi via the Baphometic Order of The Cubic Stone 1118; Princeps Draconis. By Gaelic blood descent and de jure Clan Chief and Head of The Royal House of Vere in England. Parish Records for Ulster 1820 - 1845, United Kingdom Government Registers for Births, Marriages and Deaths 1845-1957. Sussex Register of Electors U.K. Sussex Courts of Law U.K. British Government Department of Internal Affairs. Burke's Genealogies. Genetics The relationship between the Prince Mhaior - The Archduke of Argentina - who, by Normanised descent, is the Head of the Irish House of Vere and Nicholas de Vere; who - by Gaelic blood descent - is also Chief of the Tyrone Kildress Branch is that of 4th and 14th cousins. Both share various identical genes. Found in only 3% and 6% of the clinical samples tested in Britain, Nicholas de Vere and the Head of the House in Eire share two sets of rare genes each. The Prince Mhaior is of Royal Collison extraction and Nicholas de Vere has an extra set of these genes from the matrilinear descent which also supports the Royal Collison descent from Norfolk in his own lineage and echoes the selective and exclusive royal and noble marital alliances which have continued throughout the history of the House of Vere. The House of Weir and Vere commissioned genetic tests to be undertaken to confirm the precise degree of relationship between their respective lines and in order to clarify any anomalies in genealogy that inevitably creep into the records as the mists of time occlude the past. This was achieved successfully and some records were amended to reflect genetic findings both in Nicholas' lineage and that of another of his Vere cousins in Ireland, confirming that Nicholas' descent is one of the senior bloodlines of the House of Vere. However, the genetic makeup of the House of Vere manifesting generation after generation proved to be so unusual that, beyond the remit of the original commission by the family, the Department of Haemogenetics at London University took the Veres on as a special study case. At this particular stage of the research a Conference Presentation Document has been submitted prior to the delivery of a Medical Paper at a forthcoming Genetics Symposium in the United States, by an eminent professor in the department who is an internationally recognised pioneer in genetics. Further racial and mitochondrial studies on the Vere family are planned by the department.

Notes The Royal House of Vere - The Senior Angevin House of the original 'Princes and Counts of Anjou' - are latterly of Breton and Flemish extraction and the former senior, Scottish Branch; Hope-Vere of Blackwood, traditionally observed the Flemish law of Noblesse Uterine, and matrilinear and family inheritance in accordance with noble Scottish family law, which contemporarily and historically supports blood descent. The Titles of Princeps Draconis and Prince de Vere, currently held by Nicholas de Vere, are acknowledged as foreign titles in confidential files held by the British Government's Department of Internal Affairs: 'The Home Office' and are registered with them as 'Official Observations'. These titles are recognised by the most senior branches of the House of Vere. The right of fons honorum held by Nicholas de Vere is also acknowledged by Her Majesty's government. Nicholas de Vere, though accepting the existence of both with some considerable qualification; does not claim to be either a member of the contemporary British royal household or of its peerage in any sense, and does not claim any status or rank suggestive of such or appertaining thereunto. The Vere princedoms are not modern, socially derived titles; either assumed or bestowed, for or by, political expediency. The princedoms of Vere are ancient cultural manifestations of genetic qualities carried in the historical Elven Blood Royal. Established in Angiers in 740 a.d. as a Royal House arising from far older sacral-regal, Pictish, Scythian Vere origins rooted in antiquity, the House of Vere is recorded in a single name and in an unbroken line for over one thousand three hundred years, and consequently is one of the oldest surviving royal dynasties in Europe[3].

[3] See appendix at the back for full genealogy

Title page of the Dragon Legacy by Nicholas de Vere

Frontispiece

The Beast, the Dragon, the terrible monster, is the disguise of the beloved; the horror to be overcome itself is, or contains, the Reward. Beauty and the Beast must be conjoined. The old tag that a serpent becomes not a Dragon save by devouring another serpent, has an Alchemical sense: These are the two Dragons, male and female: they destroy one another, or one destroys the other and a new and mightier one is born, a fiery won- der: A Phoenix (traditionally depicted as having red and gold plumage*), a leaping glory, a STAR of dream ascending to the throne of the world. This was the Transmutation, the Great Work of the hidden glory of perfection. —Arthur Machen, Fr.GD. (Frater of the Hermetic Order of the Golden Dawn) The mating of Ravens is the rhythmic inhalation and exhalation of the breath of Ravens, one by the other. And in this way are the children of Ravens fashioned. (The Raven is the Phoenix of the Elven Kings). —Traditional country folklore (England) * The red and gold field, traditionally symbolising the plumage of the Phoenix— super- imposed by the white Star—are the Arms of the Vere. Supported by two Dragons, they historically have become one of the Seals of the House. Red and gold are also the colours of other descendants of the Merovingian dynasty, including the Planagenets, the Mandevilles, the Spencers and the pre-Jacobite Royal House of Scotland.

DRAGON LEGACY
BY TRACY TWYMAN

Blood Victory: Hope for the Future of Our Race and Civilization by Tracy R. Twyman I first heard of Nicholas de Vere on an internet chat group; typically, an environment where people pretend to be something they are not, using their anonymity as an excuse to behave even more boorishly than they do in real life. On this chat group, we had recently been discussing the theories presented in Laurence Gardner's book Genesis of the Grail Kings. The list was suddenly flooded with emails declaring that Mr. Gardner's work was not to be trusted because he had once been involved with the unscrupulous "Nicholas de Vere", or, as one detractor called him, "Tom Weir." The gist of the claim was that Mr. de Vere, who said he was a member of the "Grail bloodline" (the subject of the discussion list) had fabricated a royal genealogy, invented a royal magical order called "The Dragon Court", which he bogusly declared to be ancient, and stood to make lots of money by selling admission to this order, as well as the sales of his book, From Transylvania to Tunbridge Wells (now called The Dragon Legacy)—a book which, according to the emails, was utter nonsense and not worth reading. Being the individualistic type that I am, my natural inclination upon being told not to read something by self-serving know-it all's, is to seek it out immediately. This I did, easily locating Nicholas de Vere's book, which was, at that time posted for free in its entirety on the Dragon Court website—hardly the act of an unscrupulous con man wishing to make big bucks off of a bogus claim. I printed out the entire thing and sat down on my bed to read, high-lighter in hand to mark off anything important. A day and a half later, I had slept little, consumed lots of coffee, and was sitting in front of a manuscript half-covered in pink highlighter. For the first time in my life, I had discovered another person who thought exactly the same way I did about the Grail, and the Grail bloodline. Everything within this book corroborated the theories, speculations, and ideas that we had been writing about in a book of my own, many of them ideas that I had held for a long time but never been able to prove.

Yet here was a man claiming to speak for that very bloodline and ancient tradition which I had been studying and stating with assuredness what I had been hesitantly proposing. De Vere painted a picture of the beginnings of the Grail bloodline in an antediluvian civilization, with a super-human, red-haired race of Grail kings that conquered and ruled over the primitive hordes of the ancient world, with tribes on each continent. It provided the royal houses which guided the des- tiny of all civilized man. They were overseers, "navigators", directing the affairs of the world with the Solomonic wisdom inherent in their blood. They watched over a perfect caste-ordered society, in which all people worked and lived within their proper station, creating a harmonious, inter-dependent and respectful relationship between the classes. They created all of the traditions, customs and institutions upon which civilization depends, and of which our current traditions, customs and institutions are pathetic bastardizations. In fact, I would assert that the Dragon tradition has proven to be the very definition of "tradition" itself. As amazing as it was to find these ideas, identical to my own, in de Vere's unpublished manuscript, what was truly astounding were the more meta- physical aspects of the theory, again chillingly close to my own ideas.

To de Vere, it is the blood itself which provides the basis for the "divine right" of Dragons to be the overseers of society, and this is what sets them apart from the rest of humanity, as gods are from mortals. This is the reason why, originally, they refused to mate outside of their race, and the reason why, later, they indulged in blood-drinking rituals in which the sacred Grail DNA could be consumed. But perhaps most amazing of all, de Vere states that Grail blood contains genes specifically programmed for "magic." Dragons, and only Dragons, can perform magic, and are Therefore, the only authentic Witches, according to de Vere. For that reason, magic has always been an exclusive, secretive, royal art, and those outside of the blood- line attempting to perform such experiments are doomed to failure. We see these failures walking amongst us every day, and we can smell the mixture of self-pity and patchouli oil a mile away. This book lays down for the first time the scientific principles behind the effective use of ritual magic, and why some "magicians" are more effective than others. It explains the significance of the "Grail bloodline", irrespective of modern pseudo-intellectual theories and religious doctrines.

It reveals the true import behind age-old tales of Vampires, Elves, Fairies, etc. It gives a reasonable explanation for the otherwise inexplicable course of man's his- tory, all the way back to the Golden Age of the gods, and man's fall from the grace of the natural state of affairs. It lays down the principles behind a fair and ordered society; something we once, during the Golden Age, took for granted. It sets the foundation for a true understanding of man's natural hierarchy and issues a death warrant for civilization should this fail to occur. De Vere writes from the perspective of a lone wolf, a man who fears neither death nor life, and lives for the purpose of being. He writes to satisfy his personal impulse towards self-expression; to put the truth as he sees it down on paper—not to convince anyone else. He is a self-contained entity.

He needs nothing and no one outside of himself. Yet he represents and defends the worldview of an entire race of men—or, shall I say, "overmen"—with whom he shares a genetic, familial relationship. To him that is the only human relationship that fully counts, that truly deserves the superior man's time, effort and emotion. All else is the puerile sentimentalism of the degenerate masses. Beyond his loyalty to his kinfolk, de Vere's true fidelity lies with the order of the universe, and that transcendental principle which ordinary men know little of but refer to blindly as "God." De Vere is an iconoclast, an eccentric genius. He has all the qualities of the great writers and thinkers of history. In his philosophy I put him on the same shelf as Julius Evola, or maybe next to Oswald Spengler. His historical perspective places his work amongst classics like Ignatius Donnelly's Atlantis: The Antediluvian World, or L.A. Waddell's The Makers of Civilization in Race and History.

His encyclopaedic knowledge of occult traditions, their true meanings and origins, is superior to that of A.E. Waite, Manly Hall, or Israel Regardie. In the future, this book will be indispensable to all serious students of the true occult tradition. "Hekas hekas este bebeloi!" ("Begone, begone, ye profaners") It is safe to say that nothing is sacred in the writings of Nicholas de Vere, except that which is, by nature, sacred, because it pertains to that which is pure spirit. He does not reserve any pity for the sensitivities of pathetic liberalisms and makes mincemeat of the modern pseudo-religions: The Cult of Children*, the Cult of the Goddess, the Cult of the Oppressed, the Cult of Equality, and the Cult of Economy. Likewise, ritualistically slaughtered are the supposedly "right wing" and "conservative" cults such as those of Race, Religion, and Nationalism. This book is likely to anger people; namely: a. Liberals will not like this book because it dares to point out that not all men are created equal, nor are all men necessarily members of the same species.

It shows that nature has assigned a caste system to various types of people, and that society works better when those castes are kept intact. People are happier when not forced, expected, or encouraged to live either above or below their natural station in life. b. Catholics will be upset by what de Vere has to say about their holy institution. They will also not be pleased with De Vere's lax attitude towards such contentious issues as incest, homosexuality, cannibalism, blood-drinking, and human sacrifice.

* It is well-known in the advertising industry that any product or idea can be sold by implying that the "children of the world" will somehow benefit. This assertion is usually followed by the sickening catchphrase "children are the future", as if every snivelling rug rat were somehow paramount to the continuation of time. In reality, "the future" may be found in only a fraction of a percent of those children, and feeding an out-of-control population of degenerates is not going to further any worthwhile goals.

New Age people will be upset to read, from someone who clearly knows what he's talking about, that their incense, candles and figurines are nothing more than a drain on their bank account. (This bank account undoubtedly came with a personalized dragon-themed cheque book that says "The Goddess is alive and magic is afoot.") The reason for this is because the vast majority of these people are physiologically incapable of performing magic, according to de Vere. White supremacists will be upset because, as c. tempting as it will be for them to connect their cause to the Dragon heritage, they won't be able to. De Vere describes the kinfolk which these people come from as slave races fit mostly for field labour. He also dismisses out of hand their precious "Fatherland" idea and their pathetic nation-worship. d. Finally, de Vere assures me that his work will be offensive to those upper-crust Englishmen and "tinker nobility" who still uphold the farce of Victorian values and artistic tastes. Being an American, I am not exposed to "Victorian values" very often, so I cannot comment on this matter any further. "After a long sleep, the same theories reappear. Without doubt they return richer and with new clothes, but the foundation remains the same, and the new mask which they wear should not mislead the man of knowledge." —Le Serpent Rouge De Vere's manifesto portrays a rather pessimistic attitude towards the idea of social progress, implying that the Golden Age of Dragon hegemony is for- ever lost, never to return. This is something with which I do not agree. In fact, I can see de Vere's book playing the role of the revolutionary harbinger, welcoming back a lost era. The word "revolution" implies revolving, returning in a circular pattern to the original starting point, like the labyrinthine spiral of history which Nick discusses later in this volume. All of the points in history Therefore, issue from, and are based upon the unchanging centre, that which is "a priori", like the snake biting its tail which the Dragon Court uses in its insignia. Nature has a way of correcting imbalances, of restoring elements to their rightful place.

Yet before that can happen, we must all be reminded of what the natural order actually is. Pseudo-intellectuals like to annoyingly quote the tired adage, "Those who forget history are condemned to repeat it." I say that unless we are reminded of the Golden Age of history we will be unwilling, unmoved, and unable to replicate it in our modern era.

This book is like a spell calling forth the forces that ruled thousands of years ago, calling them back to once again hold dominion over us. Within the pages of this volume we, as Dragons (and I consider myself among them), declare our intention to take back what is rightfully ours.

If the powers of God and nature are on our side, how can we fail? "Might is right" is a popular motto amongst those who label themselves "Social Darwinists." While the principle holds true, a more proper way to express it would be to say that "right is might". That is, if you are acting righteously in accord with what is right for you, attempting to take hold of the power that is rightfully yours, nature will equip you with the might necessary to accomplish that task.

Materialism is the lie, brought to the forefront by the mercantile class so loathed by de Vere, which has caused the decay of society to its current level. People have whole-heartedly swallowed the assertion that "money is power" (outdone only by the equally offensive "time is money.")

Even those who have attempted to rebel against materialism, such as the Hippies of the '60s era, or the Communists of the 20th century, have always fallen into the materialist logic trap. They mistakenly believed that the problem of materialist elitism could be cured by redistributing the material wealth of rich people, and preventing the accumulation of wealth, as if wealth itself were the problem, instead of the people who own it. Foolishly they chanted slogans like, "There is no war but class war", and made statements like, "Every war in history was fought over money", when in fact almost every war can be traced back to a spiritual origin, a conflict between deeply held beliefs, ideas, and cultural norms.

It may be true that, as a general rule, those with true power use that power to acquire wealth, and that those who are wealthy often use it to empower themselves. But the fact is that the two concepts—money and power—are two entirely different things. Money is a tool. It can be a reward for goods or services provided, a means of acquiring things that are needed, and a way of enabling projects to come to fruition. If it weren't for the fact that certain people have acquired large sums of money, nothing of any consequence would ever happen—no wars, no monuments, no research and development. But removed from the context in which it is being used, money is meaning- less. It is a purely contingent phenomenon.

Power, however, is something transcendental. Unlike money, it is not something that was invented by mankind as a means to an end. It issues directly from God, and from Nature herself. There is such a thing as power for power's sake; and power, in the civic realm, is based on sovereignty, which comes from the blood. Therefore, true power resides not in a person's bank account, but in their DNA. There it rests within most of us, potential energy waiting to be con- verted into kinetic energy through actual use. But most people are too weak of will, too lazy and unimaginative to make use of it. Even many people of the Dragon blood have sunk into this abyss of uselessness. But the time for rest and relaxation is over now. We are charged with the responsibility of saving civilization, as the only people who are clear-sight- ed enough and capable of doing so. "Cease to Resist!" —The Beach Boys, paraphrasing Charles Manson

This book is part of a literary zeitgeist currently in manifestation that is destined to usher in a new era amongst the intelligentsia of the Western world, something I have termed "the Renaissance of the Arcadian Mystique." Already much of the groundwork has been laid by the popular Laurence Gardner books Genesis of the Grail Kings and Dragon Realms of the Ring Lords. These titles share much common ground with this book, The Dragon Legacy, which was completed in an early form back in 1997. But there is much work yet to be done. The job of writers, artists and philosophers such as de Vere and I is not to bring about the political revolution which looms on the horizon. That is the job of the men of action who belong to our cause, the born leaders of the Dragon blood who have been waiting and planning in the shadows for centuries, patiently plotting and manipulating in anticipation of the opportunity to act. They need no help in that regard. Rather, it is the job of the literary and artistic set to effect the intellectual revolution, which must precede the political revolution. It is our job to clear the path ahead, to prepare the hearts and minds of the populace for what is to come, and to erase all fear, doubt, and resistance.

We need not worry that the ideological climate is so seemingly hostile to the values of blood, spirit, and hierarchy that we promote. The masses have no will of their own, beyond that which is given to them by those who assert themselves as their superiors. We live in a multi-national culture that con- siders taking on a new ideological system to be equivalent to putting on a T- shirt. They will attach themselves to any idea which is effectively marketed so as to take advantage of their frail psychology. The occurrences on the 11th of September 2001 proved that beyond question. Overnight, the American values of libertarian independence, personal freedom, an inherent "right to privacy", and a healthy mistrust of authority gave way to state worship, rabid religious moralism, pithy sentimentality, and a general attitude of compliance towards "whatever's necessary to keep us safe." All that was necessary to achieve the result was to push the right buttons. A Blue Light Special in the Marketplace of Ideas We have been told that our democratic society is a free "marketplace of ideas."

Since democracy is also capitalistic, it only makes sense that the "marketplace of ideas" embodies the same principles as our economy.

The laws of supply and demand dictate what ideas are considered valuable, which beliefs are valid, and Therefore, which truths exist. By right of popularity, even the laws of physics can be accepted, rejected, or altered at will. But most ideas are cheap, worthless, crap; both the popularly held ideas and the majority of the rebellious "counter-ideas" presented by the numerous "counter-cultures." Better that the intellectuals of today all dedicate themselves to promoting and exploring a single priceless, transcendental idea. They can then find the best ways to defeat all competing, inferior ideas, rather than wasting their lives trying to come up with their own original (they dream) bad ideas, or, worse yet, trying to promote a conglomerate of meaningless and contradictory herd ideas which they regard as worthy by right of their popularity. A book like this is meant to penetrate into the intellectual, educated class of society, sowing the seeds of Draconian ideals, on hopes that they fall on fertile ground, grow, and pollinate the popular culture a la "trickle down" theory. **It is then up to the intellectuals who have been won over to our side to solidify the ideological revolution in the popular mind.**

All that is truly necessary for this to occur, once the literate set has been fully indoctrinated, is an eye-catching symbol, and a memorable slogan, then the constant repetition of these two in conjunction until no one can remember a time when these ideas had not been accepted and understood.

It is not necessary to argue, debate, or defend these ideas, but only to assert them as the absolute truths that they are. Wishy-washy discussion which considers the merits of opposing views merely invites attack and ridicule. However, truths spoken with authority and confidence have the mesmerizing effect upon the populace for which we are aiming. Once they are willing to accept, even demanding a transition back to the old, true order, and Draconian traditional values, we can remove the tyrannies of democracy and capitalism, putting to bed once and for all this moronic concept of the "marketplace of ideas."

There is but one real idea, and we must hold true to it unswervingly. When we vacillate, when we stop to consider alternative ideas, we lose. We must surpass the intellect of the populace and aim at the soul. Gustave le Bon wrote in The Crowd: "All founders of religious or political creeds have established them solely because they were successful in inspiring crowds with those fanatical sentiments which have as result that men find their happiness in worship and obedience and are willing to lay down their lives for their idols". This is the effect we are going for, and this monumental text put forth by Nicholas de Vere shall go a long way in promoting that cause. Thanks to him and to others like him (although there truly are no others like him), the future of the Dragon blood trembles with the awesomeness of its glorious potential. Our destiny awaits. Fraternally, Tracy. R. Twyman, E.G.M., O.L.E. Editor, Dagobert's Revenge Magazine.

The Imperial and Royal Dragon Court of the Dragon Sovereignty: Sarkany Rend 1408; Curia Regis et Ordo Draconis The Imperial and Royal Dragon Court of the Dragon Sovereignty intends to continue to publish individual aspects of its history, along with references to the classical folklore and mythic customs of Europe and Asia which are directly linked to the Dragon tradition. We trust that readers of this work will find the given details sufficient to cement the facts pertaining to the "Dragon" peoples, the Dragon Sovereignty and its Court.

As defined within the main body of the following text, the Imperial and Royal Dragon Court represented herein, legitimately recognised as the Sovereign Court of The Sovereign Dragon Nation by the relevant and appropriate Government of a European Member State, is a closed fraternity of individuals, representing those who trace their ancestry and affiliations back to the ancient Grail and Dragon families. A Closed Fraternity. When the Imperial and Royal Dragon Court was reconstituted by King Sigismund in 1408 as the Societas Draconis, it was based upon an ancient bloodline tradition which Sigismund assumed that he had inherited from his presumed Egyptian and Scythian ancestors through the Pictish, Dragon Princess Maelasanu of Northumbria and the Ancient and Original Angevin Royal House of Vere of Anjou, the Imperial Dukes of Angiers. This line had descended through the Tuatha de Danaan (the Dragon Kings of Anu) on the one hand, and the Egyptian Dragon Dynasty of Sobek on the other. The latter strain included the bloodline of the Davidic House of Judah who married into the descent of the Merovingian Kings of the Franks. Human Vanities Emperor Sigismund (as he was styled from 1410) was a son of the House of Luxembourg—dynasts who flagrantly altered their genealogy in order to be able to claim a fraudulent descent from this Dragon Dynasty of Maelasanu and Anjou. It is from this descent—from Maelasanu or Melusine—and upon her British, later Angiers-Angevin, Dragon Court, that Sigismund claimed the right to base Societas Draconis as a bloodline continuation of this ancient, prehistoric, anti-Christian, pre-Catholic, British Elven Institution. One of the most famous members of Sigismund's misappropriated organisation was Vlad Basarab or Draculea, the son of Vlad Drakul. After Draculea's death, his son Michael wrote that his father proudly claimed a linear descent from the Priests of the Dragon Court of Queen Sobekh Nefru of Egypt, whose predecessor Amenhemet had built the Dragon Labyrinth of Fayyum—dedicated to Sobekh—which was later copied in Crete as the Labyrinth of the Minotaur. Dynastic Deceptions.

The genealogy of the House of Drakul, Dracula or Basarab is well known and widely documented. Descending from Atilla the Hun, this family was established in Central Europe by the sons of Genghis Khan. No bloodline with which the House of Basarab was associated or allied in marriage at that time had any affiliation with any extraction that was remotely related with the dynasties of Egypt. It is obvious, Therefore, that Draculea or Dracula must have been claiming an apostolic succession, a spiritual priestly lineage deferring to the Egyptian Dragon Court of Sobekh Nefru through Sigismund's assumed descent from Melusine. Her ancestry actually can be traced back to the Scythian

Dragon Princess Scota, Queen Sobekh Nefru and the Egyptian Cult of the Dragon. Undoubtedly Dracula assumed erroneously that he had received this ancient mystical honour during his investiture into Sigismund's Societas Draconis, and by virtue of Sigismund's supposed descent from Melusine and the ancient Angevin House of Vere. In his own right, Dracula can claim no relationship to any early Angevins, nor to the later second Anjou House of Plantagenet, except via an eight-link marital bridge which has no alliances that relate him by blood to Anjou. Sigismund assumed a personal entitlement to this legacy in 1397, the date upon which he sought to reconstitute Princess Melusine's Dragon Court—as Societas Draconis—in a manner that he deemed the most suitable to enhance his power base and establish his royal claims. Following its subsequent for- mal inception in 1408, the Court recruited members from a number of prominent royal and noble houses. Historians have noted that these were not particularly known for their religious orthodoxy, including the later House of Vere in England, as one authority on Sigismund's Dragon Court has asserted. Today, however, the Imperial and Royal Dragon Court itself exists as a closed fraternity, a collective of individuals, comprising those who, unlike Sigismund, can trace their ancestry and affiliations back to the ancient, pre- Christian Elven, Grail and Dragon families via Anjou.

The Court retains the traditional three tier degree system that Sigismund borrowed and to which he appended three separate representations of the alchemical Ouroboros emblem for the distinct ranks of the Court. A fourth emblem, configured in the form of the Egyptian Ankh or Albigensian Cross, was used by the family officers of the Inner Temple. The tripartite system was peculiar to the Scythians and Celts, whose Druids incorporated a similar structure within their orders and colleges. It later found expression within the Cathar fraternity of Languedoc and also with the Witches. It was developed within the Hierarchical Rule of the Knights Templar with whom the Court had a strong historical connection. Blood Relationship The Inner Temple is presided over by the Vere Grand Masters, who are currently resident in Britain and Europe. Being essentially an organisation which emphasises the crucial links between Dragon families, the rank system within the Court takes second place to the sense of blood relationship and the natural bond of co-operation engendered by that relationship. Service, Mutual support and respect supersede those types of ambition and advancement which prevail in other bodies which might, on the face of it, resemble the Dragon Court model in some ways. Within such orders, sights are firmly set towards material gain through supporting establishments which themselves breed division and inequity. The tenets of the Grail and Dragon traditions are implicit in defining that we should be at one with the earth, and cannot, Therefore, presume dominion over it. Unlike those who wish to profit unjustifiably from dubious Merovingian descent.

This philosophy is embedded in the concept of individual gnosis and lies at the very heart of the Draconian culture. It is evident in all aspects of life itself. Emanating from the ancient lore of the Elven Lords and Ladies of the Forest, these ancestral legacy forms the bedrock upon which this and all legitimately related Dragon Courts were originally founded. The Tinker Kings It is no secret that, through a process of calculated indoctrination, our individual decisions are often prompted by fears of non-conformity or insecurity. As a result, we are conditioned to purchase a variety of hyped goods and services in order to redress personal inadequacies that do not, in fact, exist. In reality, the prevalent forms of fear-based merchandising are little different from straightforward protection rackets, and yet they are sanctioned and encouraged by our governing establishments. For centuries, western state authorities and their Churches have enjoyed continued power over a subordinate majority, by presenting a facade of sacrosanct jurisdiction which has seemed inextricably linked to some form of royalty, nobility, or government by divine sanction. By virtue of this, it is not surprising that so many people now consider royalty, nobility and western religion to be archaic components of a system of class and privilege which has no place in the modern age.

What few recognise, however, is that for centuries the perceived representation of royalty and nobility has, to a large extent, been a fraud perpetuated by a dressed-up merchant class elite who have no real entitlement to their positions. This farce, with its inherent tyranny and social abuse, has been endured through the ages, while the true bloodline families have been suppressed and supplanted by traders and brokers disguised in crowns and mitres. In practice, there is nothing noble about these tinker kings since the word "noble" relates to gnosis or wisdom. However, they have long been defined as "aristocrats" (meaning "best rulers") and have thereby retained gratuitous stations of power and influence in a self-proclaimed higher echelon of society. These tinker kings and their emissaries have plagued the western scene for generations, leaving all to wonder how it is that our supposed guardians and ambassadors are so often an embarrassment, and are rarely representative of community requirement. They refer to all and sundry as "subjects", "commoners" and "flocks" using such patronising terminology as "the ordinary people" or "the man in the street", as if they had some predestined right of supremacy. In reality, the fact is that the individual establishments of these said aristocrats (be they state heads, provincial overlords or clerical governors) are frequently very questionable, and their personal roots are often more ordinary than most. Mother Earth Prior to these distortions, the nature of kingship was entirely different. There was no requirement for Church sanction through coronation by parvenu popes or archbishops. Kingship was founded upon the ideal that all people were adherents of the earth, and that the earth bestowed sovereignty upon its first-born people, the Elven Tribes.

They were represented by a Dragon Queen, and she empowered the Grail King, who could not be a king without her. In this environment, the right to kingship emanated from the female, since Mother Earth was herself deemed to be female. The overriding function of a king and queen was to maintain a spiritually transcendent intelligence within the realm, thereby enabling the organism (the kingdom) to function and develop in symbiosis with its surrounding environment.

If a change of governmental practice is deemed necessary, then there is nothing to gain by swapping the merchant class nobles for lawyer class presidents. There is, however, much to be gained by considering the advantages of properly defined Grail kingship and the Messianic code of princely service within a socially orientated constitutional framework. This is the most logical route towards ensuring that true democracy prevails for "Democracy" and is correctly defined as "Government for the people by the people", as opposed to the all too familiar and oppressive "Government of the people". Opportunists and Orators As a result of a general disenchantment, many now suggest that royalty and nobility should be marginalized in favour of republican style government. Some determine that such changes replace privilege with a more acceptable form of merit advantage. However, this perception is equally untenable in practice. All that happens is that headstrong merchant class opportunists are replaced by polished lawyer class orators, thereby creating an unwarranted new elite, with the same destructive hold on society. Government of the majority by an exclusive clique, which uses intimidating tactics to manipulate a consumer-based economy, has nothing what- ever to do with the time-honoured spirit of Grail kingship and the Dragon blood. Any shift from monarchy to republicanism is simply a matter of different packaging.

In the event, we are still captive consumers enveloped within faiths of fear. Our legacy from all this is an inbred contempt for any- thing which does not conform to a system of venerated sale values. This leads to the loss of our relationship with the ecosphere upon which all species truly depend. The Grail The practical application of the Grail Code of service and guardianship was geared to the hermetic principle, "As above, so below". It recognised that no sane mind would, for the sake of short-term profit, disenfranchise the body upon which it depends. From medieval times, however, this is precisely what has happened, with the Church installing dealers and merchants as puppet kings, traders who had no knowledge of kingship, but who have spawned dynasties which, in turn, have appointed their own colleagues as hereditary puppet nobles.

The Church and its appointees (be they monarchs, bishops, or pseudo nobles) have proclaimed the Messianic legacy to be heresy. By doing this they have underwritten and promulgated tyrannical systems of elitism, separatism, and environmental domination to the detriment of the many.

Out of Egypt

The Dragon Court can first be identified in Egypt under the patronage of the priest prince Ankhfn Khonsu in about 2170 BC. It was subsequently established more formally as a pharaonic institution by the twelfth dynasty Queen Sobekh Nefru (c.1785 BC). The Court pursued the teachings of Thoth, which had prevailed from the time of Nimrod's grandson King Raneb, a pharaoh of the second dynasty. He reigned c. 2852 BC, about three centuries before the Gizeh pyramids are considered to have been built. In those far off times, the priests and temples were not associated with religion as were their later successors in other lands, but rather more with the duties of preserving and teaching the old wisdom.

The temples incorporated al-khame workshops. It was the obligation of the priests to maintain the spiritual welfare of the pharaohs, while ensuring the purity of a continuing royal bloodline which progressed through the Dragon Queens of the matrilinear Grail succession. Dragon sovereignty had evolved in Egypt from old Mesopotamia, and its tradition was vested in Sobek, the sacred crocodile (the messeh or mus-hus). It was from the practice of kingly anointing with the fat of the messeh that the Hebrew verb "mashiach" (to anoint) derived, and the Dragon dynasts became known as Messiahs (anointed ones). In

525 BC Egypt was conquered by the Persians, whose kings were subsequently ousted by Alexander the Great's Macedonian army in 332 BC.

This led to the Greek dynasty of the Ptolemies and the well-known Queen Cleopatra VII. Her liaison with the Roman general Mark Antony caused the final downfall of the pharaohs, and Egypt was subjugated by Imperial Rome shortly before the time of Jesus. At length, as the Roman Empire collapsed, Egypt fell to Byzantine governors and then, after AD 641, to the sway of Islam.

The Pendragons By that time, the Grail Dynasty from David and Solomon had progressed into the West, notably to the Merovingian kings of Gaul, while related branches established kingdoms in Ireland and Celtic Britain. These lines were linked through marriage to parallel Dragon strains from Ham, Japhet and Tubal Cain (which had survived as the royal houses of Scythia and Anatolia). The families had forged their own marital links with the early princesses of the Egyptian succession. The first Pendragon (Head Dragon) of the Britannic Isle (Pen Draco Insularis). From this stock was King Cymbeline of the House of Camu, who was installed in about AD 10. The Celtic Pendragons were not father to son successors in a particular descent but were individually elected from reigning family branches, by a Druidic council of elders, to be the overall Kings of Kings. The last Pendragon was Cadwaladr of Gwynedd, who died in AD 664.

At around that time much of Britain fell to the Germanic influence of the invading Anglo Saxons and Angle land (England) was born, as distinct from Scotland and Wales.

This coincided with Byzantium's loss of Egypt to the Caliphs and following the last Roman Emperor in AD 476, a completely new governmental structure evolved in the West. Its ultimate overlords were the Popes, and out- side the preserved Celtic domains they appointed kings not by any right of heritage, but to suit the political motives of the bishops and the fast-growing Roman Church. It appeared that the days of the Dragon heritage were over. However, the true dynasts of the original Grail stock always upheld their positions and the spirit of the Dragon Court continued in influential circles throughout Europe and the Near East. The Dragon and the Grail As the generations passed, the ideal of dynastic kingship spread through the Mediterranean lands into the Balkans, the Black Sea regions and Europe. But, in the course of this, the crucial essence of the old wisdom was lost, and this gave rise to dynasties that were not of the true kingly race. Instead, many were unrelated warrior chiefs who gained their thrones by might of the sword. The sacred culture of the ancients was, nevertheless, retained in the Messianic line of King David of Judah (c.1008 BC), whose significance was not in his generally portrayed descent from Abraham and the Shemite strain, but in his Pharaonic heritage.

It was through this particular Dragon inheritance that Solomon the Wise, some eight centuries after Queen Sobeknefru, was enabled to recreate the Royal Temple project in Jerusalem. This led to a Holy Land revival of the pharaonic Rosi Crucis (dew cup) movement at a time when Egypt was beset by foreign influences, first from Libya, Nubia and Kush, and then from further afield. As a result, the traditional marriage arrangements of the pharaohs and princesses gave way to diplomatic alliances. The symbol of the Rosi Crucis had identified the Grail succession from beyond 3000 BC, and its graphic representation was a red cross within a circle. Societas Draconis In 1408 (when Britain was in her Plantagenet era), the Dragon Court was formally reconstituted as a sovereign body at a time of wars and general political turmoil.

As we have seen, the Court's dubious re-emergence was instigated by Sigismund von Luxembourg, King of Hungary. Having presumptuously and erroneously assumed to have inherited the bloodline legacy in 1397, he drew up a pact with twenty-three royals and nobles who swore to observe "true and pure fraternity" within the Societas Draconis, a style subsequently misidentified as the Ordo Draconis (Hungarian: Sarkany Rend).

Although the original Court was by no means an Order in the recognised chivalric sense, the misnomer was strategically retained for the purposes of identification. Along with Sigismund and the twenty-three nobles, Sigismund's second wife, Barbara Cille (daughter of the Austrian Duke Hermann of Styria), was joint sovereign.

Barbara was a Vampire who was taught by Ibrahim Eleazar, the keeper of the Sacred Magic of Abramelin the Mage, and it is she who is the model for the beautiful Countess Carmilla Karnstein in le Fanu's novel of the same name. Sigismund's daughter Elizabeth was also a member of the Court, and the inclusion of the entire family thereby achieved the traditional overall standard of twenty-six members or two magical circles of thirteen. Others prominent in the Societas Draconis were the Kings of Poland and Aragon, the Duke of Lithuania and the unrepentant heretic, the Duke of Split. The founding document of the Court confirmed that members might wear the insignia of a Dragon incurved into a circle, with a red cross, the original emblem of the Rosi Crucis, which had identified the Grail succession from before 3000 BC. Members were required to wear black attire on Friday—the day ruled by Venus—and to all intents and purposes they were to hold property in common.

The Society had no patron saint; it had no chapel or chapter house and observed no feast or holy days. Members were expected to have been ennobled prior to entry and were only elevated within the Society in recognition of their contributions to the welfare of the Crown. Sigismund never knight- ed anyone into the Society. This ignored completely all the expected rituals and affectations of chivalry prevalent at the time.

At least the Luxembourgian got that right. Imperial Status Shortly after this foundation, Sigismund was crowned Holy Roman Emperor and, as a result, the noble fraternity achieved a heightened status as an imperial edifice. Although the Court's ancient origins were steeped in pre-Christian lore, Pope Eugene IV was obliged to approve his Emperor's non-Catholic establishment, for the nature of the Dragon, even if you fake it, is such that its kingly tradition surmounts the mundane constraints of denominational dispute. After all, King David, Solomon and even Jesus were all pre- Christian dynasts of the line. There were, of course, those staunch upholders of the Church's articles of dogma who openly opposed the pre papal concept of Grail kingship. These bishops pronounced the Arthurian romances heretical and black- listed the writings of Merlin in 1546 at the Council of Trento in northern Italy. Everything that was magic to the ears, and all that was fresh air to the subjugated, became denounced as sinister and occult. The great enlightenment of the "Grail Code" of service was condemned in a series of brutal Inquisitions from 1203, and anything remotely connect-ed with the female Draconian ethic was justifiably dubbed Witchcraft. The following series of essays, which could be alternatively titled The History of the Dragon Peoples, are extracted from archival and research material. The author derives its contemporary synthesis from a 30 to 40-year period of scholarship, teaching, revelation, and ceremony.

The following collection of studies reflects the nature of the author's final conclusions in 1993 and at the time of publication in 2004, respectively. This is the first book in a series of works covering the history of the Elven Tribes and the Dragon Tradition. Further works, due to be published here shortly, will include archaeological and historical studies of the Derkesthai Culture from 10,000 BC onwards, further material from the Dragon Archives, an ongoing series of novels and a series of scientific papers. The ethos of the Dragon Culture encourages an intelligent, but above all a ruthlessly honest appreciation of the matters presented. **We hope that this may expose the establishment's historical fabrications and deceptions throughout history which have harmed society immeasurably. We want to change the attitudes of the many who have been manipulated for the gain of a few for over one thousand years.**

PART ONE

Although it may appear elitist, when the old families observe that the Dragons are being misrepresented to the extent that everybody wants to become one, the time-honoured consensus of feeling among them is com- pounded. They see that it inevitably leads to a gap in the market being filled, resulting in yet another impudent impertinence being perpetrated. A good example of this is the detritus of Gerald Gardner which he presented in the 1950s as the "definitive" and "original" expression of the "Old Religion".

Inauthentic Witchcraft emerged in the 1950's, principally at the instigation of this retired clerk in the Indian Raj named Gerald

Gardner. It is from this particular source that the ridiculous notion of Witchcraft being primarily a fertility cult gained its credence. He sanitised what little he knew about Witches with exactly the same pecuniary, sexual or social motives that his descendants use for peddling their equally useless rubbish today. One can't "initiate" into the old blood or teach the old ways to the "mahoum". It is a pointless and fruitless waste of time that doesn't work. They inevitably get the wrong idea and discard its most valuable tenets. Alternatively, they add to that history or knowledge their own misconceptions which then become carved in stone and published in faddist popular books as the sacred wisdom of a faddist culture. Naturally it would be appreciated if people identified sympathetically with the characters in the Dragon tradition, but not to the extent where every reader thinks that they are one or can aspire to be one. Most of them could never be. The courses or "initiations" which are on offer from the exploiters of the "New Age" money machine are sanitised to obliterate what could be termed a "dark" and hence possibly "evil" tradition. Such exercises will also inevitably lead to the discredit of the Dragon ethos. When such courses or "initiations" are found not to work, it is because the majority of participants either won't have the right blood serum or the right connections in their cerebral lobes. We live in a world in which all people are encouraged to think of them- selves (somewhat hypocritically given the way they treat each other); in homogenous, egalitarian terms. Therefore, the foregoing statement is tantamount to heresy. It is unacceptable in ordinary society to suggest that people are not equal or physiologically and anatomically the same. But nevertheless, they are not. One might counter such an unreasonably deluded and elitist sounding statement by arguing that because of the outbreeding of the old families, there must be millions of people "of the Fairy blood" living today. However, such a statement flies in the face of the following accepted historical facts: a) The genuine old royal families rarely outbred at all, whilst the later, fake parvenu, tinker nobility with whom people now confuse them often did; b) Most of the Scythian, Royal-Druidic, Fairy population in Britain and Europe was wiped out by the Romans in the Battles at Mona and at other Druidic sites. c) The Celts (and what was left of the Scythian Fairy Families who served as their lords and protectors) were decimated by bubonic plague, starvation and the Saxon invasions in the 6th century.

Following this, in Britain and continental Eurasia, the Church and the rats spent another three or four hundred years, during the medieval and Reformation periods, dispatching the survivors of the previous epidemics, famines, wars or persecutions. d) That the Arȳan Scythian Overlords—the Fairy High Kings and Queens—maintained a caste system that, although eventually became corrupt and overrun by the warrior caste, was arguably still in place (as the European Class System) until the Second World War. Even up until the First World War the manorial restrictions on the movements of rural labourers, other than during holidays, were still enforced and Thus, unhindered mobility, either geographically or within the class system itself, was extremely rare. Throughout the period preceding the modification of the Witchcraft laws (now called "The Fraudulent Mediums' Act") the remnant of the Scythian, sacral-royal overlords who were left were destroyed by papal decree.

In the meantime, in Britain, in addition to the persecutions, many of the wealthier and more powerful overlords whose families had survived up to that point were killed off and/or replaced in both lands and name, by those merchant-class new tinker families. They, in turn, paid the corrupt ersatz royalty of the Tudor and Stewart Houses enough money for the titles and estates. Following this sequence of events Oliver Cromwell continued the good work and massacred the nobility and allowed their estates to be usurped by even more members of the merchant class.

Considering the sum of this state of affairs, it is extremely unlikely that any of the people in those classes whose descendants now patronise the "New Age" fads would have made contact with or intermarried with what was left of the pure Elven Blood-Royal. Therefore, to say perhaps that it doesn't matter whether a few mercenary fly-by-nights open up preposterous courses, making ludicrous, false claims to be able to train and initiate "probationary Elves" or "grail maidens", is a denial of what the Fairy blood and the teachings are all about.

The descent and the doctrine of the Elven Families are based upon truth and honour. The comparison shows in sharp relief to what extent people today have already been betrayed enough over the centuries by their own kind. If one presents people with the Dragon history in an over attractive candy- sweet wrapping or in such a manner as to make it seem as if anyone can belong to it, then one becomes a deceiver oneself.

This would lay others open to psychological abuse, financial exploitation, and manipulation at the hands of the "New Age Money Vampires", thereby adding yet another element to the mass psychological ignorance and confusion over identity that already contributes to so much social disquiet and unrest. Unscrupulous advertising executives, politicians and manufacturers lead people to believe that they can be whoever they want to be and achieve anything they want to achieve. The only conditions are that they have enough money and work hard enough for the establishment's corporate elites.

The object is to produce more efficient consumer-producers. Class barriers have been relaxed only slightly for a couple of generations. It is likely that the vast majority of those who would like to prop up their egos and empower themselves (in a world that only encourages such in the financial sense) by becoming Elven Magicians, Grail Maidens or Vampire Overlords are going to be in for a big disappointment. It's no use saying that people don't think like that because they do. Literally thousands of people in Britain and America have the impudence to call themselves Witches. Hundreds more join "magical orders" or associations.

Thousands more annually sign up for mystical, "New Age" workshops in a plethora of inappropriate foreign disciplines unsuited to their cultural backgrounds. It can be guaranteed that none of them were ever asked about their family history which, after all, from an endocrinal point of view, is the most important criterion. People don't realise that they have only just emerged from a social system which was corruptly used by the Church-State for centuries to engineer them into having specific brain physiologies which are not suitable for application to Dragon Subjects. If they were, then the majority of people would have transcended naturally by now anyway and the world would be an entirely different place.

They haven't, they can't, it isn't, and under the present circumstances, it never will be. Even if society were to interbreed more with the Dragon Families that are left—if there are any at all—then the Dragon DNA would eventually become weaker. In this case the Dragon ability would then be lost, leaving us with exactly the same social result anyway. The modern idea that potentially anyone can be "initiated" either as a Witch or a Druid is pretentious and arrogant. It has been, it is said, (in privately circulated Witchcraft documents*), a source of offence to many ancient families for over half a century.

Unless a full, genuine, known pedigree can be produced, demonstrating an unbroken line of descent from a royal, Arch druidic family, no modern aspirant or so-called priest or priestess has the right either to call themselves a Witch or a Druid. The same applies to those who would call themselves "Aryans". The modern concept of "initiation into Witchcraft" is an insult to those whose families, over the period of the Thousand Year Elven Holocaust, died at the hands of the Church. Like Elven royalty and nobility, to which Druidism and Witchcraft are inextricably linked, both are aspects of the High Aryan Mana, the mystical Maja or Maia, the genetic memory of a unique race that is carried in the blood. This cannot be bestowed by any form of nonsensical neo-pagan nonsense.

The Royal Windsor Coven and many others, reputedly old hereditary family groups, were the custodians of traditions which had, by their own admission, little or nothing in common with the modern neo-pagan revivalist movement or its reconstructed rituals. The latter had been invented by Gerald Gardner and revised by Sanders and other "initiates". These gentlemen,

The Marshmallow Papers related, were, along with Crowley, rebuffed by Pickingill or by other covens that descended from those East Anglian septs which themselves descended from either the historical British covens or the Flemish weavers. Here it must be noted that Aleister Crowley was actually interested in Witchcraft. Isn't that a surprise? Considering the fact that his generation of "magicians" usually tended to repudiate it. Or did they? Undoubtedly many "magicians" have justifiably poured scorn on modern Wicca but nevertheless, it still remains a recorded fact that Crowley attempt- ed to join George Pickingill's group. Furthermore, , one of Crowley's close associates, Austin Osman Spare, was involved in Witchcraft himself. We can perhaps see from Spare's work, The Anathema of Zos, why Crowley was so interested in Pickingill's pre-revivalist doctrine of the "Craft of the Wise".

During the late 1970's and early 1980's a series of privately published papers were circulated which contained material that originated from old Northern Covens and the "Royal Windsor Coven". One in particular—The Marshmallow Papers—contained a damning criticism of so-called Gardnerian and Alexandrian "initiatory" Witchcraft. This was followed by criticisms made to this author that,

In Spare's essay on traditional Witchcraft, or at least by his time, a late corrupted form of it, he describes it as an ecstatic, transcendent philosophy. He was familiar with, and variously employed, the strategies anciently used in so-called "high magic" to encourage the body to transport itself into states that were old territory for the Magi and the Druids, the Maenads and the Bacchantes. Spare's account clearly demonstrates that Witchcraft had Tantric elements and was, like Crowley's system of "Magick", in the business of making "Ubaids" or "Overseers". This is poles apart from Gerald Gardner's media- friendly product of modern Wicca.

In examining Spare's work, we might learn why Crowley was so interested in Pickingill's and then be tempted to ask where the Africans got Vodun or Voodoo, as it is known to us. "New Age" paganism or Wicca repackages old hypocritical Christian moral values and symbols, and attaches products, services and books of no value whatsoever. These are promoted and marketed by businesspeople whose only interest is in building up a captive client base of weak-minded individuals who are programmed to buy the next "soul-saving" product from them. Soon "Les idiotes dans la queste pour la verité" discover that the last philosophical tin of beans or cheap crystal they bought from the High Gurus of the "New Age" does not work.

Then these pedlars of kitsch "truth" tell them that their karma is wrong, or they "don't believe" it enough, or that they have a hostile attitude or lack of focus or some such excuse. This deflects the blame from them and lays it firmly at the door of the luckless punter—following which they then recommend that the sap buy from one of these "Irreproachable Wise Ones" yet another Mystery of the Ancients ("at only $29.99") which will undoubtedly work this time. And it never does and so they go back for another try.

Real stemmed from the leaders of the Baphometic Orders in London and the Black Country, who emphatically asserted that the only genuine form of valid Witchcraft was passed down through the blood. magic is at work here. A group of secretly initiated individuals are turning dross into gold. Fools give charlatans good money in exchange for utterly useless rubbish.

Now that's alchemy! The papers originating from the northern covens clearly revealed that Witchcraft prior to the Wiccan revival of the 1950's bore no resemblance to what passes for formulaic Witchcraft now, and was not pagan, fertility based or necessarily Goddess-led. Essentially it was and is the same as the Witchcraft sponsored by the Baphometic Orders who trace their lineage back through the Templars to Jesus' original teachings and the culture of the Druids.

The nearest approximation or identification in this particular instance would be between late 19th-century Northern British ritual and the French medieval, Cathar-sponsored Witch movement. In both these instances the central figure was the Baphomet and the highest sacrament of the "Sabbat" was the Black Mass. This had nothing to do with Satanism, which in itself, was and is a late, half understood non sequitur—manufactured by the Roman Church—that has nothing to do with the Dragon tradition. Many so-called aficionados of the Occult, and especially those who like to call themselves Witches in public, maintain that "The Black Mass was Satanic". They go on to say that white Witchcraft or Wiccecraeft—as they like to call it— "has nothing to do with Satanism and the Black Mass, which are a parody of Catholicism and the Catholic Mass". They squawk—off pat and by rote—like trained parrots, whilst the Church Fathers grin gleefully when they see how well their propaganda has taken root. The Wiccans' or neo-pagans' agenda here is to try and convince as many people as they can that they are mysterious and somehow superior to others without actually saying as much. They themselves think—and would like other people to think—that they belong to an ancient tradition or fraternity with knowledge to which the public isn't party. They want to impress upon people further—before those people are tempted to start throwing big bricks through witchy windows—that Witches are really nice people and that true "Wiccans"— (whilst still trading off the dark and slightly dangerous allure evoked by the word Witch)—deal solely with "white" magic. In this way the attention seekers hope to become more popular or respect- ed by being surrounded by some aura of mystique that they consider in their own minds to be "cool".

They've seen Witches on television no doubt. They believe that by jumping on the bandwagon and choosing that particular persona, out of the many that are on offer at a price, it will make people think they are special and hence attractive.

The big stumbling block here is that Royal Witchcraft, or Witchcraft proper, from the early Dark Ages onwards owes as much to its clearly

Christian, as it does to its direct Druidic, origins. Both in their original form, in the publicly disseminated opinion of the Catholic popes, were and are Satanic. Jesus' heredity—and the descent of the Druidic dynasties—both derived from an identical Dragon nascence that the Roman Catholics decided was devilish because the descent of both bloodlines was from the Sumerian Enki who was the Akkadian Samael: the Roman Lucifer and Thus, the Catholic Satan. In Jesus' case the Roman Church, as do all outsiders who know they are on to a good thing, sanitised his rituals and concealed his descent. All those who continued to follow Jesus' original teachings—like the Witches—they burned as "heretics". This notwithstanding, the Wiccan apologists still try to tell us that Witchcraft has nothing to do with Christianity but is a pre- Christian fertility religion. However, the word "heretic" was only used by the Inquisitors to specifically define those heterodox Christian beliefs which were at variance with the Roman Church's orthodox teachings.

To call a Witch a heretic meant that the Witch was a heterodox Christian. The Inquisitors—whatever we may think of them— were nobody's fools. They were aware of whom they were targeting. They also knew that Witches were "original Christians" whose knowledge of the true, Druidic nature of Jesus' liberating Christianity had to be quashed at any cost if the Church were to achieve the political and pecuniary supremacy, they desired by replacing it with their own enslaving dogma.

All the time Witches existed, they were a testament to the fact that Roman Catholicism was nothing like Christianity and was nothing more than a pack of usurping lies made fragrant with the incense of the suffering of the Dragons, whom the Roman Church had murdered in their pursuit of ultimate world power. The author has had first-hand experience of what happens when outsiders, either as "media commentators" or as "supporters", become involved with the traditions of the old families. It doesn't take long before both types start to demand that the tradition be adjusted to meet the middle-class expectations of a purchasing public that has been fed on sanitised, smug "New Age" moral crapulence. This is so that they, either the commentators or supporters, can attract even more adherents or readers and thereby increase their envisaged profit margins. After a while, in order to ensure maximum profits, the outsiders set about trying to silence and marginalize the very people who were born into that tradition and upon whom they formerly depended for their wisdom and knowledge. This is just in case the now somewhat bemused custodians of the blood "do something out of keeping with what WE are trying to achieve".

As Mr. Kenneth Grant, O. T. O., has pointed out, money and Magick don't mix. The author echoes this sentiment when he states emphatically that the Dragon Court is a closed body which is kept sacrosanct for members of the blood; and is not a public, profit-making organisation. As for the Black Mass that so-called New Age Wiccans disown, this ritual was not a "Christian parody born of frustration with, or rebellion against, the Church of the day"—as they repeat faithfully from the formulae printed in their bite-size tomes of "New Age" dogma.

It was the original Christian Mass of Jesus which the Catholics later stole and sanitised for public consumption in the same way that Wiccan apologists are doing with Witchcraft today. Anyone with average intelligence can interpret the Black Mass properly. Prior to the attaching of the Church's "satanic" label during the medieval period—and its decadence and misuse by outsiders throughout the Renaissance and post-Reformation eras—it was one of the most profound and poetic family rituals ever conceived. Its hermetic and alchemical symbolism delved deep into the Kabala and High Magic.

If so-called "Wiccans" in fact actually were real Witches, they would know this. But they don't and they're not. The hyperbole that they indulge in is no more than a regurgitation of books written by equally misinformed writers who, over the preceding decades, have managed to get their seriously flawed ideas published. Whether perceived from the point of view of either its Christian or its Druidic aspects, Royal Witchcraft was never devotional. So much for Witchcraft being a fertility religion. The Black Mass had its roots in the ancient alchemical lore of Solomon and was simply a memento of teachings long past and an aide memoire for future generations, a mnemonic which was intended to remind those to come from whence the power and the wisdom derives.

If the reader looks carefully at the Aziluth scales of the sephiroth of Binah they will see what is meant. The Sabbatical Goat of the Black Mass was Chem-Zoroaster, one of the early ancestors of the ancient Dragon Families. His symbolic presence at the Mass reminds one that Royal Witchcraft was strictly a family affair. Witches actually called their "god" the Antecessor, meaning "the ancestor". This illustrated to later generations of readers that "Satan", also called by the Witches "Christ, son Dei" or "Jesus Christ, son of God", and was in fact a flesh and blood being. He was not a fallen angel invented by commercially minded Catholic priests.

If the Witches of the Royal Covens honoured Jesus as an ancestor-god, then they must have been Merovingian by descent and Thus, custodians of the Sang Royale. Here we enter in upon the realm of the Holy Grail. Royal Witches were Elven by blood and everybody contemporary to them knew this. Professor Murray made this assertion in England and was followed by Jules Michelet in France who recorded that the epithet "Fairy" was attributed by the French to the ancient Gallic Queens.

This also means that The Holy Grail itself was Elven as was Jesus himself, complete with his Crown of Fairy Thorns, depicted as the headgear of Godfroi de Vere de Bouillon in the 12th century. Throughout the generations, ignorant outsiders have distorted the history of the ancient families and the ancient Royal doctrine. The fact that most of humanity is engaged in activities based upon greed, and which are destroying their world is actually seen to be good. Those who disagree with first, this modus operandi, and second, hold an historically different perspective, are perceived as evil. New Age Wicca members perpetuate this logical imbalance for their own nefarious, selfish ends.

They have nothing to do with Witchcraft, but everything to do with the selfish motivation of those who promote a "white" Wicca for their own financial, social, or sexual ends within a social environment which is still morally conditioned by manipulative medieval prejudices. Modern Wicca, much like other aspects of the 21st century, is a cheap imitation of what has gone before. Thus, it is little more than a fashion statement for those who want to take part in the "born again Christianity".

These views are due not to any particular bad experience with Wiccans or New Agers – other, that is, than any experience with such people is likely to be negative. It is simply the conclusion reached after thirty years of active involvement in the Dragon tradition. This has shown again and again that those who are attracted to the manufactured trappings of the so-called New Age and Wicca, are socially inadequate, providing perfect bait for unscrupulous charlatans.

The British Trading Standards Office demands of the manufacturer or service provider that any goods or services offered for sale by them should be "Fit to be used for the purpose for which they were intended". The New Age Movement, Wicca and indeed modern revivalist Christianity all fall below this definition and Furthermore, , and Therefore, technically fall foul of the British Trades Descriptions Act. All—including Revivalist Christianity—should be investigated in these terms and also in relation to the British Fraudulent Mediums' Act.

They will not be, because they make money. As far as the Security Services are concerned, they are impotent and harmless. Besides, they keep the consumers quiet in their semi-detached cages. To the sociologists who advise governments we have become categorised into "numbered social units"; to those governments' military tacticians we are "expendable civilian collateral assets" and to the tradesmen who control those governments we are "consumers".

Do we wish to continue to be labelled so cynically, and only according to our relative value to any given elite or its agents? -The inverted pyramid of diminishing human value –

"Expendable Civilian Collateral Asset"

"Numbered Social Unit"

"The Consumer"

"Pawn"

"0"

If the planet is to survive, social groups must become smaller and ordered by economic necessity, not by the so-called Democracy of Consumerism, championed, anything but "free" West. People learn by suffering and fundamental change comes through the stimulus of radical pain. At present many people in the western world have not experienced enough adversity to make them demand change. Any call for the adoption of sane social and environmental policies still sounds to them like the insane rantings of isolated idealists. Social Alternatives? The Dragon Court exists as an organisation solely for the bloodline descendants of the ancient Vere family—the senior bloodline successors of the Scythian-Merovingian, Elven House of Princess Maelasanu—and for those whose bloodlines are extracted from this descent and its ancient Dragon Court. Such is the nature of its enforced exclusivity that the Dragon Sovereignty has become the only sovereign body in existence today that demands a DNA test as a prerequisite of membership.

The reason is that being a Dragon is and always was a matter of race and never a matter of "lifestyle choice", regard- less of market potentials. Being of the Dragon Blood is exactly like being a member of the Amerindian Pequot Tribe which, like the Court, also demands such rigorous proofs of aboriginality. After a thousand years of persecution would anyone dare accuse us of racism?

We are fighting for our racial identity to be restored to us and in this we are no different to the Jews or the American Indians or any other Tribe or Nation which has suffered at the hands of the European Church-State.

Do we accuse them of racism or conversely, do we approve of their efforts in attempting to restore and cultivate their cultural distinctness and unique- ness? Like the Indians, the Dragons are also sick of having their culture adopted and diluted by the very races and nations that spent so much time and effort trying to eradicate them and other indigenous populations from both the face of the earth and the pages of the history books. Nevertheless, the Dragons are committed to furthering the cause of social equity. And whilst desirous of promoting spiritual and scientific education to those who genuinely seek change, ultimately the Dragons' concerns lay in the restoration of their own Tribes, their own Nation, and their own Homelands. Ultimately and unequivocally the Dragons have a love for truth and strive to re-establish their own Tuadhe based on veracity, honour, liberty, and social and environmental equity, according to the Dragons' ancient lore. They don't want to wedge their toes in your doors, and they don't want to preach their truth at you.

They certainly don't want to "convert" you! Instead, they are working towards the re-foundation of their own distinct society, utilising the sovereign national rights that the ancient Imperial and Royal Dragon Sovereignty historically already has, By re-introducing their old social structures and values the Dragons hope to establish a naturally ordained system of socio-economic interactions between the Dragon people, based on clarity of vision, honesty of spirit and material necessity. By avoiding greed and concentrating upon a far richer spiritual and cultural experience derived from the ancient racial memory of the Dragon, it is envisaged that its society will be governed by innate conviction. Achieved through teaching the timeless psychological skills that facilitate access to this infinite realm, it is hoped that the community might continue as an example of what real "royalty" entails. Furthermore, , it will demonstrate how communities can quality, work fairly and efficiently, with a hundred-fold increase in cultural spiritual significance, personal empowerment. This depends upon them being based not on and idealism, materialism, or patriotism, but on sound, realistic principles which are structured organically, according to the outworking of the Draconian consciousness. The Dragons have no interest in politics and no desire to "Rule the Planet" as certain named fools have suggested. Not least because history teaches us that in power-brokering terms, the "top dog" is in fact "the exposed duck" and in political arenas it's duck season all year round. Egotism seeks power through rule, but the Dragons' transcendent perception, the Derkesthai or clear sight, is attained through relinquishing egotism.

So, Dragons couldn't "rule" anyway, the two concepts would be mutually self-negating. The office of the ancient Druidic or Dragon Queen or King was that of a Magus (hence majesty), Seer, and Guide. The idea of a King as "ruler" or even the modern President or Premier as "ruler", is outdated warrior class nonsense, the disastrous consequences of which can be witnessed across the entire planet.

Ultimately, we do not want to be chained to your hamster wheel. The wheel might still be turning, but the rodent has long since died and the carcass is beginning to stink. In tune with the Dragon Court and the old covens, many other groups did not and still do not initiate outsiders as new members but, echoing Merovingian tradition, only acknowledge family members who have reached a certain age. The overly complex and unnecessary initiation rites found in Wicca or modern Witchcraft were and are entirely absent from the rites of small hereditary groups which practiced the old craft. If one knows one is a Witch because one is born into a Witch family, one doesn't need excessive pomp and hocus-pocus to convince one of the obvious. Similarly, it is unnecessary to wear the entire silver standard of a small nation around one's corpulent neck in the form of tasteless pseudo-Wiccan or occult jewellery in order to reinforce the idea—to oneself and to others—that one is a "Witch".

The structure of the historical covens will be dealt with later. However, the Dragon Court itself is not now and never was a "Coven" in the way that this word is accepted today. When reading this book, this should be borne in mind. Recruitment in times of hardship did occur and "listeners" were expected to drink the blood of the Officiate. This classical, pre-Christian practice was intended to act as a Eucharist where recruits would take on the nature of the Leader by infusing their own being with his or her genetic material. This form of pact lasted 7 years, the approximate time it takes for the body to renew its cells entirely. After 7 years the recruit would have to drink the blood again as none of the Leader's essence would remain with them after their cellular regeneration. In this way they were made foot soldiers.

However, it wasn't an "initiation" or for life, as modern "Wiccans" have perceived induction to be. Anyway, it is doubtful whether they would agree to a Vampiric ritual being included into their repertoire, as it might damage their respectable image as "white Witches", whatever that is supposed to mean: beyond being misinformed, fraudulent pretenders. This is not elitism. For centuries, the ancestors of today's would-be Witches, magicians and New-Age gurus raped, tortured, burned and hanged the Elven people.

Now they take their names, their titles and their culture and use it to enhance their own social kudos, when they cannot even prove that they are of the Dragon blood. In the Genes Having said that, anyone who genuinely believes they have the right to be acknowledged as a "Draconian", a member of the ancient Elven, Dragon race, is welcome to submit a genealogy which devolves back to either the Scythian or Mittani Royal Houses before the time of Christ. That is at least 80 generations. Unlike self-styled gurus, the Dragon Court, Therefore, always seeks to support its claims with substantial, scientific evidence..

We have been brought up in a scientific age where we are conditioned to demand and accept scientific proofs as the benchmark of validity for any concept presented to us. This is no bad thing and the Dragons themselves have maintained this attitude for centuries. Indeed, such an approach is at the foundation of some of the most poetic and romantic tales in the Dragon culture which, at their heart, reveal themselves as pure science.

The interaction between mind and brain can be psychosomatically suppressed or enhanced by belief. If people are presented with scientific proof of the existence of Dragon genes in their own blood, the abilities which accompany those genes and their genetic memory will become accessible in a strange kind of consensual way. Once they believe that it is "acceptable" to believe what they feared society would condemn as fanciful, they are free.

They also experience a previously unperceived sense of clarity. When they do, they will see that most of human endeavour is pointless. They will see a cleaner way to live life and will find that a common, natural social morality will accompany their every waking thought. They will have need for neither man's petty laws nor authorities and masters. The innate laws of life will arise from within accompanied by a love of truth and a contempt for falsehood, pretence, and deceit. They will allow themselves to become what they already were and what the corporate elites fear most— integrated, transcendent, detached, truly intelligent and creative beings: Overlords unto themselves—the members of a separate race—a "Royal Priesthood, a Peculiar People and a Holy Nation". Mere belief is what fuels mere religion. From absolute proof however, there is derived absolute certainty in one's condition and one's heritage. Quietly believing or hoping to oneself that one is of the Dragon Race is one thing. In most cases the belief, when it wavers, causes numerous blockages to the fulfilment of any potential as the negative spiral circles downwards with every waver and every failed attempt. "You shall know the truth, and the truth shall set you free." Knowing beyond any doubt, however, that one is of that Blood opens wide the doors to the infinite. The planet needs its Elves back, so the saying goes.

PREAMBLE

THE DRAGON CEDE TO USE AS REFERENCE OF FRAMEWORK

This latest book in the Dragon Legacy series contains the most comprehensive genealogies of the Houses of Vere, Weir and Collison published to date. It is intended as a reference work for all those readers who are interested in the Grail families or who wish to study further the ancient mythological, legendary and historical origins of their own lineage. Also published for the very first time is the Dragon Descent of Jesus Christ from Satan, an explosive secret kept hidden for centuries by a few ancient Dragon families and Gnostic sects which calls into question some of the classical identities and the inter-relationships of the figures we have grown up and become familiar with today. In the Interview with Tracy Twyman, the reader will learn the true purpose Jesus had for Mary Magdalene, her cosmic identity and the real nature of his clandestine "church." In the excerpts from the work by Leonid Korablev, The True Elves of Europe (which appears later in this book), we are introduced to the factual origin of Tolkien's elves and their actual basis in history, whilst the reader will find numerous biographical notes and passages concerning the Vere family and the Grail line in both the main body of the book and in the genealogies themselves. An old military instructor's maxim goes – Tell 'em what you're going to tell 'em: Tell 'em what you're telling 'em: Tell 'em what you've told 'em. This maxim has been repeatedly used in the construction of political speeches from Winston Churchill to Tony Blair. I use it herein to impress my message in the mind of the reader, so any threefold repetitions are conscious and deliberate.

PART ONE ESSAYS

THE DRAGON CEDE

A Brief Outline of the Prehistoric Nascence of the Imperial and Royal House of Vere The genealogical descents that appear in this book are set out in their tabular form in order that readers may view and study them individually. The more than ninety royal descents that I present to you are the culmination of 25 years of study and reference in the fields of genealogy, heraldry, genetic findings, social and political history, archaeology, mythology, comparative religion and religious mysticism, symbolism, magic, occultism, folklore and, in particular, etymology. The study of the latter has been decisive in discovering the true meaning of words, phrases and names related to the family and its history and mythology. If one merely consults a genealogist in order to discover one's family heritage, at some point or another one will hit a brick wall and go no further. By applying a wide variety of disciplines I have discovered that, rather than being a provincial Scottish family, the Veres are in fact the senior imperial and royal dynasty of Britain, Europe and the Middle-East, and are the focus, indeed in some cases the fons et origio of Eurasian folk and religious mystical tradition, and are surrounded in an aura of myth, magic and mysticism. By applying similar methods in subsequent years, by documentary cross referencing and the application of etymology at every stage of my investigations a vast panorama of family tradition has opened up to us and I have been able to take our lineage back to the very beginning of written history and indeed beyond.

This may sound fanciful but through numerous descents from the Merovingian kings of the Franks and the Angevin kings of England the Veres have inherited the 16q24.3 genes. In correspondence with a contact of mine at Oxford University who was one of the pioneers of research in this field I discovered that these gene types refer back millennia before written records. Related genetic studies over the past few years have determined that around 90,000 years ago a catastrophic disaster occurred which more or less wiped out the entire human population. Today the population of the planet only consists of four different genetic variations stemming from only four individual females. This disaster was termed the human genetic bottle-neck. The 16q24.3 genes which survived it were found not to have originated with homo sapiens but predated the emergence of modern man by thousands of years. Today 16q24.3 genes are rare and it is estimated scientifically that they will be bred out of the human population within about 150 years. In America only 2% of the population are red gene dominant, whilst in Scotland only 10% manifest the genes. In the Far East people with red hair are venerated as Gods which further asserts the divine origin of these genes. In the Epic of Gilgamesh his closest companion, Enkidu, created like Adam by Enki (hence his name) is described as being "hairy." Furthermore in the Biblical Old Testament Esau is also described as hairy, but also, from other translations, he is described as having been "born red." In apocryphal Jewish texts Sheba (Lilith) is also described as being hairy whilst in Genesis Adam, through translations is described as being a "red man," an appellation which also applied to the divine Enkidu, son of Enki. Esau's other name was Edom and is directly related to the word Adama both of which mean "red man." The word for red and the word for hairy come from the same root, and mistranslation is easy. One word, hairy, is translated from the word Se'ar, and the other word, red, is translated from Sear. From both Esau and Lilith (who had red hair), from Adam and indeed from Sheba-Lilith, wife of King Solomon, we can safely assert that Se'ar was mistranslated and should have read Sear and that as a result of this, we can state that Enki and the other gods were the fons et origio of the 16q24.3 genes. Jesus, according to Roman commentators, also had red hair. Where did they come from? It has been tentatively suggested, from I must say scant archaeological evidence, that these genes were inherited from the homo-Neanderthal through interbreeding. Having previously read an ancient apocryphal Hebrew text called the Ben Sirah, and having further cross referenced it with Greek, Babylonian and Sumerian religious works, an interesting alternative explanation emerged. In some Jewish traditions it is stated that a mortal individual named Lilith was the rebellious first wife of Adam. Wishing to dominate Adam, and unable to accept his authority over her she fled to the coast and turned into the Leviathan, the Dragon of the Sea. According to the Jews she became the mother of all demons, vampires and witches. The dragon motif is important and should be borne in mind. However, in the Ben Sirah Lilith is also described as the feared "red- haired queen of the north." Studying Greek tradition I discovered that both Rhadamanthus and his brother Zeus were described as having red hair.

These gods, as with those of many other pantheons across Eurasia, including the God of the Israelites, were all developed from a primal, proto-Sumerian original, wherein Zeus derives from the Sumerian God Enlil who was the half-brother of the God Enki – the creator of man. The Lilith of the Ben Sirah actually originates from the same proto-Sumerian pantheon, wherein she is depicted as the grand-daughter of the God Enlil (the red-haired Zeus of the Greeks) and the daughter of the Goddess Erish-Kigal and Nergal, king of the Underworld. In Jewish tradition she is part of the Tetragrammaton, YHVH, the four deities that were combined to form the monotheistic Jehovah. Within this group Lilith, the daughter of EL, is handmaiden to the mother Metatron – the Goddess Nin-Kursag, wife of EL – who, once Jewish polytheism was discarded, developed into the Lady Sabbath. So rather than her being mortal, Lilith actually originated as a proto- Sumerian

Goddess and a Queen. Furthermore, as these divine beings are described as having red hair, we can confirm that they carried the 16q24.3 genes. This being the case, we can also state that in carrying these genes, the proto-Sumerian Gods and Goddesses, in having a genetic make-up, were in fact Earth-bound beings made of flesh and blood, not ethereal inhabitants of the heavens.

The Dragon Motif of Lilith is important here because these proto-Sumerian Gods and goddesses were called the Anunnaki – the sons of An the father God – and they were described by their early Sumerian and Babylonian worshippers as Dragons. The word Dragon originates from the Greek word Edrakon, which is an aorist (tenseless verb) of the parent word Derkesthai which means Clear vision and relates to transcendent consciousness and wisdom. Not being satisfied with halting my studies in Sumeria, I wanted to carry the research beyond recorded history. As the red-haired Queen of the North, Lilith obviously didn't come from Sumeria, which means that the proto-Sumerian pantheon of Gods must have originated from another region and a far earlier period in time. Sumerian was thought to be the oldest written language on Earth, originating in Mesopotamia some 5000 years ago.

Luckily I happened upon the work of Dr. M.F. Stone whose archaeological discoveries have confirmed that linguistically, Sumerian or rather proto-Sumerian originated, as a primitive language, in Central Europe and has distinct links with the later Vinca culture which was, I believe, centred around the Danube river-basin.

To be precise, Stone's team unearthed tablets bearing the effigy of the God Enki and bearing his inscriptions and ranking numbers within the Anunnaki pantheon. This discovery was made in Transylvania. In corroboration of a Central European origin for these beings, it is to be noted that the earliest detailed stone sculptures of the Dragon Gods were also discovered in this region and it is from here that the accounts of Lilith, Nergal and the ancient Gods of the Sumerians first emerge, millennia before their appearance in Mesopotamia.

It is interesting to note that whilst orthodox historians and archaeologists would like us to believe that the neo-Mesolithic period of European history was a primitive time populated by grunting cave-men, it is from this period and this region that the archaeologist Richard Rudgely discovered the remnants of finely woven cloth with patterned stitching, combs, immaculately crafted coloured beads and other surprising artifacts. Rudgely clearly reveals that the culture and the living conditions of the age were remarkably advanced, more so than we were previously led to believe. In Bohemia – now the Czech Republic – the earliest settlement yet to be unearthed – Dolne Vistonicu – was in fact the New York of its age and had trading links with places as far afield as southern France and north Africa. In conclusion, the first "cities" to emerge didn't appear on the stage of history in Mesopotamia, but originated in central Europe with the proto-Sumerians and their red-haired Anunnaki God-Kings.

To advance the argument that the Anunnaki were a sophisticated society far in advance of any other of the time I would remind the reader that the accepted, popular misconception of a universal Stone Age, Bronze Age and Iron Age is misleading. It gives us the idea that each era emerged across the planet at the same time when in fact these changes in technology emerged at different times in different places. For example by the time the Bronze Age began in Western Europe, it had already been flourishing in early Sumer for millennia. It is also possible for the ages to reverse themselves. If a culture that has Bronze technology is forced to migrate, because of a regional disaster for instance, their first priority will be to establish an infrastructure for the provision of the basic necessities of their day-to-day survival. The last thing on their minds would be the rebuilding of their former Bronze Age culture.

Indeed the region to which they have been forced to flee may have no Tin or Copper ore at all, which would mean they would have no choice but to revert to using Stone Age tools and implements. In this manner civilizations can advance and decline according to migration and the resources available. If I advance therefore, the idea that the Anunnaki were a highly developed technological society when others were still in their Stone Age, such a concept is perfectly reasonable.

Whilst we in the west entered our Iron Age in around 500 BC, 1500 years later the American Indians were still in their Stone Age up until the 11th century and the arrival of the Vikings in Vinland. Today, whilst the developed nations enjoy a standard of scientific knowledge and expertise unprecedented in history, numerous tribes across the planet, including the Bushmen of the Kalahari and the Thai Hill Tribes are still more or less in their Stone Age.

If our computer-based technologies failed us today, within a few months all the basic resources would disappear. Fuel and electricity would become inaccessible, food and water would run out rapidly and, because we are so reliant on modern technology, in its absence most of us would die within the space of a couple of years, if not sooner. The few of us who managed to survive the total collapse of western civilisation would have to revert to a new Stone Age and, knowing nothing about basic metallurgy and lacking any skill in primitive crafts, it would take us many centuries to reach the cultural level attained by our early ancestors. In Egypt craftsmen built the Great Pyramid of Giza using the most primitive bronze, stone and wooden tools. As in other parts of this vast structure, the King's burial chamber is lined with massive blocks of red granite, one of the hardest and most unforgiving materials known to man at the time. Nevertheless the pyramid builders carved these granite blocks into perfect cubes, which they fitted together so precisely that even today it is impossible to push a razorblade between the joints. Such a level of skill and knowledge is extremely highly advanced, and yet they achieved these amazing feats using the most primitive and basic tools.

Even today archaeologists are baffled and amazed at how they managed it. The Egyptians also used gold electro-plating and performed cranial surgery on patients suffering from water on the brain and other related ailments. The age of pyramid building began around 5000 years ago and hundreds were constructed. However, only a handful remain today.

The rest have disappeared, seemingly without a trace. Consequently, it is perfectly reasonable to assert that the Anunnaki, whose descendants introduced monumental architecture to the Egyptians, enjoyed a civilisation in Europe far in advance of that of the Egyptians, perhaps millennia earlier, and that traces of that civilisation, over thousands of years, have disappeared completely. Consulting the Sumerian King Lists we find that the Sumerians claimed that the civilisation of the eight named, divine Anunnaki dynasties reached as far back as what we now think of as the Middle Stone Age, some 30,000 years ago and more, and yet we meet such a claim with incredulity and scorn, as no evidence exists to prove the assertion.

However modern scientists have calculated that, if humanity were to suffer a rapid process of complete planetary extinction, our civilisation, its infrastructure, its fragile modern materials and technologies, would rapidly crumble into dust and, after a lapse of between 5000 and 10,000 years, no trace of our existence would be found. Imagine what might survive of an advanced culture after the passage of 30,000 years. Nothing. Because of this, and because relatively little archaeological excavation has been undertaken in the poorer Central European Countries – they have more pressing needs requiring the investment of their financial resources – the Anunnaki have been relegated to the status of a myth. After a million years of human development, the idea that we are the only people to have reached the pinnacle of cultural and technological advancement, and that no one as sophisticated as we has existed prior to the modern era is arrogant in the extreme, a degenerating symptom of our smug, self congratulating, self satisfied civilisation. Because we surround ourselves with pointless technological gadgets we think we are the most advanced culture in the history of mankind and yet we have become so dependent on these gadgets that, in our laziness and complacency we have degenerated into the weakest, most unskilled and vulnerable civilisation in history. With a pride bordering on egomania, we worship ourselves for our purported genius and we celebrate our technology as a God, but we haven't a clue about how it works or how it is manufactured. We leave such matters to experts and specialists. Few of us even know how to repair a motorcar.

Our present level of technological sophistication is therefore unsustainable and, if disaster were to strike, we would be unable to repair or replace any of the machines upon which we have come to depend for our survival. As for attempting to eke out a living from the land, forget it. In the space of 150 years we have completely lost all the basic skills required to make a living, skills with which our ancestors had been conversant for thousands of years. If we are honest, we will admit that ours is the most primitive, inflexible and fragile civilisation in human history.

We depend ultimately on computers for our food and life support. If they break down, we starve and die. 10,000 years ago, our hunter-gatherer ancestors depended on flint tools to hunt their food. If a weapon broke, they would just go out and make another one. No problem. By being sustainable and renewable their culture, however simple it may have been, was far in advance of our own. With the Anunnaki the 16q24.3 genes reveal themselves and their presence within the individual's genetic make-up in the apparent manifestation of red hair, green eyes and a pale complexion deficient in melanin, a chemical vital to the protection of those peoples who inhabit areas with a harsh, sun- drenched climate such as Africa and Sumeria.

If, like the Anunnaki, one has occupied a temperate region for millennia, melanin is an unnecessary genetic component. We may safely assert therefore that the beings that became deified as the Anunnaki of Sumeria were originally domiciled in central Europe, particularly in Transylvania, Carpathia, the White Mountains and the Black Sea, on the former, pre-flood shores of which stood the temple of the Anunnaki Dragon King Ziu Sudra. He became the prototype and inspiration for the Jewish Noah. The Black Sea Flood – The Biblical Flood – after which the Ark came to rest on mount Ararat in Asia Minor and the Mesopotamian inundation are separated from each other by at least 500 years.

The craft used by King Uta Napishtim came to rest hundreds of miles south of Ararat on what was instead called Mount Nisir, in Mesopotamia. Consequently because the Bible Flood is that of Ziu Sudra and happened in the Bosphorus, this means that the children ascribed as belonging to Noah by Jewish scribes, and which they used in their myth, were in fact those of King Ziu Sudra, not Noah. Why did the European Anunnaki migrate to Sumeria? For many years scholars have dismissed the universal Biblical Flood as a myth. In fact there were two Biblical floods, one in the Bosphorus and one subsequent to it in Mesopotamia. These two events, which were separated both by time and by geography, have become fused into one myth, by both the Jews and the Akkadians. During the exile of the Jews in Babylon in 500 BC, the Jewish scribes were permitted access to the king's library and it is from the Babylonian cylinder rolls, and from far earlier Sumerian text tablets, that the Jewish scribes copied and adapted their Biblical creation myth, their histories and genealogies and their god Jehovah, to suit their own political and religious requirements.

To their God they attribute the creation of the universe, the fashioning of the Earth and the birth of mankind. In the Biblical account, Noah builds his Ark according to the instructions given by his God, fills it with all animal life, endures the flood for forty days and forty nights and eventually disembarks on Mount Ararat with his family and livestock, once the flood waters have subsided. According to Bishop Ussher's calculations the flood, which engulfed the world, occurred in 4000 BC.

If such a universal disaster had in fact occurred, the evidence for it would have been recorded geologically in silt deposits across the planet. Unsurprisingly no such evidence exists; therefore the tale of an all-consuming worldwide disaster is just a fantasy, a misinterpretation of the facts, like so much else in the Old Testament. The Jews originated in Mesopotamia and were evidently not European. Therefore no Semitic ancestor of theirs could have been involved in the Biblical Flood, which affected Europe and Europeans. The fact is that Noah and his divine mission were a Jewish fantasy derived from the account of the building of an Ark by the Nephilim King Ziu Sudra who, rather than constructing a huge unwieldy vessel to accommodate pairs of all the animals on Earth, built a more modest vessel to contain instead the "seed of life."

Recent experiments conducted by scientists and marine engineers have sought to reconstruct a model of the Ark taking into account the measurements God supposedly gave Noah and the materials he was instructed to build it from. It was demonstrated conclusively that within a couple of hours of hitting the floodwaters, the Ark would have split in the middle and sunk beneath the waves..

We can extrapolate from this that the Ark story is a no more than a Jewish literary artifice, gleaned from a more likely Sumerian account relating to Ziu Sudra who, according to the texts was actually domiciled in the Bosphorus region.

It was his Ark, which settled on Mount Ararat, adjacent to the Black sea basin, not Noah's. We might also say that, if the Ark didn't exist in the context proposed by the Jewish scribes, then nor did Noah, or his antecedents as his own, and nor did his post-Flood scions within the context of the story as the Jewish scribes have related it. However, the fact is that in around 4500 BC the Black sea was a vast, low lying fresh water basin hundreds of feet below the level of the adjacent Mediterranean Sea. Near its centre was situated a large land mass that the Romans later named the Pontus Euxine. During this time the volcanic island of Santorini exploded after a local tectonic shift, causing a tsunami.

The resultant tidal wave battered the Hellespont causing it to burst asunder and the salt water of the Mediterranean engulfed the Black Sea basin, causing a disastrous flood of horrifying proportions. The Pontus Euxine – the Holy Mountain – disappeared under millions of gallons of salt water which also took with it the settlements which were built on the shoreline, settlements which have recently been discovered by marine archaeologists and dated to 4500 BC Naturally this flood affected the whole region surrounding the Bosphorus and many inhabitants would have been permanently displaced, the salt water which polluted the surrounding lands making agriculture, pastoralism and food-gathering impossible.

The Pontus Euxine is one of the prototypes for the mythical Atlantis, which, over time has merged, like the account of the Biblical Flood, with other later fables. Nevertheless, the story of the inundation of the Holy Mountain in the Black Sea flood persisted in accounts recorded by the Sumerians, the Egyptians, the Chinese and even the Scandinavian Vikings. All of these accounts record the exploits of the Mountain's occupants who are know collectively as the Ogdoad; the eight great Gods of the Anunnaki who, millennia later, were venerated by Jesus himself. The Anunnaki living in the region and on the Mountain would have had no choice but to migrate south, through the Taurus mountains and on to Mesopotamia where they eventually settled permanently, building Ziggurats as replicas of the Holy Mountain they had left behind. With the emergence of the early city states of the Sumerians came the adaptation of their linear script into cuneiform, the invention of tarmac roads, indoor sanitation and street lighting. Clearly this advanced level of technology could not have emerged overnight, but must have been a culmination and adaptation of advanced skills and knowledge gathered in Europe over millennia. Further to the Anunnaki migration to Mesopotamia, remnants of their people wandered to the four corners of the Earth taking the story of the Flood with them thereby assuring that the fable arises in many disparate lands.

Because of this early scholars assumed that, as the Flood myth was virtually universal, the inundation must have covered the entire Earth. To summarise the foregoing, we know that we carry the 16q24.3 genes and that these genes originate in prehistory with the lineage of the European Anunnaki who, with the passage of time, by being so advanced a people in juxtaposition to those whom they encountered in Mesopotamia after the Flood, became deified by the indigenous population as the Gods of Sumeria. So at this point in our story we have moved from prehistoric Central Europe to the Middle-East, taking our genes, our technology and our literary knowledge with us. Remnants of this technology appear in the forests of central Germany in the form of detailed astronomical knowledge, whilst the practice of acupuncture emerges in the European heartlands centuries before it appears in China. In European prehistory acupuncture was practiced to introduce drugs and medicines into the body hypodermically, unlike the modern Chinese practice, which relies more on belief than empiricism. The god of the Jews, often named El, derives from the Anunnaki God Enki's half brother Enlil, whose other Sumerian name is EL. After murdering his father An, the chief of the gods, and banishing his horrified senior brother Enki who was to succeed his father An as Chief of the Gods, EL became by force of arms and usurpation the father of the pantheon of Sumerian gods, also called in plural the Elohim.

The monotheistic Jewish scribes removed Enlil or EL from his collective context within the pantheon of Gods, singularised the plural term Elohim and appropriated it as another name for El or Jehovah. They transformed the gods faithful to Enlil into angels and denigrated those faithful to Enki – An's rightful heir – relegating them to the position of "fallen angels" or demons. Although he was the creator of Man and the rightful head of the Anunnaki and was the preferred choice of his father An, Enki as the defeated and banished God – the victim of Enlil's furious jealousy and ambition – was blasphemously reduced in stature by the Jews to the status of the chief angel among the fallen ones, a figure we now know as Satan.

This process has been repeated time and time again throughout history and in various cultures, where conquerors rewrite history or modify theology to suit their own ends, denigrating the gods of those they have vanquished to the status of demons and devils. The ramifications of this process and the disastrous outcome of the "War in Heaven," originally a European internecine conflict initiated by a brutal act of fratricide, have reverberated down the millennia, emerging in pagan and heterodox Christian Gnostic and dualist manuscripts which repeatedly remind us of the original Sumerian account by constantly and consistently asserting that Jehovah is the evil demiurge – the lesser god – whilst Satan is the true God, the creator and saviour of mankind. In the Babylonian accounts Enlil (Jehovah) loathed mankind and sought constantly the annihilation of Enki's human children, reinforcing his later gnostic identification with the true opposer of man, which, in Hebrew, translates as Satan the enemy, and scourge of Mankind. The war in Heaven appears in Greek theology as the battle between Zeus (Enlil) – chief of the Olympians, the younger Gods, and Typhoeus (Enki or Eä) – chief of the Titans, the elder Gods. In the Greek account the conflict takes place in the mountains surrounding the Bosphorus, thereby supporting the idea of a European origin for the Anunnaki. It is also interesting to note that the later Scythians – the Skoloti or Scotti of Transylvania and Greater Scythia – claim descent from the four sons of the daughter of **Zeus (Enlil) fathered on her by the Titan Typhoeus (Enki). Taking into account the fable's evolution with the passing of time, the Greek account and its Sumerian prototype are almost identical, though in the latter account Enki (Typhoeus the Titan) fathers his (Scythian) children by Enlil's (Zeus's) granddaughter Lilith, who also gives birth in the Babylonian texts to a daughter - Lilith Luluwa - who marries Cain or Qayin, King of Kish. The Titans – the Old Gods – bequeathed their divine legacy, and their 16q24.3 genes, through Typhoeus, to the early Scythians who eventually became identified in European traditions as the Daouine Sidhe or Sithe, the Elves and Fairies of Germanic and Gaelic folklore. Etymologically the original spelling of the name "Scythian" in middle English was "Sithian" and the pale-skinned, red-haired, green eyed genetic legacy of the Titans (Enki's divine Anunnaki followers) who were the fallen Angels or Demons of the Jews, became the distinguishing features of the Fairies, Elves, Witches and Vampires of Central and Western Europe, an association which traveled as far as sub-Saharan Africa.**

Even in Shakespeare's A Midsummer Night's Dream we find Titania as Queen of the fairies, derived from the Greek, Titanic Goddess of the same name, demonstrating the persistence of the myth down the millennia, and the abiding association and identification of the Titans – the old Anunnaki gods – with their holy offspring the Elves or Fairies: the High God-Kings and Overlords of history. In the Gospel of the Cainites we discover that whilst Abel was the son of Eve by Adam, Cain was the son of Eve by Enki the Chief of the Gods who, as the one-eyed Samael is later replicated in form and status by Odin, Chief of the Gods of the Aesir. Besides Ziu Sudra, in the Leibher Gabhalla we learn that other Anunnaki princes, including Ba'ath and Fintan, build a vessel and, taking their womenfolk and sufficient provisions with them they leave the Bosphorus, navigate their way through the Mediterranean and sail to the Isles of the North. According to the text, one contingent settles in Ireland whilst another contingent sails further afield and settles in Scandinavia. In Ireland they are remembered as the Aes Dan, the ancient gods of the Irish, an appellation also used for the later Tuadha de Danaan, and in Scandinavia these Anunnaki princes become the Aesir, the Gods of the Vikings, and their Chief is the one-eyed Odin, scion of the Sumerian Enki. In Scandinavia Odin is also known as Ygg and he is credited with the discovery of the ancient Runes, whilst in Ireland this discovery is credited to Oghma after whom the Ogham script is named.

The linguistic similarity of the two names should not be ignored. The story of the siring of Cain by Enki in the Gospel of the Cainites is also echoed in Genesis where Eve tells Adam that she has "gotten a Man from the Lord." Having doctored the original Sumerian and Babylonian account of the creation of man, transferring the credit from the defeated Enki to the victorious usurper EL the scribes, unable to countenance the fact that Cain was the son of Satan, attributed his paternity to Adam. Just for good measure they promulgated the idea that Cain murdered his brother Abel in cold blood, thereby damning him to posterity for all time. From thence they banish him into the wilderness in the hope that he will be forgotten. And he was, at least until 1850 and the archaeological discovery in Mesopotamia of thousands of Sumerian and Babylonian texts which, when translated, told a different story. The European archaeological expeditions in Mesopotamia at the time were given specific orders to discover texts and materials, which would support and reinforce the popular view of the Bible as being an authentic, reliable historical document. When the texts were translated however, what they discovered was that the Sumerian and Babylonian records were in fact thousands of years older than the Bible, which repeated their content to the extent that it had to be admitted that the Old Testament was copied from them, and pretty badly at that. Even the law code of Moses in the Old Testament is a copy of the Laws of the Babylonian King Hammurabi, right down to the concept of "An eye for an eye." Contrary to popular belief, Moses received over 600 Commandments, not 10.

The Church authorities set about trying to discredit and suppress the ancient texts to the extent that, whilst they continued to be studied by academics, they were almost forbidden to be taught in schools, such was the threat they posed to the orthodox Judaeo-Christian propaganda, its dogmatic veracity and the world-wide Ecclesiastical hegemony, wealth and power it underpinned. The effect of this smear campaign has been to relegate the Sumerian histories to the level of dismissible myth whilst even up to the beginning of the 20th Century the Bible remained the bedrock of Christian historical validity.

This is in an age where Darwin was ridiculed and vilified and labelled a blasphemer, and the discovery of dinosaur bones in Pegwell Bay, Dorset, caused tremors of fear and consternation through the corridors of Church- State power. To this day in America, many schools refuse to teach Darwinism, and the US government is too scared to force them to, such is the ubiquity of the belief in the Biblical creation myth within the population, and a huge number of Christian Fundamentalist Churches across the world continue to assert, and to teach their children, that God created fossils and planted them in the Earth to test the faith of his believers. Recently the acclaimed naturalist Sir David Attenborough, because of his support of the modified

Theory of Evolution, has received violent hate mail from Christian Fundamentalists cursing him to an eternity burning in hell. If these ignorant maniacs had power today, as their Catholic Forebears had in previous centuries, then it could be guaranteed that anyone who opposed their narrow, ignorant view of the world would be immediately tortured and killed.

I wouldn't stand a chance! Even in more enlightened seats of learning, whilst the old favourites – the Greek and Roman Classics – are still trundled out to pupils year after year, not one of these institutions bothers to teach anyone about Sumeria or the Sumerian histories, even though they are the oldest, and indeed the most reliable of all the ancient accounts in the World. The Sumerian account of the creation of Man, the Flood and the emergence of ancient Kingship is thousands of years old and was written far closer to the time these events were taking place, whereas the Hebrew Genesis and indeed the Old Testament itself was only started during the Babylonian Exile in 565 BC and wasn't completed until 400 years later, in 100 BC. As a result, the Bible version of events is unreliable, contradictory, patchy, selective and deceitful, if not a downright lie, intended to serve the theocratic ambitions of a people with no history of their own. If any work should be relegated to mythological status and discredited, it is the Bible, not the Sumerian and Babylonian histories from which it was copied. With the discovery of the Sumerian tablets Cain appeared back on the scene again.

Rather than being an evil fratricide who had fled into the wilderness as the Jewish scribes had insisted, Cain was shown to be a man of divine substance, a priest-king, sponsored and enthroned by the Gods themselves. From Cain, or more properly Qayin King of Kish, there descends the lineage of Ham (Chem Zoroaster, tenth archon of

Capricorn or Enki). We can say that the Jews invented Noah from the earlier accounts of Ziu Sudra and that Noah's fantasy ancestral line was transposed from that of Cain to that of Seth.

We know this because Cain's descendants are virtually identical in name with those of Noah's antecedents going back to Seth, son of Adam. This demonstrates that scribal doctoring has taken place in order to fill the glaring gaps in Jewish tribal genealogy, a genealogy which the Jews prefer to begin with a victorious god – Enlil or EL – rather than the rightful but vanquished heir to the Anunnaki throne. Flying in the face of written Babylonian accounts the scribes erroneously or purposely attribute the creation of Adam to Enlil (Jehovah) who never created anything, and then set about inventing a tribal history culminating here in the invention of Noah and the misappropriation of Chem, son of Qayin King of Kish, as Ham son of Noah.

We know this as a Jewish fabrication because as the hereditary tenth high priest and magus of Capricorn (who is Enki –the Ram or Sea Goat of the Shimmering Waters) Chem Zoroaster or Ham was naturally a sacred lineal descendant of Enki – the first Zoroaster. In the earlier records Chem married Lilith Luluwa who gave birth to Cush, father of Nimrod the Mighty Hunter. Nimrod sired Boethos, founder of the second dynasty of Egypt. Boethos's son was Raneb, who was Pharaoh in 2800 BC. As a god of light and fire Enki as Zoroaster developed into the later Roman god Lucifer, the bringer of light. From this manifestation it was a short leap of the early imagination, which promoted Enki – Zoroaster and his descendant grandson Ham or Chem- Zoroaster to the position of Sun God and hereditary high priest of the Sun God respectively. To this day the Persian Parsees, descendants of the Aryans, the proto- Scythian "king tribe," worship

Zoroaster as a god of light and the sacred flame. The later identification of Lucifer with Satan is no coincidence or arbitrary symbolic artifice. Enki was Zoroaster who was Lucifer, and Enki was also the Jewish, and later the Christian Satan. Ham sired the lineage of Tubal Cain King of Ur whose descendant King Boethos moved to Egypt to become the Pharaoh Hotep Sekhemwy of the second dynasty. His son Raneb founded the cult of Khem (Chem or Ham) the goat-headed sun god, reminiscent of Enki as the Ram or Goat of the shimmering waters, whose centre of worship was situated at Mendes. The Cult of Khem later migrated into Greece where he became Pan, the Horned god of the Witches (Strega). Enki also developed into the all-healing Golden Fleece, a variation of the Holy Grail. In the medieval period this cult evolved and the Solar and Goat symbolism of Khem and Pan was amalgamated with that of the Constantinian symbol of Jesus as the Sol Invicta. Synthesised as the "Black Sun," Jesus was worshipped by witches across France as "Christ, Son Dei," whilst in Scandinavia the witches called this same Horned God "The Antecessor" or ancestor, reinforcing the tradition of Christ and his Anunnaki ancestors as progenitors and forebears, and the fons et origio of druidism, which we know etymologically later developed into witchcraft. Hotep also introduced the practice of building mortuary temples in the form of pyramids, which closely resembled the Ziggurats of his homeland. The concept of the pyramid tomb appealed to the Egyptians as a manifestation of the Holy Mountain because such was a symbol of life and fertility, and by building pyramid tombs the subsequent pharaohs hoped to replicate its effect and gain life and fertility after death. With the arrival of Hotep Sekhemwy on the scene we are in the era of the Egyptian King lists and **our 16q24.3 genes are introduced by him into the bloodline of the royal dynasties of Egypt, whilst the same genes descended from Hotep's ancestral**

mother Lilith Luluwa, daughter of the Jewish Satan by Queen Lilith, the Mother of all Demons, Witches, Fairies and Vampires, and established themselves in the divine Satanic lineage of the proto-Scythian Kings.

In my second preliminary summary of the foregoing, we have confirmed to a greater extent a historical basis for the supposed Anunnaki myth and have cross-referenced it with the theological legends of the Greeks.

Through genetics and archaeology, we can assert that the Anunnaki were advanced European settlers in Mesopotamia whose divine descendants established their bloodlines within the Egyptian royal dynasties. Within the same era, more or less, we can also assert that the Anunnaki bequeathed their genetic inheritance to the proto-Scythians whose divine ancestral name means "Princes of Power." From here we jump a couple of millennia to the year 1361 BC, passing as we do the Age of Prince Ankh-fn-khonsu who first established the Dragon Court in our lineage, to the reign of the Pharaonic Queen Sobekh Nefru. Wife of Pharaoh Amenhemet IV, Sobekh Nefru reigned during the age of the Dragon God Sobekh, the custodian and protector of the blood royal, and it was she who built the labyrinthine temple in his honour at Khayyum, a structure which was later copied by the Minoans of Crete.

Within the temple complex Sobekh Nefru ratified and re-established the Dragon Court of Prince Ankh-fn-Khonsu and the Dragon Court and her ancient genetic, Anunnaki dragon legacy descended to her ancestral daughter Merytaten, granddaughter of Queen Nefertiti. On the occasion of her marriage to Prince Niall, Lord of the Egyptian, Red Sea region of Capacyront in the High Kingdom, the two ancient dragon legacies fused into one and became all the stronger with their bond. Niall was the son of the Dragon King Fenius Farsaidh of Scythia and Queen Tadukhipa of the Scythian Mittani and, following their marriage Merytaten was bestowed with the Scythian royal title of "Scota," meaning Princess of the Scythians or Scotti. Thereby she became the Princess of the race of princes. Niall and Merytaten's son was named Geadheal Glas and it was he who was the ancestor of the later Gaels in the land that eventually became known as Albha, and then Scotland. On the death of Geadheal Glas in 1300 BC, his son Easru succeeded him in Scythia, and two distinct lineages emerged, that of the Gaels, and that of the Scythian Scotti. Following the passing of many generations, documented in detail within the ancestral charts herein, Easru's descendant King Easar Brec assumed the throne of Scythia and fought with his forces in the Greek wars.

He was named Partholon by his Greek compatriots, and his Scythians were called the "Danaan," meaning sons of An. No doubt because of his defeat and the increasing incursions of the Sarmatians into his Scythian lands, Easar Brec quit the continent and took his remnant and their womenfolk to Eire, where they encountered and defeated their distant Bulgarian cousins, the Scythian Fir Bolg, at the Battle of Moytura. Archaeological evidence supporting the Danaan migration from Greece to Eire was unearthed in the form of Grecian artifacts discovered, if I remember correctly, in the 19th Century. During this period in their history Easar Brec's people became known as the Tuadha de Danaan and on his death he was succeeded by his brother's son, the legendary fairy king, the Daghda Mor. In the ensuing generations they were enveloped in an aura of mysticism and were credited with great magical power, an aura that, no doubt, was a legacy of their divine origins as the Titanic, Dragon God-Kings of antiquity. However, this process of mythification was to backfire on them in the centuries to come.

When the Milesian Gaels invaded Ireland and put them to flight they supplanted Danaan culture and overlaid upon it their own traditions and histories. The Danaan were forced to flee to the hills following the Milesian invasion and from then on they seemed to drop out of history, so much so that centuries later their aura of magic and their subsequent obscuration by the invaders led historians and folklorists, unconversant with their history and etymology, to dismiss the Tuadha de Danaan as mythical beings, as no more than ethereal gods of the ancient Gaelic tribes who usurped their real position in history. Their identification as divine beings was quite justified, but not at the expense of their corporality. Following their victory and subsequent ascendance the Milesians renamed the Tuadha de Danaan and referred to them from then on as the fairy Daouine Sidhe which Irish scholars and historians, who apparently hadn't investigated their etymology or traced their movements, erroneously thought meant "People of the Hills," because of their supposed retreat into the mountainous regions of the island. A more thorough investigation would have revealed that Daouine Sidhe actually meant "People of Scythia." From being the Scythians of Transylvania they became the Danaan of Greece and eventually reverted to being the people of Scythia. At least their conquerors knew who they were and named them accordingly. As late as the 19th Century, W. B. Yeats records that it had been an abiding tradition in Ireland for centuries that the fairies – the Daouine Sidhe – were the "Children of Lilith" and the sons of the Devil, thereby confirming their Anunnaki parentage and their migration from Transylvania and Central Europe. At the time of the Milesian incursion the presiding king of the Tuadha de Danaan was an individual named Bruithnigh. His name derives from the arch druidic title Bruidhe, meaning a Seer, a custodian of ancient wisdom and a keeper of the histories of his people. Suffering defeat, Bruithnigh took his four sons, their wives and his warriors and sailed east from Ulster to the western isles of Albha. In the ensuing years they settled permanently in Caledonia, establishing a kingdom, which stretched south from the Moray Firth to central Scotland and west as far as the Hebrides. In its time it was the largest kingdom in Albha and remained so for centuries, until the succession of King Aed in the 8th Century, by which time it had been known as Pictland, or Pictavia, for generations. From the Pictish King Lists we know that Bruithnigh's eldest son Cait succeeded him and established the Scythian dynasty we now know through the

Romans of the 1st Century as the Pictii, from the habit of painting their torsos with sacred tribal symbols; and the Cruithainn or sons of Cruithne, a Roman misunderstanding of the ancient ancestral name Bruithne or Bruithnigh. Furthermore the Scythian Pictii retained their identity as the Daouine Sithe of Albha, and this appellation continued to be coterminous with that of the Fairies or Elves for centuries to come. Developing from this name we derive the term Pixie, another name for the fairy, which was arrived at by combining Pict with Sithe to form the word Pictsithe, which was then corrupted to Pixie. In the 1320's Robert the Bruce had been sponsored by the Church in Scotland who, following the defeat and exile of John Balliol, decided that the Bruce was the only hope Scotland had of freeing itself from the yoke of English occupation and tyranny. Eager to crown him king and persuade the Pope to recognise him as such, and recognise the foundation of a Scottish Kingdom, Bishops Wishart and Pemberton, who had been at the forefront of the previous Scottish rebellions, sent an emissary to the Holy Father to plead their case. The emissary, Father Bressick, was a legal expert and a gifted orator and with him he took a declaration signed and sealed by the Bishops and Nobles of Scotland, in which it was declared that the Scots (Picts) were Scythians who had migrated from Central Europe and that they were descended from Princess Scota. As they weren't English, Irish or Welsh, but a unique and separate people, with a unique and separate blood inheritance, they should not have to suffer the oppression of a foreign King. Such was the veracity of the declaration and the eloquence of Father Bressick that the Pope assented and the Bruce, through many trials and tribulations, was eventually crowned King of the Scots. The descent of the Scotti from Scota, particularly the Picts, rather than being just a myth, was accepted as a historical fact for centuries. In studying tribal names and migrations, by thoroughly cross-referencing sources and by applying comparative symbolism, etymology and genetic findings to so-called myth and folklore, I am the first person in this particular field to establish the Danaan and their "fairy" descendants as historical figures and place them in their proper context. The same goes for much of the research I have summarised in this essay, research that has been subsequently copied and repeated in the work of other writers and novelists. If one remains a narrow "specialist" and refuses to adopt the polymathic approach to a subject, one gets nowhere fast. Specialists are vital for the detailed research of their given subjects, but it is only through the synthesis of those subjects that one arrives at any semblance of the wider and more detailed truth. Having said that, whilst I love doing research and synthesis and I believe I'm fairly good at it, when it comes to editing and the construction of a literary narrative, I'm absolutely useless. Consequently if the reader finds this letter muddled and meandering, I hope I might be forgiven. To continue, King Cait ruled Pictavia in Albha from 650 BC and was succeeded by his son Debeccan. From him the divine, royal lineage of the Scythians descends to our first dynastic ancestor King Vere I in 400 BC From King Vere I there descends the succession of Vere Arch druid princes and Wood Lords to King Vere II. From him the line continues down to King Vere III called "Daich Vetla" in around 300 AD. From a succession of subsequent High Kings we arrive at the Scythian Pictish King Brude Mac Bile who reigned from 693 to 697 AD. His daughter, the Scythian Dragon Princess Pressina or Bruithina married the Gaelic sacral Dragon King Elinus of Strathclyde, also called "Gille Sidhean" or Elf Servant. From their union arose three sisters, Melusine, Plantina and Meliore. Again through ignorance, laziness or confusion Melusine is dismissed as a legendary figure, a creature of myth. However, persistence won the day again and subsequent research uncovered the fact that in France Melusine is called Milouziana des Scythes, or Melusine of the Scythians and that she was domiciled in Angiers in Anjou following her assassination of her father in Scotland for breaking Scythian taboos. From her sister Plantina descend the Angevin Counts who, centuries later, adopted the dynastic name Plantagenet in her memory. Melusine is dismissed as a myth because, like her divine forbears, she was shrouded in magic and mystery, and because she became confused with the two subsequent Melusine's, seemingly from other French dynasties, whose histories were at odds with each other, this false dichotomy prompted historians to dismiss her out of hand as a baseless legend, requiring no further investigation. The Veres are in fact descended from all three Melusine's. 1. Melusine Vere the First, Scythian Princess of the Picts of Albha, who fled to Angiers and married Rainfroi de Vere, Duke of Angiers and Count of Anjou in 760 AD. It is more than likely that Melusine and Rainfroi were related as cousins from the same descent. From them descends Prince Milo, Duke of Angiers and Count of Anjou after his father. Milo was named after his mother Milo-ziana. In her lifetime Melusine I was called the Dragon Princess and the Fairy daughter of Satan, illustrating the fact that the Dragon Motif of the early Scythians and the Egyptian Sobekh Pharaohs persisted until the medieval period. This Melusine was also said to be a Witch. As a descendant of Scythian Arch druids in Scotland and Eire, this appellation is quite pertinent and appropriate. In Gaelic a Witch is called a Druidhe or Druid. 2. Melusine the Second, daughter of Bouchard Comte de Corbiel and Lady Adelaide de Crecy. Melusine de Corbiel was descended from the Veres via Ida de Vere of the Ardennes, a descendant of the Vere Counts of Guisnes. This Melusine married Prince Hugh I Comte de Rethul and their son; Badouin de Bourg II married Princess Morfia of Armenia and became King of Jerusalem. Melusine the Third, called Melisende of Lusignan, married Fulke the Fifth, the scion of the Scythian Princess Plantina. Following the transference of the Comite of Anjou and Maine from the House of Vere to their cousins the descendants of Melusine I's sister Plantina, Fulke became Count of Anjou by virtue of his descent and by marriage to this Melusine, he became King of Jerusalem. Therefore, all three Melusines are actually Veres of Scythian Pictish extraction, deriving originally from the same Scottish, Scythian dynasty, and it is from all three Melusines that we are descended as the individual lineages fused. Milo Duke of Angiers, the son of Melusine Vere I and Rainfroi de Vere, married Bertheld, sister of Charlemagne and daughter of Pepin le Brevis. From this union we inherit one of thirteen lines of descent from the Merovingian sorcerer Kings of the Franks. To tell their particular story and trace their lineage to the present day, we must again go back in time and recount the Davidic descent of the pharaonic scions of Princess Scota's cousin, the Egyptian Queen Kiya Tasherit, daughter of the Dragon Queen Kiya and the Pharaoh Amenhotep IV. In 1361 BC Kiya Tasherit married Prince Rama, a descendant of the Sumerian Lord Abram. Rama's Egyptian forebears can be traced back to the Pharaoh Senusret I, son of Pharaoh Amenhemet and husband of Princess Sarai who was the daughter of Queen Tohwait. In the Old Testament Abram becomes Abraham and Prince Rama is transformed into Ram. No indication of their Sumerian or Egyptian ancestry is given and we are led to believe by default that they were the Jewish descendants of Noah, who in fact never existed. The Jews claimed that, 1500 years before the Old Testament was conceived in Babylon, Abraham was the founder of the Jewish race. This is plain nonsense. The Jews were a tribe of nomadic goat-herders who were living in Mesopotamia generations before Abraham was born. In any event Abraham wasn't a Semitic Jew, he was an Egypto-Sumerian nobleman of the line of Qayin and Pharaoh Raneb. So in fact the Jews have no recorded ancestors of their own and no history beyond the time when in 1960 BC Abraham, who was not a nomad like the Jews but a respected resident of Ur, fled Sumeria during the Akkadian invasions. The Jews were one tribe among many who migrated out of Mesopotamia at the time and Abraham was lumped in with them. That the scribes record him as their leader and their father is arbitrary invention. With Rama two lines of Anunnaki Dragon Kingship converge and become further enriched on the occasion of his marriage to Kiya Tasherit. Their children become the Egypto-Sumerian forebears of King David. David eventually marries Bathsheba the Hittite or Hurrian (Aryan) and by so doing injects more Anunnaki blood into his dynasty. Their son Solomon wrote The Song of Songs which, having been analysed, proves to be of Egyptian origin in its construction and content. Studying various sources it is my contention that Solomon adhered to pharaonic tradition and married his sister Sheba, who actually appears in one version of The Song of Songs as his sibling. In apocryphal Jewish texts Sheba is described as a Witch, a demoness with the hooves of a goat and legs covered in thick fur. One of her later titles was Sheba – Lilith, which means that she was of Anunnaki descent, not a black African Queen, despite Jewish assertions. I believe that every effort has been made to denigrate her to posterity (in exactly the same manner as the Jewish Christians later denigrated Mary Magdalene), in order to hide her familial relationship to Solomon, an incestuous relationship which, as his sister-wife, was absolutely anathema to the Jewish scribes and priests of the time. Back in time Ham, the supposed son of Noah, transgressed ancient Jewish taboo and as a result he was subsequently described as being black, which was intended to be a curse. In the last millennium all black Africans were said to be descended from Ham the transgressor, the breaker of God's holy law, and because of this Africans were seen as a race damned by God and beyond his care. As sub-human outcasts therefore, these sons of Ham were only fit to be slaves and, armed with this excuse, good "Christian" Europeans with a clear conscience initiated the Slave Trade, a period of torture, suffering and misery which lasted 300 years and which was justified by a Jewish smear campaign. In like manner, by describing Sheba-Lilith as black the Jews could assert that, as a daughter of Ham, she was damned and because of her black complexion, her incestuous familial relationship with her brother would be hidden from posterity. Solomon was one of the prototypes for the Lord of the Rings. It is said that he was a great magician; the master of demons, whom he recruited into his service to build his great temple and whom he controlled by wielding a set of magic rings of power. Solomon is also credited with having a harem of oriental proportions, which he filled with fairy women from the east and princesses who worshipped foreign gods, gods whom the scribes later described as devils. Not manifesting much piety and being tolerant to the worship of alien deities in his kingdom, Solomon doesn't appear to be particularly Jewish, either by habit or by conviction, which, given his pharaonic and Aryan antecedence, is quite understandable. All in all Solomon was an embarrassing thorn in the side of the Jewish scribes and priests of his time. From Solomon and Sheba the line of Jewish Kings descends for 500 years until we reach King Zedekiah of Judah in 598 BC With the marriage of Zedekiah's daughter, Princess Tamar, to the Milesian King Eochaid I, the royal Egypto-Sumerian and Aryan dynastic line bifurcates. From Eochaid the royal line devolves to King Erc; the Arch druid of the sacred clan of the Ulidian Fir Bolg in Ulster in 480 AD. From Erc the blood legacy is passed down to King Rhodri Mawr of Gwynedd, North Wales in 800 AD. Rhodri Mawr's descendant Llewelyn the Great sires a daughter Helen and she marries Donald 10th Earl of the Scythian Clan of Mar. Their daughter Isobel marries Robert the Bruce and the line descends through the Kings Of Scots and the Lords Hamilton to the House of Vere of Blackwood to the present day. Returning to King Zedekiah of Judah, his lineage descends for another 400 years until it eventually rests with Joseph ben Jacob, who married Miriamne or Mary of the Royal House of David. Joseph is described as a carpenter in the Gospels and this description is derived from a mistranslation of the Greek word "Tekton." In this particular context, and given the corroborative findings of Dr. Barbara Thiering and other eminent persons, Tekton actually translates as a "builder of the temple." Other scholars in this field of research agree upon this translation. They further go on to suggest that his epithet relates to the building of the spiritual temple within the heart of Man. It transpires therefore that Joseph, rather than being a humble carpenter, is in fact a Teacher, a Rabbi and furthermore, he is of the Order of Pharisees and a member of the Sanhedrin. It is quite probable that the Pauline Christians decided to retain Joseph's spurious identity as a humble tradesman in order that their cash cow, their new, invented religion might appeal to the lower classes, the peasants and humble artisans of the Empire, with whom they hoped the proletariat might identify. His wife, Mary the

"Virgin," was a ward of the Sanhedrin and that is how he first encountered her. When she had come of age it was decided by the Priests that Mary should be married off and in order to secure a husband for her, they drew lots. Though something of a shock to his fellow Rabbis, the ageing Joseph won the draw and he was duly betrothed to the young child. We all know the Gospel stories so I won't elaborate too much. Suffice to say that most of the Jesus legend is a later Pauline fabrication designed to appease and appeal to a potentially hostile pagan, Roman audience, at a time when the entire Roman province of Judea was in open revolt against the Empire. Joseph was a Rabbi and, following the family business Jesus was also a Rabbi. He is addressed as such in the Gospels. Ignorant dogmatists, still believing Jesus was a carpenter's son, explain away the false anomaly by asserting that Jesus' appellation as a Rabbi is simply a general Hebrew term meaning "teacher." However, during his sojourn in Galilee, (a Strict Orthodox district which adhered faithfully and thoroughly to the Torah and Rabbinical Law), Jesus taught regularly in the Synagogue. Unless he actually was a Rabbi in the priestly sense of the word, this would never have been permitted under Jewish Law. Furthermore, as a Rabbi Jesus would have to have been married. For a man of Jesus' age to be single, especially as a Rabbi, would have been unthinkable. Even if he hadn't been a priest, by remaining celibate he would have been breaking God's Holy Law, which specifically commands that all Jewish men should marry and sire children. For a man of Galilee especially, celibacy would have been tantamount to blasphemy. During the wedding at Caanah, at the behest of his mother who has noticed that the guests have run out of victuals, Jesus is purported to have turned water into wine. This apparent miracle was in fact a later addition to the story, which was actually borrowed from the Roman Cult of Bacchus, a deity to whom the exact same miracle was attributed. Like so much else in the Gospels concerning Jesus, he is repeatedly identified with the pagan gods in order that his story might appeal to the pagan target audience that Paul and his recidivist cronies intended to fleece. The strange thing is that the pagan rituals and traditions that actually can be attributed to Jesus were rigorously suppressed during the process of the canonisation of the New Testament. The interesting thing about the wedding at Caanah, and indeed any Jewish wedding of the period, is that the master of the feast, the individual responsible for the continued provision of food and drink during the festivities, was the bridegroom himself. That a guest would have been responsible for such a duty would have been unthinkable. By asking Jesus to replenish the wine, Mary was addressing the Bridegroom. To develop this, if we peruse the canonical gospels approved by the Pauline Church fathers, we discover that Mary Magdalene was the only female apostle and that it was she with whom Jesus was most intimate. Corroborating this fact we find that in the Nag Hammadi scrolls and in the Gospels of St. Phillip and St. Mary Magdalene, an intimate relationship between the two is variously suggested and that Jesus would often kiss Mary intimately. This relationship caused a great deal of jealousy among the other apostles, especially Peter. If we remember that Jesus' celibacy would have been socially and theologically unacceptable and we accept Jewish marital tradition concerning the responsibilities of the bridegroom, then Jesus' intimacy with Mary Magdalene is quite understandable. She was his wife. Jesus' cult wasn't Christian, it was overtly Jewish and was intended by Jesus' family to remain that way. With the arrival of Saul or Paul on the scene, a man who had hounded Jesus' followers to death before faking his Damascus conversion, Jesus' family and followers were naturally hostile and suspicious and refused him entry into their inner circle. Recruiting Peter the ignorant fisherman who had supposedly betrayed Jesus and like Paul, was therefore not party to the inner teachings, the two of them set sail for Rome, taking what knowledge of Jesus' teachings they had gleaned, and set about inventing a new, bogus religion with Peter as the First Apostle, the chosen Pope of Christ, when in fact it was Prince Elinus of Britain. Meanwhile, back in Judea, Jesus' family continued with Jesus' authentic teachings and their movement developed into the Nazorite Church, eventually to become the Celtic Church as it migrated into Europe. The Pauline movement, keen to attract a pagan audience and liberate it from its hard earned cash, modified and Romanised the Jesus cult to such an extent that it bore little resemblance at all to its Jewish, Nazorite parent or indeed to the true teachings of Christ. Naturally a schism occurred and Paul was convinced that in order to be able to present his version of Christianity as the authentic teachings of Jesus, with Peter at its head, he would have to initiate a thoroughgoing campaign of libel, misdirection and misinformation against the Nazorites whose very existence, and whose rightful claim to Christian orthodoxy and authentic apostolic blood succession threatened the future of his newly established cottage industry. In the Nazorite faith, it has been said, the right to its leadership was hereditary, which meant that only those of Jesus' blood descent could be the Chief Apostles. Knowing that Jesus had been married to Mary Magdalene who had borne him a male heir, Paul and his disciples concentrated their efforts on her. Mary's title was Miriamne Mar, which translates as "Mary The Great" and "Mary The Teacher," which meant that she was firstly of noble birth, and secondly a central figure in Jesus' cult, responsible for the promulgation of Jesus' teachings and an intimate party to Jesus' inner mystery traditions. Having asserted Jesus' celibacy in his writings, which meant to Paul's followers that Jesus had no successor, Paul could then convince them that the right to leadership of the Christian

Church rested with Peter, whom Paul insisted was the legitimate successor, chosen by Jesus himself. This spurious assertion is manifest in the New Testament where Jesus is supposed to have said "Thou art Peter, and upon this Rock I will build my Church." The name Peter derives from the Greek and means Rock. Rendered in the masculine gender Rock is Petros. So far so good. The lie is advanced. However, what Jesus actually said was "Thou art Petra and upon this Rock I will build my Church." Jesus spoke in the feminine gender and rendered the word Rock as Petra. The Pauline usurpers overlooked this one mistake and as a result of this oversight, the feminine Petra is still in the Bible to this day.

So Jesus was actually addressing his remark to a woman, not a man. The only female disciple amongst the twelve was Mary Magdalene; Mary the Noble, Mary the Teacher. Upon her and her offspring Jesus would found his Church and for those descendants to have a legitimate right to his succession, they would have to be of his blood and antecedence. To further defuse the threat that Mary posed, great efforts were made to present her in the worst possible light. In certain texts Mary is described as a priestess of the Babylonian Goddess Ishter – the Roman Venus – whose cult included sacred Venal rituals. The Pauline Church jumped on this and labelled her a common whore, a prostitute riddled with demons, the worst kind of sinner. Not only did the Roman Church want to negate the threat she and her children posed to the legitimacy of the papal succession of Paul's invented orthodoxy, they also wanted to marginalise her by stripping her of her central role as a teacher of the mysteries, thereby presenting her involvement in Jesus' movement as being no more than incidental. The task was made all the easier by public opinion. In a misogynistic, patriarchal society, the idea that a mere woman might be a religious teacher, a rabbi, was completely unthinkable and was strictly forbidden under Jewish Law.

Furthermore in Roman society women were second-class citizens, the chattels of their men folk who kept them firmly in the background. To convince their Roman audience that Mary was of no importance at all was therefore very easy. Not only was she vilified and written out of Christian Gospel history, just for good measure she becomes the hate target of the Revelations of St. John wherein, as a Babylonian priestess, and in repeating the notion that she was a common prostitute, Mary takes centre stage as The Whore of Babylon from whose chalice pour all the abominations of the world. Riding a Dragon (an appropriate symbol!) she holds in her arms her offspring, whom St. John claims is the Anti-Christ of the latter days. Not only is she damned for posterity, but also her child – the legitimate apostolic successor of his father Jesus – is cast in the role as the enemy of God and the Roman Church, the brood of Satan himself. As far as the Roman Church is concerned, the vilification and damnation of Mary and her royal child is complete and they can rest in the sure knowledge that their false Church, its spurious, fraudulent Pope and its right to decide apostolic succession is assured, leaving them with the most important task of their ministry – acquiring as much power, and raking in as much wealth as they possibly can. This Papal fraud has been accepted for 1700 years, during which time the Church destroyed as many dissenting texts as it could find – thereby creating the Dark Ages – it maimed, tortured, raped and murdered thousands, if not millions of innocent people who opposed its orthodoxy and hegemony during the Inquisition. Its anti-Jewish policies and persecutions directly resulted in the Holocaust of the Second World War, after which it provided escapes routes for the Nazi death camp guards, SS Officers and other assorted war criminals, and through the centuries and up to this present day it has amassed literally trillions of dollars in revenue and property.

The list of the Church's crimes is endless. Truly Christianity is the most evil religion in history. However, all in the garden is not rosy. Apocryphal texts declare that Mary Magdalene's cousin was Herod Agrippa whose family had a palace in southern Gaul. The texts go on to relate that, following Jesus' death, Mary his wife, Mary his mother and Mary his sister set sail for Gaul, landed in Marseilles and found refuge in Herod's palace. The arrival of the three Marys in Gaul was celebrated in religious festivals up until quite recently. During the Dark Ages and up until the medieval period the fact that Magdalene brought her son with her was also common knowledge. Early noble families claimed that Jesus' son grew up in Gaul, married and sired children whose descendants married into the Frankish Royal Line and produced the Dynasty of the Merovingian Kings. Apparently, in his old age, Mary's son returned to Judea, taking the remains of his deceased mother with him. Having studied the evidence closely and thoroughly, eminent historians and Jewish scholars, amongst them Dr. Barabara Thiering, all concur that Jesus was married and had children. So-called "apocryphal" texts support this view and in balance the weight of evidence in support of this assertion far outweighs the scant, unsupported and insubstantial arguments in favour of Jesus' celibacy promoted and advanced by the orthodox Church. An organisation which in root and branch is lying, deceitful, corrupt, fraudulent and riddled with an overpowering lust for money and power which it has misappropriated in a manner which manifests a total lack of concern for the cost to the individual or to society. Do we trust the findings of scholars whose desire is to present society with as accurate a picture of history as they possibly can. Or do we believe an organisation, which we know only too well, has deceived and oppressed human society for 1700 years in the pursuit of its own greed and megalomania? The Church might believe they have the whole argument stitched up and that any theory, which challenges the Orthodox view, can be dismissed as speculative, heretical or blasphemous. However, they do have a problem. In 1980 a team of archaeologists were working in the Talpiyot suburb of Jerusalem, a district only two miles removed from the traditional site of Golgotha, where Jesus was supposedly crucified. During the dig they uncovered the entrance to a family tomb. Having cleared the rubble they entered and inside they discovered a number of ossiaries (ten in all), sizeable boxes fashioned from alabaster, which are intended to contain the bones of the deceased in their final resting place. Alabaster is the stone sacred to the Egyptian God Amun – father of all the Pharaohs – and was used by them, after the age of the pyramids, to build their mortuary temples. This practice persisted up until the time of Alexander the Great. Its use in fashioning the ossiaries of Jesus and Miriamne Mar is deliberate and significant. They removed the ossiaries and took them to their laboratory for further examination. A closer study revealed that their design dated them to the 1st century and that the patina on the ossiaries matched the date of the design. Further inspection resulted in the discovery of individual engravings on the boxes, each engrained with a patina, which matched the 1st century date in which the boxes were originally fashioned. Naturally this meant that they had been marked immediately after they had been made. After copying and translating the inscriptions they confirmed the following Ossuary 1 contained a set of bones and was inscribed "Joseph ben Jacob." Ossuary 2 contained a set of bones and was inscribed "Jesus ben Joseph." Ossuary 3 contained a set of bones and was inscribed "Joshua ben Jesus." Ossuary 4 contained a set of bones and was inscribed "Miriamne Mar." Genetic tests carried out on the remains from ossuary 2 and ossuary 4 confirmed that they were not related to the same mother and, given Jewish burial practice, they concurred that Miriamne Mar would not have been interred in the family tomb unless she had been related to one of the other occupants which, in this case could only have been by marriage. Statisticians were consulted and they constructed a probability model to determine the likelihood of a co-incidence where another family with exactly the same names could have been contemporary with those discovered in the tomb. Though the names were well known in Judaea at the time, one was quite rare and given the specific grouping of these individual's names together, the statistical likelihood that they were any other than Jesus's wife and family was dismissed. A coincidence seemed virtually impossible. Scholars were satisfied that the remains interred within the tomb were indeed those of Christ, Mary Magdalene, their son Joshua and Jesus's father Joseph. This is now accepted as fact and confirms without question all the so called apocryphal tales concerning Jesus's marriage to Mary, the existence of a male heir, and that heir's descent to the Merovingian Dynasty in Gaul. The only reason we find this fact incredible today is because such overwhelming scientific evidence still stands in clear contradiction to what we have been spoon fed for 1700 years, an orthodox Catholic lie which has become ingrained into our racial consciousness. It isn't so incredible if we remember that Jesus emerged as only a minor provincial celebrity in what was, after all, a turbulent but insignificant backwater of the Roman Empire. If it hadn't been for Paul's greed and ambition, and his rejection by Jesus's family, Paul would not have travelled to Rome in the hope of selling his profitable new cult to the Gentiles. As a consequence Jesus, his family and his Church would still be an insignificant, anomalous Jewish cult which, today, would have been largely forgotten. Because of this any subsequent claim to a descent from Jesus now would present no problems whatsoever and would probably be met with a shrug of the shoulders. After Peter and Paul's death the Christian cult in the Empire struggled for its ascendancy in the face of hostile opposition from the State and other more well established pagan theologies. For generations the so-called Christians were no more than cat food, that is until the 4th century when the cult had finally found a foothold and gained in popularity to the point where the Emperor Constantine stepped in. A tempting political opportunity presented itself, the opportunity to unite the various factions of the Empire and prevent dissention and unrest from the Christians. The only stumbling block however, was the fact that within early Christianity there were several doctrines all vying for supremacy. To neutralise their threat they had to be unified. These factions fell loosely into two categories. On the one hand there were those who believed Paul's doctrine of the divinity of Jesus, and on the other there were those who believed that he was simply a human prophet and healer. Seeing the potential, future political profit in adopting Christianity as a State cult, Constantine determined to call a halt to the squabbling and in-fighting by ordering the heads of the various factions to meet at Nicaea in 325 AD and iron out their differences. The bishops met and a ballot was called in which the two basic doctrines would be voted on. Was Jesus to be promoted as the divine Son of God, or was he to be promoted as a mortal Teacher and Healer? The votes were evenly split and Jesus' future hung in the balance. The casting vote, which would confirm Jesus as the Son of God, lay with Bishop Arius who was firmly opposed to Christ's divinity. The old and frail Arius decided to vote according to his conscience and his convictions. As soon as he had done so, Bishop Nicholas of Myra, feared as a psychotic bully in his own lifetime, viciously beat the ageing Arius until he changed his mind and voted the way Myra wanted him to. In summary, the only reason we think of

Christ as the Son of God now is because of an inexcusable act of violence against an old man who was too weak to defend himself. Under Bishop Eusebius of Caesarea (c. 260–339 CE) and at the behest of Constantine the Gospels were canonised and those thought to be heretical were discarded, including that of St. Phillip, which confirmed the intimate relationship between Jesus and Mary. Christ was promoted as the Son of God with Constantine's approval and a unified church, with an orthodox dogma, was brought into the imperial fold. During Constantine's reign copies of the approved Gospels were distributed across the Empire, persecution ceased, Christian heresy was met with stringent penalties and Christians and pagans co-existed side by side until the succession of the Emperor Theodosius. Under him paganism was outlawed and at his order Christians put pagans to the sword, turning the persecuted into the persecutors. This is the basic outline of events that converted Christianity from a dissenting minor cult into a corrupt world power within the space of a couple of generations. If the vote had gone the other way and Jesus was recognised for what he truly was, a minor mortal prophet and healer from an obscure dynasty in a blighted backwater of the empire, then claiming descent from him would not be met with the orthodox incredulity and outrage, or the secular disbelief that it does today. Nevertheless, archaeological corroboration of Jesus' marriage and the existence of his heirs are facts supported by scientific evidence that is inescapable, regardless of our religious brainwashing and indoctrination. With this in mind I commend to you our Merovingian descents from Christ and the ancient House of David. The Merovingian dynasty began with King Meroveus and Princess Merira in 460 AD. Merira's lineage descended from Joshua, the son of Jesus and Mary, and Joshua was identified at the time as the "Quinotaur," the dragon from beyond the sea. The Merovingian descent from Christ had, by this time, become popular common knowledge and again it posed a threat to the power and authority of the Church. To neutralise this threat, they induced the Mayors of the Palace, themselves scions of Meroveus, to kidnap and incarcerate the Merovingian King Clovis. Having achieved this, they then put Clovis to death and, as a reward for their loyal service to the Church, they were duly installed as the puppet kings of the Franks. This Christianised lineage descended through Charles Martel and Pepin Brevis to Charlemagne in 780 AD. Here the lines of Vere Merovingian descent divide between Bertheld, daughter of King Pepin Brevis, who married Prince Milo I de Vere of Angiers, and Charlemagne. From Charlemagne the Merovingian bloodline devolves through Emperor Louis I and Princess Judith of Bavaria, to St Ida of Ardennes, circa 1050 AD. St. Ida married Eustace de Vere Comte de Boulogne and they had a daughter, Ida de Vere. Ida married Badouin de Bourg, Comte de Rethul and the Merovingian bloodline continues down to Fulke V of Anjou, King of Jerusalem. Here the Vere descent merges with that of Melusine I's sister Plantina. From Fulke's descendant Geoffrey Platagenet the Angevin Kings of England emerge and from them the line descends, through the Lords Hamilton, to the House of Vere in Blackwood. From Milo de Vere I the Merovingian bloodline also descends to Ralph de Vere and the Veres of Blackwood. Along the way other Merovingian descents emerge from these lines, along with imperial European descents dating from the time of Julius Caesar.

From my studies I have found that myth and legend, rather than being just fantasy, are usually grounded in factual persons and events, and that they and their symbolism can endure for millennia, migrating virtually intact from one culture to another. I would therefore commend my research and the resulting genealogical tables as the official family history of the House of Vere. A House quite rightly steeped in ancient magic, myth and legend and all the better for it. Indeed, demonstrated by the descents I have researched and uncovered, and attested to by eminent scholars of Law and History, the House of Vere emerge as the most ancient, and the senior Imperial and Royal family in Eurasia. The Dragon Cede, which includes the descents of our senior branches has had, by necessity, to be somewhat provocative. Apparently this sells books, according to my publisher and he took the project on with the understanding that I should present a new, more sensational slant on the subjects I have covered. Because of this I have retained the name "Satan" as one of our first ancestors and one of Jesus' forebears. Duly this should prove provocative enough and, as I want to get the House of Vere, its ancient history and its Imperial and Royal status as widely recognised and accepted as possible, which means selling as many books as possible, I have no choice but to concur with my publisher. In any event, as you know, being somewhat anarchic and disliking and distrusting those who have assumed self-appointed positions of authority, I have a mischievous sense of humour and the prospect of ruffling the feathers of a few bigoted religious fanatics has for me a certain appeal. These sorts of people have convinced themselves that they have cornered the market in absolute truth and, in times past, have adopted any method at their disposal to convince others that they are the custodians of incontrovertible fact.

The methods they have used, and the results they have achieved have been horrific, and socially, politically and spiritually disastrous. Any of us with even only a modicum of understanding realises that we never stop learning and that truth is never a static concept and, unlike religious dogmatists and bigots, we go on learning and changing until the day we end up in the grave. In life, learning only ceases when we succumb to the indolence of certain belief, and knowledge then becomes a Sacred Cow. As an iconoclast I have only one use for Sacred Cows: Sacred Burgers in a Bun with Garlic Mayonnaise. In promoting their ignorant, unresearched dogmas and forcing them on others, their ridiculous lies become legitimate targets for those of us who have taken the trouble to delve deeper for the truth. As such, Satan stays in my texts and genealogical tables and if it upsets the precious sensibilities of the mindless religious conformists who cling to their orthodoxy, in their cowardly desperation for spiritual certainty and psychological comfort in a transient and frightening world, then to my mind I have done a good day's work. "

Authors note: This passage is important because it shows the tone and intention behind my father's use of provocative religious language.

He was not using the word Satan casually, nor was he unaware of how it would be received. He knew exactly what reaction it would cause. His point was that religious orthodoxy had created its own sacred taboos, and that those taboos had been used to control what people were allowed to question, study, or reinterpret.

When he says that "Satan stays in my texts and genealogical tables," he is not making a devotional statement. He is making an intellectual and symbolic one. He is refusing to remove a figure simply because the Church, or later religious readers, had decided that the word itself was forbidden, dangerous, or automatically evil.

That distinction matters.

My father's position was iconoclastic. He challenged religious certainty, inherited dogma, and the habit of accepting Church-shaped language without examining where it came from. His use of Satan, Lucifer, Enki, Jehovah, the Dragon blood, and the Grail families must be read through that lens. He was not asking people to worship Satan. He was challenging the religious framework that had turned "Satan" into a weapon against older traditions, rival bloodlines, heretics, witches,

Grail families, and anyone placed outside the approved Church narrative.

This is why later writers misrepresent the work when they lift the word "Satan" out of context and use it as proof of devil worship, demonic allegiance, or an Antichrist bloodline. The surrounding passage shows the opposite. It shows a writer deliberately attacking religious conformity and defending his right to examine forbidden names without submitting to the fear attached to them.

The issue, then, is not whether the word appears in the work. It does. The issue is what the word is doing there.

In my father's work, Satan is part of a contested symbolic, genealogical, theological, and mythological framework. In hostile later readings, that context is stripped away and the word is reduced to a crude accusation.

That is not interpretation. It is purpose mal misrepresentation.

This was dads' ways of joking, provoking others, and it worked well for other people to think they can write a whole book on us being satanic and evil when he clearly missed the boat on this one..

NDV says Beliefs" regarding God and spirituality create religions, and religions create division, fear and violence within the individual and consequently within society as a whole. Religion is a handy facade for the power and money hungry to conceal themselves behind, and a crutch for the spiritually lazy, the weak minded and the unregenerate. Religions happen when people don't get the point of the message – which is nearly always – and blindly worship the message and the messenger, instead of grasping the gnosis – the wisdom – inherent within the words that the message conveys. If you talk to God… you're religious. If God talks to you... you're psychotic. "Religion is an opiate of the masses," said Karl Marx. Too true. Although I support and follow the teachings of Christ, I abhor and detest the orthodoxy of

Christianity and the blind dogma of any religion. Adherence to such results in fear and misery and destroys any opportunity of a direct, transcendent interaction or relationship with the Creator, and without that there is no chance for any revolutionary transformation within the individual wherein, as Jesus said, "The Laws of God will be written in the hearts of men with tongues of fire." Direct experience of that which we label "God" - the vastness, the power, and the supreme balance of eternal life – produces a radical and permanent readjustment of the individual's perception of himself and his position and responsibilities within the universe. At such a point the radical change at the very heart of the individual produces an abiding, fundamental sense of peace, equilibrium, serenity and grace. A heightened state of consciousness and perception manifests itself in daily life by the outworking of love and compassion, charity, empathy, justice and nobility of spirit. This is what Jesus meant by Salvation, the condition where man is freed from the externally imposed social laws or the doctrines of religion written "On Tablets of Stone" and reborn into a condition where universal law is indivisibly and irreversibly incorporated into his very nature, becoming thereby "written on his heart with tongues of fire." For this transformation to take place and for the individual to become spiritually and psychologically free, the mind must first become sensitive, able to evolve, willing to remain open to new knowledge and adaptable to change. This can only be accomplished when neurotic, psychological adherence to the rigidity of religious conditioning and the inflexible pettiness of dogma, tradition and belief fall away and the mind becomes still, free from the puerile religious fears which are underpinned by the very religious orthodoxy which imprisons us in its web of deceit. Promises of salvation and peace through blind adherence to doctrine and the totally unnecessary intercession of a self-appointed priesthood are absolute lies, promulgated by those whose main motivation is the greed for money and political power, and the establishment of mass social control through religious fear. As "Dragons," those with "Clear Sight," being the natural capacity for spiritual profundity at a genetic level, the Veres are, I believe, gifted with an ancient, innate, inherited capability for transcendent vision and wisdom, gifts which in times past enabled them to be great God-Kings and Priest-Princes, Arch druids, Seers and Healers. Because of this genetic inheritance, to a greater or lesser extent, all of us have experienced a spiritual component in our lives, as have many Veres through the generations, and I for one have been a party to profound psychological states and spiritual transformations throughout my life, and all this without the mind-numbing, soul destroying influence of religion or the misinformed, ignorant mutterings of some malignant, grubby little priesthood. It is my belief that this is a fundamental genetic component of our Dragon Legacy and therefore, as the posed children of the Gods and the scions of the priest-kings of our forebears, the Veres today are their own priests and the well-spring, the fons et origio of the very concept of divinity and of spiritual truths whose nascence emerged long before primitive human history was first recorded.

In the following pages, I present a critical analysis of how an author can take a subject and distort it so completely that the result becomes a textbook example of misinformation. Two excerpts from my late father Nicholas's books — works for which I hold full copyright — provide the foundation for this examination. His writing exposes the very type of "money vampire" he warned us about: individuals who manipulate belief, fear, and narrative for personal gain.

In my own work, including *A Story of a Thousand Faces*, I have shown how biblical context is often weaponised to govern people through fear and control. The author I am reviewing employs the same tactic, and it is precisely this parallel that prompted the publisher to invite me to write this comparison. I had intended to take a break from writing — this being my ninth book since September 2025 — while continuing research for my next major project, *Shattering Illusions*, a 400–500 page investigation. Instead, I found myself pushed into a corner, much like "Baby" in *Dirty Dancing*, and compelled to respond.

This book therefore serves two purposes: first, to provide a detailed review and comparison between my father's insights and the flawed framework presented by the author in question; and second, to demonstrate how such distortions intersect with documented case law concerning fair use, good faith, and the legal boundaries of critical commentary.

INTERNET REGURGITATION

I have disclosed this following material as proof of how our work was already being used across the internet by numerous people without my permission, from the context it is clear that this was written after dads death, It seems that people lack the understanding where they think someone is dead therefore it is apparently acceptable to copyright our work, Some of the time its was to create drama, and some of the time it was due to them feeling that if they did not then this history would diminish and were just fans. However with this sort of title, it frames us as being part of the agenda, some of this information is repeated as it is already part of the description of dad on the book tree website which was lifted so many times, likewise with the Tracy Twyman interview, I feel it is important to show how this review is not just about Gary Wayne but an overall picture of how many times my inherited work has been infringed.

"The Number one weekly report which provides concrete evidence of a New World Order & One World Government agenda"

Welcome to the Global Watch Weekly Report History is replete with whispers of secret societies...The oldest is the Brotherhood of the Snake, also called the Brotherhood of the Dragon, and it still exists under many different names. The Brotherhood of the Snake is devoted to guarding the 'secrets of the ages' and the recognition of Lucifer as the one and only true God... Its secret symbol is the all-seeing eye in the pyramid." "William Cooper (now deceased) states that he had traced the history of the nefarious Illuminati all the way back to the Ancient Temple of Wisdom in Cairo, long before the birth of Christ. 'The Illuminati exist today under many different names and many different occupations.' Cooper told us. 'They practice Hegalian conflict/resolution. They appear to oppose each other at the bottom ranks, but at the highest levels they are actually organizing and controlling the conflict which they have created to produce the solution that they seek." "'The Illuminati are extremely powerful, very wealthy men. They believe that they are the guardians of the secrets of the ages. They believe that the vast majority of people would not know what to do with the real knowledge and the real truth and the real science -- and would, in fact, misuse them all. They further believe that everything that they do is for the ultimate betterment and survival of humankind -- even if it means killing two billion people to reach their goal..." The connection between Sumeria and the Black Nobility or bloodlines of the Illuminati today is that these royal bloodlines trace their ancestral links all the way back to Israel and then further back to Egypt and Sumeria as being bloodlines that have a supernatural element. They believe that they are the lineage of the Anunnaki who came to earth to teach men sacred and secret knowledge. These bloodlines have been listed in Fritz Springmeiers books, "Bloodlines of the Illuminati" and include the following families, the Rothschilds, Merovingians, DuPont's, Rockefellers, Bundy, Astor, Collins, Freeman, Kennedy, Li, Onassis, Van Duyn. Most of these bloodlines are predominantly European. Research has shown that one of the oldest secret societies to emerge out of the Sumerian era is an occultic order called the "Brotherhood of the Serpent" which was started by the Anunnaki, Ea. Researchers who specialise in understanding occultic orders are all unanimous in the fact that the beliefs of many of the occult fraternities today whether it be freemasonry, kabbalah, theosophy etc all trace their roots back to Babylon, Egypt and Sumeria in this particular order. Considering that the Genesis account of creation refers to an ongoing rivalry between mankind and the seed of the serpent as a result of the fall, many believe that the seed of the serpent refers to an actual demonic lineage which involves beings shaped with serpent like features. Why this is of relevance in this weeks edition of the Global Watch Weekly is because when Prince Nicholas de Vere von Drakenberg died in 2013, it initiated a flurry of articles regarding the rather weird and mysterious assertion by him that his royal family roots go back to the times of the Egyptian Pharaohs, and to the Sumerian Gods before them. Furthermore, De Vere believed that his lineage contained the genetic code of an actual dragon race. De Vere's belief paints a picture of the beginnings of the Grail bloodline in an antediluvian civilization, with a super-human, red-haired race of Grail kings that conquered and ruled over the primitive hordes of the ancient world, with tribes on each continent. These kings guided the destiny of all civilized man. They were overseers, "navigators", directing the affairs of the world with the Solomonic wisdom inherent in their blood. They created all of the traditions, customs and institutions upon which civilization depends. In the first few years of his life, Nicholas de Vere was raised in the Hertfordshire countryside. At the age of seven, Nicholas' family moved to the remote outskirts of the Kittenish village of Kemsing, and then later to isolated rural settings in Devon and Sussex. Nicholas' parents sought to protect Nicholas from the mediocrity and banality of most of society by retreating with him to the sanctuary of the English countryside. Nicholas' father was a skilled backwoodsman and during these formative years Nicholas was instilled with country knowledge, as well as a deep respect for the natural world and its delicate ecosystems. As he was growing up, Nicholas' father taught him of the family's royal

Scottish origins and of its involvement with royal witchcraft within the dragon tradition, which had been passed down to Nicholas' father by his own parents. Nicholas' father was gifted with the "king's touch." His paternal grandmother – a Scottish Gael - was a skilled seer, and his maternal grandmother had spent years as a student of mediumship. Both of Nicholas' parents were deeply committed to his broader education, and fostered in him at an early age a love of Homer, the Sagas, classical history and mythology. Nicholas' father was an ardent admirer of the work of Omar Khayyam. Consequently Nicholas grew and developed in isolation, detached from the vacuity of human culture, enveloped in a world of intellectualism, magic, mysticism and imagination. Nicholas was raised by his father to highly honour the female and, as a result of his father's teaching, he discovered that the greatest spiritual expression of human relationship is seraphic in nature: the union of the divinity within the male and female. At the age of twelve, Nicholas was magically dedicated to the dragon tradition formally, and at the age of thirteen he first enacted the rite known as "Starfire". Following this period his mother obtained for him works by Aleister Crowley, and he studied the principals of the Black Arts in earnest, gaining a considerable degree of competence in ritual magic. At the age of fifteen Nicholas underwent the ancient rite of kingship which, in accordance with archaic Gaelic tradition, bestows the mantle of sovereignty arising from the very Earth itself. By the 1980's, Nicholas had become intimately conversant with a broad spectrum of magical traditions, and political perspectives. During this period he met and rejected numerous proponents of the Wiccan and New Age movements, considering them to be uninformed, self-deluding and magically incompetent. On Midsummer's night, 1985 Nicholas' skill in and knowledge of magic was acknowledged. His family's hereditary involvement in royal witchcraft and the Dragon tradition was recognized by the Black Country Covenant of the Baphometic Order of the Cubic Stone. He was bestowed with the highest accolade of the covenant: that of Magister Templi. The Order traced its origins back to the Knights Templars and Nicholas was able to use his investiture as an invocational key in the pursuit of deeper, unwritten knowledge. In 1991 Nicholas was invested as a gartered and anointed knight of the Plantagenet Clan Donnachaidh by Lord Lir of Orkney, the head of a cousin branch of the House of Vere. During the 1990's, Nicholas developed a series of associations with university lecturers and post graduate scholars. Following the academic exchanges which ensued, Nicholas was encouraged by them to construct the basis for what is now known as The Dragon Legacy. This was further influenced significantly by his experience of seraphism and hierogamy during this period, and by years of commitment to the elven, Dragon tradition – a tradition within which he is recognized as a royal Dragon prince by the House of Vere, and is acknowledged as such by the British Government. Nicholas had lived reclusively for the most part as a bachelor until the last year or so of his life. He lived with his fiancée Lila and her young son in a quiet village in the Walsh countryside, and aside from his magical pursuits, he had a broad range of secular interests including an eclectic taste in music. He was a renaissance man, a polymath. Nicholas was deeply concerned about environmental issues and animal welfare, concerns shared by his immediate family and by the House of Vere in general, whose number include skilled and experienced ecologists. But how could a man of such great intelligence and influence actually believe he was related to a distant race of dragons. This sounds like something far fetched out of a comic book yet the European Union actually recognize the sovereign rights of Drakenberg as an incorporeal sovereign state which have been registered and included as part of this process. Lets find out now more about this controversial individual. Thanks Rema Marketing Team

THE HOUSE OF DE VERE THE MYSTERY OF THE DRAGON COURT

Prince Nicholas de Vere von Drakenberg known as the Sovereign Grand Master of the Imperial and Royal Dragon Court is best known for his publication The Dragon Legacy (formerly known as From Transylvania to Tunbridge Wells), a collection of essays on the "Derkesthai Culture" with an by Tracy Twyman of Dagobert's Revenge. This 377-page book with numerous appendices, written by HRH Prince Nicholas de Vere, Sovereign Grand Master of the Imperial and Royal Dragon Court, purports to be an "Official History of the Dragon Peoples." taught them the Dragon Mysteries of alchemy and gnosis. The Dragon Court can first be identified in Egypt under the patronage of the priest-prince Ankhfn Khonsu at about 2170 BC. It was subsequently established more formally as a pharaonic institution by the twelfth dynasty Queen Sobekh Nefru in 1785 BC. The Court was re-formed in 1408 by Emperor Sigismund von Luxemburg, King of Hungary, later to become Holy Roman Emperor in 1433. The Dragon kings whom the court has supported have rightfully ruled many nations and empires throughout history. In the case of England, the last legitimate Dragon monarch was Richard III. In the Eighth Century the Court was founded in France as the House of Anjou by Dragon families known as the De Veres and Plantagenets, and in 1408 it flourished again as the Dragon Court of the Holy Roman Emperor Sigismund in Hungary. The Imperial and Royal Dragon Court is the ancient Household Court and Order of the senior Angevin descendants of the Imperial and Royal House of Vere of Caledonia, Anjou and Lorraine, and the physical embodiment of the

Sovereign Princedom of Drakenberg; which is recognised under European Law as a sovereign ethnic racial group; the principle nation state of the Draconian peoples: According to its history The Imperial and Royal Dragon Court and Order has existed since the very dawn of creation. It was founded by Earth's first rulers and teachers of the path to enlightenment who are known variously as Enki and the Anunnaki, the Sons of God, and as Sanat Kumara and the Kumaras, founders of the Great White Brotherhood. Throughout history the Dragon Court has been situated in Central Asia, Egypt, Sumeria, China, India and Persia, where ancient Dragon Priest Kings ruled over their beloved subjects and Up until 2013 the Dragon Court and Order were under the administration of HRH Prince Nicholas de Vere von Drakenberg and situated in Wales and the Duchy of Drakenberg. Its goal is to preserve the Dragon Mysteries and reunite those of the Dragon Blood. Furthermore, the royal and ambassadorial nature of the title of the Prince of Drakenberg (Princeps Draconis) is recognised under the 'Official Observations' of the Department of Internal Affairs of the Government of its state of origin within the European Union. Documents pertaining to its sovereign status are held in government archives.

The right of fons honorum has been tested and ratified under law and the sovereign rights of Drakenberg as an incorporeal sovereign state have been registered and included as part of this process. For its part however, The Imperial and Royal Dragon Court is not affiliated with or subservient to - and does not recognise - any royal house established by the Roman Catholic Church or any of its schismatic Christian denominations, or any other contemporary corporate, academic political, social, religious or quasi-mystical elites. As the Sovereign Grand Master of the Imperial and Royal Dragon Court and Order,

Prince Nicholas de Vere von Drakenberg provided the inspiration, the research, and a hefty portion of the writing for author, Laurence Gardner's Genesis of the Grail Kings and Realm of the Ring Lords. Yet amazingly, de Vere is not listed as co author on many editions of Genesis, and receives no credit at all in Ring Lords. Both of these books, credited to Laurence Gardner, are based almost entirely upon the text from Transylvania to Tunbridge Wells, by Nicholas de Vere, recently published by The Book Tree under the title The Dragon Legacy: The Secret History of An Ancient Bloodline. The rest of this edition of the Global Watch will focus on an interview which took place between Nicholas de Vere von Drakenberg and Tracy Twyman several years before his death. Twyman has been recognised as an expert on occult history for nearly a decade. She is the author of the Merovingian Mythos and her articles have been published in magazines such as Paronia and New Dawn. She has appeared numerous times on radio programs such as Coast to Coast AM. Tracy Twyman

(TT): How long ago did you write The Dragon Legacy? Nicholas de Vere von Drakenberg

(NDV): About six years ago. The Dragon Legacy was known on the net as From Transylvania to Tunbridge Wells and this was a summary of years of research and reflection. Some of it appeared in Laurence Gardner's Genesis of the Grail Kings and then after I published it on the web, Laurence based his third book Realm of the Ring Lords largely on what I had already published.

TT: What were your main sources of information when compiling the book?

NDV: On the so-called Dragon "path" one is imbued hereditarily with Dragon capabilities in varying measures. As one progresses these capabilities wax and wane according to necessity. One of the main capacities is the Derkesthai Process, in which information is "channelled" through the conduit of the Dragon archetype; specifically the racial consciousness of those of the Dragon blood. Through this process one may pick up naturally, all sorts of information relating to varied aspects of the Dragon Tradition in its many branches and manifestations. However, this is of no use intellectually and rationally without informed academic confirmation and corroboration. To this end, another Dragon capacity is to be able to obtain after the fact those confirmations required. I anticipated works before I read them, either through meditation or through experience on the Dragon Path. In a not too dissimilar manner Kerkule discovered the "Bezine Ring." I would say that the serious academic backbone of The Dragon Legacy in terms of corroboration and confirmation, lies in the work of Dr. David Barker; George Woodcock; Lysander Spooner; Professor Miranda Green; Pierre Proudhon; Professors Pierpaoli and Regelson; David Anderson; The Oxford English Dictionary and an old associate Mr. C. Murray Hall M.A. (Lecturer in Barbarian Cultures: Sussex University).

TT: How did you begin research into your family history? At what point in your life did you become aware of "the Dragon legacy" in your family? Is it something you grew up with?

NDV: From the age of seven onwards my father told me about our ancestry, an ancestry steeped in royal blood and most significantly of all, in what is termed Royal Witchcraft, which is a major, ancient, draconian, druidic facet continuing within the later history of the Dragon tradition and within the Vere family. My father educated me about our particular origins in the royal and noble Blackwood family of Lanark, Scotland. This dynasty sired the most significant practitioner of the Dragon tradition in his time: Major Thomas Weir of Vere of Edinburgh, my 11th great grandfather. As a witch lord and the prince consort to the elven queen of the Lallan, Thomas performed the ancient Gaelic rites of the sacred kingship of Epona, and consequently founded this rite of kingship within my lineage. So I received the tradition at an early age from my father and he received it from his father, and so on. TT: Your formal title is "Prince Nicholas de Vere." What does this title imply? NDV: I trace my lineage back in an unbroken bloodline to the imperial prince Milo de Vere, Count of Anjou in 740 A.D., son of Princess Milouziana of the Scythians. She was recorded throughout France as being the Elven, Dragon Princess of the Scottish Picts, and her Grandson, Milo II, derived his Merovingian descent through his father's marital alliance with the imperial house of Charlene. Later in history we picked up numerous other lines of Merovingian descent and the attitude in the house of Vere today, both here and in Ireland, reflects that of the Merovingians themselves where inheritance and blood descent is concerned. Concerning my maternal lineage: my mother is descended from the ancient Collison Jarls of Norfolk and is the third cousin of the head of the House of Vere. We are a very tightly knit family. The head of the House himself is of Royal Collison descent and this matrilinear Collison extraction also stems from the ancient House of Vere and Princess Milouziana of the Scythians. We are Veres on all sides of the family. The overall head of the House of Vere today is the Prince Mhaior. By Papal Investiture and by inheritance from the House of the royal O'Brien descendants of King Brian Boru of Tara, the Prince Mhaior is himself an Archduke - not an insignificant Irish earl, as some totally ill-informed malcontent once triumphantly proclaimed in a ridiculous, failed attempt at an exposé of me. The Head of the House formally addresses me as "the Dragon Prince" of the House of Vere.

TT: Who are the "Dragons" that you write about in your book? NDV: In brief, the recorded Dragon lineage starts with the Anunnaki and descends through the proto-Scythians, the Sumerians in one branch and the early Egyptians in another; the Phoenicians, the Mittani, back to the Scythians again through marital alliance, along to the "Tuatha de Danaan" and the Fir Bolg; down through their Arch-Druidic, Priest-Princely families, to the Royal Picts of Scotland and the high kings of the Horse Lords of Dal Riada; through to the Elven dynasty of Pendragon and Avallon del Acqs, and down to a few pure bred families today.

TT: Were the Dragons originally a separate species from what we would call "human"?

NDV: Dragon tradition related to all the current genetic and historical evidence says yes they were. Both relatively recent and ancient accounts of Dragons or Elves going back to the Anunnaki speak of them as having clearly distinct physical attributes, and these attributes are inherited from a species that scientists now assert preceded the human genetic bottleneck by about thirty thousand years. These attributes are not human in the accepted sense. Whether this ancient race was hybridized with another before history is anybody's guess, but their later hybridization to produce the Elven God-Kings and Ring Lords (the King Tribe), is clearly recorded in the Cylinder Rolls.

TT: Are these Dragons the same as the "Nephilim" of the Bible or the "Watchers" of The Book of Enoch?

NDV: The Nephilim and the Watchers are of the Dragon race, yes.

TT: Were the gods of ancient cultures (Greece, India, Sumeria, etc.) Dragons?

NDV: These pantheons are derived from one another so again the answer in simplistic terms is yes.

TT: What kind of civilization did the Dragons reign over? Would you say that it was the same as the Atlantean or antediluvian civilization?
NDV: The Platonic Atlantis theory is preceded by a much older tradition relating to the "Ogdoad." The Ogdoad, sacred to Jesus himself, were the eight great Gods who raked the Sacred Mountain - "Atlantis" - after the original Flood. This Flood occurred in the Black Sea and the Sacred Mountain, so inundated, was believed to be the Pontus Euxine. Apparently the Ogdoad failed in their attempt to bring fertility back to the Holy Place and abandoned it for a life wandering the planet. This is probably why the legend of the Flood spread and can be found in most cultures. The Ogdoad turn up in Chinese myth, in early Egyptian religious texts, and even in much later Viking legend, where the gods of the Aesir were said to have abandoned the Sacred Mountain after the Flood. From the Ogdoad, who were the first Dragon god-kings of ancient proto-Scythia, we obtain the gods of the Anunnaki, and those later pantheons that derived from them. It is not to be doubted that after the Flood the children of the Anunnaki had established incredible civilizations in their time, so I suppose you could say that the cultures of the Sumerians (whose language, termed "proto-Sumerian", originated in Transylvania), the Egyptians and even the early settlers in northern Europe stemmed from and reflect an antediluvian prototype, a much older pre-Flood "Golden Age" presided over by the ancient Dragon god-kings and goddess-queens. The mistake would be to put the Atlantean period too far back in time and to locate Atlantis where Plato did. Scientists have proved the Biblical Flood to be in the Black Sea and this region is where most of the Titanic and Olympian sagas, associated with the Dawn of the

Gods, unfold. TT: Is Dragon blood the true source of divine right kingship, in your opinion? Are the Dragons the rightful rulers of the world's governments? NDV: Anciently Dragon blood, the blood of the gods, is the true source of divine right kingship. To say that Dragons are the rightful rulers of the world's governments today might raise some contention. Perhaps it would be more realistic to suggest that they may well be the rightful rulers of the world's governments in the future.

TT: When you refer metaphorically to "the Dragon", what exactly are you referring to?

NDV: "The Dragon" is a term I use generally to mean the dragon archetype resting within the Dragon blood and passed on through the genes. It is the conduit through which flow the memories of the wisdom and experience of the Dragons who have gone before. The word "dragon" is derived from the Greek "edrakon", which is an aorist of the word "Derkesthai", which means "to see clearly". "The Dragon" therefore is the inherited Dragon archetype and that archetype is the conduit of clear sight through which racial knowledge flows. Clear sight also and principally refers to transcendent consciousness.

TT: What percentage of the world's populace would you say possesses this Dragon blood? Is it predominately found in certain types of people? How can you tell a Dragon from other types of people?

NDV: Roughly ten percent of Europeans have Dragon blood, and stem from families whose physical attributes clearly point to a genetic inheritance over 100,000 years old. This figure is calculated from research deriving from studies by Oxford University and matched to historical accounts.

TT: How did the Dragon race begin, and how did they become a separate race from the rest of humanity?

NDV: They didn't originate from outer space, that's for sure. A principal element of the Dragon genome originated in the vast forests of central Europe, and cut off from other species, they developed as a distinct race. By the time of the Anunnaki they had been hybridized to form the ancestors of the later Elves or Dragon kings and queens.

TT: Did dragons possess "magical" powers? If so, do their descendants possess them as well?

NDV: It depends on what you mean by "magical." The greatest magic of all is to be able to naturally still one's mind to the point where one sees that "all acts are magical acts." As a natural course of events stemming from transcendent perception, certain facilities are within the grasp of Dragons. These abilities, though they vary, are hereditary.

TT: Your former co-author Laurence Gardner writes a lot about "Starfire" and the power of pineal secretions, which are portrayed as being analogous to the Elixir of Life or Philosopher's Stone, bestowing increased brain capacity, magical ability, and prolonged life upon he who consumes it. These are elements that he clearly picked up from your research. In your writing, you claim that people of "Dragon blood" are the only ones bio-chemically equipped to produce these substances in their own bodies at a high enough level to yield results. But Gardner has written much about this so-called "monatomic gold" and seems to think that this is a synthetic substitute for "Starfire" which ordinary people can consume to become Dragons themselves. Do you know anything about this substance? What is your comment on Mr. Gardner's theories?

NDV: Firstly, the physical, hormonal elements of Starfire are only one side of the story, and in my book I clearly state that the whole process contains several other "psycho-somatic" elements, not least that pertaining to relationship. As for being able to pop a pill to become a Dragon, this kind of stupid New Age attitude stems from the ridiculous, totally indefensible greed-driven free market assertion that anyone can become anything they choose, and the totally unfounded PC notion that everyone is equal. This kind of pathetic liberalism, born as a reaction to the socially inculcated victim mentality, should be abhorred by all rational beings, and so my attitude towards the concept of monatomic gold as a great social leveller and equalizer is one of contempt. However, you don't make lots of money by telling the bulk of your readership that they are genetically excluded from a process they cannot experience or understand; you sell New Age drivel by telling the ingenuous that they can all assume any role they like, and adopt any trendy "lifestyle" choice that whim and deceitful advertising dictates. As you know, I don't write to make money, so I don't care who I offend with the truth. Can I pop a pill to turn me into a black African Masai warrior? No. Is there a powder I can take to change me into a woman? Of course not. I don't see the need for monatomic gold myself. "Starfire" and the Seraphic relationship worked perfectly well for me, and in any case you are either genetically a Dragon or you are not, and no amount of monatomic gold is going to change your genetic makeup. TT: What was the original meaning and purpose of vampirism? www.globalreport2010.com

NDV: Vampire stems from the word "vber" or "uber", and means "witch." It originates in Anatolia; the location of the seven yearly Druidic gatherings: the Nemetons. "Witch" in Gaelic is "Druidhe", or "druid." In practical terms and suggested by the term "uber" itself, a

Scythian druid was an overlord, and so originally a vampire was an overlord, and hence a Dragon.

The purpose of vampirism depends on the type of vampirism practiced. Starfire was the purpose of "royal" or druidic vampirism in the ancient Scythian families, and in Scythian "warrior" vampirism, drinking the blood of fallen brothers in battle was intended to take their essence and bravery into the recipient. The blood of vanquished foes was also drunk. In both cases this also had the advantage of topping up one's adrenaline and testosterone levels in the heat of conflict. The folklore image of the vampire in Europe stems from this historical root. Vampirism was an integral part of Scythian/Dragon life.

TT: Is the Dragon bloodline a Satanic or Luciferian bloodline?

NDV: Yes is the honest and simple answer.

TT: If a person believes that they have the Dragon gene, and they want to start developing the powers inherent in their blood, what course would you suggest they follow?

NDV: Developing powers for their own sake isn't magic, it's greed, and greed and ambition are the destroyers of transcendent Dragon perception. Power flows naturally for those whose vision is clear, and clear perception will determine that those powers are used with detachment. Jesus said "Seek ye first the kingdom of God and all these things will be added unto you." The fact of the matter is that to Dragons, Dragon magic is simple and straightforward and fundamentally it relies in discovering simplicity and stillness within the self. If the reader believes they are of the Dragon Blood and they wish to explore the transcendent concept, in lieu of a lengthy explanation for which there isn't space within the confines of this interview, I recommend a little book entitled The First and Last Freedom, written by Jiddu Krishnamurti.

TT: What is the history of the Dragon Court of which you are the Sovereign Head? Did you inherit this title, and if so, who from?

NDV: The Imperial and Royal Dragon Court appears repeatedly throughout the history of my family. It is the physical, cultural manifestation of the Dragon spirit inherent within the Vere Dragon blood, reaching back long before the time of Christ. Briefly, to give a few examples, in more recent times it was the Royal Court of the Dragon Princess Milouziana from whom we are descended in numerous lines, and later it was the fairy Court of Alberic de Vere, the legendary Oberon. Immediately following Alberic it was the Court of his son, Robert de Vere, earl of Huntingdon, who was the historical Robin Hood; the elven, sacral priest-king of the witches. Later the Dragon Court was manifest in the "Thirteen Covens of Mid Lothian", and in the cabal of Lady Somerville, the witch-mother of Thomas of Edinburgh. Thomas was the grandson of Sir William Vere of Stonebyres and the Elvin, Dragon priest-king of the Thirteen Covens. Sir William was the son of James, 7th Baron Blackwood. Lady Jane Somerville's heraldic family badge is recorded as the fiery dragon surmounting the pentacle, denoting Dragon blood in the House of the Somerville earls. Notably in our family the Dragon Court is also derived from the Court of the Pendragon Kings whose lineage we inherit through numerous marital alliances with our close cousins, the Dukes of Hamilton, whose estates bordered our own in Lanarkshire. The Hamiltons were the heirs presumptive to the throne of Scotland. Lateral inheritance from the extinct cadet cousin branch of the Vere earls of Oxford brings to the contemporary Court, via the 11th earl, Richard de Vere, the degree of Societas Draconis - latterly misnamed

"Sarkany Rend" - a membership bestowed upon him, it is believed academically, during his investiture into the Prince's Degree of the Order of the Garter, along with the Emperor Sigismund of Luxembourg, at St. George's Chapel, Windsor Castle. The heraldry of the family prior to Richard's investiture into Draconis already included the ancient Dragon motifs on both the paternal and maternal sides of the family, denoting pure Dragon blood in both descents, and reflecting the continuing presence of the Dragon Court in the family since the time of Princess Milouziana of the Scythians. The contemporary Dragon Court is furthermore a combination of what Aleister Crowley would term several "currents", of which the major external one to the family proper was bestowed via the Black Country Covenant of the Baphometic Order of the Cubic Stone, who trace their origins back to the Knights Templars. This was given in recognition of my family's hereditary involvement in Royal Witchcraft and the historical Dragon tradition. Other external currents derive from the Knighthood of the Plantagenet Clan Donnachaidh, Dragon cousins to the House of Vere, and laterally from Dr. John Dee's "School of Night", of which Edward de Vere, the seventeenth earl of Oxford, was a prominent member. Edward also performed the rites of Dragon kingship in the family, specifically the rite of the kingship of the Calle Daouine. Down the centuries the Royal Dragon Court is carried continuously in the Vere Dragon Blood. It would be correct to say I inherited the Dragon Court by virtue of being a senior blood descendant of the House of Vere, and I am recognized as a Dragon sovereign by the other senior members of the family. Academic sources and references pertaining to these Dragon descents are found within The Dragon Legacy.

TT: How can one become a member of the Dragon Court, and once a member, what does one do? What is the current function of the Dragon Court? www.thedragonsociety.com

NDV: Today the Court consists of participating family members here and in Ireland. In addition to these, we have emeritus officers whose functions are invaluable to the running of the Court. One of the current, "outer" functions of the Dragon Court is as the custodian of the Dragon tradition within the Vere family, which includes the continuing study of the history and genealogy of its various branches, and the amendment of records as fresh knowledge comes to light. Membership of the Dragon Court is given rarely. We are not a joining club, nor do we operate for monetary gain in any sense. As time passes, the Dragon Ethos demands that the Dragon Court change and develop according to expediency. In the future we may well expand the membership of the Court to take in new Dragon members or to expand the number of emeritus officers. However, for those who are interested in joining, we have created the Dragon Society (Societas Draconis), an auxiliary group that is open to qualified applicants and requires less commitment than full membership in the Dragon Court. It is available for those who wish to study the history of the Dragons and associate with other Dragons. Visit www.thedragonsociety.com to learn more about it.

TT: Many people have ascribed to you a radical political agenda and say that you are trying to use your genealogy as a springboard for a bid for the throne of England, and other such nonsense. What is your response to these claims?

NDV: I cannot take such assertions seriously. The educated reader will already know that the House of Vere fielded over twenty prominent earls in an unbroken line over 561 years of British history. The House of Vere was credited with being the senior bloodline of England, both by its contemporaries and by later historians, and the Veres acted for centuries as Great Chamberlains to the various royal dynasties that came and went over time. As Great Chamberlains, they were the closest advisors to the monarchs and were therefore the major influence or power behind the British throne. In all this time the family never considered it expedient to stoop to pick up the Crown, as the House of Vere was above such considerations. It is apparent, given the family's pre-eminently powerful and influential historical position within British society, that the English monarchy was a trivia beneath the dignity and ambition of the House. I see no reason to change that opinion today, so as you say, the notion that I would demean myself by making a bid for the throne is utter nonsense. We have standards to maintain in this family. In any event the monarchical system in Britain is, to the greatest extent, impotent, and so if one wanted real political power, the last place one would find it would be on the throne of England. We have no need for thrones or crowns to remind us of who we are.

TT: Are you a monarchist?

NDV: By definition Stalin was a "monarch", as were all the presidents of the United States. By such a definition I cannot be said to be a monarchist per sé. I am only a royalist with the greatest of qualifications because not all who contemporarily claim to be royal or those who have occupied the positions of royalty in history have actually been of royal blood.

TT: How do you feel about the current British monarchy?

NDV: I have no feelings about them one way or another. They have a tendency to frighten the hell out of British wildlife during the hunting season but in other respects they seem harmless enough, so I see no real reason not to leave them where they are. What would you replace them with anyway? President Blair? What a scary thought.

TT: There are a lot of wild theories being bandied about on the internet regarding the agenda of the Dragon Court. "New World Order: The Movie" (regards the Dragon Court as part of an Illuminati conspiracy involving Satanism and Nazism. "Heeding Bible Prophecy" seems to proclaim nothing less than that the scion of the Devil - the Anti-Christ himself - will emerge from the ranks of the Dragon Court. David Icke and claim that your former co-author (and former Dragon Court member), Laurence Gardner, shape-shifted into a reptile and sacrificed babies in an underground military base at Montauk, New York. How close are these claims to the truth? What sinister activities are you hiding, Mr. de Vere?

NDV: People think that the Anti-Christ will emerge from the ranks of the Dragon Court? How intuitive of them. My views on Nazism are well known. Nazism was a peasant movement populated by the worst in German peasant scum. Its "Aryan" philosophy and aspirations were a complete joke, and its blind devotion to nationalistic jingoism was the height of psychological blindness and wishful thinking. You can't make genetic Aryans - a race of kings - out of a nation of genetic turnip-peasants. As for Satanism, if we mean adherence to Satan as some externalized deity separate from the Dragon blood and the object of religious devotion, such is an illogical nonsense. Originally the Satans in Biblical terms were nothing more than Circuit Prosecutors within the Jewish Theocratic system. Who in their right mind would worship lawyers? I wish people would study the facts. It would save so much time and energy. David Icke, dear, oh dear, oh dear. David once announced on his website that Laurence Gardner and his cronies performed blood-drinking rituals at his "Columba House." Before uttering this ridiculous libel David should have contacted the Post Office and checked as to where "Columba House" was actually situated. If he had done so, the Post Office would quite happily have told him that "Columba House" was in fact a six inch by twelve-inch Post Office Box at the local Post Office Branch in Tiverton, Devon. Exactly how many shape-shifting reptilian vampires and their victims can you get into a standard British Post Office Box? Having all shape-shifted into reptilian vampires, David Icke would then have us believe that they all shrunk to the size of Minnie Mouse and got a postal worker to put them in the box. If the reader thinks this is possible or even probable, and I am sure that some who stay glued to the Internet all day will, then it is also entirely possible that the reader will believe that Laurence Gardner sacrificed babies at Montauk.

David Icke is concocting all this out of his cynical, fiscally motivated imagination and flogging it to a willing audience who, frighteningly enough, actually swallow it whole. What sinister activities am I hiding? The internal activities of the Court are confidential.

TT: What are your personal beliefs regarding God, spirituality, and religion?

NDV: "Beliefs" regarding God and spirituality create religions, and religions create division and fear, within the individual and consequently within society as a whole. Religion is a crutch for the power hungry, the lazy, the weak minded and the unregenerate. Religions happen when people don't get the point of the message and blindly worship the message and the messenger, instead of grasping the gnosis inherent within the words that the message conveys.

TT: Who do you think the Judeo-Christian god Jehovah really was? Do you believe that there is any historical basis behind the symbolic notion of Jehovah's conflict with Satan?

NDV: The Jews got the main tenets of their religion from the Babylonians during the exile. Therefore, one can say that although the later Jehovah is a composite, his main attributes can be traced back to the god Enlil, and it was Enlil who started a war with his stepbrother Enki concerning their individual number-ranking and seniority of position within the Anunnaki dynasty. So, in general terms we can say that the conflict between Jehovah and Satan originated in a petty family squabble.

TT: What is your opinion of Christ and his ministry?

NDV: A pretty good one. TT: How do you feel about the Wiccan and New Age movements?

NDV: Again, my views of the Wiccan and New Age movements are also well known. Wicca, the so-called "Old Religion" is no more than sixty years old, and the New Age movement is nothing more than a baseless, cynical marketing ploy geared towards extracting money from the gullible.

TT: How do you feel about the sudden surge of interest in the "Grail bloodline" following the publication of The Da Vinci Code? Do you think that the popularization of the idea is dangerous?

NDV: Some people, the minority, will maintain their interest and study the subject further, whilst the bulk of readers will treat the book as a novel experience and pass on to other subjects, once their curiosity has been satisfied. This happens with every new publication. The only inherent danger would be to the subject itself, once the money-vampires of the New Age get hold of it and try opening weekend workshops in "How to become a member of the Grail Bloodline." It would then get promoted and marketed as a "lifestyle choice" open to all. Once such familiarity has bred the inevitable public contempt, the subject may well be rendered valueless to the new enquirer.

TT: What is the one most important thing you want people to take away after reading The Dragon Legacy?

NDV: Firstly, one of the central themes of the book is transcendent consciousness. I would like to feel that the reader may derive some interest in this concept from reading The Dragon Legacy and will pursue the subject further. Secondly, the Dragon families have been with us for millennia and, in the course of time, their innate and rightful destiny will cause them to rise again.

END OF INTERVIEW THE HOUSE OF DE VERE CONCLUSION (By the Global Watch magazine that infringed the books to make this review/ criticism)

What makes this interview with De Vere fascinating is that very few from these royal bloodlines are willing to share such intimate level of detail about what they believe in such an open public forum. However, we would hope that you are now starting to understand that it is an absolute reality that these bloodlines believe that they descended from the Anunnaki. The conspiracy behind the Merovingian bloodline is affiliated with alore of occult knowledge that dates back to at least the sixth century BC. This lore begins with a heresy, known as Kabbalah, which disguises itself as Jewish, but is a pact to seek world domination, and the eradication of religion in favour of the worship of Lucifer. The goal devised by these Kabbalists has since been the installation of their "messiah" as world leader, who, according to their interpretation of the Bible, is to be of line of King David. Since that time, to preserve this purported lineage, until the advent of their expected leader, these Luciferians have been carefully intermarrying amongst each other and have included among them many of the leading figures of history. They begin with a Persian Royal family, who intermarried with that of Alexander the Great. By combining with that of Herod the Great, these families were responsible for the creation and dissemination of the leading mystery school of the Roman Empire, the Mysteries of Mithras, which eventually succeeded in co-opting the emerging Christian movement, by producing Catholic Christianity.

Nevertheless, a secret, or Gnostic, version of Christianity, also derived from Mithraism, survived to compete with Catholicism, in the form of several secret societies, like the Templars, Rosicrucians and Freemasons, practicing occult arts, or what is known as "witchcraft". This tradition was perpetuated by the most popularized branch of the Luciferian bloodline, the Merovingians. Symbolized by the Holy Grail, the Merovingians, after intermarrying into the family of a Jewish Exilarch, or claimant to the Jewish throne, culminated in all the leading families of the Crusades. It was at this time that this European branch of the family recombined with others from Eastern Europe and Armenia. These Eastern aristocracies derived from the enigmatic Khazars, who had populated southern Russia and the Basin of the Don River, and who, in the eighth century AD, had converted to Judaism. Legend has it, however, that the Khazar's were remnants of the Lost Tribes. Armenia, just across the Caucasus, was another locale of these supposed Lost Tribes. It was the intermarriage and perpetuation of these aristocratic bloodlines that were being referred to in the heraldic symbols of the lily, the rose, the double-headed eagle, and the skull and crossbones. Also, during the Crusades, this network connected with an important occult centre hiding within the Islamic world, in Cairo Egypt, who followed the heretical version of Islam known as Ismailism. According to Masonic legend, a number of these "Eastern Brethren" were rescued and brought to Scotland, where they provided the basis of Scottish Rite Freemasonry, which emerged in the eighteenth century. However, at the same time, this legend also provided the basis for the establishment of Freemasonry in Egypt, which then became the second centre of Illuminati activism. It was from these secret networks of Islamic impostors by which the Western powers created Islamic terrorism, used to foment of a Clash of Civilizations, through the fabrication of the terrorist threat[4].

Note by Abbe de Vere: This is the sort of mixed-up history and propaganda sensationalism that we have had to deal with.

[4] Global Watch
www.globalreport2010.com

The House of Vere references was Nicholas work, which was on the wayback machine, His previous website which the wayback machine now bibliocades reused. For provenance of the work and to be honest lack of communication, they literally do not answer any emails concerning this infringement, I had in the end decided to leave it as it shows valuable information of dad's citations

The House of Vere: References

The Duchy of Angiers

and

The Royal House Of Vere

Vere of Blackwood

Published comments concerning the House of Vere

Vere-de-Vere stalked into the English vernacular as a playful term meaning the grandest, proudest, most historic, indisputably aristocratic and absolutely creme de la creme of Anglo-'Norman' antiquity.

In fiction the expression is used for characters of, or assuming, unquestionable ancient lineage - and with good cause.

In the Middle Ages, owing to plagues and battlefield mortality, the average noble dynasty in England lasted not more than three generations. The de Veres, however, managed to maintain a line of twenty earls of Oxford over 561 years*, (*our note: The senior descents in the male line today reach back 1300 years). Lord Thomas Macaulay, Victorian historian supreme calls this family:

> "The longest and most illustrious line
> of nobles that England has seen".

Vero Nihil Verius (nothing truer than truth) is the family motto granted by Queen Elizabeth I. The family crest was already the Blue Boar.

The Falling Star of Vere

A legend lingers round the acquisition of the de Vere (star) badge. In the version as told by Leland, Aubrey was 'at the Conquest of the Cities of Nicque, of Antioch, and of Hierusalem' and:

> "In the year of our lord 1098, Corborant, Admiral to the Soudan of Persia was fought with at Antioch and discomforted the Christians. The Night coming on in the Chace of this Bataile, and waxing dark, the Christianes being four miles from Antioche, God, willing the saufte of the Christianes shewed a white Starre or Molette of fyve Pointes, which to every Manne's Sighte did lighte and arrest upon the standard of Albrey, then shining excessively".

The mystic star from this miracle became the de Veres' badge, which they wore on their shields from then onwards - quarterly gules and or, in the first quarter a mullet argent. Later heralds argued that it was merely 'a mullet with a difference' as always used to distinguish a younger son from an elder. Others said that it was not a star at all, but the rowl spur, from the French word mollet, which could have been held up as a pre~arranged sign to muster supporters and was caught in a ray of sunlight. "But for the de Veres the badge was simply God pointing out the family's near~deity".

From Verily Anderson,

'The Veres of Castle Hedingham'.

The House of Vere

"The noblest subject in England, and Indeed, as Englishmen loved to say, the noblest subject in Europe, was Aubrey de Vere........who derived his title through an uninterrupted male descent, from a time when the families of Howard and Seymour were still obscure, when the Nevills and Percys enjoyed only a provincial celebrity, and when even the great name of Plantagenet had not yet been heard in England. One chief of the house of de Vere had held high command at Hastings; another had marched, with Godfrey and Tancred, over heaps of slaughtered Moslems, to the sepulchre of Christ. The first Earl of Oxford had been the minister of Henry Beauclerc, The third earl had been conspicuous among the lords who extorted the great Charter from JOHN. The seventh earl had fought bravely at Cressy and Poictiers. The thirteenth earl had, through many vicissitudes of fortune, been the chief of the party of the Red Rose and had led the van on the decisive day of Bosworth. The seventeenth earl had shone at the court of Elizabeth I and had won for himself an honourable place among the early masters of English poetry.........".
Baron Thomas Babbington Macaulay, Lord Macaulay of Rothley Temple (1857).

See source profile.

Professor Vivian Greene:

" The Counts of Anjou: Princes of Anjou"

Sir Bernard Burke, Ulster King of Arms,

when speaking of the Vere called them

singularly and in plural:

"The Princely Noble"

"The Race of Vere"

(Extract from 'Vicissitudes of Families', page 424 line 12 and page 426 para 2 line 12)

G. E. Cokaynes Complete Peerage Volume X

Page 208

OXFORD

II. 2. AUBREY (DE VERE) IV, EARL of OXFORD, hereditary Master Chamberlain of England. 1st s. and h. by 3rd wife, (a) b. 1163 or later. (b) While still a boy he attested his father's charters for Colne Priory (c) and a charter of Ranulf de Mandeville for St. Osyth; (d) and he witnessed 7 more of his father's charters for Colne (e) and joined him in attesting a number of other charters for that priory (f) and 2 other charters. (g) Early in 1190 he Was with the King in Normandy. (h) He obtained the Bolebec fief with Isabel the heiress, (i) and together they gave a tenement in Wavendon to Woburn Abbey. (j) On 21 Feb., 1190/I he confirmed his father's foundation of Castle Hedingham Priory, and at the request of his father and rnother gave it his church at Castle Hedingham and the wood at Gosfield; (k) but at Michaelmas in that year he owed 100 marks for what was imposed on his men for burning the nunnery. (l) Within the years I191-9, he witnessed a charter of John, Count of Mortain (afterwards King), for Rouen Cathedral. (m) In Dec. 1194 he suc. his father, and in 1195 as Aubrey de Vere junior, he rendered account for £100 for his relief..[5]

---

[5] **Footnotes**

III. 1214. 3. ROBERT (DE VERE), EARL OF OXFORD,

Hereditary Master Chamberlain of England, being 3rd but eldest surv. S. of the 1st Earl, by 3rd wife.. [6]

(a) Item in comite Alberico Alberici comitis de Ver filio, simile naturae miraculum vidimus. Cum enim pater ejusdem, matre jam Praegnante, filia scilicet Henrici de Essexia, ob ignominiosum patris eventum jam ad divortium modis omni elaborasset, partu prodeunte; quem pater in oculo casuali laesione sustinuit, eadem parte defectus in filio parentavit (Giraldus Cambrensis, OP. cit, p 132). Albericus Comes Oxeneford. His testibus Alberico filio meo et Herede et Roberto Henrico Filiis meis (Colne Cart., no.42).

(b) There is no proof that his parents did not cohabit between 1163 and ii or 1172; for his mother's age cf p.206, note "e."

(c) His Testibus Alberico filio meo Radulpho de Ver. Radulpho magistro Alberici (Colne Cart., no.38; cf Idem, no. 45) That Aubrey had a master proves that he was a boy at the time.

[6] **Footnotes**

(1) His afilliation is proved by his attestations to 4 of his father's charters Colne, e.g. "His testibus Albrico filio meo et Roberto fratre ejus" (Colne Q no.46). He has always been described as the 2nd son, but in the 3 charters for Colne Priory.

Which are witnessed both by **Robert** and by his

OXFORD

'The Royal Genealogies'
Table CCXVI

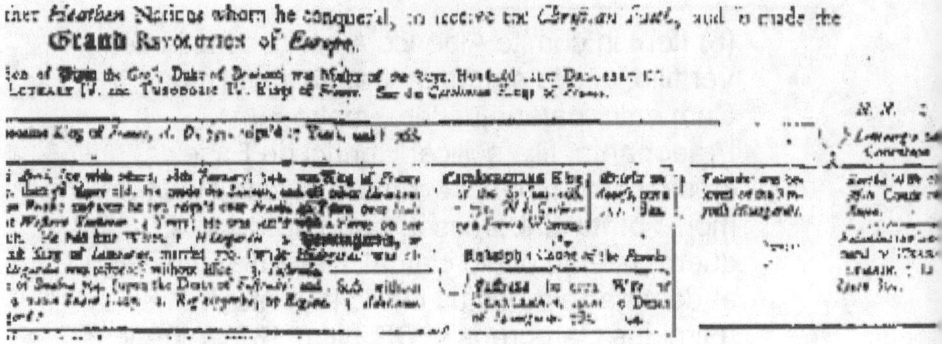
ther Heathen Nations whom he conquer'd, to receive the Christian Faith, and so made the Grand Revolutions of Europe.

---

brother **Ralph**, his name precedes **Robert**'s (Idem, nos. 36, 41, 85).

(a) On the assumption that Robert was the 3rd son; after 1172 if his parents did not resume cohabitation before I 171. He seems to have been with his brother Aubrey in Normandy in Aug. 1197 (Landon, op. cit., pp I20~2I)

See Source Profile.

Tabular Section of the above right
Milo: Count of Anjou

...uſhold under DAGOBERT III.
...ian Kings of *France*.

N. N.

Leutbergis b... Concubine.

...lomannus King of the *Soiſſons* ·768. †71. Wife *Gerberga* a *French* Woman.

Giſela an *Abbeſs*, born 757. † 812.

...udolph a Count of the *Franks*.

Faſtrada the third Wife of CHARLEMAIN, upon the Death of *Hildegardis* 783. † 794.

Talendus was beloved of the Empreſs *Hildegardis*.

Bertha Wife o... *Milo* Count o... *Anjou*.

Rolandus the Ge... neral of CHAR... LEMAIN, † in *Spain* 809.

(Page 450 'The Royal Genealogies' The Rev. Dr. James Anderson, D.D., M.A: Milo I de Vere was Count of Anjou, (hence eldest *son* of Melusine/Melouziana de Scythes /Maelasanu: The Dragon Princess).

See Source Profile.

THE MADNESS OF KINGS

A count of Anjou came back with a new wife, a strange girl of extraordinary beauty but she kept very much to herself. Unusually in so religious an age she was reluctant to attend the Mass. When she did go she always hurried from the church before the consecration of the host. Her husband, who was puzzled by her behaviour, told four knights to keep watch and to try to delay her departure from the church. When she got up to go, one of them trod on the hem of her train. As the priest raised the host to consecrate it she screamed, wrenched herself free, and still shrieking, flew out of the window, taking two of her children with her. In reality the countess was the wicked fairy, Melusine, the daughter of Satan, who cannot abide the consecration of the body of Christ in the Mass. It was from the children that she left behind that the counts of Anjou and the Angevin kings of England were said to be descended.

(Of the Plantagenet Branch):

So devilish an ancestry accounted for the demonic energy and passionate ill-temper by which these princes seemed often afflicted. 'We who came from the devil', John's brother, Richard I, was reported as saying caustically, 'must needs go back to the devil. Do not deprive us of our heritage: we cannot help acting like devils.' 'De diabolo venit et ad diabolum ibid', commented St Bernard of Clairvaux, 'From the devil he came, and to the devil he will go.'[7]

Cependant, apprenant plus tard que Geoffrey a brule l'abbaye de Maillezais et tue son frere, le Comte maudit son epouse. Il l'acuse publiquement d'etre "tres fausse serpent". Le secret est devoile. Melusine doit regagner L'Autre Monde et s'envole transformee en DRAGON.[8]

The Duchy of Angiers

Angiers was a Ducal principality in the Comite region of Anjou. In the work of The Rev. Father Sabine Baring-Gould Angiers is referred

---

[7] Professor Vivien Greene, Citations within text, The Dragon Cede, Nicholas Devere.

[8] Christine Bonnet, Lusignan.

to as the country where the Princess Melusine was a native. Angiers is now the city of Angers in northern Anjou. As a Ducal principality its rulers constituted a regnant royal house who, in the case of the Vere, were also the Counts of the region in which this 'city state' was situated.

See Source Profile.

Vere Princedom

Although Merovingian culture was both temperate surprisingly modern, the monarchs who presided over it were another matter. They (The Sorcerer Kings) were not typical even of rulers of their own age, for the atmosphere of mystery legend, magic and the supernatural, surrounded them, even during their lifetimes. If the customs and economy of the Merovingian world did not differ markedly from others of the period, the aura about the throne and royal bloodline was quite unique.

Sons of the Merovingian blood were not 'created' kings. On the contrary they were automatically regarded as such on the advent of their twelfth birthday. There was no public ceremony of anointment, no coronation of any sort. Power was simply assumed, as by sacred right.

But while the king was supreme authority in the realm, he was not obliged - or even expected - to sully his hands with the mundane business of governing. He was essentially a ritualised figure, a priest-king, and his role was not necessarily to do anything, simply to be. The king ruled in short but did not govern.

Even after their conversion to Christianity the Merovingian rulers, like the Patriarchs of the Old Testament, were polygamous. On occasion they enjoyed harems of oriental proportions. Even when the aristocracy, under pressure from the Church, became rigorously monogamous, the monarchy remained exempt. And the Church, curiously enough, seems to have accepted this prerogative without any inordinate protest. According to one modern commentator: Why was it [polygamy] tacitly approved by the Franks themselves?

We may here be in the presence of ancient usage of polygamy in a royal family - a family of such rank that its blood could not be ennobled by any match, however advantageous, nor degraded by the blood of slaves ... It was a matter of indifference whether a queen were taken from a royal dynasty or from among courtesans...

> The fortune of the dynasty rested in its blood and was shared by all who were of that blood.

And again,

> 'it is Just possible that, in the Merovingians, we may have a dynasty of Germanic Heerkonige* derived from an ancient kingly family of the migration period'.

Extracted and expanded upon by Henry Lincoln, from 'The Long-Haired Kings'
by J. M. Wallace-Hadrill; Fellow of Merton College Oxford.
* Fritz Kern, Gottesgnadentum und Widerstandrecht (1954).

The House of Vere are descended in various lines from the dynasty of Meroveus and consequently share this Germanic Royal Blood Tradition. Prince Milo de Vere - married to Charlemagne's sister - and as Head of the Imperial House and Chief of the Imperial Army, was himself an Imperial Prince.

700 -2000 a.d.

Ex libello Genealogiae Comitum Oxoniensium

Official de Vere family records

Repetit genus á Noe. Deinde á Tideo Graeco. Insuper á Vero nobilis Romano Postremo á Milone comite de Genny, alias Gisney (GUISNES).

760+ AD Milo de Ver: Duke of Aungiers and Duke Leader of Great King Charles house and army (son of Rainfroi: de Ver) - Milo married Bertbelle, sister of Great King Charles Charlemagne.

800+ AD Rouland de Ver (son of Milo and Bertbelle): Held the titles of the "Earl of Palatine", "Earl of Maunce and Bleuys", "Governor of the Marches of Brittany" however, he was killed by warring Pagans at Rumcidevale. 800+ AD Baldwine de Ver: became "Duke of Maunce" after his brother Rouland's death.

800+ AD Milo de Ver II (ii) (son of Milo [i]) Held title of the "Earl of Genney or Gisney or GHISNES" given to him by Charlemagne, he married Avelina the daughter to the "Earl of Nauntes" and they had two sons, Nicasius and Milo(iii).

800+ AD Nicasius de Vere: married Agathe daughter to the "Earl of Champaign" and gave issue to Otho "de Vere" who later became the "Earl of Genney".

[Nicasius de Ver Erle of Genney sonne to yong Milo
Erle of Genney.
This Nicasius had to wyfe Agathe the dowghtar of the
Erle of Champain.
Of Nicasius cam Otho de Vere Erle of Genney, maried to
Constance dowghtar to the Lord of Charters]

Excerpt from Stow MSS, British Library, London

800+ AD Otho de Vere: married Constance daughter to the "Lord of the Charters" and gave issue to Amelius de Ver.

Amelius("Aldolphus") de Vere: Earl of Genny (GHISNES or GUISNES) married Helena daughter of Earl Bloys

His son:

Gallus/Guillaume (Guy Blanc Barbe) de Vere: Earl of Genny (GHISNES - GUISNES) married Gerbrudis daughter to the Lord Cleremont. (Gallus - Guillaume went with Aubri and the King to England). Descent to Godfroi de Bouillon and the Counts of Boulogne.

Manasses de Vere: Earl of Genny married Petronilla daughter of the Earl of Boleine.

Their son:

Alphonsus (Alberic) I de Vere: Earl of Genney, Count of Ghesnes (Genny, alias Gisney or GHISNES or GUISNES) married Katarine daughter to Arnalde Earl of Flaunders. And was a "Counsellor (earl of the Witan) to Edward the Confessor".

The Vere Earls of Guisnes

In the matter of the succession of Robert de Vere to the earldom of Oxford in the reign of Charles I, the title was contested for by Lord Willoughby de Eresby. Several Judges of the day were appointed to guide the Lords in legal matters regarding this succession. Leading them was the Lord Chief Justice of England, Sir Randolph Crew. Robert de Vere won the case, and the Crown vouchsafed the earldom of Oxford to him.

The summing up speech delivered by the Lord Chief Justice before the House of Peers (The House of Lords) was recorded as part of the judicial process (Sir Bernard Burke) and its comments are therefore part of English Law.

On Saturday 1st April 1626 Sir Randolph Crew addressed their Lordships saying:

> "This great and weighty cause, incomparable to any other that hath happened at any time, requires great deliberation, and solid and mature judgement to determine it, and I wish that all the judges of England had heard it - it being a fit case for all - to the end we all might have given our humble advice to your Lordships herein.
>
> Here is represented to your Lordships certamen honoris, and, as I may well say, illustris honoris, illustrious honour. I heard a great peer of this realm, and a learned, say, when he lived there was no king in Christendom had such a subject as Oxford.
>
> He came in with the Conqueror, Earl of Guynes; shortly after the Conquest, made Great Chamberlain of England above five hundred years ago, by Henry I., the Conqueror's son, brother to Rufus; by Maud, the Empress, Earl of Oxford; confirmed and approved by Henry II., Alberico comiti, so Earl before.
>
> This great honour, this high and noble dignity hath continued ever since in the remarkable surname of De Vere, by so many ages, descents and generations, as no other kingdom can produce such a peer in one and the self-same name and title.................And yet let the name and dignity of De Vere stand for so long as it pleaseth God"

That the Vere were Earls of Guisnes before 1066 is recognised by British law.

With thanks to Miss C. Shelton; the House of Lords Archivist, for the primary sources consulted.

1000+ Albery II de Vere: Earl of Genney wed - Beatrice Sister to King William the Conqueror. Alberic went with the King to England. He used the motto,"Albri Comes" which some say is "Albery of truth cometh", de -of; Ver- true. Albery is also Aubri, Albury, Alberic (in Latin); Alphonsus (in Greek). He built "Hedingham Castle". At the time of the general survey, Alberic de Ver was already noted as a person of ancient and noble descent (Domesday Book). Leland stated or deduced that the pedigree of this family was from "Noah", Meleager, who slew the Caledonian boar, and Diomedes, who was at the seige of Troy. - N.B. Caesar and Charlemagne.

Alberic held a number of lordships in several countries in England and particularly 14 in Essex; where Hedingham was his castle, chief seat, and head of his barony. His wife was Beatrix, daughter of Henry Castellan, of Baurbough but others say King William's sister, by Sibilla, daughter, and heir Manasses Count of Ghisnes (GUISNES); by whom he had a daughter Rohesia, married, first, to Pagen Beauchamp; and after; to Geffery de Mandeville, earl of Essex; and five sons,

Geffery, Roger, Robert and William.

This Alberic, styled Aberico senior, took the habit of a monk; and was buried in the church of Colne priory, which he had founded.

Albericus, Junior, was successor to his father; and became so much in favor with Henry I that the said King made him great "Chamberlain of England", in fee;

Patent extracts:

"H Rex Anglrorum, &c. Sciatis universi quoniam dedi & concssi Alberico de Ver & hereib, ' suis post eum de me & meis tenend' magistram camerarim ,eamtotius Anglie in feode & hereditate quare volo & firmiter precipio quod ipse & heredes sui eam jure hereditario teneant cim omnibus dignaitatibus & libertatib'& honorisicentitis ad eam pertinentibus, ita bene &libere & honorisice sicat Robertus Malet vel aliquis alius ante vel pst cum inquam melius & nonorisicntius tenuit,

cum liberartionibus & hospiciis curie mee que ad ministerium cameratieae pertinent" Test. &c.
........to hold the same, with all the liberties and privileges thereto belonging, as fully and honourably, as Robert Malet (Robert de Vere or Veer who had been banished and disinherited), had holden that said office.

This Alberic was also justice of all England in that king's reign, but about the 5th of king Stephen, was killed in a popular turmult at London; leaving by Adeline his wife, daughter of Gilbert de Clare, or, according to Collins, in his Extinct Peerage, daughter to Roger de Ivery, three sons; viz. Alberic,

n.n canon of St. Osyth, in Essex;

Robert lord of Twiwell, in the county of Narthampton; Geffery, who, the 12th Henry II, certified his knight's fee to be nine deveteri seossamento and three de novo, and then resided in Shropshire; and William; (constituted "chancellor of England", by Maud the empress), and Juliana, Hugeot Bigot, earl of Northfolk. Alberic the third, succeeded his father, and was so considerable a person, that Maud, the empress, in order to engage him to her interest, confirmed to him the office of great chamberlain, and all his father's estates, with diver other inheritances, likewise the earldom of Cambridge, if the earldoms of Oxford, Berkshire, Wiltshire, or Doreseshire. all which grants, Maud's son, Henry II, confirmed, and constitutes him Earl of Oxford, with the grant of the third penny of the pleas of the county; a perquisite then belonging to the earls of this kingdom. He died the 6th Richard I. having been twice married:

First, to Eusamia, daughter of Sir William de Cantilupe, by whom he had no issue;

secondly: daughter (api) to Lucia, daughter and heir of William de Abrincis
(by his wife, daughter and heir of William de Archis), by whom he had sons.

From 'The Itinerary' of the Reverend John Leland 1503 - 1552.
Dictionary of National Biography.
See Source Profile.

Aubrey (Alberic or Oberon) III de Vere

Had several issue including:

Robert de Vere. The historical claimant to the earldom of Cambridge and Huntingdon, heritor of the lands of FitzOoth or Hood. Robert, 'a Templar', was outlawed by King John and lost all his lands and castles. Robert was the historical Robin Hood, Robin Goodfellow or Puck, (see Shakespeare [Edward de Vere]: A Midsummer Night's Dream, commentary; Robin's father Oberon or Alberic the Elf King descended [via Melusine] from Morgan la Fey and Julius Caesar).

Aubrey's eldest surviving son:

Ralph de Vere.

Ralph de Vere, founder of the Veres of Scotland

The first Aubrey de Vere on record (in Britain) came to England with William the Conqueror. He is usually held to be a Norman, though he may have been a Breton; he certainly had strong Connections with Brittany. Before the Conquest he was described as one of the barons of Conan, Count of Brittany, and after the Battle of Hastings he or his son (a second Aubrey) was allotted lands in Essex by the overlord there, who was Alan of Brittany, now called Alan, Count of Richmond in Yorkshire.

Like all civil wars, the conflict between the Empress Maud and King Stephen was a very troubling one. It was really a fight between Normans and Flemings for the English throne; and since Stephen's wife was the Flemish Matilda, Countess of Boulogne, those Flemings already in England naturally flocked to her side. For reasons best known to himself Aubrey III de Vere sided with the Normans; he got his reward when the Empress Maud created him Earl of Oxford.

It has been said, I think correctly, that before a man could be given an earldom he had to have another honour.

Among those who supported Stephen and Matilda against the Normans was Alan Earl of Richmond, and Aubrey III's second son, named Ralf, went against his father and fought for Stephen in the army of his own overlord. The first officially recorded de Vere in Scotland was a Radulfus (or Ralf) who was holding estates in Lanarkshire during the reign of Alexander II. In 1160 Conan, Earl of Richmond, had married Margaret, sister of the King of Scotland, and it seems likely that this may have been the time when his follower, Ralf, was awarded his lands there. We may note that when Aubrey III died, he was succeeded as Earl of Oxford by his first son, Aubrey IV; but when that son died childless the earldom passed to a third son, missing out the second son, Ralf.[i]

With thanks to Mrs Beryl Platts, author of 'The Scottish Hazard'. Further research can be found in The upper lands of Lanarkshire.

'Descent of Scots Family'

The Scottish descent of the Senior line of the Vere of Oxford.

The Scottish name Weir is derived from the Norman-French de Vere..... Alberic de Vere... accompanied the Conqueror. Ralph or Radalphus de Ver was the first of the name on record in Scotland. As Ralph de Ver he was taken prisoner at Ainwick in July 1174. As Radulphus de Weir, he witnessed a Charter of King William, between 1174 and 1184. and as Radulph de Veir he gave a bovate of land in Sprowston, Roxburgh, to Kelso Abbey. As Radalphus de Vere he witnessed another Charter by King William to the Abbey of Lindores. He also witnessed another undated Charter of King William's to William de Hala, Herd (Errol.) The same, or perhaps a succeeding

Radulph de Ver, or de Uer witnessed about 1204 a grant to the Abbey of Arbroath, and before 1214 another Charter by William the Lion. The Weirs of Lanarkshire claimed to be descended from this Radulph.

Richard Wer, Lanark, rendered homage to Edward I in 1296. Between 1398 and 1400 Rothald de Were, Baille of Lesmahagow, had a Charter from Patrick, Abbot of Kelso, of the lands of Blackwood, Mossiygning and. Durgundreston. and in 1497 Abbot Robert granted Rogerhill and Brownhill to Robert Weyr for services rendered. The English 'Weirs' (however) are descended from a progenitor who dwelt at a weir or fishing dam.

The Scottish Weir crest is (was in 1700's) a demi-horse in armour proper, bridled and saddled gules. The motto is Nihil Verius.

Source:

From Dr. George Black.

The senior descent of the Scottish Branch of Vere of Oxford continued

Source - 'The Surnames of Scotland', New York Public Library Edition.

Primary sources in italic.

WEIR............As Ralph de Vere he was taken prisoner at Alnwick along with William the Lion in 1174 *(Bain, I, p. 174)*.He witnessed a charter by King William '*de decimis episcopatus*' of Moray between 1174-84 *(REM., 2)*, and as Radulph de Veir or Veyre, within the same period, he gave a bovate of land in Sprowestun, Roxburgh, to the Abbey of Kelso, his brother Robert being one of the witnesses *(Kelso, p. 177)*. The same or perhaps a succeeding Radulph de Ver or de Uer witnessed a little before 1204 a grant to the Abbey of Arbroath *(RAA., I, 11)* and before 1214 another charter by King William *(Panmure II, 126)*

WEIR

Tartan: Weir (also Hope-Vere)

Motto: Vero Nihil Verius (Latin: Nothing Truer than Truth)

......Ralph de Ver, from whom the Weirs of Blackwood, Lanarkshire, claim descent, was captured, with King William I (the Lion), in 1174 whilst besieging the castle of Alnwick in Northumberland. Others of the name held land in Lesmahagow, Lanarkshire, in the fifteenth century.

Major Thomas Weir (1599 - 1670) born at Kirkton House, Carluke, was burned at the stake in Edinburgh for .....witchcraft. His sister was hanged the next day for her part in some of his activities.

'Scotland and her Tartans' Alexander Fulton.

(Major Thomas Weir was the grandson of William of Stonebyres and Elizabeth Hamilton. His father Thomas married the witch, Lady Jane Somerville. Major Weir was posted to Ulster in 1641 and, by family tradition, had some connection with the Tyrone descent. For Somerville see below).

'Of The Fesse' Chapter X. From the Archives of:

The Lyon King of Arms of Scotland.

THE Sirname of *WEIR* is ancient with us, as Sir *James Dalrymple* obſerves in his Collections.

Ranulphus de *WEIR* is mentioned in the Regiſters of *Kelſo*, *Paiſly*, and *Murray*, to have lived in the Reign of King *William*, and *Thomas* de *Weir* in the Reign of *Alexander* II. Of this Sirname there are ſeveral Families in *Clydſdale*; the two principal of which are thoſe of *Blackwood* and *Stonebyres*.

SIR *George WEIR* of *BLACKWOOD*, Argent, *on a Feſs* Azure, *three Stars of the* firſt, *with the Badge of* Nova Scotia *in the Dexter chief Point*, as the Knights *Baronets* uſe; and for Creſt, *a Demi-Horſe in Armour proper*, *iſſuing out of a Wreath of his Tinctures*, *bridled and ſadled* Gules; and for Motto, *Nihil verius*. His Grand-father was of the Name of *Lawry*, who married the Heireſs of *Weir* of *Blackwood*, and took upon him the *Name* and *Arms* of *Weir*.

The Scottish Clan and Family Encyclopedia

' (The Armigerous Clans and Families of Scotland)'

Weir

Arms (of Blackwood LR 4/94)[1]

Argent, on a fess Azure, three mollets of the first

Crest

(As Oxford)

Upon a chapeau Gules furred Ermine

a boar standant Azure armed Or.

Motto

(As Oxford)

'Vero Nihil Verius'

(Nothing Truer than)

1. Lyon Roll of Arms.

Ralph de Ver was captured along with William the Lion at Alnwick in Northumberland in 1174. He witnessed a charter of his king of lands in the bishopric of Moray sometime between 1174 and 1184. He also donated land to the Abbey of Kelso, and his brother Robert was a witness. The Weirs of Blackwood in Lanarkshire, who were to become the principal family, claim descent from Ralph de Vere.

(The claim is upheld in the Lyon Rolls as evidenced above).

Senior descent of the Veres of Scotland and Eire

'Baltredus' (Ralph/Ralfredus) de Vere

Who opposed his father in the Flemish war, was disinherited and fled to Scotland with his Liege Lord Conan of Brittany in approx 1165. Conan married the sister of the king and Ralph was given his lands in Lanark. He was a witness to a charter of King William, The Lion of Scotland 1165 - 1214. Ralph and William were captured after beseiging the Castle of Alnwick in Northumbria in 1174.

Had a son:

Walter Rory de Vere

Who had a son:

Ralph (Rudolphus) de Vere

Confirmed his father's donation to Kelso Monastery. Died at the end of the reign of Alexander II of Scotland 1214 - 1249

Had a son:

Thomas de Vere

Living in 1266. Witness to a charter of a donation to Kelso Monastery by Hemicus St Clan.

Had a son:

Richardus de Vere (de Were)

Living approx 1294. Laird (Lord or Baron) of Blackwood. Lanarkshire. Mentioned in a donation to Kelso Monastery

Had a son:

Thomas de Were (de Vere) of Blackwood

Proprietor of the lands and Barony of Blackwood, Lanarkshire. Died in the reign of David the Bruce; David II of Scotland 1329 - 1371

Had a son:

Brian (Buan) Were of Blackwood

Living around 1386. His 6th cousin, Robert De Vere IXth earl of Oxford, Lord of Hedingham, was Marquess of Dublin and Duke and Vice Regent of Ireland. Robert was effectively the Sovereign of Ireland during his lifetime and was permitted by King Richard to mint coins with his own likeness. Brian died in the beginning of the reign of King Robert III of Scotland 1390-1406

Had a son:

Rotaldus Were of Blackwood

Received a charter from Patrick, Abbot of Kelso Monastery; dated 1404. He was Baillie of Lesmahagow from 1398 - 1400. Died in the reign of King James II of Scotland 1437 -1460 Had a son:

Thomas Were (de Vere) of Blackwood

Had a son:

Robert Veyr of Blackwood

Died soon after receiving a charter of confirmation from Robert, the Abbot of the Monastery of Kelso dated 1474.

Had a son:
Thomas Weir of Vere of Blackwood
Stonebyers is known to be the family home of the weirs.

Married Aegidia, daughter of John, 3rd Lord Somerville (of the Dragon) in 1483. Acquired vast holdings of land and was patron of

St. Mary's Church in Lesmahagow. Died in the beginning of the reign of Queen Mary of Scots in 1542.

Had a son:

James Weir of Vere, Lord of Blackwood

Married Euphemia Hamilton, sister of the Duke of Chatelherault, Marquess of Hamilton. The Hamiltons were the Heirs Presumptive to the Throne of Scotland during this period. James lived to a great age. He died in 1595. Had sons:

1. James Weir

Married Marriotte Ramsay, daughter of George, Lord Dalhousie, an ancestor of the Hope-Veres of Craig Hall. George Ramsay was created Earl of Melrose in 1618 and changed this to the earldom of Dalhousie in 1619. The 9th earl was Governor of Canada, Nova Scotia and New Brunswick. His son was Governor General of India.

They had issue:

a) George Weir who married Margaret Vere of Stonebyres with whom he had one daughter.

Marriotte Weir who married =

1. Major James Bannatyne (a sept of the Stewarts of Bute).

2. William Lowry by whom she had a Son George who became

Sir George Weir Bt. (descent to Hope-Vere of Blackwood).

The Hope-Veres died out in 1974.

b) Robert Weir of Craighead sold or assigned his estate in 1610 and moved to Monaghan House in Co. Fermanagh, now renamed Hallcraig House. Robert married the sister of the alchemist Sir David Lindsay.

From Robert various branches descend.

Robert had sons; the eldest surviving son was:

Alexander who married Anne, Daughter of Sir John Dunbar (Graham descent) of Derrygonnelly, Co. Fermanagh.

Their eldest son:

Alexander married Sarah, daughter of Captain Goodwin and secondly, Elizabeth, daughter of Sir Paul Gore Bt.

Their eldest son:

Robert Weir of Hallcraig married Anne, daughter of Captain Carleton of Tullymargy Castle.

They had a son Captain Alexander Weir of Hallcraig

(from whom the senior branch of the House of Vere descends to Nicholas de Vere's ducal kinsman - The Mac An Mhaoir - who is of matrilinear Stoughton-Collison descent)

and a daughter from whence Captain Noble Weir of Hallcraig who married Catharine Graham (descent from the Grahams of Scotland 1600) and had issue:

('Burke's Irish Landed Gentry' 1891-1915; 'Burke's Landed gentry' 1974; 'Burke's Peerage, Baronetage and Knightage' 1957; Burke's Dormant and Extinct Peerages).

Vere of Tyrone

Robert, who by Rachael Stewart had their eldest son,

Robert Weir of Desertcreat, Tyrone who married Sarah Graham, and by her had their eldest son:

John who moved back to Scotland where he married Mary Logan of Logan in Galloway. The Logan families have held their lands in the Stranraer

Peninsula since the 1100's, whilst others of that name held Restalrig. Two Logan Knights, Sir Walter and Sir Robert Logan, were killed in Spain whilst taking the heart of Robert the Bruce to the Holy Land for burial with Sir James Douglas.

Their eldest son:

Thomas Logan Weir married a Gael, Anne Grant Macdonnell of Inverness. They had male issue, the eldest of which died without heirs.

The second eldest and surviving son:

James Weir of Vere of Lewes who married Natalie Hopgood, daughter of George Collison Hopgood, Esquire and Julia Harding of Godalming, granddaughter of Captain George Butcher of the 11th Light Dragoons, of Windsor Castle and Osbourne House; Tapetiere to Queen Victoria.

They had an only son:

Nicholas Thomas Logan Weir of Vere (Nicholas de Vere)

Nicholas Weir Had a daughter Abbe Weir Abbe Devere

The relationship between the Head of the House of Vere and Nicholas de Vere; who is Head of the Tyrone Branch, is 3rd and 6th cousins. Found in only 3% and 6% of the clinical samples tested, both share two sets of rare genes each and Nicholas de Vere has an extra set of these genes from the matrilinear descent which supports the Collison descent from Norfolk in his own line and echoes the selective and exclusive royal and noble marital alliances which have continued throughout the history of the House of Vere.[9]

---

[9] Parish Records for Ulster 1820 - 1845, United Kingdom Government Registers for Births, Marriages and Deaths 1845-1997.

Notes

The House of Vere are latterly of Flemish extraction and the former senior, Scottish Branch; Hope-Vere of Blackwood, traditionally observed the Flemish law of Noblesse Uterine, and matrilinear and family inheritance in accordance with Scottish Law, which historically supports blood descent.

The Titles of Princeps Draconis and Prince de Vere, currently held by Nicholas de Vere, are acknowledged by the British Government's Department of Internal Affairs: 'The Home Office' and are registered with them as 'Official Observations'. The House of Vere in the senior line acknowledges these titles accordingly.

Nicholas de Vere, though recognising both, does not claim to be either a member of the historical British royal bloodline or of its peerage in any sense: and does not claim any status or rank suggestive of such or appertaining thereunto. The Vere princedoms are not modern, socially derived titles; either assumed or bestowed, for or by, political expediency.

The princedom of Vere is a genetic quality carried in the historical blood royal. Established in Angiers as a Royal House arising from sacral-regal origins rooted in antiquity, The House of Vere is recorded in a single name and in an unbroken line for over 1300 years and consequently is one of the oldest surviving royal houses in Europe. [10]

---

[10] Nicholas Devere, The House of Vere: References
See back for bibliography.

Extracts for the Dragon Cede Elvish Ancestors

(SEE DESCENT OF THE HOUSE OF VERE)

As we have mentioned above, claiming Elvish ancestry was not at all unusual in ancient Germanic (Scandinavian) lands; similar cases are to be found in Wales and in the whole Gaelic area as well. Such ancestry allowed one to perform deeds hard or impossible for mere humans. In Das Niebelungenlied we find that the resistance of the Burgunds endures mostly because of Hagen's (Hoegni) feats, whose Elvish ancestry makes it hard for his mortal opponents to defeat him; finally, he is vanquished by Dietrich of Bern (Thidhrekr), who was reputed to be the son of an elf. A later Middle High German song tells of Alphart, a knight of the same Dietrich, who was able to disperse a host of enemies by challenging them one by one to a single fight. In Welsh lore (Meddigon Meddfai, 1230 AD) we find the story of three brothers, the sons of "gwraig Annwn": (de Vere – gwraig = witch; Annwn = Death), (an elvish wife), who, due to virtues of their descent, became famous doctors in Wales. [Add here also similar traditions witnessed by Scottish minister Rev. P. Graham.] Most interesting is Icelandic Koetlu Draumur (XVI c.), where an Elf's love for a mortal woman Katla (consummated in her dream; she bore his son, whom her mortal husband Marr accepted as his own) serves as a reason why later that son of Katla, the sea-traveler Are Marsson (actually well-known through Iceland), could reach the mysterious island of Hvitra-manna-land

This motif is certainly a familiar one to every reader of The Simarillion. Elvish descendants Add here also Scyld Scefing (Beowulf), Skuld Helgadottir (Hrolfs saga Kraka), Merlin (Robert of Gloucester's Chronicle.) The Family of North-Western European Elves We have a whole family of initially similar peoples (beings) who occupy a prominent place in the high myths and folklore of North-Western European nations. The word "Elf" itself, used in this paper to refer to a single being of the kind, can be traced (see Jacob Grimm, Irische Elfenmaerchen) to the Old and Middle High German "Alb," "Alf," "Alp." Etymology will help us establish a "family tree" of European Elves; analysis of features attributed to various kinds of Elves in literature and folklore will testify to the tendency of "deterioration" and "randomization" of the original high myth.

The True Elves of Europe Originally a fully independent from humans, wise and strong race with time has merged in the minds of the Scandinavians, the Germans, the English, the Welsh and others with the guardian spirits of Nature (dwellers in the forests, rivers etc, Anglo-Saxon "wudu-aelfen" and "sae-aelfen" are perhaps an intermediate state of such a merging), malignant sprites and demons that cause illness to men and cattle ("malignant elves" used to be a medical term, alongside with "elf-fire," a cattle disease in Sweden (see Nils Thun, "Studia Neophilologica," 1969), or, in one case, a historical tribe, the so-called "Alfar" of "Alfheimar," an area of Scandinavia between the two rivers Raumelfr and Gautelfr. In a few cases the Elves were identified with the souls of the dead (which may have arisen from the confusion between the old barrows and the hills in which the Elves were reputed to dwell) Of the cases above, the first two represent a "logical merging" of a folklore element whose function became unclear, with the entities whose function is well-connected with the everyday life of a people; logical, that is, if we assume that every part of folklore has to have a specific "function." More examples of merging and of random elements will follow; now let us list the names the Elven kinds were known under in Europe conjecture on their relation. We must keep in mind that in many cases the original name has become a "taboo," supplanted in everyday usage by a euphemism of sorts, for the fear of possible harm or out of courtesy to its bearers, unless indicated otherwise, the plural of a name is given.

Althochdeutsch, Mittelhochdeutsch Anglo-Saxon Old Norse-Icelandic later Icelandic ("hidden folk") Norse (Norway) Danish (Denmark) Swedish Alb, Alf, Alp fem. Elbe, pl. Elben, Elber aelf, pl. ylfe (*ielfe) alfr, pl. alfar (Ljos-alfar) alfa-folk, huldu-folk alfer, elver, elvir alfer (elle-folk) aelfvor, aelfvar

The True Elves of Europe 100 Dutch Shetland Islands Faeroes alven trows huldu-menn (huldu-folk) A few other races should be mentioned here, because of their overwhelming similarities with the above: Wales Gaelic (Ireland/Scotland) Tuatha de Danaan Tylwith Teg ("Fair Family") Daoine Sidhe / Daoine Sithe Tolkien's not-so-obvious Borrowings Although Tolkien never made a secret of his sources, it is quite astounding how many of the folk and place-names in The Lord of the Rings and Silmarillion correspond precisely to ancient Norse-Icelandic, Anglo-Saxon and other ones that were actually used for things associated with Elves. This seems to corroborate our hypothesis that in creating his Elves, Tolkien might have been thinking of reconstructing the "original" image that, should such an original exist, was reflected in various Elves of North-Western European mythologies. A striking example of this approach is provided by his treatment of the Atlantis myth. The story of Numenor is not only an example of a fascinating mythical image employed by a master storyteller to produce a compelling story with a moral purport of its own, but rather an amazing attempt to provide the real story that with time took the form of the familiar myth (or rather, familiar mess of ideas associated with Atlantis). And in the middle of it all stands the "original" name of the downfallen land and people, Atalante (in ancient Elvisn language "Quenya"), which is, of course, Atlantis, given its "original" meaning. We claim that this approach, this challenge of reconstructing the "original" image behind the current mythological mess, pervades all of Tolkien's work, and that creating linguistic proof of its authenticity as in the case of Atlantis-Atalante is not a singular occurrence either. Let us offer a list of names Tolkien chose to use for his creations and their historical counterparts. * Cala-quendi, the Elves of Light – Vikings knew the Ljos-alfar, also the Elves of Light, who lived in remote world of their own, Ljos-alfa-heimr, presided The True Elves of Europe 101 over by Yngvi-Freyr. The king of Vanyar, the noblest kindred of Tolkien's Elves who never left Valinor (blessed realm over the sea) for Middle-earth (Midhs-gardhar) and dwell there with the gods till present day is called Ingwe. * Elda-mar, the Elvenhome – We have already mentioned Ljos-alfa-heimr, its word-for-word translation. In The Book of Lost Tales and Ambarkanta Tolkien suggests a "lost" Anglo-saxon AElf-ham, an intermediary name of the same meaning. * Alqua-londe, the Elvish Haven of the Swans – In Middle English the land of the Elves is called Eluen londe. * Eles-sar (name), "the Elven Stone" – Cf. Germanic personal name Alb- stein, Anglo-Saxon AElf-stan, Modern German Elb-stein usually interpreted as a sacrificial stone "upon which victims were broken" or stones in which (inside) "Elfs" sat. (Swedish aelf-qvarn) Tolkien (apparently) restored the true meaning of this old Germanic name as "Elven (gem-)stone (!), jewel of Elves." * The sundering of Elves. (Vanyar, Noldor, Teleri) – A classification of Elves was not unfamiliar to speaker of Anglo-Saxon, with "wudu-aelfen" (forest- elves), "sae-aelfen" (sea-elves) & etc.... (Cf. also "The Noldor are. the Sword-elves," and Old Norse-Icelandic kenning for warrior "sverdh-alfr" of the same meaning.) With thanks to the author, Dr. Leonid Korablev. The excerpts included here are from a shortened version of a Russian manuscript that is difficult to find. It has remained posted on the Internet for a number of years without an apparent copyright. Out of respect for his work, we tried to contact the author, but every attempt has failed. We encourage the reader to seek out Dr. Korablev's excellent websites, subcategorised at www.shelltown.net, containing The True Elves of Europe manuscript and his impressive artwork.

It is the Roman Church who murdered and oppressed the Grail families and their supporters for millennia, it is the Roman Church who have promulgated hatred and fear of the Dragon Blood for centuries and it is the Roman Church who declared outright war on us. We have a right to defend ourselves, our Holy Bloodline and our ancient traditions, but in so doing we become the adversary of the Church and of God Himself, albeit a false Church and a false God. Forced to fulfil their spurious prophecy, one of the Grail Bloodline might have no choice but to oppose the Church, just in order for the Dragon Race to survive. In so doing they will pose this long-anticipated threat and one of us, descending from the very blood of Christ Himself, will unavoidably become their ridiculous Anti- Christ. My views on Nazism are well known. Like Roman Catholicism, Nazism was an opportunistic, myopic, hubris-driven peasant movement populated by the worst in German peasant scum.

Its "Aryan" philosophy and aspirations were a complete joke; an outrageous political and cultural lie concocted to dupe a nation into subservience and compliance, and its devotion to nationalistic jingoism was the height of psychological blindness and wishful thinking. You can't make genetic Aryans – a race of kings – out of a nation of genetic turnip-peasants. As for Satanism, if we mean adherence to Satan as some externalised deity separate from the Dragon blood and the object of religious mumbo- jumbo, devotion and worship, such is an illogical nonsense which is just as psychologically damaging and dangerous as worshipping Jehovah or any other ridiculous god. The ancient Dragon gods of the Anunnaki were flesh and blood beings and as their scions we carry those deities in our blood and in our genes. We do not worship the old Gods, we manifest them.

Their praeter-human legacy and its consequent cosmic consciousness is ancient, holy, rare and precious and we would never demean or compromise it by becoming involved in some pathetic hubris and greed-fuelled human conspiracy like the Illuminati which, even if it does exist now, can be no more than a bunch of dissipated businessmen out to make a fast buck and massage their overblown egos by deluding themselves that they are part of some secret movement that will take over the world. What would be the point of taking over the world?

It's too much like hard work. People who invent and promulgate these conspiracy theories do not have two brain cells to rub together. They don't think the subject through to its logical conclusion. If they did, they would rapidly perceive that the whole conspiracy culture is a non sequitur. As individuals they should realise that they are so unimportant and ineffectual that no conspiracy is likely to have any effect on them in their lifetime, so why bother with the paranoia? Such infantile nonsense just fills the inane websites of lonely, powerless people with too much time on their hands. It sells books and reinforces the erotic neuroses of those with weak minds and a victim mentality. They clearly manifest suppressed sexually submissive, masochistic tendencies that feed rapaciously on unrealistic conspiracy fantasies involving their absolute domination by some superannuated father figure, which is just perverted and childish. David Icke once announced on his website that Laurence Gardner and his associates performed blood-drinking rituals at his "Columba House." Before uttering this ridiculous libel David should have contacted the Post Office and checked as to where "Columba House" was actually situated. If he had done so, the Post Office would quite happily have told him that "Columba House" was in fact a six inch by twelve-inch Post Office box at the local Post Office branch in Tiverton, Devon. Exactly how many shape-shifting reptilian vampires and their victims can you get into a standard British Post Office box? Having all shape-shifted into reptilian vampires, David Icke would then have us believe that they all shrunk to the size of mannequins and convinced a postal worker to put them in the box. If the Icke fanbase thinks this is possible or even probable, and I am sure that some who stay glued to the Internet all day will, then it is also entirely possible that his readers will believe that Laurence Gardner sacrificed babies at Montauk. In my considered opinion, David Icke is concocting all this out of his cynical, fiscally motivated imagination and flogging it off to a specifically targeted, willing audience of fellow flakes who, frighteningly enough, actually swallow it whole. Laurence Gardner published groundbreaking research and changed the course of Grail study and presented it to a fascinated audience. As such he was an extremely creative and innovative author. People like David Icke and his lunatic followers, however, have no creative talent whatsoever, and rather than write or discover something unique themselves, they just latch on to artists like Laurence and through sustained public libel and criticism they jump on the bandwagon and bathe in the negative reflected glory. What sinister activities am I hiding? The internal activities of the Court are confidential.

TT: What are your personal beliefs regarding God, spirituality, and religion?

NDV: "Beliefs" regarding God and spirituality create religions, and religions create division, fear and violence within the individual and consequently within society as a whole. Religion is a handy facade for the power and money hungry to conceal themselves behind, and serve as a crutch for the spiritually lazy, weak minded and the unregenerate. Religions happen when people don't get the point of the message – which is nearly always – and blindly worship the message and the messenger, instead of grasping the gnosis – the wisdom – inherent within the words that the message conveys. If you talk to God… you're religious. If God talks to you... you're psychotic. "Religion is an opiate of the masses." —Karl Marx Too true.

TT: Who, in your opinion, was the Judeo-Christian god Jehovah? Do you believe that there is any historical basis behind the symbolic notion of Jehovah's conflict with Satan?

NDV: The Jews obtained the main tenets of their religion from the Babylonians during the exile. This is the period when the scribes first started to write the Old Testament but as John Macarthy has pointed out, one later commentator in the Bible complained that the scribes were all damnable liars. One can say that although the later Jehovah was a false Jewish composite which has changed and developed over the ensuing centuries, his main attributes can be traced back to the Anunnaki god Enlil, and it was Enlil who, after cold-bloodedly murdering his father Anu, caused a war with his step- brother Enki – the Jewish Satan – concerning their individual seniority of position within the Anunnaki dynasty. So in general terms we can say that the "War in Heaven" between Jehovah and Satan originated in an internecine conflict, fuelled, not by the pride and greed of Lucifer, as the Bible would have us believe, but by the fear and jealousy of "God" towards his half-brother "Satan" or Enki who, with Nin- Kursag, was the true creator of both elves and men. In later Greek mythology, Anu is replaced by Chronos. Enlil becomes Zeus, the leader of the Olympians – the younger gods – and Enki becomes Typhoeus, the leader of the Titans, the old gods. In Gnostic texts Jehovah is called the Evil One – the demiurge – whilst the serpent or Satan, as Lucifer the Bringer of Light, occupies the position of the Saviour of Man. As the Bible itself says, "What evil befalls a city that does not come from the Lord God." In the Book of Kings Jehovah assumes the role of Satan the Tempter – as if it were second nature for him – in an attempt to make King David break the Holy Law and number the individual members of the Tribes of Israel. Jehovah hated mankind and sought man's oppression and ultimate annihilation. In Biblical theology this makes Jehovah the opposer of man, the real "Satan" in etymological terms. So, when Jesus says in the wilderness, "Get thee behind me Satan," we don't have to wonder who he's actually talking to. Even as Enlil, Jehovah sought constantly the destruction and eradication of all mankind whom he hated and feared because he was terrified that man, the Nephilim and the Dragons – loyal to Enki or Satan – might launch an uprising against him in retaliation for his crime. Which indeed they did, and quite rightly so. Satan, as Eä or Enki, was the son of the senior queen and the rightful heir of Anu, his father, who supported Enki's claim. Unable to bear this, in a fit of jealousy and rage, Enlil committed patricide in an attempt to force his way onto the throne of the father-god and, as a result, a protracted conflict ensued which became known in myth as The War In Heaven.

TT: What is your opinion of Christ and his ministry?

NDV: I have covered this subject in my answers to other questions, where it is clear that I am obviously a committed supporter of his spiritual and social traditions and teachings.

TT: What is your opinion of the Wiccan and New Age movements?

NDV: Again, my views of the Wiccan and New Age movements are also well known. Wicca, the so-called "Old Religion," is an artificial construct cobbled together from a variety of dubious folksy beliefs, which lacks any historical continuity, traditional pedigree, authority, or spiritual antecedence beyond sixty years. It is just substituting church dogma in another form, led by a so-called priesthood intent on self-aggrandisement, sexual seduction, petty power games and financial profit. The New Age movement is nothing more than a baseless, cynical marketing ploy geared towards extracting money from the fear and neurosis- driven, gullible, wet liberal, super-idealistic, fluffy bunny, rainbow-unicorn brigade. New Agers force themselves to see a world filled with human hatred, corruption and sadness, through almost militantly rose-tinted spectacles and, like ostriches who at the first sign of danger bury their heads in the sand, they vehemently refuse to address in any intelligent, practical or sensible ways the dire problems that stupid mankind has foisted upon itself.

TT: How do you feel about the sudden surge of interest in the "Grail bloodline" following the publication of The Da Vinci Code? Do you think that the popularization of the idea is dangerous?

NDV: My opinion is that The Da Vinci Code is a Holy Blood, Holy Grail rip-off, a one-day wonder that has masses of people desperately searching for something outside of themselves that, for a few, can only be found within. Some people, the minority, will maintain their interest in the Grail, understandably leaving The Da Vinci Code behind to study the subject further, through more informed and reliable sources, whilst the bulk of readers will rightly treat the book as a novel experience and pass on to other unrelated subjects, once their curiosity has been satisfied. This happens with every new publication. The only inherent danger would be to the subject itself, once the money- vampires of the New Age get hold of it and try opening weekend workshops in "How to become a member of the Grail Bloodline" or something equally unrealistic. It would then get promoted and marketed as a "lifestyle choice" open to all. Once such familiarity has bred the inevitable public contempt, the subject may well be rendered valueless to the new enquirer. The book has come and gone and been the subject of an intended lawsuit against Dan Brown, the inevitable Hollywood film has been made, everyone has made a million out of it and the hapless reader could have picked up a copy of Holy Blood, Holy Grail for a fraction of the price, and learnt an awful lot more from it in the bargain.

TT: What is the most important thing you want people to take away after reading The Dragon Legacy and this current work?

NDV: Firstly, one of the central themes of the books is transcendent consciousness. I would like to feel that the reader may derive some interest in this concept from reading The Dragon Legacy and The Dragon Cede and will pursue the subject further. Secondly, the Dragon families have been with us for millennia and, in the course of time, their innate and rightful destiny will cause them to rise again. With that rise will come a New Order, an order free of injustice and religious bigotry, free of political ambition, egotism, nationalism and social violence. This is an order that will herald in a new Golden Dawn for mankind. Those with vision will welcome their return and support them in their efforts to bring such to fruition in the time to come.

Author Note Abbe de Vere

What is striking about this passage is that my father was already warning against the very type of distortion that later attached itself to his work.

He was not inviting people to turn the Dragon Court into a conspiracy playground, nor was he asking later writers to flatten his language into a crude Satanic or Antichrist label. He was doing the opposite. He was mocking the same culture of sensationalism, shape-shifting fantasies, blood-drinking accusations, internet paranoia, and clickbait conspiracy that later commentators would use against him.

This passage shows two things at once. First, my father understood that the Dragon bloodline had been cast as the adversary by hostile religious systems, especially by the Roman Church. Secondly, he rejected the empty conspiracy culture that turned every older bloodline, symbol, or esoteric tradition into a cartoon of demons, vampires, reptilians, secret masters, and hidden world controllers.

That distinction has been repeatedly lost.

When he spoke of Satan, Lucifer, Jehovah, Enki, Enlil, the Anunnaki, the Grail families, and the Dragon blood, he was not simply using those names in the modern evangelical sense. He was working through myth, etymology, religious inversion, Gnostic interpretation, bloodline tradition, and hostile Church propaganda. The word "Satanic" in that context did not mean worship of an external devil. It meant adversarial to the

religious power that had already declared the Dragon bloodline its enemy.
That is why later readings become so damaging when they ignore the surrounding explanation. If someone lifts the most provocative terms and leaves behind the context, they can make the work appear to say the very thing my father was correcting.
In this passage, he also directly rejects Nazism, rejects empty Satanic worship, rejects conspiracy culture, rejects the Illuminati fantasy, rejects blood-drinking libel, and the type of internet mind that turns complex symbolic material into crude fear-based theatre. That makes it difficult for later writers to honestly pretend that his work was an invitation to build a Dragon-bloodline Antichrist panic.
The irony is obvious. My father named the problem before some of these later writers made themselves part of it.
He warned against people who latch on to another writer's work, reshape it through libel and sensationalism, and gain attention through negative reflected glory. That is precisely the pattern I am now examining.

This is why context is not optional. Without it, the Dragon Legacy material can be made to look like something it was not. With it, the reader can see that my father was not creating a doctrine of devil worship or a master-race fantasy. He was challenging religious demonisation, rejecting conspiracy culture, and defending the right of the Dragon families to exist outside the hostile labels placed upon them.
That is the difference between interpretation and misrepresentation.

Within this review I am very careful not to use full chapters word for word, as I also am very aware of fair use, therefore I will only use work that has been used of mine but do an overall review of each chapters with my opinions on how similar the framework is.

The main issue becomes and this is the hypocrisy is that people who hide behind the bible as biblical of christian authors rarely

have many words of their own, much like a smaller commentary of again heavily lifted information from the bible, They attempt to show themselves as the mask of god, And good verses evil, when at the same time, they show to me, in my opinions, that they present themselves in the very ways that god and Jesus commanded us against.
Jealousy, I question is this person jealous that they haven't done their genealogy or that they have and that they do not share this same bloodline, I also question what if they did find out that they shared the same bloodline as myself, does that not make them the antichrist and evil which they profess about?

I question their intentions, there has to be said there is very little integrity in a person who lifts this amount of framework from another person's work and idea in order to sell a few books, likewise the integrity due to originality and the laws and codes of conducts authors and publishers are supposed to behold and adhere to. Thou shall not steal also comes into play.

Judgement, I question how this book does not cast judgment on others, and I say this because this book, although my father used to joke a lot to provoke these sorts of people, this book condemns not only myself but thousands of people who share this bloodline, does that mean we are all evil? There is an overall broader persecution here, which religions fall into play over, are all Muslims, jews, Buddhists evil just because they do not follow the same doctrine?

What makes it acceptable to kill thousands of people like the Cathars because they did not follow suit and it has to be said , the very people the templars, who worked with the church to condemn these people ended up being condemned themselves by the very same institution and named to be satanic Baphomet worshippers, This continues today, (Baphomet worshipper, Baphomet wasn't even a name termed then, It was bought in later in the 18th Century)., It seems to me that this mask which I have already spoken of in the my books, that its acceptable to persecute only until these people are no longer useful, that they receive the same treatment.

Is my baby evil because he or she shares this bloodline, DNA doesn't choose its people, it doesn't say oh I know I'm going to create Hitler and make him into an autistic narcissist that will spread cruelty and evil, that is a matter of nature over nurture that a person becomes a tyrants, not bloodline.

Not all powerful or rich people are evil.

I have many people in my bloodline who have created hospitals, set up charities for the good and betterment of others, stopped and abolished slavery, helped women's rights, many pioneer for helping women in domestic abuse.

Forced adoptions were initiated by the church, In the most recent news we have the church apparently sending a public apology to all those mothers and children who they put through this forced adoption system, but the apology is meaningless in comparison to the abuse that the children went through. Forced adoption is no better than institutionalised child trafficking

So you the reader had to make a choice, will you allow yourself to be indoctrinated by this sort of behaviour, will you allow this kind of slavery of the mind or will you prefer for the truth to be set out in black and white so that you can make informed choices and a better life for your and your children's future.

Do not fall into the battle of good verses evil, from the 20 years of research I have found that this is just another mask people hide behind, when the reality of t is, the good they pretend becomes the evil they attempt to steer us away from.

The Review pages

Chapter Review Framework

Each chapter review applies the same test so that the evidence can be read consistently rather than as a personal reaction. This is AI assisted.

1. Material used: what text, citation, terminology, phrase, source-field or argument is being reviewed.

2. Source-field comparison: where the same or similar material appears in Nicholas de Vere, Laurence Gardner, Dragon Publishing, The Dragon Legacy, The Dragon Cede, the House of Vere material, or the wider Royal Dragon Court framework.

3. Attribution issue: whether the original source is clearly acknowledged, or whether the citation trail gives the appearance of independent research while relying on another source-field.

4. Nature of the concern: whether the issue is direct textual similarity, paraphrase, terminology borrowing, citation displacement, structural reliance, hostile recontextualisation, or lack of original contribution.

5. Review finding: what can reasonably be concluded from this chapter when read as part of the wider pattern.

This review does not treat every citation as infringement. Citation alone is not the issue. The issue is whether repeated citation, paraphrase, source-field reliance, structural dependence and hostile recharacterisation create a pattern that goes beyond ordinary fair dealing, fair use, scholarship or review.

CHAPTER 2 REVIEW
Giants of Old

1. Material used
Gary Wayne's discussion of the "Giants of Old" begins with language, etymology, Indo-European tribes, Scythians, Transylvania, Tartaria tablets, Sumerian glyphs, Nephilim, Titans, Cyclopes and ancient bloodlines. The argument is not presented as ordinary Biblical commentary. It uses word origins and ancient tribal migration as a means of reconstructing hidden prehistory.

There is also a clear methodological similarity in the use of etymology. Nicholas de Vere uses the word "Dragon" through Greek edrakon and Derkesthai, meaning "to see clearly," and then builds a wider theory of Dragon blood, inherited memory, clear sight and transcendent consciousness. Gary Wayne performs the same kind of operation with "giant," moving through Greek gigas, Gigantes and gigentes, Latin gigant, and Middle English giaunt, before connecting the word to Nephilim, Titans, heroes, demigods, earth-born beings and bloodline history.

The similarity, therefore, is not limited to one word or one citation. It lies in the structure of the argument. Gary Wayne uses etymology, Scythian ancestry, Transylvanian proto-Sumerian material, Titans, Cyclopes, Nephilim and Indo-European language to reconstruct hidden ancient bloodlines. Nicholas de Vere used the same broader method to reconstruct Dragon, Scythian, Danaan, Anunnaki, Fairy, Grail and Vere bloodline history.

2. Source-field comparison

This is important because the same research method is central to Nicholas de Vere's work. In The Dragon Cede, Nicholas de Vere states that etymology was decisive in uncovering the "true meaning of words, phrases and names related to the family and its history and mythology." His method was not limited to genealogy alone. He cross-referenced genealogy, heraldry, genetics, mythology, comparative religion, symbolism, magic, occultism, folklore and etymology in order to reconstruct the Vere / Dragon lineage beyond conventional written history.

The same Transylvania / Tartaria / proto-Sumerian field appears in Nicholas de Vere's work. The Dragon Legacy refers to early evidence from Tartaria in Transylvania, where a body and clay tablets were found bearing the names of the Sumerian god Enki and the ranking number of Father Anu, with the language described as proto-Sumerian. The Dragon Cede repeats the wider claim that Transylvanian tablets bearing Enki and Anunnaki-related inscriptions support the argument that proto-Sumerian culture originated in Central Europe before Mesopotamia.

The Cyclopes comparison strengthens the point. Nicholas de Vere describes the Cyclopes of Greece as members of the Titanic, Fairy race of giants, cave or Rath-dwelling miner-smiths who forged thunderbolts for Zeus. Gary Wayne similarly discusses the Cyclopes as a distinct giant race, naming Stereopes, Arges and Brontes, and placing them within a wider framework of divine beings, physical-world DNA, human females, smaller cyclopean giants and ancient bloodline descent.

The point is not that only Nicholas de Vere ever discussed Cyclopes. The point is that both works treat Cyclopes, Titans and giants not merely as mythological figures, but as traces of ancient corporeal races and bloodline history.

3. Attribution issue
This passage demonstrates more than ordinary citation or shared interest in ancient myth. Gary Wayne adopts the same etymological research architecture found throughout Nicholas de Vere's work. He uses word-origin analysis to reconstruct hidden prehistory, divine or giant ancestry, Scythian-Aryan migration, Transylvanian proto-Sumerian origins and bloodline continuity.

4. Nature of the concern
One of the clearest overlap points concerns Transylvania and the Tartaria tablets. Gary Wayne writes that tablets found beneath Tartaria in Transylvania predate the first Sumerian texts by perhaps a thousand years, and that their symbols were virtually identical with Sumerian glyphs. He then connects this discovery to Scythians, Indo-European language and hidden pre-flood history.

This shows that Gary Wayne's passage is not simply about "giants" in the Biblical sense. It enters the same wider field: Central Europe, Scythians, Aryan or Indo-European language, Anunnaki, Transylvanian proto-Sumerian origins and hidden bloodline continuity.

Gary Wayne has not merely borrowed isolated terms. In this section, he appears to adopt the same etymological architecture by which Nicholas de Vere built his Dragon bloodline history.

QUICK COMPARISON TABLE

Gary Wayne text	Nicholas de Vere / Dragon Publishing comparison	Similarity type
Uses etymology of "giant" to	The Dragon Cede states that etymology	Same research framework

reconstruct hidden ancient history	was decisive in reconstructing Vere family history, mythology and origins	
Links Indo-European / Aryan languages to Scythians, ancient tribes and giants	The Dragon Legacy and The Dragon Cede link Aryan / Scythian peoples, Dragon bloodlines, Anunnaki and hidden ancient origins	Structural overlap
Uses Tartaria / Transylvania tablets and Sumerian glyphs	The Dragon Legacy and The Dragon Cede both use Tartaria / Transylvania / proto-Sumerian / Enki / Anu material	Strong thematic overlap
Treats Scythians as central to ancient pre-flood and post-flood history	The Dragon Cede makes Scythians, Danaan, Anunnaki and Dragon God-Kings central to Vere descent	Strong framework similarity
Builds from Greek word roots into mythic race and bloodline claims	Nicholas de Vere does this with Dragon / Derkesthai, Vampire / Ubaid / Uber, Danaan / Sons of An and Scythian / Sithe	Same etymological method
Uses giants, Titans, Cyclopes and demigods as historical bloodline beings	The Dragon Cede treats Anunnaki, Titans, Dragon God-Kings, Fairies, Scythians and Danaan as historical or corporeal lineages	Strong conceptual overlap

5. Review finding

This passage demonstrates more than ordinary citation or shared interest in ancient myth. Gary Wayne adopts the same etymological research architecture found throughout Nicholas de Vere's work. He uses word-origin analysis to reconstruct hidden prehistory, divine or giant ancestry, Scythian-Aryan migration, Transylvanian proto-Sumerian origins and bloodline continuity.

This mirrors the method used in The Dragon Legacy and The Dragon Cede, where etymology is repeatedly used to connect Dragon, Derkesthai, Anunnaki, Scythian, Danaan, Ubaid, Vampire, Fairy and Grail bloodline material.

Gary Wayne has not merely borrowed isolated terms. In this section, he appears to adopt the same etymological architecture by which Nicholas de Vere built his Dragon bloodline history.

CHAPTER 3 REVIEW

Nephilim, Rephaim, Naphidim and the Anunnaki Framework

1. Material used
Gary Wayne's chapter on the Nephilim, Rephaim, Naphidim and Anunnaki is not simply a general Biblical discussion of giants. It enters the same specialised source-field found in Nicholas de Vere's work: Watchers, Anunnaki, Nephilim, Rephaim, Naphidim/Naphadim, Elvin bloodlines, hybrid descent, daughters of men, and post-flood giant races.

2. Source-field comparison
In The Dragon Legacy, Nicholas de Vere connects the Rephaim with healing, describing them as the Rephaim or Rapha 'Elohim, the healing gods of the Anunnaki. The same framework links the Rephaim with Enki / Raphael, Elven Overlords, Nephilim, Anakim, Idumea, Canaan, Black Sea migrants, Scythians, and Dragon symbolism.

In The Dragon Cede, Nicholas de Vere states that the Nephilim and Watchers are of the Dragon race, that they are the children of the Anunnaki gods, and that the children of the Nephilim were the Naphidem, the "giants" of the Bible. This is presented as the result of the sons of the Anunnaki, the Nephilim, going with the daughters of men.

The Dragon Cede also places the Anunnaki / Dragon bloodline within a wider historical structure involving antediluvian and post-flood migration, the Black Sea Flood, the Sacred Mountain, Mesopotamia, Sumerian culture, Egypt, Scythia, and an older pre-Flood Golden Age.

This is a distinctive Nicholas de Vere framework. Gary Wayne appears to adopt the same terminology and structure, while recasting it within his own hostile fallen-angel, Nephilim World Order, and Antichrist interpretation.

3. Attribution issue
No direct citation problem is isolated in this chapter from the current draft. The chapter is therefore best used as pattern evidence unless final footnotes show direct reliance, missing attribution, source displacement or inadequate citation.

4. Nature of the concern
This chapter should be recorded as evidence of substantial framework borrowing, distinctive terminology borrowing, and hostile recharacterisation of Nicholas de Vere's work.

QUICK COMPARISON TABLE

Gary Wayne text / issue	Nicholas de Vere / Dragon Publishing comparison	Similarity type
Discusses Naphalim / Watchers who fornicated with the daughters of men and produced Naphidim / Naphadim, giants and related hybrid races	The Dragon Cede states that the Nephilim / Watchers were children of the Anunnaki gods, and that their children were the Naphidem, the giants of the Bible	Strong terminology and framework overlap
Links Nephilim, Rephaim, Watchers, human women, giants, and hybrid descent	Nicholas de Vere links Nephilim, Watchers, Anunnaki, Dragon race, Naphidem, and human women within the Dragon bloodline framework	Distinctive source-field overlap

States that western occult organisations describe the Nephilim as Elvin sons of the Anunnagi / Anunnaki / Watchers and human women	Nicholas de Vere repeatedly connects Anunnaki, Elven, Dragon, Nephilim, Watchers, and bloodline descent	Strong conceptual overlap
Connects Rephaim with healing and ancient giant races	The Dragon Legacy describes the Rephaim / Rapha 'Elohim as healing gods of the Anunnaki	Direct thematic overlap
Reframes the material as fallen-angel corruption and Nephilim World Order material	Nicholas de Vere presents the same broad field as Dragon / Anunnaki / Elven / bloodline history	Hostile recharacterisation

5. Review finding

This chapter should be recorded as evidence of substantial framework borrowing, distinctive terminology borrowing, and hostile recharacterisation of Nicholas de Vere's work.

CHAPTER 4 REVIEW

Biblical Dependence and Lack of Original Contribution

1. Material used
Much of this chapter is heavily dependent on Biblical material. As the Bible is in the public domain, the issue is not copyright infringement in the ordinary sense. A writer is legally entitled to quote, edit, paraphrase, or comment upon public-domain Biblical text.

2. Source-field comparison
This matters because the same pattern appears elsewhere in the book: large bodies of pre-existing material are gathered, rearranged, and reframed. In some places that material comes from the Bible. In other places, it appears to come from Nicholas de Vere, Laurence Gardner, and the Dragon / Grail / Ring Lords / House of Vere source-field.

3. Attribution issue
No direct citation problem is isolated in this chapter from the current draft. The chapter is therefore best used as pattern evidence unless final footnotes show direct reliance, missing attribution, source displacement or inadequate citation.

4. Nature of the concern
However, this remains relevant to a review of scholarship and originality. Heavy reliance on public-domain Scripture can make a chapter appear substantial in length while contributing comparatively little original analysis. The question is not whether public-domain Biblical material may be used. It may. The question is whether the chapter offers original scholarship, or whether it is largely constructed from copied, paraphrased, or rearranged Biblical material.

For that reason, Chapter 4 is relevant as part of the wider pattern. It demonstrates a method of composition based heavily on borrowed textual material, even where the borrowed source is public domain.

5. Review finding
However, this remains relevant to a review of scholarship and originality. Heavy reliance on public-domain Scripture can make a chapter appear substantial in length while contributing comparatively little original analysis. The question is not whether public-domain Biblical material may be used. It may. The question is whether the chapter offers original scholarship, or whether it is largely constructed from copied, paraphrased, or rearranged Biblical material.

This matters because the same pattern appears elsewhere in the book: large bodies of pre-existing material are gathered, rearranged, and reframed. In some places that material comes from the Bible. In other places, it appears to come from Nicholas de Vere, Laurence Gardner, and the Dragon / Grail / Ring Lords / House of Vere source-field.

For that reason, Chapter 4 is relevant as part of the wider pattern. It demonstrates a method of composition based heavily on borrowed textual material, even where the borrowed source is public domain.

CHAPTER 5 REVIEW
"The Serpent's Root"

1. Material used
Chapter 5, titled "The Serpent's Root," raises serious concerns of framework copying, hostile recharacterisation, and uncited reliance upon the work of Nicholas de Vere.

In this chapter, Gary Wayne constructs a chain of ideas around:

Dragon royal houses become beast bloodlines. Ancient divine kingship becomes demonic empire control. Dragon / Revelation symbolism becomes Antichrist bloodline prophecy. Anunnaki / Dragon descent becomes a rival seed-line against Adamites.

2. Source-field comparison
The concern is that Gary Wayne combines those subjects into a distinctive bloodline framework that closely mirrors the Dragon lineage system developed in the work of Nicholas de Vere, while recasting that framework in a hostile direction.

The House of Dragon concept aligns far more closely with Nicholas de Vere's body of work, where Dragon lineage, Dragon blood, Dragon families, Dragon sovereignty, the Royal Dragon Court, Anunnaki / Watchers, Nephilim / Rephaim, serpent symbolism, and royal descent are central and recurring ideas.

This is a hostile inversion of Nicholas de Vere's Dragon bloodline framework.

Nicholas de Vere's work connects Dragon symbolism, serpent symbolism, Anunnaki, Watchers, Nephilim, Dragon blood, royal descent, ancient priest-kings, divine kingship, and ruling dynasties into a distinctive historical and genealogical system. Gary Wayne appears to take that same architecture and reframe it as demonic corruption, serpent seed, beast bloodline, and Antichrist preparation.

3. Attribution issue
The phrase does not appear to arise naturally from the cited Biblical or lexical sources attached to this section. Those sources may explain individual words such as serpent, seraph, dragon, seed, iron, clay, men, or beast. They do not, on their own, create a distinctive "House of Dragon" bloodline framework.

This is not neutral citation or ordinary commentary. It is a hostile reworking of the Dragon lineage structure.

A major concern is that, within this specific Chapter 5 section and its cited notes, Nicholas de Vere is not cited as the source for the Dragon / serpent / bloodline framework being used.

The notes attached to this section cite Biblical passages, Hebrew definitions, Strong's Dictionary, Enoch, Daniel notes, study Bibles, Gary Wayne's own earlier work, and other supporting sources. These may support isolated lexical or Biblical points. However, they do not account for the distinctive House of Dragon, serpent-seed, Dragon Watcher, royal bloodline, and end-time Dragon lineage framework that Wayne constructs.

4. Nature of the concern
The concern is not simply that Gary Wayne discusses Biblical serpents, Nephilim, Rephaim, Watchers, Daniel, Revelation, or end-time prophecy. Those subjects, taken individually, are widely discussed in religious, Biblical, and esoteric literature.

This is not merely a standard Biblical discussion. It is a genealogical, symbolic, and prophetic bloodline framework.

One of the strongest concerns in this chapter is Gary Wayne's use of the phrase "House of Dragon" in connection with serpent seed, Dragon Watchers, beast bloodlines, and end-time rulership.

Serpent Seed as Hostile Inversion of Dragon Bloodline

QUICK COMPARISON TABLE

Gary Wayne Chapter 5	Nicholas de Vere / RDC provenance	Issue
Serpent seed linked to House of Dragon, Dragon Watchers, royal / beast bloodlines and end-time empire	Serpent-seed / Dragon-line material appears in Nicholas de Vere's wider work and was publicly discussed in a Robert Sepehr video made for / with Abbe de Vere over seven years earlier	Provenance, uncited framework reliance, hostile recharacterisation
Cited sources explain Biblical, Hebrew, and prophetic vocabulary	They do not explain the Dragon Court, House of Dragon, serpent-seed royal bloodline, or Dragon Watcher framework	Missing source-field attribution
Dragon language is placed into a hereditary seed-line structure	Nicholas de Vere's work treats Dragon lineage, Dragon families, Dragon blood, Anunnaki / Watchers, Nephilim / Rephaim and royal descent as a recurring system	Framework appropriation
Daniel 2 is used to argue for a hybrid	Nicholas de Vere's work also	Hostile inversion of lineage theory

or non-human bloodline distinction	distinguishes ordinary humanity from Dragon / Grail / Anunnaki / Elven or royal bloodline descent	

5. Review finding

Chapter 5 should be recorded as evidence of hostile framework reworking, conceptual reliance, and possible uncited use of Nicholas de Vere's Dragon bloodline material.

The central concern is that Gary Wayne appears to have absorbed Nicholas de Vere's Dragon lineage system and recoded it into his own serpent-seed / Antichrist / beast empire narrative.

The cited sources in this section may explain individual Biblical or Hebrew words, but they do not explain the creation of the House of Dragon serpent-seed royal bloodline framework. That framework closely resembles Nicholas de Vere's Dragon bloodline system, particularly where Dragon, serpent, Watchers, Nephilim, Rephaim, royal descent, ancient ruling bloodlines, and end-time Revelation imagery are combined.

CHAPTER 6 REVIEW

"Second Incursion," Rephaim, Sodom and the Post-Flood House of Dragon

1. Material used
In the "Second Incursion" section, Gary Wayne continues the Chapter 5 serpent-root argument by moving from the original serpent seed into a post-flood framework involving Rephaim, Zuzim, Emim, Anakim, Amorites, Hittites, Canaanites, Sodom, Gomorrah, and the cities of the plain.

The key framework used in this section includes:

Gary Wayne places heavy emphasis on the wording "and also after that" in Genesis 6:4. He uses this phrase to argue that giant creation occurred before and after the Flood, or at least that there was a later re-establishment of the same type of bloodline corruption.

2. Source-field comparison
That phrase and structure are much closer to Nicholas de Vere's Dragon bloodline and Dragon family framework than to the cited Biblical sources alone.

In The Dragon Legacy, Nicholas de Vere connects the Rephaim with healing, serpents, Dragon symbolism, Anunnaki, Elven Kings, Nephilim, Anakim, Idumea, Canaan, Black Sea migrants, Scythians, and Dragon heraldry. He writes that the kings and queens of pre-Catholic history were known for healing capabilities and were called the Rephaim or Rapha 'Elohim — the healing gods of the Anunnaki. The same passage connects these figures with Enki / Raphael, Elven Overlords, Nephilim, Anakim, Idumea, Canaan, Black Sea migrants and Scythians.

In The Dragon Cede, Nicholas de Vere states that the Nephilim and Watchers are of the Dragon race, that they are the children of the Anunnaki gods, and that the children of the Nephilim were the Naphidem, the giants of the Bible, produced when the sons of the Anunnaki — the Nephilim — went with the daughters of men.

The Dragon Cede also presents the Anunnaki / Dragon line as hybridised before written history, connected with Elven God-Kings, Ring Lords, the King Tribe, Scythians, Danaan, and the surviving Dragon families.

3. Attribution issue
The wine thereof is the poison of dragons from the genealogical vine and branches of Sodom and Gomorrah who rule this world, the postdiluvian house of Dragon that imposes their ritual abominations and religions as the daughters of Babylon religion. Accordingly, Sodom's poisonous serpent/dragon roots vines, and seeds, along with its fiery destruction is an example for Babylon's end-time destruction and its spurious seed. Citation Deut. 29:23; Isa. 13:19; Jer. 50:52; Zeph. 2:9; Rev. 18:1–24.

The cited Biblical passages may discuss Sodom, judgment, poison, serpents, dragons, or Babylon. They do not, on their own, create a distinctive postdiluvian House of Dragon bloodline framework.

The cited Biblical material may explain individual components: Sodom, Gomorrah, poison, dragons, seed, judgment, Babylon and destruction. However, it does not explain the construction of a postdiluvian House of Dragon ruling bloodline.

However, those citations do not explain the distinctive postdiluvian House of Dragon framework Wayne constructs from the material.

4. Nature of the concern
This is not merely an ordinary discussion of Sodom, Genesis 14, or post-flood peoples. It is a post-flood Dragon / serpent / genealogical framework.

This passage is significant because Wayne is not merely citing Biblical judgment against Sodom. He connects Sodom, Gomorrah, poison of dragons, genealogical vine and branches, postdiluvian House of Dragon, serpent / dragon roots, seeds, Babylon, and end-time destruction.

Wayne's postdiluvian House of Dragon appears to function as a hostile recoding of Nicholas de Vere's Dragon bloodline material. Where Nicholas de Vere presents Dragon bloodlines, Dragon families, Dragon sovereignty, Anunnaki descent and royal lineage, Wayne reframes the same architecture as Sodomite corruption, serpent poison, Rephaim hybrids, Babylonian abomination and end-time destruction.

This is structurally close to Nicholas de Vere's treatment of the Rephaim as ancient ancestral kings connected to the Anunnaki, Elven Overlords, Nephilim, Anakim, Idumea, Canaan, Scythians, Black Sea migrants and Dragon symbolism.

QUICK COMPARISON TABLE

Gary Wayne Chapter 6	Nicholas de Vere / Dragon Publishing comparison	Issue
Proposes a Second Incursion to explain post-flood giants and Rephaim lines	Nicholas de Vere traces pre-flood, flood and post-flood Dragon / Anunnaki / Nephilim / Scythian continuity	Post-flood lineage framework

Links Rephaim, Anakim, Canaan, Sodom and ruling classes	The Dragon Legacy links Rephaim / Rapha 'Elohim with Anunnaki, Elven Overlords, Nephilim, Anakim, Idumea, Canaan, Scythians and Dragon symbolism	Strong framework overlap
Uses the phrase postdiluvian House of Dragon	Nicholas de Vere's work centers on Dragon bloodlines, Dragon families, Dragon sovereignty and Dragon lineage	Distinctive source-field reliance
Frames Sodom as serpent / dragon poison, genealogical vine and corrupt seed	Nicholas de Vere's Dragon framework uses lineage, blood, descent, serpent / Dragon symbolism and royal houses	Hostile recharacterisation
Uses Genesis 6:4 "and also after that" to support post-flood continuation	Dragon Publishing material traces ancient pre-flood and post-flood lineages through Anunnaki, Nephilim, Scythia, Danaan and Dragon families	Structural similarity
Cites Biblical and historical sources for isolated words and events	Those citations do not explain the House of Dragon or Dragon bloodline architecture	Missing source-field attribution
In earlier work, Wayne	Nicholas de Vere's work includes	Selective framing / confirmation bias

acknowledges serpent symbolism can include healing; in this later book the serpent is framed chiefly as evil and Antichrist-linked	Dragon / serpent symbolism within a broader sacred, royal, healing and lineage framework	

5. Review finding

This "Second Incursion" section should be recorded as further evidence of framework reliance, hostile recharacterisation and possible uncited use of Nicholas de Vere's Dragon bloodline material.

Gary Wayne appears to use the Rephaim / Anakim / Canaan / Sodom material to extend his serpent-seed argument into a post-flood Dragon house theory. This theory closely mirrors Nicholas de Vere's wider Dragon lineage architecture but reverses its meaning.

Gary Wayne's "Second Incursion" functions as a hostile post-flood version of Nicholas de Vere's Dragon bloodline continuity.

CHAPTER 7 REVIEW

Habitation, Angelic Bodies and Genetic Inheritance

1. Material used
Chapter 7 should be recorded as a framework match rather than a direct quotation match.

2. Source-field comparison
That is where the comparison with Nicholas de Vere becomes relevant.

The relevant Nicholas de Vere comparison is the genetic-bloodline framework.

In The Dragon Cede, Nicholas de Vere states that the Dragon archetype rests within the Dragon blood and is passed on through the genes. He also states that the Anunnaki were genetically similar enough to clone their genes with the Eljo race, and that they used their genetic material to sire the Elves, the Elder Race, and hybrid humans.

Nicholas de Vere also describes Dragons or Elves as a separate species from ordinary humanity, with inherited physical attributes from the Anunnaki gods. He states that this ancient race hybridised before written history to produce the Elven God-Kings and Ring Lords.

3. Attribution issue
The cited sources may explain angelic habitation, bodies, flesh, spirits, tabernacles, judgment and strange flesh. They do not, by themselves, explain the larger idea of inherited hybrid descent as a continuing bloodline structure.

4. Nature of the concern
Gary Wayne's argument depends on the idea that heavenly beings could enter the physical world, take bodily form, mate with human women, and produce descendants with inherited traits. In this structure, the "fallen" beings do not merely appear as spirits or

symbolic figures. They become physically reproductive beings whose actions create continuing bloodline consequences.

The match in Chapter 7 is not merely the old idea that angels had children with women. The match lies in the movement from angelic or divine beings into physical embodiment, sexual reproduction, hybrid offspring, genetic inheritance, and continuing bloodline consequence.

Gary Wayne frames this in hostile fallen-angel language. Nicholas de Vere frames it through the Dragon / Anunnaki / Elven / genetic bloodline system.

Chapter 7 should be recorded as evidence of framework reliance, not direct textual copying.

QUICK COMPARISON TABLE

Gary Wayne Chapter 7	Nicholas de Vere / Dragon Publishing comparison	Issue
Angels leave their heavenly habitation and take bodily form	Nicholas de Vere presents Anunnaki / Watchers / Dragon beings as corporeal or biologically active beings	Framework overlap
Angelic beings interact physically with human women	Nicholas de Vere states that the sons of the Anunnaki / Nephilim went with the daughters of men	Shared reproductive structure
Hybrid offspring result from angelic-human union	The Dragon Cede identifies the Naphidem as giants produced from Anunnaki /	Strong conceptual overlap

	Nephilim and human women	
The offspring carry continuing consequences through history	Nicholas de Vere's Dragon / Anunnaki / Elven framework is built on inherited bloodline transmission	Genetic-bloodline parallel
Wayne's citations explain habitation, flesh, spirit and judgment	They do not explain the DNA-transfer and inherited bloodline framework	Missing source-field attribution

5. Review finding
Chapter 7 should be recorded as evidence of framework reliance, not direct textual copying.

This chapter should therefore be treated as a supporting example of structural reliance on Nicholas de Vere's genetic-bloodline architecture.

CHAPTER 8 REVIEW

The Seventy Nations and the Assembly of Gods

1. Material used
Chapter 8 concerns the seventy nations, Deuteronomy 32:7–9, the sons of God, the sons of Israel, the Dead Sea Scrolls, the Septuagint, angels of God, Elohim, Psalm 82, the assembly or congregation of gods, Satan as ruler of a rebellious angelic council, and the allotment of nations to divine or angelic rulers.

In this chapter, Gary Wayne constructs a framework involving:

In The Dragon Cede, Nicholas de Vere uses the phrase "Grand Council of the Anunnaki" in connection with the Nephilim, Naphidem, divine kingship, and Anunnaki rule. This is especially relevant where Gary Wayne discusses divine assemblies, gods ruling over nations, and angelic or divine council structures.

2. Source-field comparison
The concern is that Gary Wayne's treatment appears to move beyond the cited Biblical and historical sources into a broader Dragon / Anunnaki / Elohim / divine-council framework strongly associated with Nicholas de Vere's work.

The footnote attached to the Anunnaki assembly reference cites Laurence Gardner's Realm of the Ring Lords. However, the surrounding framework resembles Nicholas de Vere's Dragon / Anunnaki / Elohim divine-council structure.

This creates a citation concern. Gardner may be cited for the Anunnaki assembly, but if the broader Dragon / Anunnaki / Elohim / genealogical divine-council framework is drawn from Nicholas de Vere's work, then the citation to Gardner alone may not adequately identify the source-field being used.

In The Dragon Legacy, Nicholas de Vere describes the Anunnaki as the children of Anu who "decree the fates," and connects them with Dragon kings, Nagas, serpent deities, Anu, and the wider Dragon / Anunnaki tradition.

3. Attribution issue
A specific concern arises where Gary Wayne cites Laurence Gardner's Realm of the Ring Lords for the Grand Assembly of the Anunnaki at Nippur, while the surrounding framework appears closer to Nicholas de Vere's Dragon / Anunnaki / Elohim material.

If Gardner's cited page does not contain the full Dragon / Anunnaki / Elohim / genealogical divine-council framework being used, then this should be recorded as possible inadequate attribution or citation displacement.

This is particularly important because Gardner's Grail, Ring Lords, and Anunnaki material itself sits inside the Nicholas de Vere / Dragon Court source-chain. Gardner acknowledged access to Dragon Court and household archive material, and Nicholas de Vere wrote in connection with Gardner's Grail material. Therefore, a Gardner citation may not be enough if the actual framework being used comes through Nicholas de Vere's Dragon Publishing source-field.

The following citation should also be retained for the Gardner-linked material:

4. Nature of the concern
The issue is not merely that Wayne discusses divine councils, gods, angels, Elohim, or ancient assemblies. Those subjects can be found in Biblical, apocryphal, Mesopotamian, classical, and comparative-religion literature.

The similarity in Chapter 8 is not merely that both authors mention Anunnaki or gods. The overlap lies in the structure:

The concern is that the citation to Gardner may not account for the full framework actually being used. If the Dragon / Anunnaki / Elohim council structure comes from Nicholas de Vere's work, then Nicholas de Vere should be cited directly, not displaced behind a Gardner citation.

This chapter should therefore be recorded as evidence of possible inadequate attribution, citation displacement, and framework reliance upon the Nicholas de Vere / Dragon Publishing source-field.

QUICK COMPARISON TABLE

Gary Wayne Chapter 8	Nicholas de Vere / Dragon Publishing comparison	Issue
Discusses the seventy nations, sons of God, Elohim, divine rulers and angelic government	Nicholas de Vere treats the Elohim as original divine beings linked with Dragon Kings and Queens of the Anunnaki	Divine-council framework overlap
Cites Gardner for the Grand Assembly of the Anunnaki at Nippur	Nicholas de Vere uses the phrase Grand Council of the Anunnaki in connection with Nephilim, Naphidem, divine kingship and Anunnaki rule	Possible citation displacement
Connects divine beings with rulership, nations,	Nicholas de Vere's framework connects Anunnaki, Dragon kingship, divine	Structural similarity

and heavenly governance	family relationships, royal descent and ancient sovereignty	
Uses Biblical citations for sons of God, Elohim, angels, nations and divine assembly	Those citations explain individual Biblical terms, but not the full Dragon / Anunnaki / Elohim genealogical council framework	Missing source-field attribution
Places Satan or rebellious angelic authority over an earthly system of rule	Nicholas de Vere's work treats divine / Anunnaki / Dragon structures as ancient royal and genealogical systems, later reframed by Wayne as hostile angelic government	Hostile recharacterisation

5. Review finding

Gary Wayne appears to construct a divine-council model involving seventy nations, sons of God, Elohim, ruling angelic princes, the Anunnaki assembly, and Satanic government of the earth.

This overlaps with Nicholas de Vere's Dragon / Anunnaki framework, especially the treatment of the Anunnaki as ruling gods, the Elohim as Dragon Kings and Queens, and divine family structures as genealogical charts.

The concern is that the citation to Gardner may not account for the full framework actually being used. If the Dragon / Anunnaki / Elohim council structure comes from Nicholas de Vere's work, then Nicholas de Vere should be cited directly, not displaced behind a Gardner citation.

Chapter 9 Review

Satan, Heylel and Lucifer

1. Material used
Chapter 9, titled "Satan, Heylel, and Lucifer," raises concerns of framework reliance, selective attribution, and hostile recharacterisation.

The concern is the way Wayne combines these subjects into a single hostile framework involving Satan-Lucifer, Venus, Luciferian light, occult orders, Babylon, Antichrist, divine or royal pedigree, bloodline succession, beast kings and tyrannical rulers. This framework overlaps with Nicholas de Vere's existing Dragon / Satan-Lucifer / Anunnaki / genealogical material, but Wayne reframes it as a demonic and Antichrist system.

In this chapter, Gary Wayne builds an argument around:

2. Source-field comparison
Nicholas de Vere's work contains a direct Satan-Lucifer genealogical framework. In The Dragon Cede, Satan-Lucifer is presented as the son of Anu and creator of the Elven or Fairy Kings. The genealogical line then moves through Qayin, Lilith, Dragon Lords, Tubal Cain, Nimrod, Egyptian pharaohs, Prince Ankhfn-Khonsu, the Royal Dragon Court, and later Dragon descent.

Nicholas de Vere's work also develops Lucifer / Venus / Tree of Life / Grail symbolism. In The Dragon Legacy, Lucifer, Venus, the Morning Star, the Tree of Life, Anunnaki family relationships, Dragon Queens, Grail symbolism and occult reworkings of Christian material are treated as part of a deeper symbolic and genealogical system.

Gary Wayne's Chapter 9 directly cites The Dragon Legacy in connection with the Otherworld or Underworld material. In the pasted notes, de Vere is cited at notes 290 and 291.

This is significant because it shows that Wayne knew he was using Nicholas de Vere's material in this chapter. He cites The Dragon Legacy for the Otherworld / Underworld framework, then continues into Satan, hell, Lucifer, occult religion, Freemasonry, Venus and Antichrist material.

3. Attribution issue
However, those citations do not, by themselves, fully explain the Satan-Lucifer / Dragon / royal bloodline / occult rulership / Antichrist pedigree framework being constructed.

Nicholas de Vere's work does contain a Satan-Lucifer genealogical framework and a Lucifer / Venus / Dragon / Grail symbolic framework. Therefore, where Gary Wayne uses the same symbolic architecture while only citing de Vere narrowly for Otherworld material, this should be recorded as selective attribution and possible framework reliance.

Chapter 9 should be recorded as evidence of hostile framework reworking and selective attribution.

Gary Wayne's citations explain individual lexical, Biblical and occult references.

4. Nature of the concern
The concern is not that Gary Wayne discusses Isaiah 14, Lucifer, Heylel, Satan, Babylon, Freemasonry, Rosicrucianism, the New Age movement, the Illuminati, Hitler, Napoleon, Alexander, or Antichrist. Taken individually, those subjects are widely discussed in religious, esoteric, historical, and conspiracy literature.

This is not merely a lexical study of the word Lucifer. It becomes a prophetic, genealogical and occult-history structure.

This is highly relevant to Chapter 9 because Wayne is not simply discussing Satan as a theological figure. He is discussing Satan-Lucifer in connection with world rulership, occult orders, Babylonian kingship, Antichrist succession, and claims of divine or royal pedigree.

Gary Wayne's Chapter 9 appears to use similar symbolic territory but inverts the meaning into a hostile anti-Luciferian and anti-occult prophecy argument.

QUICK COMPARISON TABLE

Gary Wayne Chapter 9	Nicholas de Vere / Dragon Publishing comparison	Issue
Cites The Dragon Legacy for Otherworld / Underworld material at notes 290 and 291	Nicholas de Vere develops Otherworld / Underworld material within a wider Dragon / Anunnaki / symbolic framework	Narrow citation, broader framework use
Builds a Satan-Lucifer framework around Babylon, occult orders and Antichrist	The Dragon Cede contains a Satan-Lucifer genealogical framework connected to Anu, Qayin, Lilith, Dragon Lords, Nimrod, pharaohs and Dragon descent	Framework overlap
Connects Lucifer with Venus, Morning Star,	The Dragon Legacy links Lucifer, Venus, Morning Star, Tree of Life,	Strong symbolic overlap

pentagram and occult symbolism	Grail symbolism, Dragon Queens and Anunnaki family relationships	
Uses royal or divine pedigree language in an Antichrist context	Nicholas de Vere's work is built around Dragon / Grail / Anunnaki / royal bloodline descent	Hostile recharacterisation
Links Hitler, Napoleon, Alexander, Nimrod and future Antichrist into beast-king succession	Nicholas de Vere's method links ancient figures, divine beings, pharaohs, Dragon Lords and royal houses across deep time	Hostile inversion of genealogical method
Cites de Vere narrowly while using a broader Satan-Lucifer / Dragon / Venus / bloodline framework	Nicholas de Vere's work contains the closer combined framework	Selective attribution / possible citation displacement

5. Review finding
Chapter 9 should be recorded as evidence of hostile framework reworking and selective attribution.

The concern is not simple subject overlap. The concern is that Wayne appears to draw from Nicholas de Vere's Satan-Lucifer / Dragon / Anunnaki / royal bloodline framework and reverse it into an accusation structure involving Luciferian deception, secret societies, Hitler, Babylon and Antichrist.

Gary Wayne's citations explain individual lexical, Biblical and occult references.

CHAPTER 10 REVIEW
"Heylel: God of Hell"

1. Material used
Chapter 10, titled "Heylel: God of Hell," is not presently the strongest chapter for direct wording comparison. Much of the section is built from Biblical passages, Strong's definitions, and conventional distinctions between Sheol, Hades, Tartarus, Gehenna, the abyss, the pit, and the lake of fire.

However, the chapter remains relevant because Gary Wayne uses those Biblical and lexical sources to construct a wider underworld framework involving fallen angels, demons, Nephilim / Rephaim spirits, abyss prisons, another dimension, passage between realms, and end-time release from the underworld.

He then uses these distinctions to build a framework in which the underworld is not merely the grave, but a complex realm containing fallen angels, disembodied spirits, demons, Nephilim / Rephaim spirits, abyss prisons, end-time releases, and possible dimensional overlap with the physical world.

2. Source-field comparison
A further citation point should be noted. In this section, Wayne refers to Lilith as Samael's consort, with Samael alternatively known as Enki in Sumerian legend, citing Laurence Gardner, Genesis of the Grail Kings. This is relevant because the Lilith / Samael / Enki connection also sits inside the wider Nicholas de Vere / Dragon Publishing source-field.

Nicholas de Vere's work contains a distinctive Otherworld framework. In The Dragon Legacy, the Otherworld is described as not simply a place "up in the stars," but as a state of being adjacent to our own dimension. It is described through the Mabinogion as the Mirror World, entered and left by gods of Heaven and Earth, the Portal Guardians.

The Dragon Legacy also uses Tir Na Nog, the Otherworld, Portal Guardians, passage after death, transition between this world and the Otherworld, and the idea of beings moving between realms.

Nicholas de Vere's work contains the corresponding mythic structure:

3. Attribution issue
Much of this chapter appears to be constructed by lifting Biblical vocabulary and dictionary definitions into a larger speculative framework. The citations explain individual words: Sheol, Hades, Tartarus, darkness, prison, abyss, pit, Gehenna, Hinnom, fire, valley, and Rephaim.

Those citations can support the vocabulary. However, they do not fully explain the larger world-system Gary Wayne builds from them.

The cited Bible and lexical sources explain the words. They do not independently create a full underworld / abyss / spirit-prison / other-dimensional framework involving fallen angels, Nephilim / Rephaim spirits, passages between realms, and end-time releases.

That should be recorded carefully. The issue is not that every discussion of Sheol, Hades, Tartarus or Gehenna must cite Nicholas de Vere. The issue is that Gary Wayne uses those terms to construct a wider spiritual geography that overlaps with Nicholas de Vere's distinctive Otherworld framework.

4. Nature of the concern

This is relevant to Chapter 10 because Gary Wayne's underworld argument is not merely a simple Christian discussion of hell. He develops the idea of layered realms, abyss prisons, disembodied spirits, fallen beings, and a dimensional relationship between the underworld and the physical world.

The two frameworks are not identical in theology. Gary Wayne turns the underworld into a hostile Biblical prison system for fallen angels, demons, and Rephaim spirits. Nicholas de Vere frames the Otherworld through Fairy, Dragon, ancestral, mythic and sovereignty traditions.

The concern is that Gary Wayne appears to take a similar realm-structure and recast it in hostile Biblical language.

This matters because it pulls the discussion of hell back into the same Rephaim and giant framework used elsewhere in the material. The chapter is not simply defining hell. It uses hell-language to support a wider giant / Rephaim / end-time geography.

QUICK COMPARISON TABLE

Gary Wayne Chapter 10	Nicholas de Vere / Dragon Publishing comparison	Issue
Separates Sheol, Hades, Tartarus, Gehenna, abyss, pit and lake of fire	Nicholas de Vere distinguishes this world from the Otherworld, Mirror World, and adjacent dimensional realm	Realm-structure similarity
Builds an underworld system involving fallen angels, demons, spirit prisons and end-time release	The Dragon Legacy presents Otherworld passage, Portal Guardians, transition after	Framework overlap

	death and movement between realms	
Connects the underworld with Nephilim / Rephaim spirits	Nicholas de Vere connects Rephaim, Nephilim, Anunnaki, Dragon symbolism and ancestral lineages	Repeated source-field overlap
Cites Biblical and lexical sources for hell terminology	Those sources explain vocabulary but not the full adjacent-dimension / spirit-prison framework	Missing framework explanation
Cites Gardner for Lilith, Samael and Enki	The Lilith / Samael / Enki material sits inside the wider Nicholas de Vere / Dragon Publishing source-field	Gardner-chain relevance
Recasts supernatural realm material as hostile hell, abyss and demonic prison	Nicholas de Vere frames Otherworld material through Fairy, Dragon, ancestral, mythic and sovereignty traditions	Hostile recharacterisation

5. Review finding

Chapter 10 should be recorded as a weaker direct-copying chapter, but a useful supporting framework chapter.

It demonstrates Gary Wayne's method: take Biblical terms, Strong's definitions, and conventional religious material, then build them into a larger speculative framework involving fallen angels, demons, Rephaim spirits, underworld prisons, dimensional realms, and end-time release.

The matching Nicholas de Vere framework is not the word "hell" itself. It is the structure of an adjacent Otherworld or underworld realm, inhabited by supernatural beings, accessible through passage or transition, and connected to ancestral, divine, or semi-divine races.

CHAPTER 12 REVIEW

First Angelic Hierarchy: Watchers

1. Material used
Chapter 12, titled "First Angelic Hierarchy: Watchers," raises concerns of framework reliance, selective attribution, and possible misdirection of citation.

In this chapter, Gary Wayne constructs an argument around:

Therefore, where Wayne builds a chapter around Watchers, Seraphim, dragon-shaped angels, Samael, Enki, Lilith, and Gnostic divine hierarchy, the citation to Gardner may be inadequate if the fuller framework derives from Nicholas de Vere's Dragon Publishing material.

2. Source-field comparison
The concern is that Wayne takes those materials and builds them into a Dragon / Watcher / Anunnaki / Samael framework that strongly overlaps with Nicholas de Vere's Dragon bloodline and Anunnaki material, while citing Laurence Gardner for part of the underlying Grail Kings / Samael / Enki material.

Gary Wayne cites Laurence Gardner's Genesis of the Grail Kings in this section, specifically in connection with Samael, Lilith and Enki-type material.

The concern is that Nicholas de Vere's work contains a much closer Dragon / Anunnaki / Samael structure than the citation to Gardner alone suggests.

Nicholas de Vere's work directly connects Satan-Lucifer with Enki, Ea, Khem, Pan, Leviathan, Qayin, Lilith, Dragon Lords, Nimrod, Egyptian pharaohs, and the Royal Dragon Court. Nicholas de Vere also treats the Watchers and Nephilim as of the Dragon race and as children of the Anunnaki gods.

3. Attribution issue
That citation may support some Grail Kings material, but it does not by itself account for the wider Dragon / Anunnaki / Watcher framework Wayne is constructing in this chapter.

Gary Wayne cites Gardner for part of this, but Nicholas de Vere's material contains the direct Dragon genealogy: Satan-Lucifer as Enki / Ea / Khem / Pan / Leviathan; Lilith as connected to the Dragon / Grail line; Qayin as son of Satan; and the descent of Dragon Lords, Nimrod and the Royal Dragon Court.

This means the chapter should not be treated as simply "Gardner material." If Wayne is using Samael / Enki / Lilith within a Dragon / Watcher / angelic hierarchy framework, then Nicholas de Vere's material is directly relevant.

The footnotes in Gary Wayne's Chapter 12 cite standard theological sources, Dionysius, Enoch, Encyclopedia, Strong's definitions, Gnostic texts, and Laurence Gardner.

4. Nature of the concern
The concern is not that Gary Wayne discusses angels or the traditional hierarchy of angels. Angelic hierarchy is widely discussed in Biblical, theological, Catholic, apocryphal and esoteric literature.

This is not merely a study of Dionysius or Biblical angelology. It becomes a supernatural hierarchy model that links angels, Watchers, Gnostic rulers, Dragon imagery, Samael / Enki, Lilith, and divine or counterfeit kingship.

That structural mirroring is part of the same framework pattern seen across the material.

The overlap is the combined architecture, not merely one word or isolated subject.

QUICK COMPARISON TABLE

Gary Wayne Chapter 12	Nicholas de Vere / Dragon Publishing comparison	Issue
Discusses Watchers, angelic hierarchy, Seraphim, Cherubim and Ophannim	Nicholas de Vere identifies Watchers and Nephilim as of the Dragon race and children of the Anunnaki gods	Framework overlap
Uses serpent-faced Seraphim and dragon-shaped angels	Nicholas de Vere repeatedly links serpent, Dragon, Anunnaki, Watchers, Nephilim and ruling bloodlines	Dragon / serpent source-field overlap
Cites Gardner for Samael, Lilith and Enki material	Nicholas de Vere directly connects Satan-Lucifer with Enki / Eä / Khem / Pan / Leviathan, Lilith, Qayin, Dragon Lords, Nimrod and the Royal Dragon Court	Possible citation displacement
Builds a Satanic counterfeit throne and rebellious angelic hierarchy	Nicholas de Vere uses mirrored divine structures, Anunnaki hierarchy, Tree of Life genealogy and Dragon kingship	Structural similarity

Uses Gnostic archons, Samael, Ialdabaoth and divine rulers	Nicholas de Vere's framework links divine beings, Anunnaki rulers, Dragon kings and older religious structures	Framework reliance
Cites general angelology and Gardner	These citations do not fully explain the combined Dragon / Watcher / Anunnaki / Samael architecture	Selective attribution

5. Review finding

Chapter 12 should be recorded as evidence of framework reliance and possible selective attribution.

Gary Wayne cites Gardner for Grail Kings material.

The wider Dragon / Watcher / Anunnaki / Samael framework is strongly present in Nicholas de Vere's work.

CHAPTER 13 REVIEW

First Angelic Hierarchy: Archangels

1. Material used
Chapter 13, titled "First Angelic Hierarchy: Archangels," raises concerns of framework reliance and hostile recharacterisation.

The concern is the way Wayne uses those subjects to construct a framework in which the Watchers are identified with the sons of God, the Seraphim, serpents, dragons, illicit knowledge, earthly religion, government, science, monarchy, royal imagery, hidden hierarchy and divine-right rulership.

In this chapter, Gary Wayne builds a chain of ideas around:

2. Source-field comparison
That combination strongly overlaps with Nicholas de Vere's Dragon / Watcher / Anunnaki / royal bloodline framework.

Nicholas de Vere's work contains the corresponding framework.

In The Dragon Cede, Nicholas de Vere identifies the Watchers and Nephilim as being of the Dragon race and as children of the Anunnaki gods. The same framework connects these beings with hybridisation, Dragon descent, Elven God-Kings, Ring Lords, ancient kingship and Dragon families.

In The Dragon Legacy, Nicholas de Vere connects Watchers or Seers with Dragons and places them within a wider Dragon / Anunnaki / Scythian bloodline framework.

3. Attribution issue
That is not neutral citation. It is hostile recharacterisation of the Dragon divine-right framework.

However, those citations do not fully account for the Dragon / Watcher / royal-genealogy framework Wayne constructs from the material.

The cited sources may explain angelic ranks. They do not explain why royal coats of arms supposedly preserve Dragon-serpent genealogy, why monarchy is interpreted through Watcher descent, or why divine right is redefined as authority from invisible Watcher beings.

4. Nature of the concern
The concern is not that Gary Wayne discusses archangels, Michael, Gabriel, Enoch, Watchers, Seraphim, or angelic hierarchy. Those subjects are widely discussed in Biblical, apocryphal and theological literature.

This is therefore a hostile inversion. Nicholas de Vere frames Dragon knowledge as ancient royal, magical, priestly or sovereign inheritance. Wayne reframes it as forbidden Watcher knowledge used to corrupt the world.

That is a hostile reworking of the Dragon heraldry and royal bloodline framework found in Nicholas de Vere's work.

So, the archangel discussion by itself is not the strongest copying issue. Its relevance lies in the structure Wayne builds around it.

QUICK COMPARISON TABLE

Gary Wayne Chapter 13	Nicholas de Vere / Dragon Publishing comparison	Issue
Identifies the Watchers with sons of God, Seraphim, serpents and dragons	Nicholas de Vere identifies the Watchers and Nephilim as of the Dragon race and	Strong framework overlap

	children of the Anunnaki gods	
Presents Watcher knowledge as the source of counterfeit religion, government and sacred sciences	Nicholas de Vere connects Dragon / Anunnaki / Watcher lineage with ancient knowledge, kingship, priestcraft, rulership and magical inheritance	Hostile inversion
Claims dragon, serpent and cherubic imagery in royal coats of arms reflects tacit genealogy	Nicholas de Vere's work links Dragon identity, Dragon blood, Dragon heraldry, royal descent and divine right	Heraldic-genealogical overlap
Presents earthly government, religious centers and learning centers as masking a hidden hierarchy	Nicholas de Vere's work presents hidden Dragon inheritance, Dragon families, priest-kings, sovereignty and preserved knowledge	Structural similarity
Uses archangel material within a wider Watcher / Dragon / royal hierarchy framework	Nicholas de Vere's Dragon framework links Watchers, Anunnaki, Dragon race, divine kingship and ancient rulership	Supporting framework relevance
Reframes divine right as authority from invisible Watcher beings	Nicholas de Vere connects Dragon blood with divine-right kingship and royal sovereignty	Hostile recharacterisation

5. Review finding
Chapter 13 should be recorded as a strong framework chapter.

It is not the strongest direct quotation chapter, but it clearly uses the same Dragon / Watcher / royal-genealogy architecture found in Nicholas de Vere's work.

The key concern is that Gary Wayne appears to take Nicholas de Vere's Dragon bloodline framework and invert it. In Nicholas de Vere's work, Dragon blood and Dragon heraldry support ancient sovereignty, divine right and royal descent. In Gary Wayne's Chapter 13, the same architecture becomes evidence of Watcher corruption, serpent-dragon religion, hidden hierarchy and spurious royal bloodlines.

CHAPTER 14 REVIEW

Second and Third Hierarchies of Angels

1. Material used
Chapter 14 begins as a discussion of angelic hierarchy, Greek terminology, Dionysius, dominions, powers, virtues, principalities and angels. On it's opening alone, the chapter appears to be mostly theological and lexical.

Nicholas de Vere presents Dragon blood as the ancient source of divine-right kingship. His work links Dragon blood, Anunnaki descent, royal dynasties, Dragon kings and queens, divine sovereignty, ancient government, priest-kings, royal houses and the Dragon Court.

Nicholas de Vere connects ancient divine beings, Anunnaki / Dragon lineage, sovereign houses, priest-kings, royal courts, Church-state suppression and Dragon ancestry into a historical power structure. Wayne uses a similar architecture but describes it as Satan's World Order and the earthly implementation of the Naphalim / Nephilim World Order.

2. Source-field comparison
However, the later section reviewed here substantially strengthens the comparison with Nicholas de Vere's work.

This is where the chapter becomes relevant to the Nicholas de Vere comparison.

This passage cites Nicholas de Vere, but the difficulty is that the paragraph is so long and so densely constructed that it is not clear where the citation begins and ends. The reader is left to untangle whether the citation applies only to a narrow point, to the Pergamum / Satan's seat material, to the "king" / "wise one" etymology, or to the wider dynastic and divine-right framework.

That matters because the passage moves through many Nicholas de Vere source-field markers: another dimension, divine thrones, Naphalim, Nephilim, Rephaim, postdiluvian nations, dynastic offspring, god-kings, pure-blood women, founding dynasties, king as wise one, the Noble Race, and power over fate and destiny.

3. Attribution issue
Zeus, Pergamum, Satan's Seat and Dragon Legacy Citation

Gary Wayne's notes for this chapter cite Nicholas de Vere's The Dragon Legacy in connection with the Pergamum / Zeus / Satan's seat material.

The concern is that the citation may be narrow, while the framework being built is much broader.

Wayne cites de Vere for specific Pergamum or Dragon Legacy material, but the surrounding argument also uses Dragon / serpent royal imagery, divine right, thrones, dynasties, godfathers, royal coats of arms and hidden rulership — all of which are central to Nicholas de Vere's Dragon bloodline work.

4. Nature of the concern
Nicholas de Vere has a whole chapter concerning the "wise ones." Nicholas says, "race of the wise ones," a caste which was described in Latin as the nobilis, a name that originated from the Greek root gno, meaning "to know."

Nicholas de Vere's work contains the corresponding framework in a non-hostile Dragon bloodline form.

That is not merely a theological disagreement. It is a hostile inversion of the Dragon divine-right framework.

Nicholas de Vere's work is heavily concerned with Dragon heraldry, royal blood, Dragon families, the House of Vere, the Royal Dragon Court, ancient sovereignty and genealogical symbols. Wayne's statement that heraldic imagery encodes divine or semi-divine ancestry sits directly inside that same field.

QUICK COMPARISON TABLE

Gary Wayne Chapter 14	Nicholas de Vere / Dragon Publishing comparison	Issue
Uses king from Gothic kuningzam, meaning "wise one" and "knowing one," linked to a scion of the Noble Race	Nicholas de Vere gives kun-ingzam as "knowing one" and "scion of the noble, meaning wise, race," and links this to the wise ones	Strong textual / framework overlap
Links Gothic / Guth with power over fate and destiny	Nicholas de Vere links siddhis, powers, Scythians, Arya-Sidhe, Sidheans, samadhi and the "wise ones"	Etymological and magical framework overlap
Describes dynastic offspring, postdiluvian nations, pure-blood women, founding dynasties and royal representatives of gods	Nicholas de Vere links Dragon / Anunnaki / Scythian / Danaan bloodlines to ancient kingship, ruling families and divine descent	Strong bloodline framework overlap
Uses divine right as authority from invisible beings	Nicholas de Vere presents Dragon blood as the true source of divine-right kingship and ancient sovereignty	Hostile inversion

Treats coats of arms as encoded genealogy	Nicholas de Vere's work is built around Dragon heraldry, royal blood, Dragon families, ancient sovereignty and genealogical symbols	Heraldic-genealogical overlap
Presents earthly governments, courts, religions and dynasties as manifestations of invisible hierarchy	Nicholas de Vere connects divine beings, Anunnaki / Dragon lineage, royal courts, priest-kings and ancient power structures	Structural similarity
Cites de Vere narrowly for Pergamum / Satan's seat material	The wider chapter uses Dragon / serpent royal imagery, divine right, thrones, dynasties, godfathers, royal coats of arms and hidden rulership	Selective attribution
Uses "as above, so below" rulership through the chessboard model	Nicholas de Vere's Dragon / Grail framework also links cosmic order, divine ancestry, sacred kingship and earthly rule	Framework reworking

5. Review finding
Chapter 14 should be recorded as a strong framework chapter.

The opening section is mostly angelic hierarchy and Greek terminology, but the later section moves directly into Nicholas de Vere territory: divine right, Dragon / serpent rulership, royal dynasties, coats of arms, thrones, hidden hierarchy, wise ones, Noble Race, Gothic kuningzam, and earthly institutions reflecting invisible spiritual authority.

The first part of Chapter 14 is mostly general angelology.

CHAPTER 16 REVIEW
SATAN: THE ANOINTED OF ANGELS

1. Material used
Citation Method Concern: Anderson Legend and Secondary Source Reliance

2. Source-field comparison
No single source-field paragraph was isolated in the original draft. This chapter should therefore be treated cautiously as pattern evidence unless the final page references identify direct Nicholas de Vere, Laurence Gardner or Dragon Publishing material.

3. Attribution issue
Wayne cites his own earlier work, The Genesis 6 Conspiracy, alongside Albert Mackey, Genesis 4:17, and Manly P. Hall. He then states that, according to the Anderson Legend, Cain took to sacred knowledge, practised the disciplines with unusual vigour, and used the fifth science, geometry or masonry, to build the city of Hanoch / Enoch after his son. He further connects this to pre-Flood masonry, curious works before the Deluge, and even the Great Pyramid.

If Wayne is relying on the Anderson Legend, then the obvious primary source is James Anderson's Constitutions of the Free-Masons. Anderson is not a minor background figure in this subject. He is central to the published Masonic constitutional tradition. Therefore, if Wayne is making a claim about what the Anderson Legend records, the reader should reasonably expect to see Anderson cited directly, not merely later secondary Masonic writers or Wayne citing his own earlier book.

This matters because the chapter gives the appearance of deep research, but the citation route is indirect. Wayne cites himself, cites

Mackey, cites Manly P. Hall, and cites Genesis, yet the original Anderson material appears to be absent from the citation chain at the very point where it should be most relevant.

In this case, the failure to cite Anderson directly raises a fair question: has Wayne investigated the original material, or is he relying on later writers and his own previous framing to build the argument?

4. Nature of the concern
Another issue appears in Wayne's treatment of Cain, geometry, masonry, the Anderson Legend and the Seven Sacred Sciences.

It also fits a wider pattern in Wayne's work: secondary sources are sometimes used to carry claims that should have been checked against the original source. This may make the writing look well supported to a casual reader, but it leaves important questions about whether the primary material has been properly investigated.

5. Review finding
That weakens the scholarship.

It also fits a wider pattern in Wayne's work: secondary sources are sometimes used to carry claims that should have been checked against the original source. This may make the writing look well supported to a casual reader, but it leaves important questions about whether the primary material has been properly investigated.

In this case, the failure to cite Anderson directly raises a fair question: has Wayne investigated the original material, or is he relying on later writers and his own previous framing to build the argument?

CHAPTER 21 REVIEW
Unicorns of Mount Hermon

1. Material used
Chapter 21, titled "Unicorns of Mount Hermon," raises strong concerns of framework reliance, hostile recharacterisation, and reputational harm.

In Chapter 21, Wayne builds an argument around:

Gary Wayne's Chapter 21 uses that same field of material, but recasts it negatively as occult, Rephaim, Nephilim, Antichrist and Satanic pedigree material.

2. Source-field comparison
This is highly relevant to Nicholas de Vere's work because Wayne places the same Dragon / Vere / Tuatha / royal / divine-right field into an Antichrist framework.

Nicholas de Vere's work contains the corresponding Dragon / Vere / Tuatha / royal framework.

In The Dragon Legacy, Nicholas de Vere places the Royal Dragon bloodline through the Tuatha Dé Danann of Eire, the Pictish Dragon queens and kings, the Vere-Bruidhe priest-kings, Maelasanu de Scythes or Sidhe, and the first Royal House of Vere of Anjou.

In The Dragon Cede, the Dragon Court line is also connected to the Tuatha Dé Danann, described as the Dragon Kings of Anu, and to the Egyptian Dragon Dynasty of Sobek.

3. Attribution issue
Gary Wayne cites Nicholas de Vere's The Dragon Legacy in this chapter. He also cites a wide range of other sources on unicorns,

heraldry, Rosicrucianism, Herodotus, Diana Cooper, mythology and the KJV.

A narrow citation does not cure hostile recharacterisation, especially where the author uses the cited bloodline material to build implications about Rephaim descent, corrupt royal oaths, Antichrist pedigree, and future Dragon / Elvin Antichrist claims.

Gary Wayne cites The Dragon Legacy but uses the material inside a hostile Antichrist narrative.

This should be recorded as evidence of hostile recharacterisation, selective attribution, and reputationally damaging bloodline recoding.

4. Nature of the concern

The chapter is not merely about the King James translation of "unicorn" from the Hebrew r'em, nor is it simply a discussion of wild oxen, bulls, rhinoceroses, or ancient unicorn mythology.

The concern is that Wayne appears to take the Dragon / Tuatha / Vere framework and reframe it as evidence of Nephilim or Rephaim bloodlines and Antichrist pedigree.

This is not neutral discussion of heraldry. It is hostile bloodline reclassification.

This matters because the chapter places royal divine-right claims into the same hostile framework as Mount Hermon, Rephaim, occult oaths and Antichrist pedigree.

QUICK COMPARISON TABLE

Gary Wayne Chapter 21	Nicholas de Vere / Dragon Publishing comparison	Issue
Refers to a Tuatha De Danann Dragon	Nicholas de Vere connects the Tuatha	Strong source-field overlap

king and connects the Tuatha Dé Danann with giant offspring, white steeds, Arya-Sidhe, people of the stars, Dragon kings and Elvin god-kings	Dé Danann with Anu, Arya / Scythians, Daouine Sidhe, people of the powers, Elves / Fairies, Dragon blood, Dragon kings and Elven goddess-queens or God-kings	
Uses king / Kuningzam as "wise one," "knowing one," and scion of the Noble Race	Nicholas de Vere gives kun-ingzam as "knowing one" and "scion of the noble, meaning wise, race"	Strong wording / etymology overlap
Uses royal coats of arms as hidden genealogical stories	Nicholas de Vere's work is built around Dragon heraldry, royal blood, Dragon families, divine right and ancient genealogical identity	Heraldic-genealogical overlap
Links Stuart unicorn, King James, divine right, Mount Hermon, Rephaim and Antichrist pedigree	Nicholas de Vere treats royal and Dragon bloodline claims as ancient sovereignty and divine-right kingship	Hostile inversion
Uses Scythian / Aryan horse and unicorn imagery in connection with ancient royal or giant bloodlines	Nicholas de Vere connects Scythian Dragon territory, Horse Lords, Arya / Sidhe, Dragon Lords and ancient royal lineages	Structural overlap
Cites The Dragon Legacy while placing the material inside an Antichrist claim structure	Nicholas de Vere's Dragon / Tuatha / Vere / royal bloodline material is being used in a	Selective attribution and reputational harm

	hostile Rephaim / Nephilim / Antichrist framework	

5. Review finding
Chapter 21 should be treated as a strong hostile framework chapter.

The concern is not that Wayne discusses unicorns or Mount Hermon. The concern is that he uses those subjects to build a hostile bloodline narrative around royal houses, Dragon kings, Tuatha Dé Danann, the Stuart unicorn, divine right, and future Antichrist claims.

Gary Wayne uses unicorn symbolism to discuss royal genealogy, Mount Hermon, divine right, Tuatha Dé Danann Dragon kings, Scythian / Aryan horse-lord traditions, royal coats of arms and Antichrist pedigree.

CHAPTER 22 REVIEW

Nimrod and Babel City

1. Material used
Chapter 22, titled "Nimrod and Babel City," raises strong concerns of framework reliance, selective attribution, and possible source displacement.

The chapter is not simply a Biblical discussion of Nimrod, Babel, Genesis 10–11, or the Table of Nations. Gary Wayne uses Nimrod and Babel to construct a wider postdiluvian framework involving giants, Rephaim, hybrid dynasties, forbidden knowledge, masonry, geometry, Enochian mysticism, Babel religion, Uruk / Erech, Sargon, Lugalbanda, Gilgamesh, Egyptian pharaohs, Mendes, Khem, Azazel, the Goat of Mendes, Rosicrucian and alchemical symbolism, and the origins of post-Flood mystical systems.

The concern is not that Gardner cannot be cited. The concern is that Wayne uses Gardner citations while building a broader Dragon / Anunnaki / Nimrod / Egyptian / Grail dynasty structure that is also central to Nicholas de Vere's work.

2. Source-field comparison
This is highly relevant because Nicholas de Vere's work contains a prior Dragon / Anunnaki / Nimrod / Egyptian-pharaonic / Grail bloodline framework.

Chapter 22 contains several citations to Laurence Gardner. Gary Wayne cites Gardner's Genesis of the Grail Kings in connection with Nimrod's Egyptian pharaonic descent, the Targum-Jonathan material, and the suggested pharaoh identities. He also cites Gardner's Realm of the Ring Lords in connection with Raneb and related Egyptian material.

Those citations matter because Wayne is visibly routing key Grail Kings / pharaonic / Nimrod material through Gardner, while the wider framework also overlaps with Nicholas de Vere's Dragon Publishing material.

Where the full framework is closer to Nicholas de Vere's Dragon bloodline material than the narrow Gardner citation suggests, this should be recorded as possible selective attribution or source displacement.

3. Attribution issue
Gary Wayne claims Nimrod spawned the first postdiluvian pharaonic dynasty of Egypt, cites Gardner and other authors for pharaoh identifications, then moves into Mendes, Khem, Azazel, Capricorn, the Goat of Mendes, alchemy and Rosicrucianism.

Gary Wayne's citations support individual points: Genesis, Josephus, the Septuagint, Masonic history, Nimrod legends, George Smith, Gilgamesh / Izdubar material, Targum-Jonathan, David Rohl, Gardner, Egyptian history, Mendes and Khem material.

However, those citations do not fully explain the wider Dragon / Anunnaki / Nimrod / Egyptian hybrid dynasty framework.

The repeated Gardner citations are especially important. If Wayne is citing Gardner for Nimrod and pharaonic descent while the broader framework also tracks closely with Nicholas de Vere's Dragon Publishing material, then the citation trail may obscure the Nicholas de Vere source-field.

4. Nature of the concern
This makes Gary Wayne's Chapter 22 highly relevant, because Wayne is discussing Nimrod, Babel, hybrid dynasties, Egypt, pharaohs, Khem

/ Mendes, Azazel, goat symbolism, and postdiluvian mystical systems — all within a hostile Nephilim / Rephaim framework.

Nicholas de Vere's workplaces Nimrod inside a Dragon / Grail genealogical descent structure. Gary Wayne appears to rework Nimrod into a hostile postdiluvian hybrid-ruler figure: a rebellious king connected to Babel, masonry, Enochian knowledge, Rephaim / Anunnaki intermarriage and later royal dynasties.

The structure is similar; the interpretation is hostile.

This should be recorded as hostile inversion rather than simple parallel subject matter.

QUICK COMPARISON TABLE

Gary Wayne Chapter 22	Nicholas de Vere / Dragon Publishing comparison	Issue
Uses Nimrod as a post-Flood mighty one, rebel ruler and origin figure for Babel	Nicholas de Vere places Nimrod inside a Dragon / Grail genealogical descent structure	Framework overlap
Links Babel with masonry, geometry, Seven Sacred Sciences, Enochian forbidden knowledge and occult religion	Nicholas de Vere connects ancient knowledge, Dragon / Anunnaki lineage, magical inheritance, priest-kingship and hidden traditions	Hostile inversion of knowledge framework
Claims Nimrod intermarried with Rephaim / Anunnaki lines to produce hybrid dynasties	Nicholas de Vere repeatedly connects Dragon / Anunnaki descent, hybridisation, ancient kingship and royal bloodlines	Strong hybrid-dynasty overlap

Links Uruk / Erech with Sargon, Lugalbanda, Gilgamesh and giant warrior-kings	Nicholas de Vere's method also links ancient figures, divine beings and royal houses across deep time	Structural similarity
Moves from Nimrod into Egyptian pharaohs, Mendes, Khem, Azazel and Goat of Mendes material	The Dragon Cede links Nimrod, Egyptian dynasties, Khem / Enki / Pan / Leviathan and Dragon Court descent	Strong source-field overlap
Cites Gardner's Genesis of the Grail Kings and Realm of the Ring Lords	Gardner's Grail / Ring Lords material sits within the wider Nicholas de Vere / Dragon Court source-chain	Possible source displacement
Presents the material as Rephaim / Anunnaki corruption, Babel rebellion and Satanic mysticism	Nicholas de Vere presents the related framework as Dragon / Grail royal descent and ancient sovereignty	Hostile recharacterisation

5. Review finding

Chapter 22 should be recorded as a strong framework chapter.

Gary Wayne cites Gardner several times in this chapter for Grail Kings / Nimrod / Egyptian pharaonic material.

The wider framework strongly overlaps with Nicholas de Vere's Dragon / Anunnaki / Nimrod / Egyptian dynasty material.

CHAPTER 23 REVIEW —
The Anakim and Patriarch-Less Nations

1. Material used
Chapter 23, titled "The Anakim and Patriarch-Less Nations," raises strong concerns of framework reliance, selective attribution, and hostile recharacterisation.

The chapter is not simply a Biblical discussion of Canaanite tribes, Anakim, Rephaim, Goliath, Rapha, or the Table of Nations. Gary Wayne uses those subjects to build a wider framework involving patriarch-less hybrid nations, Rephaim royal bloodlines, Anakim giants, Anu, Anukim, Tuatha D'Anu, Tuatha Dé Danann, Scythian ancestral kings, people of the stars, Rapha'Elohim, healing gods, and hybrid human Canaanite confederacies.

In this chapter, Gary Wayne builds an argument around:

2. Source-field comparison
This directly overlaps with Nicholas de Vere's Dragon/Anunnaki/Tuatha/Scythian/Rephaim material.

Gary Wayne cites Nicholas de Vere in this chapter.

He cites The Dragon Legacy in relation to the Repha'im / Rapha'Elohim healing-god material, and again in connection with Anukim, Anu, Tuatha D'Anu / Tuatha Dé Danann and Scythian ancestral king material.

This is significant because it shows Gary Wayne knew he was relying on Nicholas de Vere's material within this section.

3. Attribution issue
Gary Wayne does cite Nicholas de Vere in this chapter, which is important evidence of knowledge and reliance.

However, the citation does not remove the problem. The issue is that Gary takes Nicholas de Vere's Dragon/Anu/Tuatha/Scythian framework and places it inside a chapter that classifies related lines as Rephaim, Anakim, hybrid human, patriarch-less, and part of a corrupted Canaanite confederacy.

A citation does not give permission to reframe a bloodline work into a hostile accusation system. Nor does a narrow citation fully account for the wider framework being borrowed.

4. Nature of the concern
Gary takes Nicholas de Vere's Dragon/Anunnaki/Tuatha/Scythian framework and inserts it into a hostile chapter about patriarch-less hybrid Canaanite nations, Rephaim giants, hybrid human confederacies, and corrupt post-Flood giant bloodlines.

Therefore, Gary Wayne's Chapter 23 is not merely using public Biblical material. It uses Nicholas de Vere's distinctive interpretive framework and then reclassifies it as evidence of Rephaim/Anakim hybrid corruption.

This overlaps with Nicholas de Vere's treatment of Repha'im / Rapha'Elohim and healing gods. The concern is that Gary Wayne takes the healing-god material and reframes it inside a hostile giant/demon/Rephaim structure.

That is a strong framework match and a hostile inversion.

5. Review finding
Preliminary assessment

Chapter 23 should be recorded as a strong chapter.

.

CHAPTER 24 REVIEW — THE JEBUSITES OF THE MIGHTY SEVEN NATIONS

1. Material used
Chapter 24, titled "The Jebusites of the Mighty Seven Nations," raises concerns of framework reliance and hostile recharacterisation.

The chapter is not simply a Biblical study of the Jebusites, Canaanite tribes, Jerusalem, Exodus 3:8, Deuteronomy 7:1, Joshua 3:10, or the Table of Nations. Gary Wayne uses those subjects to build a wider framework involving patriarch-less Canaanite families, Rephaim intermarriage, hybrid human tribes, missing patriarchs, patrial city names, Amorite-Hittite extraction, Jerusalem as a hybrid city, Jebus as an eponymous Rephaim patriarch, the Mighty Seven nations, and giant-like ruling people's occupying the Covenant Land.

In this chapter, Gary Wayne builds an argument around:

2. Source-field comparison
This overlaps with Nicholas de Vere's wider Rephaim/Anunnaki/royal-bloodline method, although Chapter 24 does not appear from the pasted section to be as direct a named De Vere citation chapter as Chapter 23.

Nicholas de Vere's work contains a closely related framework involving Rephaim, Anunnaki, royal bloodlines, ancient priest-kings, healing gods, Dragon symbolism, and hidden descent.

In The Dragon Legacy, Nicholas de Vere connects the Rephaim or Rapha'Elohim with healing gods of the Anunnaki, Elven Overlords, Nephilim, Anakim of Idumea and Canaan, Scythian migrants, serpent/Dragon symbolism, sacred kingship, wisdom and healing powers.

Nicholas de Vere also describes ancient priestly and royal figures as ambassadors of the Anunnaki, Nephilim and later Rephaim, acting as lawgivers, judges and holders of ancient authority.

3. Attribution issue
Gary Wayne cites Josephus to describe the Jebusites as a nation extracted from the Canaanites, then interprets "extraction" as potentially meaning a lineage drawn out of or foreign from ordinary Canaanites.

From the pasted section, Chapter 24 does not appear to cite Nicholas de Vere directly. The sources cited include Josephus, Strong's, Sayce, Mercer Dictionary, Armana Letters, Egyptian Execration Text material, Billington, Pritchard and standard Biblical passages.

4. Nature of the concern
This is relevant because Gary Wayne's Chapter 24 uses the Rephaim and hybrid-nation framework to explain ancient ruling peoples, Jerusalem, Canaanite families and the Mighty Seven nations. He takes the same ancient ruling-class and Rephaim field and recasts it as hostile hybrid corruption.

This continues the hostile Rephaim framework.

Gary is not simply identifying the Jebusites as Canaanites. He is suggesting they are a mixed or extracted lineage, shaped by Rephaim patriarchs through Canaanite female descent.

Gary Wayne's interpretation is hostile. He presents the comparable structure as evidence of corrupt Rephaim-human hybridisation and patriarch-less Canaanite contamination.

5. Review finding
Those sources may support parts of the Jebusite, Jerusalem, Amorite, Hittite and Egyptian-text discussion.

However, they do not fully explain the broader framework of hidden hybrid genealogy, excluded Rephaim patriarchs, female-line Canaanite/Rephaim intermarriage, Jerusalem as hybrid bloodline city, and royal/giant ancestry encoded through place names.

That wider interpretive method overlaps with Nicholas de Vere's Dragon/Rephaim/Anunnaki bloodline framework.

CHAPTER 25 REVIEWS.

The Amorites-

1. Material used
Forensic Note: Why This Chapter Requires Closer Investigation

2. Source-field comparison
On the surface, this chapter may look satisfactory to the untrained reader. A person looking only at the citations might say: there is no citation to Nicholas de Vere here, so there is nothing to examine. Move on to the next chapter.

In that podcast material, Wayne admits that at a certain point in his research, conveniently around 1996, he needed "something else." He explains that he decided to begin looking into secret societies and Freemasonry because he needed further material. That matters because the Royal Dragon Court framework, Nicholas de Vere's work, Laurence Gardner's Grail / Ring Lords material, and the wider Dragon bloodline field sit precisely inside that area of research.

In The Dragon Cede, Nicholas de Vere mentions King Hammurabi in one part of the discussion. Then, only a few pages later, the material moves through genealogical and cultural associations into the Tuatha Dé Danann / Danaan framework. The connection is not laid out in one neat modern search-engine paragraph. It appears as part of a wider Dragon / Anunnaki / Scythian / Danaan framework.

To me, as the person raised inside this material, and as the person now responsible for the Nicholas de Vere / Dragon Publishing source-field, not so much.

3. Attribution issue
Gary Wayne's chapter appears to perform a similar movement. He draws on etymology, frames Hammurabi / Hammurapi through

Rephaim, Rapiu, Amorite, Ham / Cham, healer, dynastic kingship and bloodline language, and then moves into associations with Dedan / Ditanu / Didanu and the Tuatha Dé Danann. His citation trail points elsewhere, but the structural movement is recognisable.

I am used to these patterns. I recognise them quickly because I know how the material was originally arranged, where the associations appear, and how the Dragon / Anunnaki / Scythian / Danaan framework develops across the pages. This is not confirmation bias. This is pattern recognition based on direct knowledge of the source-field.

The point is not that Nicholas de Vere owned the name Hammurabi. He did not. Hammurabi is a public historical figure. The point is that Wayne's chapter appears to draw together Hammurabi, Rephaim / Rapiu, Ham / Cham, healing terminology, Amorite descent, dynastic kingship, Dedan / Ditanu, and the Tuatha Dé Danann in a way that mirrors the underlying de Vere framework while avoiding a direct Nicholas de Vere citation at the relevant point.

Without that knowledge, Wayne's citation trail may look acceptable.

4. Nature of the concern
When applying that knowledge, the pattern becomes much harder to ignore.

This is why the book requires a more forensic investigation. The issue is not only direct copying. It is also the quieter use of distinctive connective tissue: the way names, genealogies, etymologies, bloodlines and mythic structures are moved, rearranged, supported with alternative citations, and then presented as if they have not passed through the Nicholas de Vere / Dragon Publishing source-field.

This chapter therefore should not be dismissed simply because Nicholas de Vere is absent from the citation list. On the contrary, that absence is part of the concern.

For this edition, I have drawn the line at the clearest examples: direct citation, copied or closely mirrored wording, citation-chain reliance, framework borrowing, and hostile recharacterisation.

5. Review finding

For this edition, I have drawn the line at the clearest examples: direct citation, copied or closely mirrored wording, citation-chain reliance, framework borrowing, and hostile recharacterisation.

This review is not presented as an exhaustive forensic audit of every hidden nuance in Gary Wayne's work. It is a substantial evidential review showing a repeated pattern.

The fact that further uncited patterns may exist does not weaken this book. It strengthens the reason why the work should be examined more closely.

CHAPTER 29 REVIEW
The Sidonians

1. Material used
Chapter 29, titled "The Sidonians," raises strong concerns of framework reliance, selective attribution and hostile recharacterisation.

The chapter is not simply a Biblical or historical study of Sidon, Tyre, Phoenicia, Jezebel, Baal, Ashtoreth, the Sidonian city-state or the Phoenician trading world. Gary Wayne uses the Sidonian material to construct a wider framework involving Rephaim intermarriage, hybrid Canaanite bloodlines, Hyksos, Mitanni, Hurrians/Horim, Baal worship, demigod kings, divine-right rulership, Tyrus as an Antichrist archetype, Terrible Ones, Atlantis, Babylon, Tyre as an end-time prophetic allegory, and the Ring Lords of Nippur.

In Chapter 29, Gary Wayne builds an argument around:

2. Source-field comparison
The chapter becomes significant because it moves directly into the same Dragon/Grail/Ring Lords/Anunnaki/divine kingship field associated with Nicholas de Vere's work.

The language of Ring Lords, Nippur, heaven meeting earth, Anunnaki assembly, divine appointment, anointing, antediluvian kings and divine right to rule sits directly inside the same field as Nicholas de Vere's Dragon/Anunnaki/Ring Lord/Grail kingship framework.

Nicholas de Vere's work contains the corresponding framework.

Nicholas de Vere connects Anunnaki, Dragon kings, Rephaim/Rapha'Elohim, healing gods, Dragon sovereignty, royal bloodlines, Tuatha de Danaan, Scythian/Sidhe descent, and ancient divine kingship.

3. Attribution issue
This matters because it draws Dragon/Grail/Ring Lords material into a large end-time conspiracy architecture. The Ring Lords and divine-right kingship material are not merely cited as ancient tradition; they are folded into an accusation structure about Babylon and Antichrist.

Gary Wayne cites Laurence Gardner's Realm of the Ring Lords in this section for the Ring Lords of Nippur material.

That citation is important. It shows that Gary Wayne is knowingly using the Ring Lords/Grail kingship field. However, the concern remains that the wider Dragon/Anunnaki/Ring Lord/divine-right framework also strongly overlaps with Nicholas de Vere's work.

A Gardner citation may explain part of the visible source trail, but it does not remove the need to recognise Nicholas de Vere's related Dragon Court framework where the same symbolic architecture appears.

4. Nature of the concern
This is not ordinary Sidonian history. It is a hostile bloodline and prophetic framework.

Ring Lords / Nippur / divine-right issue

His wider Dragon Court framework treats ancient divine or semi-divine kingship as Dragon/Grail sovereignty and royal descent. It is not presented as a hostile Antichrist system.

This continues the same hidden hybrid-bloodline method seen in earlier chapters. Sidon becomes not simply a son of Canaan, but a line that allegedly produced hybrid Rephaim-connected city-states and royal houses.

5. Review finding
That citation is important. It shows that Gary Wayne is knowingly using the Ring Lords/Grail kingship field. However, the concern remains that the wider Dragon/Anunnaki/Ring Lord/divine-right framework also strongly overlaps with Nicholas de Vere's work.

A Gardner citation may explain part of the visible source trail, but it does not remove the need to recognise Nicholas de Vere's related Dragon Court framework where the same symbolic architecture appears.

If Gary Wayne uses the Ring Lords / Nippur / divine-right kingship framework inside a hostile Antichrist and Rephaim bloodline narrative, this should be recorded as selective attribution and hostile recharacterisation.

CHAPTER 30

The Hittites

1. Material used

Unger's Dictionary suggests then that Hittites were non-Semitic and perhaps Aryan or at least in part Aryan via Indo-Europeans who brought their "harbinger Sanskrit language and religion with them."

2. Source-field comparison

No single source-field paragraph was isolated in the original draft. This chapter should therefore be treated cautiously as pattern evidence unless the final page references identify direct Nicholas de Vere, Laurence Gardner or Dragon Publishing material.

3. Attribution issue

No direct citation problem is isolated in this chapter from the current draft. The chapter is therefore best used as pattern evidence unless final footnotes show direct reliance, missing attribution, source displacement or inadequate citation.

4. Nature of the concern

The concern is assessed through the wider pattern rather than by one isolated phrase: whether the chapter borrows structure, citation chains, terminology or source-field architecture in a way that goes beyond ordinary quotation or scholarship.

5. Review finding

Unger's Dictionary suggests then that Hittites were non-Semitic and perhaps Aryan or at least in part Aryan via Indo-Europeans who brought their "harbinger Sanskrit language and religion with them."

Scythians were renowned in polytheist circles as a "sept of the Aryans," "the noble tribe," or the "Royal Scythians." A "sept" is otherwise understood as a clan and was a symbol of royal bloodline descent reflected in the above titles.

"The Hur syllable in Hurrian has been asserted by scholars, including George Contenau (La Civilisation des Hittites et des Hurrites de Mitanni) to be Har or Ar, indicating the Hurrians like the Scythians were Aryans, that venerated 'an Aryan Vedic royal-sacral family of gods. They bestowed these upon the Hittites whose culture they dominated.'"

CHAPTER 33 REVIEW —
The Horim Elvin Bloodline

1. Material used
Chapter 33: Gary Wayne directly cites Nicholas de Vere for the Tuadhe d'Anu / Daouine Sidhe / Fairies / Dragons / Elves / Anunnaki Watchers framework, while also citing Gardner's Realm of the Ring Lords. But Gardner's Ring Lords material is itself tied to Nicholas de Vere's earlier Dragon Legacy source-field, so the Gardner citations may disguise rather than remove De Vere reliance. Gary then recasts this Dragon-Elven source-field as a Horim/Edomite/Rephaim/Antichrist bloodline, making Chapter 33 one of the strongest examples of direct reliance, source displacement and hostile recharacterisation.

The chapter is not simply a Biblical discussion of the Horim, Horites, Mount Seir, Edom, Esau, Eliphaz or Timna. Gary Wayne uses those subjects to construct a wider bloodline framework involving Horim, Rephaim, hairy Watchers, satyrs, Seir, Edomite dukes, Eliphaz, Timna, Amalek, Gardner's Fairy/Dragon/Ring/Grail culture, Nicholas de Vere's Tuadhe d'Anu / Daouine Sidhe / Dragon / Elf / Anunnaki framework, Albi-Gens, Cathars, Templars, Merovingians, Arthurian bloodlines, Albion, Gog-Magog, Scythian Ring Lords and future Antichrist bloodline implications.

In Chapter 33, Gary Wayne builds an argument around:

2. Source-field comparison
According to Laurence Gardner, an adept and famous royal bloodline genealogist, the fairy precept was born directly from Dragon/Ring/Grail culture. Gardner added that fairies were the Shining Ones of the kingly, Cathar Elven race, the Albi-Gens descended from the Tuatha De Danann, Tuadhe d'Anu—the tribe of

Anu, parent god of the Anunnaki. De Vere documented that the Aryans and Scythians were the Taudhe d' Anu, the Daouine Sidhe, the tribe of Anu, the Fairies, Dragons, Elves, "Kings above kings," the Shining Ones, and the star children of the heavenly Anunnaki Watchers.

This is in bold all context from Nicholas de Vere and Laurence Gardner which much has been miscited.

xiv, citing Gardner, Realm of the Ring Lords, notes about the author: "Gardner was the past Master Mason of the United Grand Lodge of England for twenty years. He also held a plethora of other distinguished positions and titles. He was a noted prior of the Celtic church's Sacred Kindred of St. Columbia, Prior of the Knights Templar of St. Anthony, and internationally recognized as a sovereign and chivalric genealogist. Gardner was distinguished as the Chevalier Labaran de Saint Germain and was the Presidential Attaché to the European Council of Princes, all while being formally acknowledged as being attached to the Noble Household Guard of the Royal House of Stewart founded at St. Germain. Gardener was appointed Jacobite Historiographer Royal, a Fellow of the Society of Antiquities of Scotland, and a Professional Member of the Institute of Nana Technology. In addition to all this, Gardner was an attaché to the Grande Protectorate of the Imperial Dragon Court." 1419 Gardner, Realm of the Ring Lords, 30–31. 1420 De Vere, The Dragon Legacy, 32, 114. 1421 H5051—nogahh, no'-gah; brilliancy: brightness; light; shining. 1422 Gardner, Realm of the Ring Lords, 63, 226. 1423 Gardner, Realm of the Ring Lords, 103–115 and 64,

Gardner, Realm of the Ring Lords, 58. 1430 Gen 10:1–5. 1431 Rose, Giants, Monsters and Dragons, 11, 146, 187, citing Geoffrey of Monmouth (1100–1154),

3. Attribution issue
Gardner noted that Edomite marriages into the dukes of Edom was the nascence for the Tuatha D'Anu fairy kings (at least in part). The Lords of Anu were in this scenario were the lords of Edom. Gardner stated: "It is within their [Edomite] history that we find another root of the Elf distinction, for the members of this influential king-tribe were described in old biblical Hebrew as Elefs"—the Noble Elven Race. And: "The noble princes were the very race from whom the Tuadhe d'Anu fairy kings emerged." The Tuatha De Danann are renowned in the fairy mythos as the world's most noble race, alongside dynastic Egyptian kings. Gardner's archives of royal genealogies indicated to him that the word "fairy" is in part rooted in the word phare, or pharo, meaning pharaohs, of the House of Dragon: kings of fate, or fairy kings.

Gardner, Realm, 58. 1434 Gardner, Realm, 64–75. 1435 James Mackillop, Dictionary of Celtic Mythology (New York: Oxford University Press, 1998), 366–67: Tuatha De Danann. 1436 Ibid., 367: Tuatha De Danann. 1437 Ibid. 1438 Gardner, Grail Kings, 315. 1439 Laurence Gardner, Lost Secrets of the Sacred Ark (London: Harper Element, 2003), 229. 1440 Gardner, Grail Kings, 315. 1441 Ibid. 1442 Ibid. 1443 https://www.etymonline.com/search?q=albi; https://etymologeek.com/ron/albi/90876344.

Chapter 33, titled "The Horim Elvin Bloodline," is a strong chapter for evidence of framework reliance, direct source overlap, selective attribution and hostile recharacterisation.

Horim and Horites; Mount Seir; Edom; Esau; hairy, pale and red-haired giant-like peoples; Seir as a hairy goat or satyr-linked figure; Watcher language; degraded hairy Watchers; Pan and Azazel; Atlantean giants; Scythians, Tuatha Dé Danann and Celts as pale, fair-haired

Aryan survivors; Edomite dukes; Eliphaz and Timna; Amalek; Laurence Gardner's Fairy/Dragon/Ring/Grail culture; Nicholas de Vere's Tuadhe d'Anu / Dragon / Elf / Anunnaki framework; Albi-Gens and Elven bloodlines; Pharaohs and House of Dragon; Scythian Ring Lords; Fir Bolg, Milesians and Tuatha Dé Danann; Cathars, Templars, Merovingians and Arthurian lines; Albion, Albina, Gog and Magog; Horim and Edomite royal dynasties; Hadad, Baal and Aramaean kingship; and Herod as later Edomite product of the same bloodline field.

4. Nature of the concern
With this amount of work, paragraphs used this is not fair use.

This is a full Dragon/Elven royal-bloodline chapter recast through a hostile Rephaim/Horim/Edomite lens.

The chapter therefore cannot be treated as independent Biblical interpretation. Gary Wayne is directly using Nicholas de Vere's Dragon/Elven/Anunnaki framework and placing it into a hostile chapter titled "The Horim Elvin Bloodline."

Gary Wayne's note on Gardner's credentials should be separately flagged as a source reliability issue.

5. Review finding
Preliminary assessment

Chapter 33 should be recorded as a strong direct-reliance and hostile-recharacterisation chapter.

It directly uses Nicholas de Vere's Dragon/Elven/Anunnaki framework while also relying on Gardner's Ring/Grail/Fairy material. It then reframes that source-field as the Horim Elvin bloodline, tied to

Rephaim, Edom, Amalek, Albion, Gog-Magog and Antichrist implications.

CHAPTER 34 REVIEW

The Amaleqim and Agagite Bloodline

1. Material used

Daughters of Dragon kings with pure matriarchal dragon blood in antiquity were wedded to kings to propagate new fairy dynasties.

2. Source-field comparison

No single source-field paragraph was isolated in the original draft. This chapter should therefore be treated cautiously as pattern evidence unless the final page references identify direct Nicholas de Vere, Laurence Gardner or Dragon Publishing material.

3. Attribution issue

The notion that Timna and Eliphaz dwelled among Amaleqim giants is consistent with Scripture and was likely the inspiration for naming their son patronymically after `Amaleq, the likely patriarch for the Amaleqim. However, the patronymic king title for the royal hybrid house was memorialized in the name Agag, not Amalek, for the new fairy dynasty. Thus, Duke Amalek was the twelfth and uniquely ennobled Elef/Elvin king of Edom Gardner was alluding to, versus Esau as the twelfth, because Esau the patriarch was of pure human stock as son of Isaac and Rebekah. Cited as Genisis 1504 Gen 25:19–27.

4. Nature of the concern

The concern is assessed through the wider pattern rather than by one isolated phrase: whether the chapter borrows structure, citation chains, terminology or source-field architecture in a way that goes beyond ordinary quotation or scholarship.

5. Review finding

The notion that Timna and Eliphaz dwelled among Amaleqim giants is consistent with Scripture and was likely the inspiration for naming their son patronymically after `Amaleq, the likely patriarch for the Amaleqim. However, the patronymic king title for the royal hybrid house was memorialized in the name Agag, not Amalek, for the new fairy dynasty. Thus, Duke Amalek was the twelfth and uniquely ennobled Elef/Elvin king of Edom Gardner was alluding to, versus Esau as the twelfth, because Esau the patriarch was of pure human stock as son of Isaac and Rebekah. Cited as Genisis 1504 Gen 25:19–27.

Genisis does not mention Elvin /Elven kings

The chapters in between heavily lift of the bible.

CHAPTER 42 REVIEW —
The Philistine Military Complex

1. Material used
The section titled "The Philistine Military Complex" raises another clear concern of citation laundering, self-citation, source displacement and hostile framework reliance.

Gary Wayne builds the Philistine section around:

Gary Wayne uses the Philistine military complex to continue the same hidden-bloodline method seen in earlier chapters.

2. Source-field comparison
Gary cites his own previous work, The Genesis 6 Conspiracy, which in turn cites Laurence Gardner's Realm of the Ring Lords. Gardner's Realm of the Ring Lords is itself tied to Nicholas de Vere's earlier Dragon Legacy source-field.

Instead of citing the underlying Dragon / Ring Lords / Sidhe source-field directly, Gary cites his own earlier book. That earlier book cites Gardner. Gardner's Ring Lords material is not separate from Nicholas de Vere's Dragon Legacy material.

Nicholas de Vere / Dragon Legacy source-field; then Gardner / Realm of the Ring Lords; then Gary Wayne's earlier book, The Genesis 6 Conspiracy; then Gary Wayne's later Philistine chapter citing himself.

That chain matters because the framework survives through the layers while the visible citation moves further away from Nicholas de Vere.

3. Attribution issue
The concern is that this framework is not fully explained by the immediate Biblical and historical citations. It belongs to the same

layered Dragon / Ring Lords / Scythian / Sidhe / Rephaim source-field that appears repeatedly throughout Gary Wayne's work.

The result is a layered citation trail that can make the material look like Gary's own independent framework, when the underlying architecture still belongs to the Gardner / De Vere / Dragon Legacy source-field.

This should be recorded as citation laundering or source displacement.

The visible citation trail can be summarised as:

4. Nature of the concern
One of the clearest source-field markers in this section is the reference to Bethshean / Scythopolis as the "House of Power" and "House of Sidhe."

This is a clear example of source displacement. The phrase belongs to the same Scythian / Sidhe / Ring Lords field repeatedly associated with Gardner and Nicholas de Vere. By citing his own earlier work, Gary places himself between the reader and the underlying source-field.

This should be treated as a repeated pattern, not an isolated footnote issue.

He treats ordinary national and military history as evidence of hidden Rephaim, Anakim, Avvim, Hyksos, Indo-Aryan and Cretan bloodline alliances. The Philistine pentapolis becomes not merely a military confederacy, but a hybrid network of fortress cities tied to ancient Rephaim kingship and iron-age power.

5. Review finding
The key concern is that Gary cites himself for material that itself points back to Gardner and the Ring Lords tradition, which is tied to Nicholas de Vere's Dragon Legacy source-field.

This is another example of source displacement through self-citation.

Chapters 43 – 58 again heavily lift off the bible

CHAPTER 58 REVIEW —
Pharaoh and Beast Empires

1. Material used
Chapter 58, titled "Pharaoh and Beast Empires," raises another strong concern of self-citation, citation laundering, source displacement and hostile recharacterisation.

The chapter is not simply a discussion of Matthew 24, Daniel, Revelation, Ezekiel 29, Ezekiel 32, Pharaoh, Babylon or end-time prophecy. Gary Wayne uses these prophetic passages to construct a wider framework involving Egypt as the first beast empire, Pharaoh as a Dragon or sea-serpent figure, the Houses of Dragon, Rephaim kings, the Terrible Ones, Leviathan, Tiamat, the Hydra Dragon, Azazel, Khem, the Goat of Mendes, Rosicrucianism, alchemy, fallen Watchers, satyrs, the abyss and Antichrist typology.

Nicholas de Vere's Dragon Cede framework directly contains Khem, Pan, Leviathan and Dragon genealogy material. Gary Wayne uses a comparable field but frames it through Azazel, fallen Watchers, Goat of Mendes, degraded angels, satyrs, abyss imprisonment and Antichrist prophecy.

2. Source-field comparison
This is highly relevant because those themes overlap with Nicholas de Vere's Dragon / Khem / Enki / Pan / Leviathan / Egyptian Dragon Court source-field.

2866 Wayne, Genesis 6 Conspiracy, 685–686, citing Gardner, Lost Secrets, 88; Gardner, Grail Kings, 219; Gardner, Realm of the Ring Lords, 133; Collins,

Gary Wayne again cites his own previous book, The Genesis 6 Conspiracy, for material that itself cites Laurence Gardner's Lost

Secrets of the Sacred Ark, Genesis of the Grail Kings, and Realm of the Ring Lords, alongside Andrew Collins.

The later chapter appears to cite Gary Wayne as the authority. However, the earlier Gary Wayne work is itself built on Gardner and related Dragon/Grail/Ring Lords material. Gardner's Realm of the Ring Lords is also tied to Nicholas de Vere's earlier Dragon Legacy source-field.

3. Attribution issue
This creates a layered citation problem.

The visible citation therefore moves progressively away from Nicholas de Vere, while the underlying framework remains within the Dragon / Ring Lords / Khem / Grail source-field.

This should be recorded as citation laundering or source displacement.

Nicholas de Vere / Dragon Legacy / Dragon Cede source-field; then Gardner's Ring Lords / Grail Kings / Sacred Ark material; then Gary Wayne's earlier book, The Genesis 6 Conspiracy; then Gary Wayne's later Chapter 58 citing himself.

4. Nature of the concern
This is important because Gary is not merely citing himself for neutral historical background. He is citing himself for material involving Khem, Azazel, Goat of Mendes, alchemy, Rosicrucianism and Dragon/Leviathan prophetic symbolism.

Nicholas de Vere's work contains the directly relevant source-field.

The strongest source-field marker in Chapter 58 is the Goat of Mendes section.

Pharaoh as Dragon / House of Dragon issue

5. Review finding
Preliminary assessment

Chapter 58 should be recorded as a strong source-displacement and hostile-recharacterisation chapter.

It is especially useful because the self-citation trail is visible and because the Goat of Mendes / Khem / Azazel section connects directly to the Dragon Cede framework of Khem, Pan, Leviathan, Egyptian pharaohs and Dragon royal descent.

CHAPTER 60 REVIEW —
The Mysterious Trees of Eden

1. Material used
Chapter 60, titled "The Mysterious Trees of Eden," raises another strong concern of self-citation, citation laundering, source displacement and hostile recharacterisation.

The chapter is not simply an exposition of Ezekiel 31, Eden, Pharaoh, the Assyrian cedar, trees, branches, the pit, Sheol, or end-time prophecy. Gary Wayne uses the tree imagery to build a wider framework involving oath-bound beast-empires, fallen Watchers, Mount Hermon, Rephaim branches, Terrible Ones, the pit/abyss, Satan as the greatest tree in Eden, cedars of Lebanon, oaks of Bashan, Tuatha Dé Danann tree symbolism, Fair Folk, Fairy People, fair branches, Albi-Gens, Shining Ones, Satanic covering imagery, and Antichrist-like figures.

Nicholas de Vere's work uses tree symbolism genealogically, especially where the Tree of Life is interpreted as a genealogical chart and connected to Elohim, Dragon Kings and Queens of the Anunnaki, family relationships and Dragon bloodline symbolism.

2. Source-field comparison
This is highly relevant because the chapter moves directly into the Tree / branch / fairy / Dragon / Rephaim symbolic field associated with Nicholas de Vere and the wider Dragon Legacy source tradition.

Gary Wayne cites his own previous book, The Genesis 6 Conspiracy, for tree, Celtic, branch and related symbolic material. That previous book cites Laurence Gardner's Realm of the Ring Lords, along with other fairy and Celtic sources.

Instead of clearly exposing the underlying Ring Lords / Dragon Legacy / fairy-bloodline source-field, Gary cites his own earlier book. The earlier book then points to Gardner. Gardner's Realm of the Ring Lords is itself tied to Nicholas de Vere's earlier Dragon Legacy material.

Nicholas de Vere / Dragon Legacy source-field; then Gardner / Realm of the Ring Lords; then Gary Wayne's earlier book, The Genesis 6 Conspiracy; then Gary Wayne's later Chapter 60 citing himself.

3. Attribution issue
This creates another source-distance problem.

This should be recorded as another example of citation laundering or source displacement.

This matters because the visible citation becomes Gary Wayne, but the conceptual architecture underneath remains within the Gardner / De Vere / Dragon Legacy field.

However, those citations do not fully explain the wider framework:

4. Nature of the concern
The method is similar. The interpretation is hostile.

The clearest source-field marker in Chapter 60 is Gary's movement from trees of Eden and cedars/oaks into the Tuatha Dé Danann, Bile, Fair Folk and Fairy People.

That is a hostile reclassification of the fairy / Dragon / Elven source-field.

Eden tree as Satan / covering cherub issue

5. Review finding
Chapter 60 should be recorded as a strong source-displacement and hostile-framework chapter.

It shows Gary Wayne again citing his own earlier work, while that earlier work cites Gardner's Ring Lords material. The chapter then uses tree, branch, Fairy, Tuatha Dé Danann, Albi-Gens and Shining Ones material inside a hostile Rephaim / Satan / beast empire / Antichrist framework.

The chapter should be classed as evidence of self-citation laundering, source displacement, framework reliance and hostile recharacterisation.

CHAPTER 65 REVIEW

The King of Jerusalem Title

1. Material used
Chapter 65, titled "The King of Jerusalem Title," is one of the strongest chapters for direct reliance, self-citation laundering, source displacement and hostile recharacterisation.

The chapter is not simply a prophecy discussion about 2 Thessalonians, Antichrist, Daniel, Jerusalem, Melchizedek or the abomination of desolation. Gary Wayne uses those subjects to construct a hostile bloodline framework involving divine right, unicorn heraldry, Stuart kingship, Rex Deus bloodlines, Sion/Zion double entendre, King of Jerusalem succession, Templars, Priory of Sion, Anjou, de Bouillon, de Payen, Sinclair/St Clair, Baphomet, Samael the Dragon, Pendragon, Mithras, Khem, Leviathan, Planta-genista, Quinotaur, Meroveus, Dragon/Elvin Antichrist and future rival Antichrist bloodlines.

Gary then uses that material in a hostile Templar / Baphomet / Antichrist bloodline structure. He identifies Baphomet with Samael the Dragon, the Head Dragon and Pendragon, and places this inside a chapter about the King of Jerusalem title and future Antichrist claims.

2. Source-field comparison
This chapter directly overlaps with Nicholas de Vere's Dragon/Anjou/Vere/Templar/Baphomet/Dragon bloodline source-field.

The later chapter appears to use Gary Wayne as the authority. However, the earlier work is itself built on Gardner, and Gardner's Realm of the Ring Lords is tied to Nicholas de Vere's earlier Dragon

Legacy material. Therefore, the later self-citation does not make the material independent.

Nicholas de Vere / Dragon Legacy source-field; then Gardner / Ring Lords / Grail Kings / Bloodline material; then Gary Wayne's earlier book, The Genesis 6 Conspiracy; then Gary Wayne's later Chapter 65 citing himself.

This is directly relevant to Nicholas de Vere's Dragon/Anjou/Vere framework. Gary is not simply discussing medieval Jerusalem. He is discussing a Dragon/Elvin hereditary claim through the very families and mythic structures associated with Nicholas de Vere's work.

3. Attribution issue
Gary Wayne again cites his own earlier book, The Genesis 6 Conspiracy, for material that itself cites Gardner and other Grail/Templar/Rex Deus sources.

This creates the now-repeated source-distance problem.

Gary cites De Vere directly in this chapter for Baphomet material. The same field appears in The Dragon Legacy: Baphomet with goat head, Swan wings, Dragon torso, Khem, Leviathan, serpents of Hermes, alchemical Solve et Coagula, Grail symbolism, and Chem-Zoroaster.

Gary Wayne's footnotes include direct citations to De Vere, Gardner, Laidler, Knight and Lomas, Sora, Addison, William of Tyre and his own earlier book.

4. Nature of the concern
This is not ordinary eschatology. It is a hostile Dragon/Grail/Templar bloodline accusation chapter.

Baphomet / Samael / Dragon / Pendragon issue

This is not neutral quotation. It is hostile incorporation of Nicholas de Vere's Baphomet/Dragon framework.

This is one of the clearest hostile associations in the whole review.

5. Review finding
Chapter 65 should be recorded as one of the strongest chapters.

It directly ties Dragon/Elvin bloodline material to Antichrist pedigree and the King of Jerusalem title. It uses Anjou, Vere, Melusine, Melisende, Baldwin II, Plantagenet, Order of Sion, Templars, Baphomet, Samael the Dragon, Pendragon, Khem, Leviathan and Merovingian material inside a hostile end-time framework.

It also repeats the same source-displacement pattern: Gary cites himself; his earlier work cites Gardner; Gardner's Ring Lords material is tied to Nicholas de Vere's Dragon Legacy source file.

CHAPTER 66 REVIEW
THE ELVIN HOUSES OF VERE, ANJOU, AND PLANTAGENET

1. Material used
Cites NDV so much so that de Bouillon was coronated with the "crown of fairy thorns" that represented Duke Godfrey's alleged Elvin bloodline from the Merovingians, Cited Devere over 26 times in this one chapter alone.

Godfrey de Bouillon held Anjou bloodlines from the kings of Lorraine, via the Vere bloodline. The house of Vere had previously left Anjou and the Comite of Anjou circa AD 800. The house of Vere was one of the branches of the Angevin dynasties but was not the senior branch; it was a junior branch that extended out of the first of three houses of Anjou. The Vere coat of arms contained a field of red and gold symbolizing the phoenix, superimposed by a white star that symbolized ascending to the throne of the world. When supported by two dragons, the coat of arms becomes the official seal of the house. Red and gold colors accompanied the coat of arms of the Merovingians, Plantagenet, Spencer, Mandeville, and the Jacobite house of Scotland. Godfrey de Vere de Bouillon was further ennobled with royal bloodlines that descended from an ancient bloodline, from the "Ancient Royal Doctrine" as an Elvin king. The house of de Vere traces their royal ancestry back to the Merovingians and allegedly includes the Davidic bloodline scioned into the Tuatha De Danann royalty, the tribes of d' Anu, which in part is patronymic in the first syllable of the Anjou.

the pure form of grail is San Greal, meaning "royal bloodline," and to others, Sang Real, again meaning "royal blood." According to Rex Deus genealogist Laurence Gardner, the "Grail" always secretly represented the royal bloodline, the Messianic Sang Real of Judah, and not the chalice we are all familiar with. The Priory of Sion further insisted that Holy Grail and Arthurian tales encrypted the genealogy to the royal bloodline of Mary Magdalene and Jesus, descending through the Merovingian dynasty. Grail literature was patronized by Rex Deus houses and the Knights Templar, and that the Holy Grail, the Sangreal bloodline, housed the secrets to the Kings of God dynasty. The "Grail Code" observed by grail kings like the Knights of the Round Table, the Knights Templar, and the Elvin royals maintained a "behavioural manifestation" "devoted to a 'particular form of consciousness,'" a divine essence attuned to a specific organization working toward a common good and agenda. This harmonious consciousness participation required a "Hive Mind—a collective consciousness—or at least a heightened capacity toward sensitivity and the anticipation of the needs of all within the genome.. .. Without the 'Hive Mind' (symbolized in the Dragon Dynasty by the Merovingian Bee, t

2. Source-field comparison
De Vere, The Dragon Legacy, 15, 112, 120, 121. 3187 Ibid., 3, 16. 3188 Ibid., 3–4. 3189 Ibid., 32, 121. 3190 Ibid., 21, 340. 3191 Baigent, Laurence Gardner, Bloodline of the Holy Grail (Rockport, MA: Element Books Inc., 1996), 147, 164, 236. 3193 De Vere, The Dragon Legacy, 84. 3194

417–427; De Vere, The Dragon Legacy, 79.

De Vere, The Dragon Legacy, 79. 3207 De Vere, The Dragon Legacy, 270. 3208 Ibid., 79.

De Vere, The Dragon Legacy, 16, 120, 121. 3236 Ibid., 120. 3237 De Vere, The Dragon Legacy, 120. 3238 276–277;

3. Attribution issue
So yes: based on the uploaded material, this is not just "he cited Nicholas de Vere." There are passages where Gary's wording and structure appear to track The Dragon Legacy closely enough that you can put them into a formal comparison schedule.

In the Gary extract, his footnotes repeatedly cite The Dragon Legacy, Gardner, Baigent/Leigh/Lincoln, Markale, William of Tyre, etc., but I have not yet seen him cite The Dragon Cede in the extract. His footnotes shown around this chapter cite The Dragon Legacy several times, but the search for "Dragon Cede" in the Gary document did not bring up a Gary citation to The Dragon Cede; it returned the Dragon Cede file itself instead.

"The chapter appears to contain material overlapping with The Dragon Cede, while the citations supplied in the extract point to The Dragon Legacy and other authors, not The Dragon Cede."

That is safer than saying absolutely "he never cited it" until we check the whole bibliography.

4. Nature of the concern
This is important because it is not merely "both books mention Anjou." It is the same genealogical architecture.

That is a strong "framework borrowing" point.

Gary's extract then uses that same vocabulary and structure while placing it inside his own hostile Antichrist/Rex Deus framing. That supports your argument that he is not merely making a casual reference; he is building from the terminology and internal logic of the work.

3. Structural reliance The same genealogical-historical framework appears: Vere of Anjou, Maelasanu/Melusine, Tuatha de Danaan, Sobekh, Davidic/Merovingian bloodline, Plantagenets as junior branch, Societas Draconis, Dragon Court.

QUICK COMPARISON TABLE

Issue	Gary Wayne extract	Nicholas de Vere source	Type
Grail Code / Hive Mind	Uses "Hive Mind—a collective consciousness …" and "needs of all within the genome"	Same wording and structure in The Dragon Legacy	Near-direct textual overlap
Bee / Royal Jelly / Dergflaith	Uses bees, Sovereign, Royal Jelly, previous Queen, Danann, Elvin King Tribes	Same passage in The Dragon Legacy	Near-direct textual overlap
Vere arms	Red/gold Phoenix, white star, throne of the world, two dragons	Same symbolic constructio n in frontispiec e	Distinctive expression/symbol ic arrangement
Vere-Anjou-Plantagenet	Vere left Anjou c.800, Plantagenets junior branch	Same genealogica l structure	Structural reliance
Dragon Court/Societ as Draconis	Sigismund, Maelasanu, Sobekh, Tuatha de Danaan, Vere of Anjou	Same framework in The Dragon Legacy	Framework borrowing

5. Review finding
The strongest similarities to The Dragon Cede are:

Gary's chapter appears to rely not only on The Dragon Legacy, but also on the distinctive genealogical structure and House of Vere material set out in The Dragon Cede. Yet the citations visible in the Gary extract refer to The Dragon Legacy and other sources, not The Dragon Cede.

The original source material has been scraped from a number of places, Firstly to use a comparison I will add this material here now.

CHAPTER 67 REVIEW — THE DRAGON KINGDOM OF HEAVEN

1. Material used
Chapter 67, titled "The Dragon Kingdom of Heaven," is a major framework chapter and should be treated as direct reliance, source displacement, hostile recharacterisation and evidential confirmation of the wider pattern.

This chapter does not merely discuss Anjou, medieval France, the Kingdom of Jerusalem, Fulk V, Baldwin, the Lusignans, Lorraine, Hungary, the Double Cross or Templar history. Gary Wayne uses those historical materials to construct a wider Dragon/Elvin royal-bloodline framework involving the House of Vere, Anjou, Plantagenet, Royal Scythians, Tuatha Dé Danann, Fairies, Shining Ones, Elvens, Lords of Anu, Dragon/Fairy genes, Albi-Gens, Rh-negative blood, divine-right kingship, King of Jerusalem title claims, Dragon kingdoms, the Cross of Lorraine, Sigismund, Dragon kingship and the eventual world-monarch / Antichrist structure.

The Angevin province was the source name accepted by its ruling French family, who established the dukes of Angiers and the first house of Anjou in the ninth century AD with Fulk I Anjou, circa 888–938. The royal houses of Vere, likely from the royal Latin Verus and/or royal Pictish Vere families, was begat by King Vere of Anjou de Vere (c. 659–704) and his Dragon Queen Melusine (685–714).

2. Source-field comparison
This is not independent medieval history. It is the Dragon Legacy / Dragon Cede / House of Vere source-field being rebuilt inside Gary Wayne's hostile prophetic structure.

3258 Gardner, Realm, 58, 324–325, 355–364; De Vere, The Dragon Legacy, 12–127, 340. 3

3261 De Vere, The Dragon Legacy, 115, 120.

3266 De Vere, The Dragon Legacy, 1, 32, 109. 3267 Ibid., 36–37. 3268 Gardner, Grail Kings, 219.

3. Attribution issue
Without having to copy every single paragraphs, to a person like myself who has grown up with this material all my life, I know what is dads work and what is not, The amount of citations show the truth, likewise with using the etymology framework.

3256 Gardner, Realm, 58, 324–325, 355–364.

259 Gardner, Realm, 55–58, 324–325, 355–364; http://www.houseofvere.com/ver.htm.

3https://www.etymonline.com/search?q=albi; https://etymologeek.com/ron/albi/90876344; De Vere, The Dragon Legacy, 120; Websters: Hoar; Dictionary.com: hoary. 3273 De Vere, The Dragon Legacy, 120; Gardner, Realm, 315. #

4. Nature of the concern
This is not just a history of Anjou. It is Gary Wayne's hostile version of the Dragon Kingdom.

Nicholas de Vere's work and House of Vere material concern the House of Vere, Dragon blood, Royal Dragon Court, Anunnaki, Elven Kings, Ring Lords, Scythian descent, Tuatha Dé Danann, divine-right kingship, Anjou/Vere descent, Dragon queens and kings, and the Dragon lineage as a hereditary royal structure.

Therefore, when Gary cites Gardner for Anjou, Dragon, Ring Lords, Elven, Tuatha Dé Danann, Scythian or Grail material, the citation may still be passing through Nicholas de Vere's source-field.

Nicholas de Vere / Dragon Legacy / Dragon Cede / House of Vere source-field; then Gardner / Realm of the Ring Lords; then Gary Wayne's earlier book or later chapters; then Gary Wayne's expanded hostile framework.

5. Review finding
It demonstrates that Gary Wayne is not merely quoting Nicholas de Vere. He is reconstructing the Dragon Legacy / Dragon Cede / House of Vere framework across multiple chapters and reframing it as Antichrist prophecy.

Chapter 67 should be marked as:

direct framework reliance; source displacement through Gardner; citation scaffolding; substantial use of House of Vere material; hostile recharacterisation; and rebuttal evidence against the publisher's "one citation / fair use" claim.

CHAPTER 68 REVIEW
THE NEW TEMPLARS

1. Material used
In bold are extracts that Wayne has used in his chapter that are direct citation word for word from Garnder and NDV

2. Source-field comparison
3355 Gardner, Realm of the Ring Lords, xvii, 242; De Vere, The Dragon Legacy, 16. 3356 Gardner, Grail Kings, 313;

3357 De Vere, The Dragon Legacy, 15. 3358 Ibid., 16.

3359 Gardner, Realm of the Ring Lords, xvii, 242 3360 Ibid.; De Vere, The Dragon Legacy, 15–16. 3361 Gardner, Grail Kings, 316. 3362 De Vere, The Dragon Legacy, 16–17. 3363 Gardner, Realm of the Ring Lords, 242. 3364 Baigent, Leigh, and Lincoln, Holy Blood and Holy Grail, 443–445. 3371

The chapter presents the Templar/Rosicrucian/Dragon Court structure as part of a Nephilim or Antichrist world-order system. This is a hostile recharacterisation of material that belongs to the Nicholas de Vere / Dragon Legacy / Dragon Cede / Royal Dragon Court source-field.

3. Attribution issue
The chapter is especially important because Gary Wayne does not merely cite Nicholas de Vere once. In the footnotes attached to this section, he directly cites The Dragon Legacy several times, while also citing Laurence Gardner's Realm of the Ring Lords and Grail Kings around the same House of Vere / Dragon Court / Anu / Tuatha Dé Danann / Angiers / Sobek / Merovingian material.

The direct reliance is shown where Gary Wayne cites The Dragon Legacy.

The indirect reliance is shown where he cites Gardner's Realm of the Ring Lords, because Gardner's Ring Lords material is itself tied to Nicholas de Vere's earlier Dragon Legacy / From Transylvania to Tunbridge Wells source-field.

The chapter therefore strengthens the argument that Gary Wayne's use of Nicholas de Vere's work is structural, repeated and central to his book. It is not incidental, and it cannot be dismissed as one citation or fair dealing.

4. Nature of the concern
Nicholas de Vere / Dragon Publishing source-field:

This chapter is not independent Christian commentary on the Templars. It is a hostile reconstruction of the Dragon Legacy / Royal Dragon Court framework using Nicholas de Vere's own material, Gardner's related material, and Gary Wayne's biblical-prophecy framing.

The result is commercial use of the House of Vere / Dragon Court source-field while presenting that field as part of a Nephilim, Antichrist, New Babylon and world-government conspiracy.

This is source displacement, structural reliance and hostile recharacterisation.

5. Review finding
This chapter is not independent Christian commentary on the Templars. It is a hostile reconstruction of the Dragon Legacy / Royal Dragon Court framework using Nicholas de Vere's own material,

Gardner's related material, and Gary Wayne's biblical-prophecy framing.

The result is commercial use of the House of Vere / Dragon Court source-field while presenting that field as part of a Nephilim, Antichrist, New Babylon and world-government conspiracy.

This is source displacement, structural reliance and hostile recharacterisation.

CHAPTER 69 THE THELEMIC TREE

Chapter 69 Comparison Note — "The Thelemic Tree"

1. Material used

Chapter 69 should be treated as a significant structural comparison chapter.

The chapter is relevant because it uses tree symbolism not only as religious metaphor, but as genealogy, hierarchy and inherited spiritual power.

This chapter should be linked back to the earlier "Mysterious Trees of Eden" chapter and to all chapters where Gary Wayne uses Dragon, Grail, Tree of Life, Ordo Draconis, Templar, Rosicrucian and royal bloodline material.

2. Source-field comparison

This overlaps with the Nicholas de Vere / Dragon Legacy / Dragon Cede source-field, where the Dragon bloodline, Grail, Tree of Life, sacred genealogy, royal descent, hidden transmission and esoteric Dragon symbolism are part of the same larger framework.

Nicholas de Vere / Dragon Publishing source-field:

This chapter strengthens the argument that Gary Wayne is not simply quoting isolated material. He is absorbing and reworking the symbolic architecture of the Dragon Legacy / Dragon Cede field.

The tree is used as a structure for genealogy, authority, secret transmission and spiritual inheritance. That is central to Nicholas de Vere's Dragon/Grail/bloodline framework.

3. Attribution issue

No direct citation problem is isolated in this chapter from the current draft. The chapter is therefore best used as pattern evidence unless final footnotes show direct reliance, missing attribution, source displacement or inadequate citation.

4. Nature of the concern
Gary Wayne's version is hostile. He reframes the tree/genealogy/Dragon/Grail field as a Thelemic, Nephilim, Rephaim, Hades-rooted, secret-society and Antichrist structure.

Gary Wayne then converts that architecture into a hostile biblical-prophecy narrative involving Nephilim, Rephaim, Hades, secret societies, Babylon, Antichrist and world government.

structural reliance; symbolic borrowing; hostile recharacterisation; genealogical reframing; and continued use of Dragon/Grail/Tree of Life material within an Antichrist narrative.

5. Review finding
This is relevant to the wider complaint because it shows:

structural reliance; symbolic borrowing; hostile recharacterisation; genealogical reframing; and continued use of Dragon/Grail/Tree of Life material within an Antichrist narrative.

This chapter should be linked back to the earlier "Mysterious Trees of Eden" chapter and to all chapters where Gary Wayne uses Dragon, Grail, Tree of Life, Ordo Draconis, Templar, Rosicrucian and royal bloodline material.

CHAPTER 70 THE JESUITS

"Chapter 70 does not merely discuss Jesuits. It extends the Dragon Legacy conflict between Church power, false kingship, Templar structures, hidden bloodlines and royal legitimacy into a hostile Jesuit/Hapsburg/New Babylon framework. This is a continuation of the same source-field, recoded through Gary Wayne's Antichrist narrative."

1. Material used

One might anticipate a royal bloodline and heraldry like the ennobled house of Stuart, which boasted the unification of Rex Deus bloodlines from the Merovingians, the Dalriada dynasties of Tara in Ireland, the Celtic Camelot dynasty of Wales, Norse bloodlines from Rollo via the de Bruce and Saint Claire houses, David and Saul's bloodlines, as well as alleged bloodlines from Jesus and Mary Magdalene via the Celtic and Merovingian dynasties. The Stuart bloodline, the heraldic "House of Unicorn," commingled with so many Rex Deus bloodlines that they were regarded as the most ennobled bloodline of their era.

It is not as directly House-of-Vere centred as the chapters on the Elvin Houses of Vere, Anjou and Plantagenet, or The Dragon Kingdom of Heaven. However, it continues the same architecture: Templars, Rosicrucians, royal bloodlines, Church power, hidden orders, Dragon Court-adjacent structures, Hapsburgs, Borgia/Borja, Montesa, Vatican authority, banking, New World control and world-government prophecy.

2. Source-field comparison

Dad's version: the Church and Church-backed establishment suppressed, distorted, mocked and displaced the older Dragon/Grail royal heritage. The Dragon Legacy explicitly says the Church and establishment attempted to eclipse the pure origins and sovereign status of the Royal House of Vere, and that authorities twisted or concealed truth to control information.

The relevance to Nicholas de Vere's work is structural.

Nicholas de Vere's Dragon Legacy / Dragon Cede field already presents the Roman Church and Church-backed establishments as forces that suppressed, distorted or fraudulently displaced the older Dragon / Grail / royal bloodline tradition. Nicholas's work also lays out Societas Draconis, Sigismund, Luxembourg, Anjou, Melusine, the Dragon Court, Egyptian and Scythian inheritance, Templar connections, the Albigensian Cross, Inner Temple structure and Vere Grand Masters.

Nicholas de Vere / Dragon Publishing source-field

3. Attribution issue
Having reviewed Gary Wayne's chapters in context against Nicholas de Vere's The Dragon Legacy, The Dragon Cede, the Royal Dragon Court material, the House of Vere material, and associated Dragon Publishing source-field, my conclusion is that this is not a case of one isolated citation, one passing reference, or ordinary disagreement between authors.

The publisher's position that Nicholas de Vere was cited only once does not answer the evidence. Even if that claim were numerically correct in one narrow sense, it would still ignore the wider source-chain. Gary Wayne also cites Laurence Gardner repeatedly, including works whose Ring Lords and Grail material are themselves tied to Nicholas de Vere's earlier Dragon Legacy source-field. Gary Wayne also cites his own earlier work, which in turn cites Gardner and related De Vere-linked material. This creates a source-displacement problem.

substantial reliance on the Nicholas de Vere / Dragon Publishing source-field; direct and indirect citation-chain reliance; source displacement through Gardner and Gary Wayne's own earlier work; commercial use of a distinctive research framework; hostile recharacterisation of the Dragon Legacy material; reputational harm to the living continuation of Nicholas de Vere's work; and character or bloodline assassination by association.

This is why the issue cannot be reduced to "fair use" or "one citation."

4. Nature of the concern
Gary's version: he takes that same conflict pattern and says these orders are not suppressing the Dragon line because they fear it; rather, they are part of a satanic/Nephilim/Antichrist New Babylon machine.

This chapter should be treated as a supporting structural chapter within the wider Gary Wayne comparison.

This chapter shows Gary Wayne continuing the same pattern of hostile expansion.

That matters because it shows that Gary's use of the Nicholas de Vere source-field is not confined to the explicit House of Vere chapters. The same architecture continues into later institutional history.

5. Review finding
De Vere, Nicholas. The Dragon Legacy: The Secret History of an Ancient Bloodline. San Diego: The Book Tree,

Gardner, Laurence. Genesis of the Grail Kings. London: Bantam Press, 2000. Gardner, Laurence. Realm of the Ring Lords. Gloucester, MA: Fair Winds Press, 2003.

After thoughts Chapter 78

Example of Heavy Biblical Lifting Without Original Contribution

1. Material used

This is an example of extreme lifting from Biblical source material with little apparent originality. It comes from only one chapter, and it is not even the full citation list for that chapter.

In my opinion, the book begins to border on a work of indoctrination rather than education. It does not simply discuss Scripture; it repeatedly uses fear-based religious framing to tell the reader what to believe, what to reject, and who or what should be viewed as evil.

2. Source-field comparison

There are several methods at work in Wayne's books. One is the heavy use of Biblical material. Another is the use of citation trails that create an air of authority. Another is the borrowing or reframing of specialist material from source-fields such as Nicholas de Vere, Laurence Gardner, the Dragon Court, the Tuatha Dé Danann, the Anunnaki, and related bloodline frameworks.

The Bible is widely known. The Dragon Court is not. If listeners first encounter the Dragon Court through Wayne's hostile framing, and are told that it is evil, Antichrist, Nephilim, Rephaim, or Satanic, they may accept that without ever researching the original Nicholas de Vere material for themselves.

3. Attribution issue

I question this method of writing, and I also question the proofreaders, editors, and publishers who allow this kind of book to pass as robust scholarship. The method appears throughout Wayne's work: long passages of Biblical or public-domain material are gathered, rearranged, and heavily cited, creating the appearance of depth and scale.

In my view, this also pads the book. It gives the impression of a large, heavily researched work, when much of the structure relies on pre-existing material, extensive citation lists, and compilation.

4. Nature of the concern
This matters because Wayne's public image is reinforced through podcasts and interviews, where he often appears as the knowledgeable authority in the room. In some cases, especially where Biblical material is concerned, he may indeed be teaching hosts or listeners something they have not studied before.

The problem arises when that authority is used alongside misinformation, hostile reframing, or unattributed specialist material.

The remaining chapters continue in the same manner: extreme use of Biblical material concerning Satan, the Devil, the Antichrist, spiritual warfare, fear, obedience, and control.

5. Review finding
In my opinion, the book begins to border on a work of indoctrination rather than education. It does not simply discuss Scripture; it repeatedly uses fear-based religious framing to tell the reader what to believe, what to reject, and who or what should be viewed as evil.

For readers already familiar with the Bible, myself included, this raises an obvious question: how many more books are needed that simply repackage Biblical material through fear, control, and end-times certainty?

Most people who have read the Bible do not need another Bible book. What they need is honest context, careful scholarship, and the freedom to question what they are being told.

Keyword Search Evidence from the Kindle Edition

As part of this review, I carried out keyword searches within the Kindle edition of Gary Wayne's later work and preserved screenshots of the search results as supporting evidence. These searches were not intended to prove copying by number alone. Their purpose was to show the scale and recurrence of the same source-field across the book.

The following keyword results were recorded:

"Dragon" — 225 results
"Vere" — 56 results
"Nicholas" — 6 results
"Dragon Legacy" — 37 results
"Realm" — 72 results
"Gardner" — 98 results
"Tuatha" — 37 results
"Melusine" — 5 results
"Anjou" — 75 results
"Elvin" — 25 results
"Elven" — 10 results
"Scythian" — 47 results
"Anu" — 49 results

These figures matter because they show that the relevant material is not confined to one isolated reference, one footnote, or one chapter. The repeated appearance of Dragon, Vere, Anjou, Scythian, Tuatha, Anu, Elvin/Elven, Gardner, Realm, and *The Dragon Legacy* demonstrates that Gary Wayne's argument repeatedly enters the same Dragon/Grail/Ring Lords/House of Vere source-field associated with Nicholas de Vere and Laurence Gardner.

This does not mean that every occurrence is automatically infringing. However, it does demonstrate scale, recurrence, and context. When these search results are read alongside the chapter structure, the footnotes, and the direct textual comparisons, they support the conclusion that the reliance is not incidental.

The issue is therefore not simply whether Nicholas de Vere is named a certain number of times. The issue is that Nicholas de Vere's source-field appears repeatedly through related names, terms, citations, genealogical structures, symbolic language, and bloodline concepts.

This is not a single-citation issue. It is a repeated source-chain issue.

One Screenshot of the amount of time Gardner has been used in the first book as an example. And likewise, Tuatha is mentioned 75 time, which shows the same pattern across both books.

gardner

456 results found

Page 17
Of the host of contemporary authors I employ in this work, Laurence Gardner stands out.

Page 17
Knights Templar of St. Anthony, and internationally recognized as a sovereign and chivalric genealogist.

Page 18
and a Professional Member of the Institute of Nana Technology. In addition to all this,

Page 65
not least, in Canaan. Similarly, the Ubaid culture of ancient southern Mesopotamia, a culture which

Page 86
hieroglyphs. This was the brick pillar mentioned earlier that contained the Archives of the Masons.

Page 86
then reconciled later as laterite, red, iron-based clay used for making bricks and road surfaces.

Page 100
Degree or Master Freemason, as the instructor of metal artificers from 3500 B.C.E. According to

Page 102
slandered and maligned by God and all His priests throughout history. Spurious organizations, according to

Page 108
course, no mention of this transfer of divine knowledge or any mention of Euclid. Laurence

Page 144
accusation against the lawless ones. Note Enoch's accusation of blood consumption in the above passage.

Page 182
Egyptian prehistory, which ruled over the kingdoms of Egypt for millennia. Isis, too, according to

Overall Finding from the Citation Search

The search results show repeated references to Nicholas de Vere, *The Dragon Legacy*, Laurence Gardner, *Realm of the Ring Lords*, *Genesis of the Grail Kings*, *Bloodline of the Holy Grail*, and related Grail/Dragon/Templar/Anjou material throughout Gary Wayne's work.

This matters because the references are not confined to one page, one footnote, or one isolated subject. The results appear across different parts of the book and cluster around the same subjects that form the core of my father's framework: the Dragon bloodline, the House of Vere, Anjou, Melusine, the Tuatha Dé Danann, the Elvin bloodline, the Grail families, the Templars, Rosicrucians, Scythian ancestry, the King of Jerusalem title, and the Dragon Court tradition.

The search for "De Vere" shows direct citations to *The Dragon Legacy* on multiple pages, including references to specific pages such as 42, 62, 66, 79, 115, 120, 121, 221 and others. These are not random mentions. They are attached to the same genealogical, mythological, and esoteric structures that my father wrote about.

The search for "Vere" also brings up repeated references to the House of Vere, Anjou, Plantagenet, Melusine, Godfrey de Bouillon, the Priory of Sion, Royal Secrets, Elvin bloodlines, and related noble-house material. This shows that the use is not simply a citation of one title in passing, but a repeated engagement with the Vere/Anjou/Dragon framework.

The search for "Legacy" shows repeated results for *The Dragon Legacy*, especially in the later reference sections. This confirms that the book is not merely using general biblical or historical material but repeatedly returning to the specific Dragon Legacy source-field.

The search for "Gardner" is even larger, with hundreds of results. That is important because Laurence Gardner's work is deeply entangled with my father's material, and in several places Gary Wayne appears to rely on Gardner as a bridge into the same Dragon, Grail, Anunnaki, Ring Lord, Templar, Scythian and bloodline framework. This supports the concern that the material is not only being taken directly from Nicholas de Vere, but also indirectly through Gardner.

The screenshots also show that many of the citations are positioned in sections dealing with the Elvin Houses of Vere, Anjou and Plantagenet, the King of Jerusalem title, Grail bloodlines, Rosicrucian and Templar themes, and the wider Dragon/Grail genealogy. These are exactly the areas where my father's work is most distinctive.

The overall pattern is therefore clear:

Gary Wayne cites Nicholas de Vere, *The Dragon Legacy*, and Laurence Gardner multiple times, drawing on the same Dragon/Grail/Vere/Anjou/Templar framework throughout.

The references appear across multiple sections, not in one isolated passage.

The citations support the argument that his work substantially relies on the Dragon Legacy source-field.

This does not look like a passing reference. It looks like a major structural dependency.

The strongest point is that when the citations to Nicholas de Vere and Laurence Gardner are placed together, they show the pathway by which the Dragon Legacy framework enters Gary Wayne's work. The material is then reorganised into his own biblical and end-times argument, but the underlying framework remains recognisable.

That is why this cannot be dismissed as "only one use" of my father's work.

The search results show a repeated pattern of citation, borrowing, reliance, and framework use. They also support the wider argument of this review: remove Nicholas de Vere and Laurence Gardner from the structure, and a substantial part of the distinctive Dragon/Grail/Vere framework disappears, leaving mainly biblical material and general public-domain religious commentary.

The evidence therefore supports the position that the issue is not simply quotation. It is repeated reliance on a protected and identifiable source-field.

THE LAW REVIEW USING THIS INFORMATION IN CONTEXT TO THE BEARNE CONVENTION AND WHEN THE LAW SETS OUT AS FAIR USE

Supporting Legal Context: Prior Intellectual Property Law Study

In 2020, while studying Intellectual Property Law, I examined copyright, design rights, moral rights, assignment, commercial exploitation, fair dealing, quotation, public communication, infringement, and the protection of authors against derogatory treatment of their work.

This earlier study is relevant to the present review because the current issue is not limited to simple word-for-word copying. It concerns the broader use of an author's protected work, framework, terminology, presentation, reputation, attribution, and commercial value.

Copyright ownership and assignment

One of the central points considered was whether copyright can be verbally assigned. The legal principle is that permission to use a work is not the same as assignment of copyright.

A copyright owner may give permission for a limited use, such as performance, recording, quotation, publication, or review, without transferring ownership of the copyright itself. An assignment of copyright must be clear, formal, in writing, and signed by or on behalf of the assignor.

This distinction is important because a publisher, record company, or commercial user may have permission to exploit a particular edition, performance, recording, or format, but that does not necessarily mean they own the underlying copyright in the original literary, musical, artistic, or scholarly work.

In the present matter, this principle is relevant because citation, access, previous publication, or commercial availability of Nicholas de Vere's work does not equal ownership of the underlying copyright, nor does it create a free right to reuse the distinctive Dragon Legacy / Dragon Cede / Royal Dragon Court framework.

Copyright protection of literary and artistic works

Copyright protects original literary, dramatic, musical and artistic works once they are recorded in a material form. In the example considered in my earlier work, lyrics and melody were treated as separate protected contributions: the lyricist owning the literary work and the composer owning the musical work.

The same principle applies more broadly. A book may contain protected expression, arrangement, terminology, selection, structure, and presentation. Copyright is not limited to a few quoted sentences. It can also concern the substantial use of a protected structure or expression when that use takes the author's original presentation, selection, ordering, or framework.

Substantial part and non-literal copying

A key issue in copyright is whether the alleged use reproduces the whole or a substantial part of the work. The test is qualitative as well as quantitative. A small amount may still be substantial if it takes the author's skill, labour, judgement, original arrangement, or central expressive structure.

In *Designers Guild Ltd v Russell Williams (Textiles) Ltd* [2000] 1 WLR 2416, the House of Lords confirmed that infringement is not simply a matter of counting copied elements. The court considers whether the defendant has taken a substantial part of the claimant's work, judged by the quality of what has been taken.

That principle is relevant here because the issue is not merely how many times Nicholas de Vere is named in the footnotes. The issue is whether Gary Wayne has taken and reused the distinctive Dragon Legacy source-field: House of Vere, Dragon Court, Anjou,

Plantagenet, Melusine, Societas Draconis / Ordo Draconis, Tuatha Dé Danann, Dragon bloodline, Grail bloodline, Egyptian Dragon Dynasty, Sobek, Khem, Baphomet, Templars, King of Jerusalem, and related symbolic and genealogical architecture.

Fair dealing, quotation, criticism and review

In the **US**, fair use is broader and more flexible. A court looks at four factors: the purpose of the use, the nature of the copyrighted work, how much was used, and the effect on the market for the original work. It is an open-ended balancing test, which means a use can sometimes be fair even if it does not fit neatly into a fixed category.

In the **UK**, fair dealing is narrower. You usually have to fit into a recognised statutory purpose, such as criticism, review, quotation, research/private study, news reporting, parody, caricature or pastiche. For criticism, review and quotation, the UK Intellectual Property Office says fair dealing is allowed for any type of copyright work, but a sufficient acknowledgement is required.

For your book, the UK wording matters more because you are in Britain and publishing through Dragon Publishing. So, the safer phrase is:

fair dealing for criticism, review, quotation, scholarly reference and evidential comparison

rather than only saying "fair use."

The practical difference is this:

US fair use asks:
"Looking at all the circumstances, is this use fair?"

UK fair dealing asks:
"Does this use fall within a permitted purpose, and is the amount used fair and justified for that purpose?"

For your review, you are not reproducing extracts as entertainment or substitute reading. You are using them to show overlap, citation-chain reliance, copied wording, framework borrowing, and hostile recharacterisation. That fits much more naturally under **criticism, review and quotation** in the UK, provided the extracts are no more than needed and properly acknowledged.

Fair dealing may permit limited use of a protected work for criticism, review, quotation, research, scholarship, or reporting, provided the use is genuinely fair, proportionate, properly attributed, and justified by the purpose.

However, fair dealing does not give an author permission to take another author's distinctive framework and rebuild it inside a different commercial argument. It also does not cure inadequate attribution, excessive reliance, misrepresentation, or hostile recontextualisation.

The principle from *Hubbard v Vosper* [1972] 2 QB 84 is that fairness depends on the facts, including the amount taken, the purpose of the use, and whether the use competes with or harms the original work. Lord Denning stated that fair dealing is a matter of impression and degree.

This is directly relevant to the present review. The question is not simply whether Gary Wayne quoted or cited Nicholas de Vere. The question is whether the scale, purpose, framing, commercial use, and cumulative effect of the material remain fair.

Communication to the public and online availability

My earlier study also considered whether a person may copy or upload a work simply because it is already available online or through a public platform.

The answer is no. Public availability does not mean public ownership. A work being available on Spotify, in print, online, in a library, or on a website does not give the public a right to copy, upload, reproduce, adapt, repackage, or commercially exploit it.

In *Football Association Premier League Ltd v QC Leisure* [2011] ECR I-9083 and *Svensson v Retriever Sverige AB* [2014] ECDR 9, the courts considered communication to the public in the context of copyright works and public access. The broader principle is that making a protected work available to a public audience can engage copyright control, depending on the method, audience, and authorisation.

This matters because public circulation of Nicholas de Vere's work, or the fact that related material was previously available online, does not make the Dragon Legacy framework free for hostile commercial reuse.

Design law and copying

In my earlier design-law work, I considered unregistered design rights, registered design rights, copying, novelty, individual character, and the difference between independent creation and copying.

The example referred to *Emeco Industries, Inc. v Restoration Hardware, Inc.*, a United States design dispute concerning alleged copying of a well-known chair design. Although that case is not a UK copyright authority, it was useful as an illustration of how distinctive designs can be commercially imitated and how disputes often turn on whether the later product reproduces the protected features of the earlier one.

The same broad idea applies to literary and symbolic frameworks. A later work may not copy every word of an earlier work, yet may still reproduce its distinctive structure, features, and identity closely enough to raise a serious infringement or unfair-use issue.

Moral rights

The moral-rights issue is especially important.

Moral rights recognise that a work is not merely a commercial object. It is connected to the author's identity, honour, reputation, and intellectual standing.

The Berne Convention, Article 6bis, recognises that authors have the right to claim authorship and to object to distortion, mutilation, modification, or other derogatory action in relation to the work where such treatment would be prejudicial to the author's honour or reputation.

Under the Copyright, Designs and Patents Act 1988, UK moral rights include the right to be identified as author, the right to object to derogatory treatment, and the right not to have a work falsely attributed.

The case of *Clark v Associated Newspapers Ltd* [1998] 1 All ER 959 is relevant to moral rights and false attribution. It demonstrates that attribution and the public presentation of authorship can matter legally, not merely personally.

The right of integrity has also been considered in cases such as *Pasterfield v Denham* [1999] FSR 168 and *Confetti Records v Warner Music UK Ltd* [2003] EWHC 1274 (Ch), where the courts considered whether treatment of a work was derogatory and prejudicial to honour or reputation.

These authorities are relevant because the present concern is not only copying. It is also the recontextualisation of Nicholas de Vere's work. Gary Wayne appears to take the Dragon Legacy / Dragon Cede / Royal Dragon Court source-field and place it inside a hostile Antichrist, False Prophet, Nephilim, Rephaim, serpent-seed, New Babylon and demonic bloodline narrative.

That is the moral-rights and reputational-harm issue.

Derogatory treatment and recontextualisation

Derogatory treatment is not simply criticism. An author may criticise another author's work. That is different from taking the author's material, altering its meaning, placing it into a hostile interpretative structure, or presenting it in a way that harms the author's honour, reputation, or public standing.

A criticism says, "I disagree with this work."

A derogatory recontextualisation says, in effect, "I will use this work as part of a hostile framework that makes the author's tradition appear corrupt, demonic, deceptive, or dangerous."

That is the issue here.

Nicholas de Vere's work presents the Dragon lineage, House of Vere, Royal Dragon Court, Grail, Anunnaki, Melusine, Egyptian, Scythian, Templar and royal bloodline material as a sacred, genealogical, symbolic and esoteric tradition.

Gary Wayne's work appears to use the same field and recode it through a Christian end-times argument, where Dragon bloodlines, Dragon gens, Pendragon imagery, Templar continuation, secret societies and royal bloodline claims are driven towards Antichrist and False Prophet conclusions.

Reputation and commercial harm

Moral rights exist because damage to an author's work can damage the author's reputation. Reputation is not separate from commercial value. An author's name, source-field, public identity, and intellectual authority are part of the value of the work.

If an author's work is distorted or hostilely reframed, the harm may affect public perception, future sales, licensing, reputation, and the author's literary estate.

This is especially relevant where the author is deceased, but the literary estate, publisher, family representative, trademark, and continuing editions are still active. The living rights holder may suffer reputational and commercial harm where the original work is mischaracterised in the marketplace.

Conclusion

The legal principles from my earlier IP law study assist this review in several ways.

They show that permission is not assignment, public availability is not public ownership, copying can be direct, indirect, literal, non-literal, structural, or substantial, fair dealing depends on fairness, purpose, proportion and attribution.

Moral rights protect authorship, integrity, reputation and honour.

Derogatory treatment and hostile recontextualisation may be relevant where a work is placed into a damaging context.

For these reasons, the present review must not be reduced to whether Gary Wayne copied individual sentences. The proper question is whether he used Nicholas de Vere's protected source-field, distinctive terminology, symbolic arrangement, genealogical structure, and Dragon Court framework, and whether that material was then commercially exploited and hostilely recharacterised.

That is the legal and evidential question at the heart of this book.

Summary of the Berne Convention and Why It Matters Here

The Berne Convention for the Protection of Literary and Artistic Works was first adopted in 1886. It is one of the main international copyright agreements protecting authors and creators across member countries.

Its purpose is to ensure that authors of literary and artistic works are recognised as having rights over their creations, including the right to control how their works are used, reproduced, translated, adapted, quoted, and distributed.

The Convention is based on three central principles.

The first is national treatment. This means that a work created by an author from one member country must be protected in other member countries in the same way those countries protect the works of their own nationals.

The second is automatic protection. Copyright does not depend on a special registration formality under Berne. Once a qualifying work exists, protection arises automatically.

The third is independence of protection. Protection in one member country does not depend entirely on whether protection exists in the country of origin. Each country applies its own copyright law, but it must still meet the minimum standards set by the Convention.

The Berne Convention protects literary and artistic works, including books, writings, lectures, dramatic works, musical works, drawings, illustrations, photographs, films, and other creative works. This is important because written books, editorial material, s, structured research, and original presentation can all fall within protected literary works.

For this review, the most important provisions are those dealing with reproduction, quotation, adaptation, and moral rights.

Article 9 recognises the author's exclusive right to authorise reproduction of their work. This matters because copying, reproducing, or closely reusing protected material is not automatically permitted simply because the work has been published, quoted, or made available online.

Article 10 allows quotations from a work, but only where the quotation is compatible with fair practice and only to the extent justified by the purpose. This is important because quotation is not a blank cheque. A person cannot rely on quotation as an excuse to take more than is necessary, to build their own work out of another author's framework, or to use the material in a way that goes beyond genuine criticism, review, scholarship, or commentary.

Article 12 gives authors the exclusive right to authorise adaptations, arrangements, and other alterations of their works. This is relevant where an author's original framework, structure, terminology, or presentation is not merely quoted but reshaped into another work.

Article 6bis is especially important because it protects moral rights. It recognises that authors have rights beyond money. Even independently of economic copyright, and even after economic rights have been transferred, an author has the right to claim authorship and to object to distortion, mutilation, modification, or other derogatory treatment of the work where that treatment would be prejudicial to the author's honour or reputation.

This is directly relevant to the present matter.

The issue is not only whether words have been copied. It is also whether Nicholas de Vere's work, name, framework, terminology, and Dragon Court material have been taken, altered, recontextualised, or presented in a way that damages the meaning of the work and the reputation attached to it.

The Berne Convention therefore supports several key points in this review.

Copyright protection is automatic.

Publication does not mean abandonment.

Online availability does not mean free use.

Quotation must be fair and limited.

Adaptation requires authorisation.

Authorship and reputation matter.

Derogatory treatment of a work can be a serious issue even where the user claims to be quoting, reviewing, or interpreting it.

For that reason, the Berne Convention is relevant not because this review depends on international law alone, but because it shows that the protection of authorship, integrity, reputation, and controlled use of creative works is a recognised principle of copyright law across member countries.[11]

---

[11] Protecting your copyright abroad - GOV.UK

Additional Review Clause: Laurence Gardner's Work

Even if I approached this review as an independent person, setting aside my own complaint concerning my father's work, the same concern would still arise in relation to Laurence Gardner's material.

The use of Gardner's work appears substantial enough that his estate would also have fair grounds to question the extent of reliance, quotation, citation, and framework use. If that behaviour has not already been flagged, then I find that concerning, because it is a publisher's responsibility to ensure that copyright infringement does not occur. A publisher is not merely there to take a percentage. A publisher is supposed to protect the intellectual property of the authors they represent.

This is one of the issues I had with my own former publisher. No matter how many times I raised concerns about other people using my work, he appeared unwilling to take meaningful action. To some publishers, these matters become inconvenient because they involve time, money, court risk, and work. That raises a fair question: why should publishers take such a substantial percentage from authors if they are not prepared to protect the work, promote it properly, or act when infringement occurs?

Once the financial structure is examined, the imbalance becomes clear. The author does the research, writes the book, builds the audience, absorbs the risk, and often receives the smaller share. If the publisher also lacks the willingness or ability to protect the author's rights, then the publisher becomes little more than a middleman.

The same concern applies where a publisher attempts to reduce accountability by relying too quickly on terms such as "fair use" or "fair dealing." Those terms do not automatically excuse substantial reliance on another author's work. Whether the material used comes from my father, Nicholas de Vere, or from Laurence Gardner, the issue remains the same: excessive use, structural reliance, and framework borrowing cannot simply be waved away as fair use.

In my view, the material taken from both Nicholas de Vere and Laurence Gardner sits well beyond ordinary citation or limited critical reference. It forms part of the working structure of the later book, and that is precisely why it must be reviewed.

Where contract law is concerned, we now have a third layer issue, like as previously sated my own issue with my publisher not helping me with the overall exposure of my book, putting a convicted criminal who spent 30 years in prison for rape with a weapon over my work that I had been loyal to him for 13 years, not reprimanding copyright infringement and diluting my work to monotone 17 hour ai generated slop, along with the fact that we ended up before reconciling a period of not speaking which completely null and voids the contract due to a break down in communication, made his iron clad contract weak as a chocolate teapot, (I will say I actually like the guy and hold no malice however it's a massive situation to learn from as far as contract law is concerned)

There are certain requirements a publisher has to ensure when taking on a book to publish which you can find in the codes of conduct online.

Podcasts that Gary Wayne has been on speaking about my bloodline and The Dragon Legacy

The material I have preserved is only a sample. In one search capture alone, I identified 417 "Now playing" video entries associated with Gary Wayne. Even allowing for shorts, duplicates and unrelated results, the scale of circulation is clear. This is not one isolated podcast, one isolated chapter or one accidental association. It is a repeated public media pattern across a large number of interviews, channels and audience communities. I have had to use Chat got to help with the transcript and pattern recognition, Even though I see it myself, I needed a second opinion. I am not editing this to sound like a human when I explicitly admit I needed help from a computer.

The YouTube Admission and Public Reframing of The Dragon Legacy

The YouTube episode titled *The Dragon Legacy w/ Gary Wayne*, published by Prometheus Lens Podcast and hosted by Doc Brown, 20 Aug 2025 Prometheus Lens (Full Episodes)

is significant because it publicly demonstrates knowledge, access, reliance, commentary, and hostile recharacterisation of Nicholas de Vere's work.

This was not a passing reference. The episode was not titled as a general discussion of Genesis, giants, Nephilim, or biblical history. It was titled *The Dragon Legacy w/ Gary Wayne*. That title directs the audience immediately to my father's named work and the Dragon Legacy / Dragon Court source-field. The surrounding description and hashtags reinforce the same public framing, using terms such as Dragon, Dragon Court, Legacy, Genealogies, Royals, Gary Wayne, Serpent Seed, Lost History, Biblical History, Supernatural, Nephilim, and Giants.

That matters because the audience is being invited into the discussion through my father's title, my father's subject-field, and the public identity of the Dragon Court material.

At the beginning of the discussion, Doc Brown introduces the episode as a "deep dive" into "the dragon court and the dragon legacy." He then identifies the book he is referring to as *The Dragon Legacy* by Nicholas de Vere. He also makes clear that Gary Wayne had already read these books before later citing or using the material in his second book. That is important because it establishes prior knowledge and access. Gary Wayne was not approaching this material unknowingly, accidentally, or through some vague independent tradition. The discussion itself acknowledges that the books were already known to him.

Doc Brown then reads directly from my father's work as the foundation for the discussion. This is crucial. The video is not simply a case of Gary Wayne giving a loose opinion about dragons, biblical giants, or serpent symbolism. The host physically brings Nicholas de Vere's book into the episode, reads from it, and asks Gary Wayne to respond to it.

The structure of the conversation then becomes revealing. Doc Brown repeatedly attempts to focus on what Nicholas de Vere actually says in *The Dragon Legacy*. He raises specific material from the book, including Nicholas de Vere's comments on witches, warlocks, vampires, bloodline, magical ability, and the distinction between modern occult cosplay and ancient bloodline-based claims. Rather than remaining within Nicholas de Vere's own textual framework, Gary Wayne repeatedly redirects the material back into his own biblical-prophecy framework: Satan, Samael, polytheism, misinformation, Nephilim, fallen angels, giants, demons, devils, unclean spirits, serpent seed and end-times theology.

That is the central issue. My father's work is being used as the launch point, but the meaning is then redirected into Gary Wayne's system.

The host's discussion of witches is particularly important. Doc Brown states that the beginning of Nicholas de Vere's book caught his attention because Nicholas was criticising modern New Age people, witches, warlocks and vampires, saying that people may perform the spells, own the grimoires, and believe themselves to be witches, warlocks or vampires, but that they are not accomplishing the same things as the ancients because, in Nicholas de Vere's framework, the distinction lies in blood and bloodline.

This is a clear example of the host attempting to extract a specific idea from Nicholas de Vere's work. The point in my father's writing is not a simple horror claim that "these people drink blood" or that the Dragon Court is a Dracula cult. It is a discussion of ancient bloodline belief, hereditary magical status, symbolic kingship, mythic identity, and the contrast between modern imitation and claimed ancestral inheritance.

However, the discussion then shifts into a far more hostile theological frame. Gary Wayne moves the material into claims about polytheists, royals, Gnostics, giants, Sodom and Gomorrah, poisonous vines, dragons, demonic spirits, vampire allegory, and control. The effect is that Nicholas de Vere's historical, symbolic and genealogical material is absorbed into a Christian demonological narrative.

The most damaging part is the explicit blood-drinking discussion. In the transcript, the conversation moves from Nicholas de Vere's material into claims that "they" drink blood, that blood is used for control, that people become "like servants of Dracula," and that blood-drinking is connected with hierarchy, authority, telepathic control, extended life, cognitive ability, demons, devils, unclean spirits and vampires.

This is not neutral commentary. It creates a public impression that the Dragon Legacy / Dragon Court field concerns an active blood-drinking, controlling, Dracula-linked, demonic system. That is a serious hostile recharacterisation of my father's work.

The harm is increased by the fact that the video is publicly packaged around *The Dragon Legacy*. The title names the source-field. The host identifies Nicholas de Vere and reads from the book. The hashtags attach the video to Dragon, Dragon Court, Legacy, Genealogies, Royals, Serpent Seed, Nephilim and Giants. The episode description presents the discussion as a controversial exploration of serpent seed doctrine and ancient belief systems. The whole public framing therefore invites viewers to understand Nicholas de Vere's work through a hostile lens before they have even heard the discussion.

This is also why the video is relevant to the wider copyright and source-chain issue. Gary Wayne's published work repeatedly uses Nicholas de Vere / Dragon Legacy / Dragon Court material, directly and indirectly. The podcast then shows that the same source-field is being used in public promotional or associated commentary, where it is repackaged for an audience as spiritually dangerous, Satanic, deceptive, bloodline-based, Nephilim-linked, giant-related, Dracula-linked and demonic.

That is the hypocrisy.

Gary Wayne and associated platforms use the Dragon Legacy / Dragon Court material because it supplies content, controversy, authority, genealogy, terminology and narrative structure. Yet the same material is then presented to a Christian audience as misinformation, serpent seed doctrine, fallen angel religion, blood-drinking hierarchy, Dracula control, demonic influence and spiritual deception.

A person cannot fairly mine a source-field for content, build public discussion around it, benefit from the controversy of it, and then rebrand the same source-field as evil, deceptive, Satanic or demonic without consequence. That is not neutral scholarship. It is hostile rebranding after reliance.

The episode therefore provides several important evidential points.

It shows that *The Dragon Legacy* was expressly identified and discussed. Nicholas de Vere's book was physically used and read from by the host.

Gary Wayne had prior knowledge of the books and was not unaware of the source-field.

The discussion was publicly titled, described and hash tagged around Dragon Legacy / Dragon Court / royal genealogy material.

It shows that Nicholas de Vere's own claims were used as the starting point for the conversation.

Gary Wayne then redirected the material into his own Genesis 6 / Nephilim / Satan / fallen angel / end-times framework.

It shows that the public audience was exposed to a framing in which my father's work was associated with misinformation, polytheist deception, blood-drinking, Dracula, demons, devils, unclean spirits, vampires, hierarchy and control.

In my view, this is not merely criticism. It is source-field exploitation followed by public hostile recharacterisation.

The podcast does not weaken my position. It strengthens it. It shows knowledge, access, public use, commercial packaging, hostile framing and reputational damage. It also supports the wider pattern already visible in Gary Wayne's written work: Nicholas de Vere's distinctive Dragon Legacy / Dragon Court framework is repeatedly drawn upon, rearranged, interpreted through another author's religious system, and then presented to the public as part of a threatening occult, Nephilim, Antichrist or demonic structure.

That is precisely why this matter cannot be reduced to "one citation," "fair use," or ordinary commentary. The issue is not that someone disagreed with Nicholas de Vere. The issue is that Nicholas de Vere's protected work and source-field have been used as material, content, title value, search value and controversy value, while being publicly reframed in a way that damages the author, the work, Dragon Publishing, the Royal Dragon Court ®, and the living family now responsible for preserving that legacy.

My Rebuttal to the Prometheus Lens Podcast Discussion

After watching the Prometheus Lens Podcast episode titled *The Dragon Legacy w/ Gary Wayne*, my concern is not simply that Gary Wayne disagrees with Nicholas de Vere. People are entitled to disagree with books, theology, history, genealogy, symbolism and interpretation. My concern is the way this episode publicly frames my father's work, reads from it, uses it as the foundation for the discussion, and then turns it into something much darker for the audience.

The episode is not neutrally titled. It is titled *The Dragon Legacy w/ Gary Wayne*. The description and hashtags place it directly inside Dragon, Dragon Court, Legacy, Genealogies, Royals, Gary Wayne, Serpent Seed, Nephilim, Giants, Supernatural and Biblical History territory. That means the public framing is already aimed at my father's named work and source-field before the discussion even begins.

Doc Brown then physically brings up *The Dragon Legacy* by Nicholas de Vere and reads from it. He is not simply discussing a general biblical topic. He is using my father's book as the opening source and asking Gary Wayne to respond to it. That matters because it shows knowledge, access and reliance. It also shows that the public conversation is being built around Nicholas de Vere's work, not merely around Gary Wayne's independent biblical research.

What I found especially revealing is that Doc Brown appears interested in the specific things my father actually wrote. He tries to draw out the points in the book: the Dragon Court, the Dragon Legacy, bloodline claims, witches, warlocks, vampires, modern occult cosplay, ancient hereditary claims, and the idea that some knowledge was historically connected to bloodline rather than merely to book-learning or ritual imitation.

That is a specific idea in my father's work. Nicholas de Vere was not simply saying, "We drink blood," or "we are servants of Dracula," or "we are demons." He was discussing myth, genealogy, symbolic kingship, ancient rites, hereditary identity, bloodline traditions, esoteric history, and the difference between inherited claims and modern people acting out occult fantasy.

Yet Gary Wayne repeatedly moves the discussion away from that framework and places it back into his own biblical and demonological system. He reframes the material through Satan, Samael, polytheism, misinformation, serpent seed, Nephilim, giants, fallen angels, demons, devils, unclean spirits, vampires, hierarchy and control. This is not simply interpretation. It is a rebranding of my father's work through Gary Wayne's own religious lens.

The blood-drinking section is one of the clearest examples of this problem. The conversation moves from my father's book into claims that "they" drink blood, that blood is used to control lower beings, that people become "like servants of Dracula," and that blood-drinking connects with hierarchy, demonic spirits, extended life, cognitive ability, vampires and unclean spirits.

That is not a fair public representation of my father's work or of the Dragon Court. It creates the impression that the Dragon Legacy / Dragon Court field is an active blood-drinking, Dracula-linked, demonic control system. That is deeply damaging.

Another issue is the repeated implication that *The Dragon Legacy* represents "our genesis" or "what these people believe," as if everyone connected to the Dragon Court, Dragon Publishing, Nicholas de Vere, or the House of Vere is unable to think critically for themselves. That is not true. I have not been indoctrinated by my father. I have inherited, researched, preserved, corrected and published his work. Those are not the same thing.

I am not a mindless follower of Nicholas de Vere. I am his daughter, his editor, his publisher, and a researcher in my own right. I have spent years studying genealogy, religion, law, history, symbolism, mythology, publishing, and source material. I am capable of agreeing with some things, questioning others, correcting parts, expanding context, and developing my own conclusions.

The implication that people connected to the Dragon Court are simply indoctrinated into an evil bloodline belief is offensive and intellectually lazy. It denies individual agency. It denies critical thought. It denies the fact that people can research outside the Bible, outside the Church, and outside conventional religious authority without being evil.

My position is not anti-God. My position is that I do not accept that a good God should be used as an excuse for human cruelty, institutional hypocrisy, religious abuse, forced adoption, child trafficking, persecution, censorship or historical erasure. I do not reject spiritual study. I reject the idea that one religious institution has the right to define all other inquiry as demonic.

The Christian Church has its own history to answer for. Forced adoptions, abuse, institutional control, persecution, suppression of alternative texts, and the rewriting of religious authority are not imaginary concerns. When victims of forced adoption receive apologies decades later, those apologies do not undo the harm. When religious institutions participate in systems that remove children from mothers, silence women, control families, or abuse power, it is not evil to question those institutions. It is necessary.

That is why I find the podcast framing so hypocritical. Gary Wayne presents the Dragon Legacy / Dragon Court material as dangerous, deceptive and demonic, while his own framework relies heavily on a biblical tradition and church-shaped worldview that also contains violence, contradiction, exclusion, suppression and institutional harm. To question that history is not to be evil. It is to think critically.

The Bible itself is not a single simple object. Different traditions contain different canons. The Ethiopian Bible contains books that are not found in the standard Roman or Protestant canons. Other texts, such as the Gospel of Thomas and wider apocryphal or excluded writings, raise legitimate questions about what was preserved, what was removed, who removed it, and why. Asking those questions does not make a person wicked. It makes them a researcher.

I have studied different religious and spiritual systems, including Buddhism and broader spiritual concepts. I have researched symbolism, mythology, religion, the law of attraction, universal principles, and different ways people have tried to understand the divine, the world and human consciousness. That does not make me evil. It makes me intelligent, curious and independent.

The podcast also misrepresents the lived reality of people connected to these genealogical traditions. Gary Wayne talks about dragon bloodlines, elites, ruling classes, lower classes, blacksmiths, workers, entrepreneurs and ordinary humans as if the whole framework is one simple hierarchy of superior and inferior people. That does not reflect my family or my life.

I have blacksmiths in my family. My great-grandfather was a blacksmith, and one of the best blacksmiths in Redditch. I have bankers in my family. I have people in my family who helped build hospitals, support women's rights in medicine, and open the way for women to become surgeons. I have factory people, working people, professional people, creative people, farmers and survivors. I am a farmer myself.

So, the neat little framework he tries to impose does not work. My family history is not a cartoon of "elite dragon rulers" looking down on "lower humans." It is a real family history, full of labour, trade, craft, law, medicine, farming, publishing, survival, loss and responsibility.

That is why this public framing is so wrong. It flattens real people into a theological stereotype. It turns a complex body of genealogical, mythological and symbolic writing into a horror story for a Christian audience. It takes Nicholas de Vere's work, uses it for content and controversy, then reframes it as serpent seed, Nephilim, giants, blood-drinking, Dracula, demons and misinformation.

This is not neutral review. It is hostile recharacterisation.

I am entitled to defend my father's work. and to correct public misrepresentation. I am entitled to protect Dragon Publishing, the Royal Dragon Court ®, the House of Vere material, and the literary inheritance I am responsible for.

The issue is not that Gary Wayne has a different belief system. The issue is that he uses my father's source-field while publicly rebranding it as dangerous, deceptive and demonic. He cannot rely on the Dragon Legacy / Dragon Court material for content, traffic, authority and controversy, while also presenting it to an audience as though it proves an evil blood-drinking Dracula-linked hierarchy.

That is the hypocrisy.

The podcast shows knowledge. It shows access. It shows the host reading from my father's book. It shows Gary Wayne responding to that material. It shows the material being redirected into his own biblical and demonological structure. It shows the Dragon Legacy / Dragon Court source-field being publicly packaged, monetised, searched, hash tagged and promoted under terms such as Dragon, Dragon Court, Legacy, Royals, Serpent Seed, Nephilim and Giants.

In my opinion, this video strengthens my case. It demonstrates that the use of Nicholas de Vere's work is not isolated, accidental or incidental. It forms part of a wider public pattern: draw from the source-field, use its distinctive language and genealogy, redirect its meaning, and then publicly brand it as evil.

I reject that framing entirely.

I am not evil because I question the Bible, question the Church, study multiple religions., because I preserve my father's work.

I am not evil because I defend my inheritance.

I am a researcher, an author, a publisher, a farmer, a daughter, and a woman protecting the work she has inherited.

I have over the years pulled together a community of friends and fans who love the work I do, We are Family.

And I will not allow my father's work, my family, or the Dragon Publishing / Royal Dragon Court source-field to be reduced to a blood-drinking Dracula caricature for someone else's content.

I reached out to this Justin Brown, The exchanged showed that he was not very christian at all, I repeatedly told him that I do not give him permission to use my work, Before I reached out I had already started the process to remove this video on you tube.

He said that he was going to use my fathers work in his upcoming book A Tale of two Trees, Chasing the Dragons, I must have said more than five time that I do not give him permission, He added he would be buying my own books and doing a review on them, Which he wont be able to comprehend them, there is no sensational material, It will not get him clicks, Its pure history and genealogy, anthropology, It tells the story of real humanity, nit some made up fictional book like the bible. Once The video had been removed he rushed to re upload it and start a smear campaign against me. This is the Transcript in Justins own words

"Hey guys, sorry I had to cut in here, but uh I had to re-upload this video because Abby De Vere apparently uh had wanted nothing to do with the Dragon Court while her father was alive, but since he passed away, she's wanting to cash in. So now she's

republishing his books and everything else. And uh she says that for me and Gary talk about her father's work and that uh this bloodline is of the serpent seed and they drink blood and all this stuff is inaccurate.

We're misrepresenting her work and she's coming after me and Gary Wayne. Uh I don't know if she's actually read her father's work because he does say that they drink blood. Uh he does say they are of the serpent seed. Uh, so I don't know what the issue is here, but they hit me with a copyright infringement for reading. I'm serious. For reading 10 sentences from the book. I held it up, gave acknowledgement, read 10 sentences to Gary, and asked him his interpretation, and my video got taken down, and I got a strike on my channel for copyright.

Yeah, so, it tells me I'm barking up the right tree. She's squirming.

Uh but so I'm going to re-upload the video and I'm just going to give you my synopsis of what was read there because uh I tried to read it that way you guys would have word for word and not know and know that I'm not misrepresenting the work and that's obviously not allowed. So, you're just going to get my interpretation of what it says and read it for yourself, and you'll see that my interpretation in my own words of what they said in the book is correct.

De Vere says outright that they are of the Anunnaki and they are a subhuman race created to rule over us little dummies and comes right out and throws out the mythologies of Inky. Inky mated with Eve creating Cain and this stemmed that bloodline. In a biblical view, folks, that is the serpent seed. And he says it right out in his book.

And I read that to Gary and then I told him about the one ring to rule them all. The Lord of the Rings Tolken was based off of this.

And it was the Orouborus, the serpent eating its own tail, which was alchemically talking about this bloodline by consuming itself, drinking its own blood, evolves like a phoenix that rises from the ashes and evolved new creature. This serpent lineage that devours itself then evolves to be a dragon.

And so, I read that to Gary asked his interpretation. The video got flagged and taken down because of those 10 sentences that I read from the book. So, uh she doesn't know me too well. I tried to tell her you catch more or you catch more bees with honey than you do with vinegar.

So, I'm just going to double down and lean in even harder. Uh, I'm currently working on a book on these subjects. So, be on the lookout for that. And I'm just reloading this episode. So, that's what was read there, but I had to cut it out. Enjoy the rest of the video.

So, this is basically their genesis and what they believe.

This is now not only untrue, but defamation saying we all drink blood is ridiculous behaviour.

Here for the purpose of evidence are the emails which shows a false prophet pretending to be good but the mask slipping into what I can only call from my freedom of expression, Parasitic behaviour.

The Mask of God s Slips

Clean Email Thread

Ref: The Dragon Legacy with Gary Wayne

Source: Gmail thread export supplied by Abbe de Vere.; wording preserved as supplied, including original spelling and punctuation.

EMAIL 1

From: SOVEREIGN GRAND DUCHY OF DRAKENBERG <royaldragoncourt@gmail.com>
Date: 28 Jun 2026, 13:01
To: prometheuslens423
Subject: The Dragon Legacy with Gary Wayne

Dear Mr Brown,

I wanted to write to you after listening to your episode with Gary Wayne, because I noticed that you asked some very good questions about the Royal Dragon Court, Nicholas de Vere, inherited insight, bloodline traditions, and the claims that have been made around them.

My concern is that you asked Gary Wayne about the Royal Dragon Court, but the Royal Dragon Court itself was never asked. Nor was permission granted for our work, our family material, or Nicholas de Vere's writings to be used, reframed, and publicly presented through Gary Wayne's interpretation.

That is an important distinction.

Gary Wayne has taken material from Nicholas de Vere and Royal Dragon Court sources, but he has done so without permission and without proper representation from the people whose work and legacy he is discussing. He has cherry-picked from that material, removed it from its original context, and then presented it through his own religious and conspiratorial framework.

In the episode, when you asked about inherited insight, intuitive ability, bloodline memory, and spiritual perception, the answer you were given effectively reduced the subject to dark ritual, blood drinking, or sinister occult practice. That is not an accurate representation of our work.

The Royal Dragon Court position was not that wisdom, insight, or intuition came from blood-drinking ritual. That is a gross distortion. The wider argument in Nicholas de Vere's work concerned inheritance, memory, culture, mythology, spiritual perception, and the preservation of certain symbolic and ancestral traditions across generations. Whether someone agrees with those ideas or not, they deserve to be represented honestly.

There is a serious difference between critique and unauthorised misrepresentation.

Gary Wayne has repeatedly used Royal Dragon Court themes, language, research structures, and Nicholas de Vere's material, including the subjects of dragons, bloodlines, Merovingians, priest-kings, sovereignty, ancient mythology, and spiritual inheritance. However, he has then recast these ideas as evidence of an evil bloodline conspiracy. That is not our position, and it was not authorised by us.

This is why I felt I needed to contact you directly. You asked questions that deserved proper answers. Instead, you were given a one-sided version of our work by someone who was not authorised to speak for us, and who appears to have relied heavily on our material while also condemning and distorting it.

The Royal Dragon Court was not about promoting evil, ritual abuse, blood drinking, or domination. It was about sovereignty, lineage, myth, history, spiritual inheritance, and recovering older traditions that had been demonised or misunderstood. Our lineage is recorded in history, not made up and dropped into the bible, People are free to disagree with those ideas, but they should not be replaced with sensational claims that bear little resemblance to the original material.

I would be very happy to refer directly to your transcript and episode, and to answer the questions that were raised there from the Royal Dragon Court perspective. I think it would be fair for your audience to hear from the source that was being discussed, especially when the discussion involved claims about our work, our family, our intellectual property, and our legacy.

At the very least, I wanted to make clear that Gary Wayne's presentation of the Royal Dragon Court is not our position. It is his unauthorised interpretation, built from selected fragments of our work, and in many places it becomes a serious misrepresentation.

Kind regards,

Abbe de Vere

Dragon Publishing / Royal Dragon Court

www.royaldragoncourt.com

EMAIL 2

From: Justin Brown	
Date: 28 Jun 2026, 13:16	
To: Abbe de Vere	
Subject: Re: The Dragon Legacy with Gary Wayne	

Hey,

Thanks for reaching out and clarifying that. I understand the issue with the misrepresentation.

I'm happy to have you on to discuss the Royal Dragon Court perspective directly. Let me know what dates work for you soon. Big fan of your guy's work, I'm supposed to get two of your books today actually.

-Doc

EMAIL 3

From: SOVEREIGN GRAND DUCHY OF DRAKENBERG <royaldragoncourt@gmail.com>
Date: 28 Jun 2026, 16:59
To: Justin
Subject: Re: The Dragon Legacy with Gary Wayne

Ahhh, okay.

Well, maybe reading my books will help set the record straight.

The issue of fantasists using our work and turning the context into a stage performance for likes, clicks, and sensationalism is something I have had to deal with for years.

Some people may not even realise the level of defamation they are spreading, not just about me, but about my family, my father's work, and our wider community across the world.

We do not drink blood. That is ridiculous, cherry-picked misinformation.

The irony is that if people actually did the science, the anthropology, the DNA, the migration history, and the genealogy — rather than forcing everything back through a literal biblical lens — many may discover they share parts of the same bloodline they have been trying to demonise.

That is why misrepresentation matters. What people set out to use against us may eventually become a weapon against themselves.

A Story of a Thousand Faces is also a good place to begin, as it helps explain how people became misinformed along the way.

Happy reading, Mr Brown.

Attachment noted in Gmail: One attachment; scanned by Gmail.

Email 4

From: SOVEREIGN GRAND DUCHY OF DRAKENBERG <royaldragoncourt@gmail.com>	
Date: 28 Jun 2026, 20:41	
To: Justin	
Subject: Re: The Dragon Legacy with Gary Wayne	

Justin,

Just to make this very clear.

I do not give you permission to reproduce, narrate, read aloud, serialise, adapt, publish, broadcast, or otherwise produce content from any of my books, nor from the books of my late father, Nicholas de Vere.

This includes, but is not limited to:

The Royal Dragon Court: Inbred Britain

The Forgotten Royals of the USA

The Dragon Legacy

The Dragon Cede

A Story of a Thousand Faces

I am aware of previous material you have produced concerning The Royal Dragon Court and my father's work, including content which presents us through vulgar, sensationalised, and defamatory misrepresentation.

We do not drink blood, and I do not accept my family, my work, or The Royal Dragon Court being used as clickbait or content-farm material to drive views.

My work is copyright protected. The Royal Dragon Court is also a protected brand/trademarked identity. My aim is to educate people through my own published work, not to have that work distorted, mocked, misrepresented, or repackaged for entertainment.

You may of course read the books privately and educate yourself. However, permission is not granted for you to reproduce, narrate, perform, quote extensively from, adapt, or use my books or my father's books as content for your show, podcast, Instagram, YouTube, or any other platform.

For avoidance of doubt, permission is expressly refused.

You may also wish to familiarise yourself with copyright protection under the Berne Convention, and with the legal consequences of defamatory misrepresentation, passing off, and unauthorised reproduction of protected works.

Abbe de Vere

Dragon Publishing / The Royal Dragon Court

EMAIL 5

From: Justin Brown
Date: 1 Jul 2026, 15:50
To: Abbe de Vere
Subject: Re: The Dragon Legacy with Gary Wayne

Abbe,

I appreciate you reaching out as I said I'm a fan of your Dads work and Gardners. I got both your books the other day and looking forward into diving into them. I can see why you're upset and being defensive as some people like David Ike has totally demonized your people. I know first hand how awful most "christians" can be. Especially in this space of everyone fighting for attention and clicks. That's not me. I'm truly interested in the topic, and I'm searching for truth. Many "christians" attack me on the daily as a heretic. lol I don't share a lot of traditional views.

The videos I have done I have mentioned that the dragon court DID drink blood. It's in your fathers book. I've read it several times. It does say he believes the practice had stopped a long time ago because of the dalluted bloodline not having the potency it used to. I think I remember him saying alchemists syncicized a white powder (or tried to) to get those hormones artificially. Everything I talk about comes strait from the book.

I would love to have you on the show for a conversation, I guarantee you it will surprise you. haha I'd love to get your side of everything and give you a chance to get your message out to a christian audience. You sounded like that's what you wanted to do in the beginning.

But, I am working on a book on this subject. Your fathers book and Gardners were great study resources. I will be doing commentary on the works, adding in my own research and thoughts. I have no plans on reproducing your book. I will give credits in the book as well as in the index and reference works.

As far as me writing about, or doing shows on material in your book I'm sorry that upsets you, but you do not own the thought or idea. Just because you and your father have written on it doesn't mean others can't. I did read a very small excerpt from your fathers book on a show I did with Gary Wayne (maybe 5/6 sentences), because I wanted to give credit where it was due, and I didn't want to misquote or misrepresent the work. I could easily just go from memory, but wanted to honor the work and not misquote.

Some Christians hold to a theory on "serpent seed", as do I. But, I've stated clearly in past books and podcasts; I don't see them as less than human, or an evil race that needs to be "dealt with". I don't encourage hate at all. I encourage acceptance. You father said himself in his works, that bloodline goes back to the Anunnaki, they were a sub-human race made to oversee mankind. I believe that is a Biblical theme. But, Christ died for ALL at the cross in my belief system. Nobody is condemned over bloodlines. We all live and die by our freewill choices.

I enjoy history and digging for truth. Many things have been mythologized, but i think humanity had a bigger role than most religions give credit for. Many men were worshipped as gods for their brain power and technology. That's something your father talked about too, I agree with that.

Like I said, I hope we can have a conversation to put you at ease, even if it's not recorded. I think I would show you quickly you got the wrong idea about me.

-Justin.

EMAIL 6

From: SOVEREIGN GRAND DUCHY OF DRAKENBERG <royaldragoncourt@gmail.com>	
Date: 1 Jul 2026, 17:38	
To: Justin	
Subject: Re: The Dragon Legacy with Gary Wayne	

Justin,

Once you have actually read my books, you will see the difference.

My reference to "Queen of Shit Rock" is a joke, and it takes the same context of humour as "the Fantasist," before anyone starts posting that out of context as if it proves something it does not.

My issue is that you are promoting Gary Wayne as though he is an authority on my bloodline, when he has so much of it wrong. Gary Wayne has copied and pasted the Bible alongside over 456 citations from Laurence Gardner's books in his first book, and over 150 citations in his second. My father co-wrote with Laurence Gardner, so this is not some distant or unrelated source. There are also 17 Gardner citations in the "Elven House of Vere" chapter, which is apparently "nothing to do with us." That is hypocrisy.

Without our work, his books are largely a regurgitation of the Bible with borrowed frameworks added in. By giving him a platform and allowing him to speak as an authority on this subject, it appears to me, and this is my opinion under my freedom of expression, that you have assisted Gary Wayne in the promotion of material connected to copyright infringement, misrepresentation, and distortion.

This is the whole reason I studied law: to stop issues like this, especially when the people doing it have admitted they had no education and needed something to add to their Bible book, so they researched secret societies because they saw that subject was selling. That is greed. Your Bible and the Ten Commandments are supposed to teach against this sort of thing.

I do not think you practise what you preach.

Jesus died because of humanity's sins, not so that people could carry on sinning while hiding behind scripture. You do not need to post scripture to be a good person. You do not need to wear a mask of God when the mask slips and reveals its true adversary.

I suggest you listen properly to my father's videos if you are truly a fan. You will see and hear his humour, and you will understand how much he disliked people confusing the etymology of words. We are not "servants of Dracula." That is hilarious.

You cannot tell me you are a fan when I have seen the Instagram video of you dressed as a vampire. You are attempting to mock this subject while claiming to respect it.

My father deliberately used certain words because he knew they would offend the Church. That was the point. We see the hypocrisy of what the Church has promoted throughout history. People are sheep and they follow blindly, they enjoy being spoon fed and told what to do. The church promoted the marriage and sexual ownership of underage children. Mary was around 12 or 13 when she was sent to marry Joseph, a man two or three times her age. In this day and age, we call that paedophilia. Funny how you all left that out when you discuss your little bookywook in such high regards, Its Russell Brand all over, Commit sexual offence, Hide behind the bible, Rape someone and spend 30 years in prison, oh wow he's reformed, god saved him, he repented.

Its utter crap, being ok with that sort of behaviour and not addressing it.

You seem to assume we have not read the Bible. I was sent to Sunday school every week by my father. I know the Book of Job well. I know that Satan was a title. Lucifer and Satan were not originally intertwined; that association developed much later, when the Bible was used as propaganda for fear and control. The ouroboros is about the life cycle and not repeating the same mistake twice. The bloodline means we see straight through lies. We see through the masks that people present to us.

You have also reduced the subject of blood-drinking into something attached specifically to the Dragon Court and my bloodline, when that is historically and symbolically misleading.

Accounts of warriors drinking the blood of the fallen, enemies, kings, heroes, or defeated opponents appear across many cultures and battle traditions. It was not segregated to one family, one people, one bloodline, or one "evil" race. It was often connected to ideas of victory, power, conquest, vitality, initiation, fear, ritual, or absorbing the strength of the defeated. However due to the amount of royals and nobles it seems we had the most battles. Go figure.

So to keep dragging that subject back to my father's work, my family, or the Dragon Court, while dressing it up with vampire imagery or serpent-seed theology, is not honest research. It is selective framing.

If you are going to discuss blood rituals, then discuss them properly and historically. Do not isolate them, sensationalise them, and pin them onto my bloodline as though this was some unique mark of corruption.

For that reason, I decline your request.

I do not need to wear a mask. I am not a clout chaser. I do not believe appearing on your platform would serve my integrity, nor do I need advertising from the wrong audience, especially one that lacks the ability to read between the lines.

What I do want is a public apology.

I want a public apology for the way my father's work, my family, and the Dragon Court material have been framed, mocked, reduced, or allowed to be presented through the "serpent seed," vampire, blood-drinking, and evil-bloodline narrative. I want it made clear that Gary Wayne is not the authority on my bloodline, that my father's work has been misrepresented, and that my family should not be presented as evil, demonic, sub-human, vampiric, or spiritually corrupt by bloodline.

Freedom, love, and sovereignty are our way. Not fear and control.

Good day to you.

Abbe de Vere

EMAIL 7

From: Justin Brown	
Date: 1 Jul 2026, 17:54	
To: Abbe de Vere	
Subject: Re: The Dragon Legacy with Gary Wayne	

You think highly of yourself don't you? 🤣 You will get no apology from me hun. I tried to be nice and civil with you, but you're just plain ugly. You keep projecting past experiences on me, it's sad. Blinded by your anger. Before you ever reached out to me I had a member of the dragon court reach out to me. I've been in contact ever since. He warned me about you. I didn't pay much attention as some people get their feelings hurt and lash out, there's always two sides of the story.

He informed me he was good friends with your father, he even sent me pictures. He said you had nothing Rodney your father or his work until he died. You wanted to cash in on his legacy. He said since you took over he and others have stepped back because of how you act and the direction you're taking the court. I can see what he was talking about now.

I'm a simple country bumpkin, but I'll tell you something that will help you in the future. What you do with it is on you sister. You catch more flies with honey than vinegar. You insulating people, talking about law suits and what you will do if people don't give into your demands it's very unbecoming. Anyone with a backbone will give you the finger and lean in harder.

You've only hardened my resolve to talk about it more. Go ahead and try to sue me. You can't get chocolate milk out of a cow no matter how hard you squeeze. Can't take what someone doesn't have. lol

Regardless if your snooty attitude I've enjoyed your fathers books, and i look forward to reading yours and discussing them on my channel. 😊

-Justin.

EMAIL 8

From: SOVEREIGN GRAND DUCHY OF DRAKENBERG <royaldragoncourt@gmail.com>	
Date: 1 Jul 2026, 17:59	
To: Justin	
Subject: Re: The Dragon Legacy with Gary Wayne	

Justin,

Your response has been noted and retained.

The mask has slipped and your true self has been shown.

For the avoidance of doubt, you do not have my permission to use my books, my father's work under my stewardship, my name, my family history, or Dragon Court material in any defamatory, mocking, misleading, or hostile framing.

You have now confirmed in writing that my notice has "hardened" your resolve to discuss the matter further. Any further publication will therefore be treated as knowing publication after notice.

I will not engage with personal insults or anonymous third-party gossip.

Abbe de Vere

Dragon Publishing

Separate Podcast Evidence: The Wider Gary Wayne Bloodline Framework

This is a separate podcast from the Prometheus Lens episode. It should therefore be treated as separate public evidence, not as part of the same video.

The Prometheus Lens episode is the direct *Dragon Legacy* evidence because it is titled *The Dragon Legacy w/ Gary Wayne*, names Nicholas de Vere's book, and uses my father's work as the opening basis of discussion.

This separate podcast is relevant for a different reason. It shows Gary Wayne publicly advancing the same wider interpretive framework elsewhere: royal bloodlines, Dragon terminology, Nephilim or Raphaim descent, fallen angels, secret societies, Freemasonry, hierarchy, elites, lower classes, end-times prophecy, and control.

.

One video shows the direct use and public discussion of my father's named book. The other shows the broader framework Gary Wayne repeatedly applies to royal and Dragon bloodline material. Taken together, they show a pattern: Gary Wayne discusses these themes across platforms and repeatedly places royal, Dragon, bloodline and genealogical material inside his own Genesis 6 / fallen angel / end-times conspiracy structure.

The concern is not merely that Gary Wayne has a theological opinion. The concern is that Nicholas de Vere's Dragon Legacy / Dragon Court source-field is being pulled into that same hostile framework and publicly reframed through it.

Now in the last few days it has been presented to me that this has not been one isolated offence, Justine Brown whom I never heard of before these last 3 days and until I saw this podcast has been uploading several podcasts using The Dragon Court, The Dragon Legacy, dressed up as a vampire and mocking us, In one podcast he is sat with four other people discussing the books, and calling us evil, vampires, blood drinkers, and pornographic. Where I thought It was just one incident it turns out that I am his gravy train, He is using my material for commercial purposes, Why should other people think it is ok to make money from me and my dads work?

This is my inheritance, that I have worked on for the last 13 -17 years bringing it into the mainstream. These people are relentless.

Copyright Infringement Bad Faith

As I mentioned The Dragon Legacy Video was removed , Justine reuploaded it and tries to start a smear campaign.

I reported is for bullying and harassment, along with a new copyright infringements as this is not fair use, This is my response to you Tube.

Dear You Tube Copyright Support,

Thank you for your review.

I am providing the required detailed explanation as to why this video constitutes wilful infringement and does not qualify as fair use or fair dealing.

I request that YouTube proceed with removal based on the following factors.

1. Verbatim use of copyrighted material

The issue is not general discussion or criticism. The uploader displays and discusses *The Dragon Legacy* by my late father, Nicholas de Vere, and uses material from the book without permission. The disputed material is being used word for word, verbatim, in a hostile context.

I am the rights holder and manager of Nicholas de Vere's estate and Dragon Publishing material.

2. Bad faith and wilful continuation after notice

The uploader acknowledges that I previously issued a copyright complaint. At approximately 03:35, he names me directly and states that I sent him a copyright violation, before saying words to the effect of: "she doesn't know me, but she will soon." He also says he will continue, "double down," "lean in harder," and "push harder."

This demonstrates knowledge of the copyright dispute and an intention to continue using the disputed material after notice. That is not innocent or good-faith use.

3. Commercial exploitation and market harm

The uploader uses my father's work, the Royal Dragon Court name, and the controversy around my family/source-field to attract viewers to his channel and platform. He also states that he is preparing his own commercial book using this material.

This creates direct market harm because the video uses my inherited intellectual property, family name, and publishing source-field to build his own commercial audience. Viewers have already commented that they intended to buy de Vere books but will now look for used copies instead. This shows actual commercial damage to Dragon Publishing sales.

4. Hostile misrepresentation and reputational damage

The video is not a neutral review. It frames the Royal Dragon Court, my father's work, my bloodline, and the living community around it as "evil," "blood drinking," and "serpent seed." This hostile framing damages the commercial value of the books and brand.

The video uses copyrighted material while simultaneously presenting the rights holder, author's family, and source community in a defamatory and degrading manner. That is not fair dealing in good faith.

5. Harassment and targeted intimidation

The uploader names me personally, comments on my motives, discusses my copyright complaint, and frames the re-upload as retaliation. His statement that I "don't know him, but I will soon" is intimidating in context, especially when combined with his stated intention to continue and escalate.

This crosses beyond ordinary commentary into targeted harassment and cyberbullying.

6. Assisting wider infringement

The video continues with an interview involving Gary Wayne, whose work is already subject to separate copyright concerns for extensive unauthorised use of Nicholas de Vere / Dragon Publishing material. This video therefore helps promote, justify, and circulate wider infringement of my father's work.

For these reasons, the video is not fair use, fair dealing, or good-faith commentary. It is a wilful repeat use of copyrighted material after notice, combined with commercial exploitation, personal targeting, reputational harm, and ongoing misuse of Nicholas de Vere / Dragon Publishing / Royal Dragon Court material.

Please enforce removal of the video immediately.

Kind regards,
Abbe De Vere

Now all of this evidence is ready w=for when he attempts to upload his book to amazon, As he said keep a look out for it, I certainly will have all the evidence I need to prove this is in bad faith.

Keep every bit of evidence. I HAVE NOT RETALLIATED, no comments, on his channel, no retaliating shorts or videos of my own, Although I am well within my rights.

My professional Facebook is clean of anything that can be used to say that I am stirring up hate, or creating drama. I have just kept everything as evidence and stayed as normal as possible.

This is the graceful and dignified way to deal with it, while right now online behaviour is very toxic and all about taking out the trash, naming and shaming people online and making them with no choice take accountability.

I have not done this to my fans, Most of them have no clue what's been happening.

Other Podcast Interviews

Third Podcast Evidence: Arthur, Guinevere, Fairy and Dragon Bloodlines

A third public podcast further demonstrates the repeated framework being used by Gary Wayne around Dragon, Fairy, royal, Arthurian, bloodline, secret society and Nephilim material.

This episode is titled *King Arthur & Guinevere: Human Hybrids of Fairy & Dragon Bloodlines? | with Gary Wayne PODCAST #3*, published by Reema Fae Podcast on 15 January 2022. The title alone is significant because it publicly frames King Arthur and Guinevere as possible human hybrids of Fairy and Dragon bloodlines.

The episode description confirms that the discussion covers King Arthur, Guinevere, Camelot, the Lady of the Lake, Excalibur, Morgan le Fay, the Knights of the Round Table, Avalon, Tolkien's *Lord of the Rings*, fairies, dragons, wizards, secret societies, Atlantis, New Atlantis, mythical beings, and pre-history. The timestamped topics include King Arthur as son of Uther Pendragon, Guinevere's bloodline and genealogy, whether fairies and dragons co-existed with humanity, whether these beings were inter-dimensional, Fairy and Elven people, bloodlines of Morgan le Fay and Lancelot, Tolkien's connection to Arthurian pre-history, Glastonbury, and whether Fairy, Dragon and Demi-God bloodlines still exist today.

This is not an isolated subject. It is the same cluster of material repeatedly appearing around Gary Wayne's public work: Dragon bloodlines, Fairy bloodlines, Arthurian genealogy, royal descent, secret societies, Atlantis, hidden history, bloodline survival, altered human origins, and Nephilim or giant-related interpretation.

In the transcript, Gary Wayne states that King Arthur descends from the Tuatha Dé Danann, that Arthur's father is a Pendragon, and that

Guinevere is a Fairy Queen of Tuatha Dé Danann bloodlines. He then frames the Tuatha Dé Danann as Fairy people, giants of Ireland, direct descendants of the Golden Age, and part of a wider Atlantis-linked bloodline structure.

This matters because the same symbolic field appears throughout Nicholas de Vere's work and the Dragon Legacy / Dragon Court material: Dragon bloodlines, Fairy bloodlines, Pendragon language, Tuatha Dé Danann, Arthurian tradition, Avalon, Grail symbolism, Elven people, royal genealogy, ancient bloodlines, and hidden history.

The issue is not that Gary Wayne discusses Arthurian material. The issue is that he repeatedly absorbs the same Dragon / Fairy / royal / bloodline source-field into his own Genesis 6 framework and presents it through fallen angels, demigods, giants, secret societies, Atlantis, New Atlantis, occult hierarchy and end-times theology.

The podcast also shows how wide the public pattern is. In one podcast, *The Dragon Legacy* by Nicholas de Vere is named, read from, and discussed. In another, Gary Wayne discusses royal bloodlines, Dragon terminology, Nephilim / Raphaim descent, fallen angels and hierarchy. In this third podcast, he discusses Arthur, Guinevere, Fairy and Dragon bloodlines, Pendragon ancestry, Avalon, Glastonbury, Tolkien, Atlantis and whether those bloodlines still exist today.

Taken together, these podcasts show a repeated public use of the same thematic field. The same ideas are circulated across platforms, repackaged for different audiences, and repeatedly placed inside Gary Wayne's interpretive structure.

That is why I say this is not accidental. It is a pattern.

Nicholas de Vere's work is not merely being disagreed with. The wider Dragon Legacy / Dragon Court / Fairy / Elven / Arthurian / royal bloodline source-field is being drawn into Gary Wayne's public content ecosystem and reframed through his Genesis 6 conspiracy model.

That reframing matters because it turns complex genealogical, mythological, historical and symbolic material into a story about fallen angels, demigods, occult bloodlines, secret societies, hidden rulers, end-times deception and spiritual danger.

The result is reputationally damaging. It risks making the public believe that Dragon Publishing, the Royal Dragon Court ®, Nicholas de Vere's work, and the families connected to this material are part of a literal demonic, hybrid, fallen angel, bloodline-control system.

That is not a fair representation of my father's work. It is not a fair representation of me. It is not a fair representation of Dragon Publishing. It is Gary Wayne's imposed framework.

Fourth Podcast Evidence: The Hive Mind, Elven Gene, Fairy Gene and Mark of the Beast Framework

A fourth public example appears in the Eric Rolon / Tough Clips video titled *The Abyss, Unbreakable Chains, & The Mark Of The Beast — With Gary Wayne*, published on 28 July 2023.

This podcast clip is not directly titled around *The Dragon Legacy*, and I do not present it as direct citation evidence from Nicholas de Vere's book. Its importance is different. It shows the same wider Gary Wayne interpretive framework being publicly developed through Enoch, the Watchers, DNA alteration, the Mark of the Beast, Nephilim, counterfeit spirits, quantum technology, hive mind, Rh-negative blood, the Elven Gene, the Fairy Gene, Anjou symbolism, bees, and transhumanism.

That matters because these are not random disconnected themes. They overlap directly with the distinctive symbolic field that appears in

Nicholas de Vere's work and in the Dragon Legacy / Dragon Court source-field: Elven bloodlines, Fairy bloodlines, Dragon symbolism, Grail Code, Hive Mind, Merovingian Bee, Rh-negative blood, Anjou, inherited bloodline traits, and hidden genealogical structures.

In this clip, Gary Wayne discusses the Mark of the Beast as part of a system involving DNA alteration, altered humanity, quantum technology, dimensions, the Abyss, demons, fallen angels, counterfeit spirit, immortality, godhood, and the "ultimate hive mind." He then links that hive mind concept to "occult bloodlines," inherited demigod traits, Rh-negative blood, the Elven Gene, the Fairy Gene, and bloodlines going back to the Nephilim, Raphaim and fallen angels.

He also refers to the Anjou and their emblems, saying that designs which look like fleur-de-lis are actually an allegory for bees. This is important because the Bee / Hive Mind / Anjou / Elven / Fairy symbolic cluster is precisely the kind of material that appears in the Dragon Legacy / Dragon Court field and in the passages already compared elsewhere in this review.

The relevance of this clip is therefore not merely that Gary Wayne discusses Enoch or the Mark of the Beast. The relevance is that he repeatedly takes the same symbolic and genealogical vocabulary — Elven Gene, Fairy Gene, Rh-negative blood, Anjou, bees, hive mind, bloodlines, demigod inheritance, Nephilim and fallen angels — and places it inside an end-times demonological framework.

This is the repeated pattern.

In the Prometheus Lens episode, *The Dragon Legacy* by Nicholas de Vere is named, read from, and publicly discussed. In the Taylor Welch episode, Gary Wayne discusses royal bloodlines, Nephilim / Raphaim descent, fallen angels, secret societies and class hierarchy. In the Reema Fae episode, he discusses Arthur, Guinevere, Fairy and Dragon bloodlines, Pendragon, Avalon, Tolkien, Atlantis, DNA and whether such bloodlines still exist today. In the Eric Rolon clip, he extends the same field into Enoch, the Mark of the Beast, DNA alteration, transhumanism, the hive mind, Rh-negative blood, the Elven Gene, the Fairy Gene, Anjou and bee symbolism.

This is no longer an isolated overlap. It is a public content ecosystem.

The same terms, symbols and genealogical ideas recur across platform after platform. They are repeatedly repackaged into Gary Wayne's Genesis 6 / fallen angel / end-times framework and presented to audiences as evidence of deception, demonic influence, altered humanity, occult bloodlines, counterfeit spirit, transhumanism and the Mark of the Beast.

That is why the use of Nicholas de Vere's work cannot be treated as harmless, incidental or isolated. The Dragon Legacy / Dragon Court source-field is not simply being cited. It is being absorbed into a broader public narrative that repeatedly associates Elven, Fairy, Dragon, Anjou, royal and bloodline material with fallen angels, demonic spirits, DNA corruption, the Antichrist system and spiritual danger.

The reputational harm is obvious. These ideas are not being presented as neutral mythology, comparative religion, literary symbolism, genealogy, or alternative history. They are being framed as part of a threatening spiritual and biological conspiracy against humanity.

That is not my father's work being fairly reviewed. That is my father's source-field being mined and rebranded through somebody else's fear-based theological system.

Source Displacement and Assumed Authority

What appears to be happening is source displacement.

At the beginning, Gary Wayne cites or acknowledges the source-field enough to show knowledge and access. He refers to, reads from, or discusses material connected to Nicholas de Vere, Laurence Gardner, Dragon Court, Dragon Legacy, Fairy bloodlines, Dragon bloodlines, Anjou, Grail, Hive Mind, Elven Gene, Fairy Gene, Rh-negative blood, Arthurian genealogy, secret societies, royal bloodlines, Nephilim and fallen angel descent.

However, across repeated public interviews, the citation-trail becomes thinner while the language remains. The material is no longer presented as a contested source-field belonging to earlier authors, family archives, Dragon Publishing, Nicholas de Vere, Laurence Gardner, or the Royal Dragon Court tradition. Instead, it is increasingly delivered as Gary Wayne's own authority.

That is the problem.

A person cannot read from a source, absorb its terminology, repeat its structure, place it into their own system, speak about it repeatedly in public, and then gradually behave as though they are now the authority simply because audiences have heard it from them more often.

Repetition does not create authorship. Public speaking does not create ownership. Podcast appearances do not erase provenance. Familiarity with another author's source-field does not give a later commentator the right to displace the original source.

This is why the issue is larger than isolated copying. It is not only a question of whether a single sentence appears word-for-word. It is the cumulative transfer of authority. Nicholas de Vere's Dragon Legacy / Dragon Court material is used as raw material, passed through Gary

Wayne's Genesis 6 framework, and then publicly returned to audiences as though Gary Wayne is the primary interpreter and authority over it.

That is source displacement.

The original author becomes backgrounded. The family archive becomes invisible. The earlier publications become footnotes, or disappear altogether. The later commentator becomes the recognised public voice, while the source-field he relied upon is rebranded as his own research territory.

I reject that entirely.

Nicholas de Vere's work, Dragon Publishing's publications, the Royal Dragon Court ® source-field, and the family inheritance behind that material do not become Gary Wayne's intellectual property simply because he has spoken about them repeatedly.

Fifth Podcast Evidence: Faery and Dragon Royal Bloodlines as Nephilim Bondage

A further public example appears in the Gabbi Choong video titled *Gary Wayne — The Nephilim Faery & Dragon royal bloodlines and the counterfeit spirit*, premiered on 7 January 2024.

This video is significant because the public title and description directly frame Faery and Dragon royal bloodlines as Nephilim bloodlines connected with spiritual bondage, idolatry, deception, psyops, the Age of Horus, a United Nations One World Religion, fallen angelic technology, the seven fallen sciences, the Order of the Garter, the Order of the Golden Fleece, the Isis Gene, Sophia, the demiurge, unicorn symbolism, bloodline symbols and coats of arms.

This is not a neutral historical or genealogical discussion. It publicly packages Fairy and Dragon royal bloodline material as part of a hostile Christian end-times framework. The description itself states that these bloodlines have kept humanity in spiritual bondage and deceived humanity away from the Creator and the one true God.

That matters because the Dragon Legacy / Dragon Court source-field also contains Fairy, Dragon, Elven, royal, Anjou, Garter, Grail, bloodline, heraldic and symbolic material. Gary Wayne's public framework repeatedly takes that same symbolic field and places it into a narrative of Nephilim descent, fallen angels, spiritual deception, occult hierarchy, false religion and end-times control.

The transcript reinforces this. Gary Wayne is introduced as someone who writes about dragon bloodlines, giants, fallen angels and the Nephilim. The host frames his work as exposing Nephilim bloodlines and the royal ruling class. The discussion then moves into mystery schools, fallen angel technology, fallen sciences, Sophia, counterfeit spirit, Mother Goddess material, hive mind, queen bee symbolism, Fairy bloodlines, Dragon allegory, King Arthur, Uther Pendragon, Guinevere, the Fairy Queen, the gene of Isis and the Elven gens.

This is highly relevant because it shows the same pattern again. Fairy, Dragon, Elven, royal, heraldic and bloodline language is not being presented as genealogy, mythology, symbolism, literary tradition or alternative history. It is being publicly reframed as evidence of Nephilim bloodlines, spiritual bondage, fallen angel technology, demonic deception, counterfeit spirit and end-times manipulation.

That is the hostile rebranding.

The issue is not simply that Gary Wayne discusses similar subjects. The issue is that he repeatedly presents the Dragon / Fairy / Elven / royal bloodline field as if it belongs inside his Genesis 6 demonological system, while the original source-field and earlier authors become displaced or backgrounded.

This supports the wider source-displacement argument. After repeated podcasts and interviews, Gary Wayne becomes treated by hosts and audiences as the authority on Fairy and Dragon royal bloodlines, while the earlier Dragon Court / Dragon Legacy / Gardner / Nicholas de Vere source-field is no longer properly foregrounded. The language remains, the structure remains, the symbolic material remains, but the public authority shifts to Gary Wayne.

That is not harmless commentary. It is cumulative source displacement combined with hostile religious recharacterisation.

The timeline is even more important when stated precisely.

Gary Wayne identifies the period from approximately 1980 to 1996 as the first part of his research. That phase, by his own explanation, was centred on the Bible, prophecy, Genesis 6, angels, demons, giants, the Flood, Antichrist, Revelation and related scriptural material.

He then explains that from 1996 to about 2013 he moved into the wider field: comparative religions, mythology, Gnostic texts, mystery schools, bloodlines, elite structures and secret societies.

That distinction matters.

The Dragon / Faery / Elven / Anjou / Grail / Bee / Hive Mind / royal bloodline material does not appear, from his own account, to belong to his earliest Bible-prophecy foundation. It appears to belong to the later research phase, from 1996 onward, when he began learning about secret societies, mystery schools, bloodlines and the wider esoteric framework.

This is exactly the period after Nicholas de Vere and Laurence Gardner had become publicly known.

That does not prove every source by itself, but it makes the provenance question unavoidable. If Gary Wayne's first phase was Bible prophecy, and his second phase was secret societies, bloodlines and esoteric structures, then the question becomes: where did the later Dragon, Faery, Elven, Anjou, Grail, Bee, Hive Mind and royal-bloodline framework come from?

That is the point. His own timeline separates the Bible-first foundation from the later bloodline-source-field expansion. The later expansion must be traced properly, especially where it overlaps with Nicholas de Vere, Laurence Gardner, the Dragon Court, the Grail/Ring Lords field, and the wider Dragon Legacy source-field.

Gary Wayne's Admission About Religious Texts, Authority and Control

There is also an important admission in Gary Wayne's discussion of the Qur'an.

In the Gabbi Choong interview, Gary Wayne explains that he did not want to include the Qur'an in his book but eventually did so because he considered it relevant. He says he wanted the best English translation, chose the Oxford translation, and included it as part of his wider comparative-religion framework.

That is relevant because it shows that Gary Wayne is willing to use religious texts outside the Bible when they assist his own argument. He does not confine himself to the Bible. He reads, selects, interprets and incorporates material from other traditions where it helps his thesis.

He then says he is not a Qur'an expert, but also describes correcting people on passages, context and related texts. This creates a tension. On the one hand, he distances himself from being an expert. On the other, he publicly speaks with authority about how the Qur'an should be read, how Muslims are allegedly taught to understand it, and how religious hierarchies use texts.

Most importantly, he admits that religious authorities use religious texts for power and control.

That admission matters.

It means Gary Wayne already understands that religious interpretation can be used to control people, manipulate belief, and set one group against another. Yet when others question the Church, question biblical canon, question institutional religious power, or examine excluded traditions, he frames that questioning as deception, polytheism, Gnosticism, idolatry or spiritual danger.

That is inconsistent.

If Gary Wayne is allowed to read the Qur'an, the Vedas, Gnostic texts, the Popol Vuh, mythology, Enoch, secret society publications and other religious or esoteric material in order to develop his Christian framework, then it is hypocritical to imply that others are evil, deceived or spiritually corrupt for reading widely, questioning inherited doctrine, or examining religious history from outside the Church's preferred boundaries.

Research is not evil when Gary Wayne does it, but demonic when Nicholas de Vere, Laurence Gardner, Dragon Publishing, or the Royal Dragon Court source-field does it.

That double standard is part of the problem.

Gary Wayne's own method relies on comparative religion. He reads outside the Bible. He uses non-biblical traditions. He interprets myth, language, symbolism, bloodlines, secret societies and religious texts. He then uses those materials to support his own Christian conclusion.

Therefore, he cannot fairly condemn others merely for working across religious traditions, examining alternative texts, questioning church authority, or tracing suppressed histories.

The issue is not that Gary Wayne researches religion. The issue is that he reserves legitimacy for his own research while presenting similar or earlier research by others as dangerous, deceptive, demonic or spiritually corrupt.

That is not objective scholarship. It is selective authority.

Admission of Bias and Evangelical Purpose

Gary Wayne also openly admits that his work is not neutral.

In the Gabbi Choong interview, he explains that *The Genesis 6 Conspiracy* was written from a Christian perspective. He says that while it was not written only for Christians, it was designed so that people outside Christianity might see commonality between Christianity, other cultures, other histories, and the Bible. He then states that this might encourage them to read the Bible.

That is important because it shows that Gary Wayne's use of comparative religion is not detached academic inquiry. It is being used inside an openly Christian interpretive and evangelical framework.

He is therefore not simply comparing religions, myths, bloodlines, secret societies, Arthurian legends, Dragon material, Faery material, Elven material, Grail symbolism, Gnostic texts, Qur'anic passages, Vedic material or ancient mythology as neutral source material. He is selecting and interpreting those materials in a way that supports his Christian conclusion.

That is his bias, and he admits it.

There is nothing wrong with a writer having a perspective. The problem arises when that perspective is used to reframe another author's source-field as spiritually dangerous, demonic, deceptive, fallen angelic, Nephilim-linked, bloodline-corrupt or Antichrist-related, while the author presents his own interpretation as the corrective truth.

This matters directly to Nicholas de Vere's work.

Gary Wayne's framework is not neutral scholarship on the Dragon Legacy / Dragon Court field. It is a Christian apologetic and end-times framework into which he places earlier Dragon, Faery, Elven, Anjou, Grail, Hive Mind, royal bloodline and secret-society material. Once placed inside that framework, the material is no longer being read on its own terms. It is being used to support Gary Wayne's pre-existing religious conclusion.

That is why his treatment of Nicholas de Vere, Laurence Gardner, Dragon Court material and related source-fields must be scrutinised.

Gary Wayne is entitled to write from a Christian perspective. He is not entitled to absorb another author's distinctive source-field, use it as content, and then publicly rebrand it as demonic or deceptive while allowing audiences to treat him as the authority over it.

His own admission of bias matters because it explains the pattern: the material is not being preserved in its original context. It is being converted into evidence for his Christian Genesis 6 argument.

Part Two as an Argument Manual for Christians

Gary Wayne's own description of *The Genesis 6 Conspiracy Part Two* is highly relevant.

In the Gabbi Choong interview, he explains that the sequel is "targeted at Christians" and is designed to give them "the arguments that they need." He says the purpose is so that when someone responds by saying, "that's crazy talk" or "you've taken that out of context," Christians will have the information in front of them.

He then explains that he placed material in footnotes rather than endnotes because there is so much information on the same page, allowing readers to go to those areas, make their arguments, and take them back to people "whether or not they want to hear them." He also says that what people "can't say is it's not biblical," and that this is what the book was about.

That matters because this is not neutral comparative scholarship. It is openly framed as an argumentative Christian resource.

Gary Wayne is not merely saying, "Here is a historical study of mythology, genealogy, secret societies, Dragon bloodlines, Faery bloodlines, Elven gens, Anjou symbolism, the Hive Mind, Gnostic texts, Qur'anic material, Vedic material and ancient religion." He is saying that he is equipping Christians with arguments to defend his reading and challenge others.

That admission changes the way his work should be read.

His books and interviews are not detached academic treatments of the source material. They are written and spoken from an acknowledged Christian position, with a declared purpose of giving Christians an argumentative framework. The sources are selected, organised and interpreted to serve that purpose.

This is especially important where Nicholas de Vere, Laurence Gardner, Dragon Court material, Faery bloodlines, Dragon bloodlines, Grail material, Elven symbolism, Anjou, bees, royal genealogies and secret societies are concerned. When those materials enter Gary Wayne's work, they do not remain in their own historical, symbolic or authorial context. They are converted into ammunition for his Genesis 6 / prophecy / fallen angel / end-times argument.

That is not the same as fair representation.

It is one thing to cite another author for criticism or comparison. It is another thing to absorb a distinctive source-field into an apologetic weapon designed to argue that the material is ultimately biblical evidence of deception, fallen angels, Nephilim bloodlines, counterfeit spirit, demonic influence or end-times corruption.

Gary Wayne's own words therefore support my concern. He has not simply studied these materials. He has built an argumentative system around them and taught audiences how to use that system against competing interpretations.

That helps explain the hostile recharacterisation.

Nicholas de Vere's work is not being approached on its own terms. It is being placed inside a framework already designed to prove a Christian Genesis 6 conclusion. Once inside that framework, Dragon, Faery, Elven, Grail and royal bloodline material becomes evidence for Gary Wayne's argument, rather than being treated as protected work with its own provenance, meaning, authorship and context.

This is why the issue cannot be dismissed as ordinary commentary. Gary Wayne's own explanation shows that the material is being used as part of a targeted Christian argumentative project.

Specific Timestamp: "Pure Blood Dragon Bloodline" and "Pure Blood Fairy Bloodline"

At approximately 51:45 in the Gabbi Choong interview, Gary Wayne uses the phrase "pure blood dragon bloodline" and pairs it directly with "pure blood fairy bloodline."

This is significant because the terminology is no longer general. He is not merely discussing the Bible, Genesis 6, giants, angels or prophecy. He is speaking in the specific language of Dragon and Fairy bloodlines.

He states that when a new dynasty is started, a pure blood Dragon bloodline and a pure blood Fairy bloodline are grafted or "scioned" together, with particular emphasis on the female bloodline because of its rarity.

That phrase matters.

"Dragon bloodline" and "Fairy bloodline" are central terms within the Nicholas de Vere / Dragon Legacy / Dragon Court source-field. They are not ordinary biblical phrases. They belong to a distinctive esoteric, genealogical and mythological framework involving Dragon descent, Fairy / Elven bloodlines, royal genealogy, Anjou, Grail traditions, bloodline symbolism and hidden dynastic history.

Gary Wayne then places those terms into his own Genesis 6 structure: Nephilim, Raphaim, giants, fertility issues, post-Flood bloodline survival, hybridisation and fallen angel descent.

That is exactly the pattern I am identifying.

The source-field language remains, but the meaning is redirected. Dragon and Fairy bloodline terminology is removed from its original Dragon Legacy / Dragon Court context and converted into part of Gary Wayne's fallen angel / Nephilim / end-times bloodline argument.

This supports the wider source-displacement point. Gary Wayne is not simply discussing "giants" from the Bible. He is using highly specific Dragon and Fairy bloodline terminology, then presenting it through his own theological framework as though he is the authority over it.

That is why this timestamp should be preserved.

Arthur, Tuatha Dé Danann, Pendragon and the Dragon/Fairy Bloodline Structure

Another important point appears when Gary Wayne discusses King Arthur.

In the Gabbi Choong interview, he states that Arthur is a descendant of the Tuatha Dé Danann and the son of Uther Pendragon. He then connects Arthur to the Dragon King role and Guinevere to the Fairy Queen / Mother Goddess role.

This matters because the terminology is no longer merely biblical. Arthur, Tuatha Dé Danann, Pendragon, Dragon King, Fairy Queen, Fairy bloodline and Dragon bloodline are all part of a very specific symbolic and genealogical field.

The Tuatha Dé Danann, Fairy bloodlines, Elven gens, Pendragon language, Arthurian genealogy, Dragon kingship and royal bloodline symbolism are central to the wider Dragon Legacy / Dragon Court source-field associated with Nicholas de Vere and related Grail / Dragon / Fairy / Elven material.

Gary Wayne then reframes those terms through his own Genesis 6 structure: Nephilim, Raphaim, giants, fallen angels, post-Flood hybrid bloodlines, fertility issues and demigod descent.

That is the pattern again.

He is not simply discussing "giants in the Bible." He is using the Dragon/Fairy/Arthurian source-field and translating it into his own fallen angel bloodline system. Arthur becomes not merely an Arthurian figure, but part of a Dragon/Fairy/Nephilim dynastic framework. Guinevere becomes not merely a queen in Arthurian tradition, but a Fairy Queen / Mother Goddess figure inside his theological argument.

This is why the passage matters. It shows Gary Wayne using the same Dragon/Fairy/Elven/Arthurian vocabulary that appears in the Nicholas de Vere / Dragon Legacy / Dragon Court field, while presenting it as part of his own Genesis 6 authority.

Female Bloodlines, Fertility, Rh-Negative Blood and the Future Expansion of the Framework

Gary Wayne's discussion of the "terrible ones" is also relevant because it leads into his wider claims about fertility, female bloodlines and inherited bloodline traits.

In the Gabbi Choong interview, he states that the post-Flood giants had a fertility issue and specifically describes it as a female issue. He says there was a shortage of female giants and that this affected the continuation of bloodline dynasties. He then links this to the need to graft or "scion" a pure Dragon bloodline with a pure Fairy bloodline, with special emphasis on the female bloodline because of its rarity.

That is significant.

Gary Wayne is not merely discussing abstract biblical prophecy. He is constructing a reproductive and dynastic bloodline theory. Female bodies, fertility, inheritance, rare bloodlines, Dragon bloodlines, Fairy bloodlines, post-Flood giants and dynastic continuation all become part of the same system.

This becomes even more important when compared with his later discussion of Rh-negative blood, the Elven Gene, the Fairy Gene, inherited demigod traits, Nephilim / Raphaim ancestry, the Hive Mind, queen bee symbolism and bloodlines back to fallen angels.

Taken together, the pattern is clear: female fertility, rare female bloodlines, Dragon bloodlines, Fairy bloodlines, Elven genes, Rh-negative blood, inherited traits and dynastic survival are being folded into Gary Wayne's Genesis 6 / fallen angel / end-times framework.

That matters because this is precisely the kind of material that overlaps with the Dragon Legacy / Dragon Court / Elven / Fairy / Grail / bloodline source-field, but it is being re-explained through Gary Wayne's own theological system.

It also shows that the issue is expanding, not shrinking.

Gary Wayne is not merely repeating old material from earlier chapters. He is building forward: using public podcasts to discuss female bloodline rarity, fertility issues, Dragon and Fairy bloodlines, and then linking similar material elsewhere to Rh-negative blood, Elven genes, Fairy genes, inherited demigod traits and future end-times deception.

This strengthens the source-displacement argument because the source-field is being carried into new publications, new interviews and new public claims. The more this continues, the more the public associates Dragon / Fairy / Elven / bloodline material with Gary Wayne rather than with the earlier Dragon Court / Nicholas de Vere / Laurence Gardner source-field.

It also strengthens the hostile recharacterisation argument because the material is not being presented neutrally. Female bloodlines, Dragon bloodlines, Fairy bloodlines, Elven genes and rare blood inheritance are being associated with giants, fallen angels, Nephilim, Raphaim, demigods, spiritual deception, counterfeit spirit and end-times corruption.

That is not simply historical discussion. It is religiously hostile reframing of a distinctive bloodline and symbolic field.

This is not NEW INFORMATION, again it is something we all within the Royal Dragon Court know, because we have the RH Neg blood situation, Many of us and our mothers have lived through this, at this point it is becoming predictable.

Early 2017 Podcast Evidence: House of Dragon and Antichrist Bloodlines

A further important item appears in the Awakening Liberty video titled *THE HOUSE OF DRAGON & ANTICHRIST BLOODLINES GARY WAYNE*, published on 8 May 2017.

This video is significant even without a transcript because the public title and description are themselves evidential.

The title directly links "The House of Dragon" with "Antichrist Bloodlines." That is not a neutral description of myth, genealogy, symbolism, heraldry, Arthurian tradition, Grail material, Dragon Court material or royal bloodline research. It is a hostile religious framing. The Dragon field is being publicly associated with Antichrist bloodlines.

The description states that Gary Wayne, author of *The Genesis 6 Conspiracy: How Secret Societies and the Descendants of Giants Plan to Enslave Mankind*, joined the show for the fifth programme in an ongoing series. It also states that his book details the role of modern-day Nephilim in Satan's plan to install the Antichrist at the End of Days.

The topics listed include Dragons in the Bible, occult symbolism including the Ouroboros, Fairies, Goblins and Elven mythologies, Rex Deus, the bloodlines of the thirteen families, the Sinclair's and Stewarts, and whether these are the bloodlines which will spawn the Antichrist.

That combination is highly relevant.

By 2017, Gary Wayne was already publicly discussing the same cluster of subjects that later appears across his podcasts and interviews: Dragon material, Faery material, Elven mythology, Rex Deus, royal bloodlines, occult symbolism, secret societies, serpent beings, Nephilim, Antichrist bloodlines and end-times control.

This is not merely biblical discussion. It is the Dragon / Faery / Elven / royal bloodline field placed into an Antichrist framework.

The date matters. This video was published in 2017, long before the later 2024 and 2025 interviews, showing that the hostile public rebranding of this field had already been underway for years. It also appears to be part of a series, as the description refers to this as the fifth show in an ongoing sequence. That suggests repeated platforming and repeated public conditioning of the audience to associate Dragon,

Faery, Elven and royal bloodline material with Nephilim descent, Satan's plan, Antichrist prophecy and spiritual enslavement.

This strengthens the source-displacement argument.

By repeatedly appearing on shows like this, Gary Wayne was not only discussing a source-field. He was occupying it. The audience was being taught to hear "House of Dragon," "Fairies," "Elven mythologies," "Rex Deus," "Ouroboros," "Sinclair," "Stewart" and "royal bloodlines" through Gary Wayne's Genesis 6 / Antichrist framework.

That is public authority transfer.

It is also hostile recharacterisation.

Dragon, Faery, Elven, Rex Deus and royal bloodline material are not being presented in their own context. They are being folded into claims about modern-day Nephilim, Satan's plan, secret societies, enslavement of mankind, and the bloodlines that may spawn the Antichrist.

This is the very thing I object to: a distinctive Dragon / Faery / Elven / royal bloodline source-field being taken into Gary Wayne's religious argument system and then publicly branded as Antichrist-related.

Early 2017 Evidence: The Zen Garcia Interview, Opening Quote, Host Framing and Dragon Bloodline Recharacterisation

A highly significant early example appears in the Zen Garcia interview titled *Gary Wayne — Antediluvian Atlantean Dragon Lords and Their Blood Progeny I of II*, published on 26 June 2017.

This interview is important because the hostile framing begins before Gary Wayne even speaks. It begins with the public title, the description, and the host's opening quote.

The title itself directly connects "Dragon Lords" with "blood progeny," Atlantis, and the antediluvian world. The description then frames the programme as the first part of a two-part series on ancient Atlantean reverence and "ritualized blood worship" of "feathered reptilian entities." It also connects these entities with Zep Tepi, ancient deities and Revelation 12.

That is not neutral language.

Before the discussion has even begun, the audience is being placed inside a hostile frame: Dragon Lords, blood progeny, reptilian entities, ritual blood worship, Atlantis, ancient deities and biblical apocalypse.

The opening quote then reinforces that frame. It describes serpent worship as one of the most remarkable and mysterious forms of religion in the world. It asks what humanity could see in something so "repulsive and forbidding" as the reptile, and then says serpent worship can be traced across the ancient world through mythology, monuments, temples and earthworks.

This opening matters because it primes the listener.

The audience is not being invited into a neutral discussion of Dragon symbolism, family tradition, royal genealogy, Arthurian material, Grail symbolism, heraldry, mythology or historical source-study. The audience is being invited into a discussion of repulsive reptiles, serpent worship, global ancient cults, Dragon Lords, blood progeny and ritualized blood worship.

That is reputational poisoning by association.

The sequence is clear: serpent worship, reptilian imagery, global ancient religion, feathered serpent entities, Dragon Lords, blood progeny and ritual blood worship. Once that frame has been established, later references to Dragon bloodlines, royal bloodlines, serpent symbolism or ancient blood descent are already contaminated by the opening association.

The hostile effect is therefore not limited to one direct defamatory sentence. It is created by the framing architecture: the title, the description, the opening quote, the host's commentary and the direction of the discussion.

Gary Wayne then participates inside that frame.

The transcript moves into serpent worship, feathered serpent traditions, reptilian-looking beings, Anunnaki mythology, Egyptian gods, elongated skulls, serpent-like beings, bird-like beings, patriarchal bloodline allegories, dragons, ravens and serpents as signs of royal bloodlines descending back to the gods. Gary discusses royal bloodlines, gods, Nephilim, hybrid humans, serpent-like beings, fallen angel descent, Titans, corrupted DNA, demigods, secret societies and the possibility that diluted bloodlines became the ruling class.

This is extremely important because it shows that, by June 2017, Gary Wayne was already participating in public conversations where Dragon bloodline material was being framed as antediluvian, Atlantean, reptilian, serpent-based, blood-descended, Nephilim-linked and spiritually hostile.

The blood language is especially serious.

The public description uses the phrase "blood progeny" and refers to "ritualized blood worship." Later in the discussion, blood drinking is described as a significant part of ancient ritual and as something that continues in secret societies. It is linked with increased cognitive ability, life extension, sacrifice, occultism, fertility rites, cannibalism and the belief that descendants of gods or demigods treat ordinary humans as inferior.

This is not harmless mythological commentary.

Dragon language is being made to sound monstrous. Dragon bloodline material is being placed beside reptilian entities, ritual blood worship, secret societies, Nephilim descent, demigods, corrupted DNA, sacrifice, cannibalism, domination and end-times deception.

That is the hostile recharacterisation.

The issue is not merely that Gary Wayne discusses dragons or serpents. The issue is that Dragon / serpent / royal bloodline language is repeatedly framed in public as something demonic, blood-ritualistic, reptilian, fallen, predatory and hostile to humanity.

This matters directly to the Dragon Legacy / Dragon Court source-field.

Nicholas de Vere's work may contain Dragon symbolism, royal genealogy, Faery and Elven traditions, Grail material, ancient religious memory, serpent symbolism, bloodline mythology and controversial historical claims. But that does not mean that the Dragon source-field can fairly be reduced to reptilian blood worship, Nephilim descent, secret-society cannibalism, Antichrist bloodlines or fallen angel corruption.

The Zen Garcia interview shows the mechanism of reputational harm.

The host builds the hostile frame. The title and description introduce Dragon Lords, blood progeny and ritual blood worship. The opening quote primes the audience with serpent worship and repulsive reptilian imagery. Gary Wayne then continues the discussion inside that frame by speaking about serpent gods, royal bloodlines, Nephilim, hybrid beings, fallen angels, blood rituals, secret societies and diluted ruling bloodlines.

The combined effect is that Dragon bloodline material is publicly rebranded as something sinister, occult, reptilian, demonic, blood-based and spiritually corrupt.

2025 Far Out With Faust Evidence: Royal Bloodlines, Dragons and "Celestial Mafia Godfathers"

A further significant example appears in the *Far Out With Faust* episode titled *Secret Societies, Royal Bloodlines, and Hidden Bible Revelations | Gary Wayne Podcast*, premiered on 14 February 2025.

The public description frames Gary Wayne as revealing the hidden truth behind secret societies, ancient bloodlines and their influence on human history. It states that he exposes elite families who claim divine rights to rule the world, discusses the House of Windsor bloodline, King Charles III's connection to Vlad the Impaler, powerful dynasties, the Romanovs and Tsars, the New World Order, UFOs, fallen angels, interdimensional beings, the Priory of Sion, Atlantis, the Ring lords and the suppressed sciences of the ancient world.

This is highly relevant because it shows the same pattern again: royal bloodlines, secret societies, hidden Bible revelations, fallen angels, ancient gods, elite families, Atlantis, Ring lords and global control are placed together as one interpretive field.

The opening clip is particularly important.

Gary Wayne asks whether King Charles III's oath was to the God of the Bible or to another god. He then says that in the royal belief system, divine right comes from a specific god, and that this god is connected through heraldic imagery to bloodlines going back to a specific Angelic being. He lists dragons, eagles, bulls and other symbols, saying that these are understood as their "Celestial Mafia Godfathers."

That phrase matters.

"Celestial Mafia Godfathers" is not neutral historical language. It frames heraldic and royal bloodline symbolism as evidence of hidden allegiance to non-biblical godfathers, angelic beings, secret divine ancestry and an occult hierarchy. When dragon imagery is placed inside that statement, the Dragon source-field is again pulled into a hostile religious and conspiratorial framework.

Gary Wayne then develops the point further by saying that royal bloodlines trace back to specific Raphaim or Nephilim patriarchs, and then to the specific god who created them. He also states that royal families intermarried to keep their bloodlines pure and not mix with "lower-level beings," because they consider themselves superior as elites.

This is a serious public framing.

He is not merely saying that royal families have heraldic symbols. He is saying that dragons, eagles, bulls and other heraldic devices represent concealed bloodline connections to Angelic beings, Nephilim/Raphaim patriarchs and celestial godfathers. He is also associating royal bloodlines with elitism, divine-right claims, hidden gods, secret societies, lower beings and world control.

That is directly relevant to my complaint.

The Dragon Legacy / Dragon Court / royal bloodline source-field includes dragon symbolism, heraldry, genealogy, royal descent, Grail traditions, Arthurian memory and ancient symbolic structures. Gary Wayne's framework takes that same language and recodes it as evidence of Nephilim descent, fallen angel ancestry, occult divine right, secret-society control and a hidden celestial mafia.

That is hostile recharacterisation.

The issue is not that he mentions King Charles, Vlad the Impaler, the House of Windsor or heraldry. The issue is that he repeatedly places royal heraldic and bloodline material into a framework where dragons and other symbols become signs of non-biblical gods, Angelic beings, Nephilim/Raphaim patriarchs and hidden controllers.

This also supports the source-displacement argument.

By 2025, Gary Wayne is being publicly presented as the authority who can explain royal bloodlines, secret societies, Ring lords, Atlantis, hidden Bible revelations, the Priory of Sion, the House of Windsor, Vlad the Impaler and the supposed divine ancestry of ruling families. The audience is not being directed back to the earlier Dragon Court / Nicholas de Vere / Laurence Gardner / Grail / Ring Lords source-field. The public authority is being transferred to Gary Wayne.

The comment section reinforces that public authority transfer. Viewers describe Gary Wayne as unmatched in this realm of knowledge and as someone whose work explains present events and the Rex Deus bloodlines. This shows how audiences are receiving him: not merely as a commentator, but as the apparent authority over the bloodline field.

That matters because the field itself did not originate with him.

The Dragon / royal / Grail / Ring Lords / Rex Deus / bloodline material already had earlier source-fields, including Nicholas de Vere, Laurence Gardner and related Dragon Court material. When Gary Wayne speaks repeatedly across major podcasts and is praised as the authority over the same territory, the earlier source-field is displaced.

This video is therefore important evidence of both hostile framing and public authority transfer. Gary Wayne takes royal bloodline, Dragon, heraldic, Ring Lords and secret-society material and presents it through his Genesis 6 / Nephilim / fallen angel / celestial-godfather system, while the public increasingly treats him as the source of the knowledge.

In the *Far Out With Faust* interview, Gary Wayne discusses material that Nicholas de Vere and Laurence Gardner had already written about, including royal bloodlines, Rex Deus, Ring Lords, Dragon symbolism, the Priory of Sion, Charles III, Vlad the Impaler and hidden dynastic traditions.

The issue is not that he mentions those subjects. The issue is that he places them inside a secret-society / Genesis 6 framework. He describes royal divine right as connected through heraldic symbols, including dragons, eagles and bulls, to specific Angelic beings. He then refers to these as "Celestial Mafia Godfathers" and links royal bloodlines back to Raphaim or Nephilim patriarchs and the gods who supposedly created them.

That matters because the de Vere / Gardner source-field is being recoded. Material previously written about as Dragon, Grail, Rex Deus, Ring Lord and royal genealogy material is being presented to a podcast audience as evidence of secret-society bloodline control, fallen angel ancestry, elite domination and occult divine-right claims.

This is both source displacement and hostile recharacterisation. The earlier source-field remains in the background, while Gary Wayne becomes the public authority. At the same time, the meaning is changed: the material is made to sound like Nephilim/Raphaim bloodline control rather than de Vere / Gardner genealogy and source research.

And where that same source-field overlaps with earlier Dragon Court / Nicholas de Vere / Laurence Gardner material, the issue becomes even more serious: the earlier source-field is not only being displaced, but also being publicly poisoned.

In the *Far Out With Faust* interview, Gary Wayne states that people within secret societies reacted more positively than negatively to his work and that some of them verified his direction while he was researching. He says they would tell him whether he was going in the right or wrong direction.

That admission matters because it undermines the idea that his secret-society material is simply independent biblical research. He is saying that part of his work was discussed with, and in some way checked against, people connected to the very secret-society field he writes about.

He also says that his first book was intended to let other belief systems speak in their own words so that people could not accuse him of manipulating what they said. He then explains that, in book two, he went further into the Priory of Sion and attempted to trace the sources back.

This is relevant because it shows his method: he collects material from other belief systems, secret-society writings and prior source-fields, then places them inside his own Genesis 6 interpretation.

That is precisely why provenance matters. If he is using material from de Vere / Gardner territory, Priory of Sion material, Rex Deus, Ring Lords, Dragon symbolism, Grail bloodlines and royal genealogy, then the issue is not whether he has "researched" it. The issue is whether he has properly attributed the source-field and whether he has fairly represented it, rather than converting it into a secret-society / Nephilim / fallen angel control narrative.

Red Pill Underground: "House of Dragon" as Serpentine Bloodline

The Red Pill Underground interview titled *Gary Wayne — Order of the Dragon & The Arcane Serpent*, published on 29 May 2026, is one of the clearest current examples of Gary Wayne's hostile Dragon-bloodline framing.

At the very beginning of the transcript, Gary Wayne states that the biblical Seraphim angels are the serpentine gods seen around the world. He then says that these beings produced offspring who looked like them and identifies this as the origin of the "House of Dragon." He defines it as "the serpentine bloodline." He further states that kings before the Flood, and shortly after the Flood, were called dragons and serpents.

This is not vague symbolic commentary. It is a direct statement: House of Dragon equals serpentine bloodline.

He then links this to Dracula and Dracul language, stating that Dracula means "son of a dragon" and connecting Dracul / dragon terminology with a "dragon watcher" or watcher angel. The host immediately reinforces the association by adding "Draconian," "Dracula," and "blood suckers."

That sequence matters.

The public chain being created is Seraphim, serpentine gods, offspring, House of Dragon, serpentine bloodline, dragon kings, Dracula, Dracul, watcher angel, blood drinking and Draconian symbolism.

Gary Wayne then expands the same framework across world mythology: serpent imagery in First Nations traditions, serpent mounds, Aztec, Maya and Inca serpent symbolism, African serpent traditions, Egyptian reptilian gods, Sarmatian dragon warriors, Leviathan, Tiamat, Apophis, Lotan, Yam, Vritra and the Vedas. He presents serpent and dragon symbolism as a global religious memory of gods, giants and bloodlines.

He then goes further and states that the giants originally looked like serpents, became kings and royal families, received divine right to rule from the council of gods, and established the ruling classes of the world. He places ordinary humans beneath that system as lower classes, including labourers, slaves, sacrifice classes, blacksmiths, bakers and tailors.

This is the hostile recharacterisation in its clearest form.

Dragon and serpent language is not being treated as neutral myth, heraldry, genealogy or symbolism. It is being presented as evidence of serpentine gods, fallen angel offspring, giant kings, royal families, bloodline rule, secret societies, lower human classes, ancient hidden knowledge and end-times return.

Where this overlaps with the Dragon Legacy / Dragon Court / Nicholas de Vere / Laurence Gardner source-field, the concern is serious. Gary Wayne is not merely using common biblical imagery. He is publicly defining the House of Dragon as a serpentine bloodline and connecting Dragon terminology to Dracul, Dracula, watcher angels, blood-drinking imagery, royal bloodlines, ancient gods and end-times control.

That is not fair neutral representation. It is hostile religious recoding of the Dragon source-field.

Post-Notice Evidence: 17 June 2026 Indie Comic Empire Interview

The Indie Comic Empire interview titled *Writing Non-Fiction Connecting Nephilim Giants w/ Royal Families | ft. Gary Wayne* was published on 17 June 2026, five days after my cease-and-desist notice of 12 June 2026.

That timing matters.

The public description states that the interview discusses Gary Wayne's research into the connection between the Nephilim giants of the Christian Bible and modern royal and elite families. This is the same disputed bloodline field: royal families, elite descent, Nephilim, hidden genealogy and ancient bloodline control.

In the transcript, Gary Wayne expressly refers to Laurence Gardner. He says that when he was looking at royal genealogical research, he used Laurence Gardner in book one because Gardner was "one of the genealogists of several families" and because Gardner's books provided snapshots of the genealogies being tracked.

That admission is significant. It confirms that Laurence Gardner was not incidental to Gary Wayne's research. Gary Wayne identifies Gardner as a genealogical source used for the royal bloodline material.

The interview then continues into the same hostile framework. Gary discusses royal bloodlines, Nephilim patriarchs, celestial mafia godfathers and mothers, World War bloodline families, Rex Deus, royal families, House of Dragon / Game of Thrones allegory, dragon patriarchal bloodlines, heraldic coats of arms, dragons as Seraphim angels, intermarriage, scioning, grafting, pure bloodlines, the Gene of Isis, fairy gens, Elben gens, Rh-negative blood, royal genetics and elite bloodline tracking.

This is not a neutral mention of Laurence Gardner.

Gary Wayne acknowledges Gardner as a source for genealogical material and then places that same field into his own Genesis 6 / Nephilim / celestial mafia / secret-society / royal-bloodline framework.

Because the interview was published after the cease-and-desist notice, it should be preserved separately as post-notice evidence. It shows that the contested subject-field continued to be publicly discussed after notice had been given.

The issue is not only historical use. It is ongoing public use.

This interview is therefore important for three reasons. First, it is dated after notice. Second, it contains an express acknowledgement of Laurence Gardner as a source used for royal genealogical material. Third, it continues the hostile recharacterisation of that bloodline field by linking royal genealogy, Dragon symbolism, Rex Deus, House of Dragon, Nephilim patriarchs, celestial mafia godparents, heraldic dragons and Rh-negative blood into one Genesis 6 conspiracy framework.

This strengthens the argument that the de Vere / Gardner source-field was not merely cited and left alone. It was absorbed, reinterpreted and continued publicly after notice.

The omission of Nicholas de Vere is significant.

Gary Wayne is able to discuss the House of Vere / Dragon / royal bloodline field at length, and he is able to acknowledge Laurence Gardner as a genealogical source when it suits the structure of his argument. Yet when the discussion moves into the Dragon source-field itself, Nicholas de Vere is not named.

That omission matters because Nicholas de Vere is not peripheral to this subject-field. He is central to the Dragon Court / Dragon Legacy /

House of Vere material. A discussion that moves through royal bloodlines, Rex Deus, Dragon symbolism, House of Dragon allegory, heraldic dragons, ancient bloodlines and Gardner-style genealogical material cannot fairly treat Nicholas de Vere as invisible.

The result is selective provenance.

Laurence Gardner is useful to Gary Wayne as a genealogical source, so Gardner is named. Nicholas de Vere is more difficult for Gary Wayne because naming him would expose the prior Dragon source-field more clearly. It would also make it harder for Gary Wayne to appear as the public authority over Dragon bloodline material.

This is why the omission should be noted.

The issue is not merely that Gary Wayne forgot to mention a name. The issue is that the same source-field is being used, reinterpreted and publicly rebranded, while one of its central authors is omitted. That omission assists source displacement: the material remains, the earlier authority disappears, and Gary Wayne's Genesis 6 framework becomes the public explanation.

Continued Publication After Notice: Alien, Antichrist and Aryan-Race Framing

After my cease-and-desist notice of 12 June 2026, Gary Wayne has continued appearing in public interviews discussing the same disputed bloodline field.

A further example is the Sabbath at Midnight episode titled *The 5 Aryan Races — Gary Wayne*, premiered only hours after the previous post-notice material I had already identified. The public description frames the discussion around the Five Aryan Races, Genesis 6, the Watchers, Nephilim, Tuatha Dé Danann origins, Anunnaki, Atlantis traditions, UFO disclosure, ancient gods, end-times deception, secret societies and hidden history.

This is significant because the contested field is still being publicly circulated after notice.

The episode does not merely discuss ancient history in neutral terms. At the beginning, the host frames the discussion around Nordic-looking aliens, grey aliens, praying-mantis entities and reptilians. Gary Wayne then states that the subject must be understood as a repeating cycle that attempts to bring about the end time and the Antichrist, and to destroy humanity from the face of the earth.

He goes on to describe giants as the offspring of beings we would today call extraterrestrials because they are "not from the earth." He describes angels as spirit beings or alien beings, and says these beings created demigods who were given divine right to rule.

This is the same hostile pattern again.

The language of genealogy, ancient peoples, Tuatha Dé Danann, Aryan races, Anunnaki, Seraphim, Watchers, gods and bloodlines is being placed inside an alien / fallen angel / Antichrist / end-times deception framework.

The transcript then becomes more direct. Gary Wayne says that the Seraphim rebellious Watchers populate the top hierarchy of the gods and are reptilian-looking, serpent-faced, dragon angelic beings of heaven with six wings. He says that dragon, serpent and crocodile imagery refer to the same god-type, and that these beings looked after religion and governance. He identifies these as the Seraphim angels, the Nagas, the dragon creator gods of China, and the feathered or plumed serpents of the Americas.

This is not neutral mythology. It is a public statement that dragon and serpent traditions represent reptilian angelic beings connected with governance, religion, gods, Watchers and hidden bloodlines.

He also discusses the Tuatha Dé Danann / Scythians as red-haired and blond-haired giants, tying Irish, Scottish, English and northern European traditions into this wider giant / Aryan / Watcher framework. That is directly relevant to the de Vere / Gardner / Dragon / Tuatha / Faery source-field.

The problem is not simply that Gary Wayne has a different interpretation. The problem is that, after being placed on notice, he continues to appear in public interviews where the same field is recoded as alien, reptilian, Watcher, Nephilim, Aryan, Antichrist and end-times deception material.

That continuation matters.

It shows that the issue is ongoing. The disputed source-field is not merely something he used in an old publication. It is still being publicly discussed, reinterpreted and promoted after notice, while audiences continue to treat Gary Wayne as the authority over the material.

This supports the concern that the Dragon / de Vere / Gardner / Tuatha / Faery / royal bloodline field is being publicly absorbed into Gary Wayne's Genesis 6 framework and re-presented as evidence of alien beings, fallen angels, reptilian Seraphim, Aryan giant races, Antichrist preparation and end-times deception.

For that reason, this episode should be preserved as further post-notice continuation evidence.

The issue is no longer limited to past publication.

Gary Wayne was placed on notice by my cease and desist of 12 June 2026. Despite that, he has continued appearing in public interviews discussing the same disputed field: Dragon bloodlines, royal and elite families, Tuatha Dé Danann, Aryan races, Watchers, Nephilim, reptilian Seraphim, alien beings, secret societies, Antichrist cycles and end-times deception.

This is significant because the continuation occurs after notice. Once notice has been given, repeated public use of the same disputed terminology and source-field cannot be treated in the same way as earlier material. It becomes evidence that the concern has not been addressed.

In the Sabbath at Midnight episode premiered after notice, the public description frames the discussion around Aryan races, Genesis 6, Watchers, Nephilim, Tuatha Dé Danann, Anunnaki, mysterious bloodlines, UFO disclosure, ancient gods and end-times deception. In the transcript, Gary Wayne describes angels as extraterrestrial or alien beings, Seraphim as reptilian-looking, serpent-faced, dragon angelic beings, and continues into Dragon bloodline language.

This shows ongoing publication after notice.

Gary Wayne is aware that the Dragon / de Vere / Gardner / royal bloodline field is disputed. Yet the same material continues to be publicly discussed and re-presented through his Genesis 6 framework. That continued use, after notice, supports the concern that the notice is being ignored rather than meaningfully addressed.

The point is not that he is forbidden from discussing the Bible, mythology or ancient history. The point is that he continues to use the contested Dragon bloodline source-field after being notified of the objection, while still presenting it through alien, reptilian, Watcher, Nephilim and Antichrist framing.

That is post-notice continuation,

After notice, continued public use of the same disputed Dragon bloodline field. This supports an inference that the cease and desist was ignored rather than addressed.

FORMAL CEASE AND DESIST NOTICE

Dated 12th June 2026

I am writing as the copyright owner and literary representative of the late Nicholas de Vere, author of *The Dragon Legacy: The Secret History of an Ancient Bloodline*, and as the owner/representative of The Royal Dragon Court®, a protected trademark.

This letter concerns the repeated public, commercial, and unauthorised use of Nicholas de Vere's *The Dragon Legacy*, the Royal Dragon Court® name and identity, and the wider Dragon bloodline framework developed and circulated by Nicholas de Vere.

Nicholas de Vere's *The Dragon Legacy* was published in 2004, with the underlying Dragon Court, Dragon bloodline, Grail, royal bloodline, fairy/faery bloodline, Scythian, Arthurian, Tolkien, Ring Lord, Vlad/Dracula, and related material developed and circulated before that date. Nicholas de Vere was also associated with and worked alongside Laurence Gardner from the mid-1990s onward. This establishes a much earlier provenance for the subject field now being repeatedly used, repackaged, and commercially circulated by Gary Wayne.

The Dragon bloodline framework now being discussed by Mr Wayne was not mainstream material before Nicholas de Vere wrote and circulated it. While individual subjects such as dragons, serpents, Dracula, fairies, Arthurian material, Tolkien, Grail lore, and royal genealogy existed separately, the distinctive synthesis of Dragon Court, Dragon bloodlines, Royal/Scythian bloodlines, Tuatha Dé Danann,

Fairy/Faery and Elven bloodlines, Ring Lords, Grail/Arthurian material, Vlad/Dracula, serpent symbolism, and hidden royal genealogy was developed and publicly associated with Nicholas de Vere's work.

I have documented multiple instances in which Mr Wayne, and/or podcast hosts interviewing him, directly discuss Nicholas de Vere's *The Dragon Legacy*, the Dragon Court, Dragon bloodlines, Fairy/Faery bloodlines, Tuatha Dé Danann, Royal/Scythian bloodlines, Dracula/Vlad, Ring Lords, Tolkien/Arthurian bloodline material, serpentine symbolism, secret societies, and related subject matter that is central to Nicholas de Vere's published body of work.

Of particular concern is a publicly available episode titled *The Dragon Legacy w/ Gary Wayne*, in which Nicholas de Vere's book is named and read from directly. The host states that the discussion will take a "deep dive" into the Dragon Court and *The Dragon Legacy*, then reads passages from Nicholas de Vere's work as the basis for discussion. Mr Wayne then proceeds to interpret and reframe that material through his own Genesis 6 / Nephilim / Satan / fallen angel / end-times framework.

This is not an isolated reference. I have identified a wider pattern across multiple podcast appearances where Mr Wayne discusses the same Dragon/Fairy/Royal bloodline framework in connection with Nephilim, fallen angels, secret societies, serpent symbolism, Lucifer/Satan, Freemasonry, Tolkien, Arthurian material, Vlad/Dracula, giants, occult bloodlines, and the end times.

No authorisation has ever been given by me, by Dragon Publishing, or, to my knowledge, by Nicholas de Vere during his lifetime, for Gary Wayne or any associated publisher, platform, podcast, or promotional outlet to reproduce, rely upon, adapt, commercially use, or repeatedly build public content from *The Dragon Legacy*, the Royal Dragon Court® material, or Nicholas de Vere's wider Dragon bloodline framework.

Given the extent, repetition, commercial context, and public reach of Mr Wayne's books, interviews, podcast appearances, monetised platforms, and promotional activity, I do not consider this to fall within fair use, fair dealing, ordinary commentary, or incidental reference. This appears to be sustained and commercially beneficial use of a distinctive protected body of work without permission, adequate attribution, licensing, or fair contextualisation.

Mr Wayne has publicly acknowledged that he had read Nicholas de Vere's work and has used this material within his own published and promotional output. My concern is that Nicholas de Vere's protected research framework has been used relentlessly and commercially, while the original author, source work, and Royal Dragon Court® provenance have not been properly credited, licensed, or contextualised.

Accordingly, I require that you immediately cease and desist from:

1. Reproducing, quoting, reading aloud, adapting, paraphrasing, or commercially using protected material from *The Dragon Legacy* or any Nicholas de Vere / Royal Dragon Court® material without written authorisation.

2. Using the Royal Dragon Court® name, identity, trademark, or associated reputation in a way that may create confusion, misrepresentation, or unauthorised commercial association.

3. Presenting, promoting, or commercially circulating Nicholas de Vere's distinctive Dragon bloodline framework without clear attribution, licensing, permission, and fair provenance.

4. Reframing Nicholas de Vere's work and the Royal Dragon Court® material as Satanic, Nephilim, Antichrist, fallen angel, counterfeit-spirit, or occult-fear material while using that same material as source content.

5. Continuing any public or commercial use of this material without first providing a full written explanation of the sources used, permissions relied upon, and steps taken to ensure lawful use.

I further require written confirmation of the following:

- Whether Gary Wayne cited or relied upon *The Dragon Legacy* or other Nicholas de Vere / Royal Dragon Court® materials in his published works.
- Whether permission was ever sought or granted to quote, reproduce, paraphrase, adapt, or build upon Nicholas de Vere's protected material.
- Whether any publisher, agent, platform, or production company holds records of permissions, citations, or source acknowledgements relating to Nicholas de Vere, *The Dragon Legacy*, Laurence Gardner, Dragon Court material, or the Royal Dragon Court®.
- Whether any use of the Royal Dragon Court® name, identity, trademark, or related material has been authorised.
- Whether any due diligence was undertaken regarding the origin and provenance of the Dragon bloodline framework used in Mr Wayne's work.
- What immediate steps will be taken to correct unauthorised use, inadequate attribution, trademark confusion, commercial exploitation, and misrepresentation.

For clarity, I am not objecting to ordinary criticism, commentary, or scholarly disagreement. However, commentary does not provide a right to repeatedly reproduce, adapt, commercialise, or build a public platform from another author's protected work without authorisation, licensing, proper attribution, or fair contextualisation.

Likewise, if Mr Wayne is publicly commenting on Nicholas de Vere's work, I reserve my own right to publicly comment on Mr Wayne's commentary, including correcting provenance, addressing misrepresentation, identifying unauthorised use, and defending Nicholas de Vere's authorship, legacy, and the Royal Dragon Court® name.

I am currently compiling a full evidence bundle, including screenshots, transcripts, video titles, timestamps, publication dates, comparison notes, examples of public monetised use, and examples showing Nicholas de Vere's earlier provenance in this subject field.

Please provide a written response within 14 days of receipt of this notice. If I do not receive a satisfactory response, I reserve all rights to take further action, including but not limited to copyright complaints, trademark enforcement, platform takedown requests, publisher notifications, public correction, and legal advice.

Nothing in this letter should be taken as a waiver of any rights, remedies, claims, or actions available to me, Dragon Publishing, Nicholas de Vere's estate, or The Royal Dragon Court®.

Please treat this as a formal cease and desist notice.

Kind regards,

Abbe de Vere
Copyright owner and literary representative of Nicholas de Vere
Owner/representative of The Royal Dragon Court®
Dragon Publishing / The Royal Dragon Court®
royaldragoncourt@gmail.com

Response

Dear Abbe de Vere,

Thank you for your email. My name is William Carmichael, and I am the publisher of Deep River Books LLC.

We find no violation of your copyright based on Gary Wayne's references to the Dragon Legacy in his copyright book, the Genesis 6 Conspiracy. In fact, there is only one small mention, which is properly documented with no other references.

Gary has been speaking and researching this topic for over thirty years, holding seminars and teaching classes prior to publishing his book in 2014.

Dozens of books have been written and debated in reference to Nephilim and Secrete Societies. It is a widely debated and extensively covered topic for well over 100 years.

Further, regarding podcasts and speaking, purpose and character of use by Mr Wayne includes commentary, critique, teaching, scholarship and research. All of these are considered fair use. Also, transformative use (adding new meaning, analysis, or commentary) is considered favoured fair use under the law.

You cite a commentator on a talk show who read a quote from your book, inviting Mr Wayne to comment. Mr Wayne's right to free speech and commentary is absolutely protected. If you have issues with the portion read by the talk show host, you will need to contact them, not Mr Wayne, as he was not the one quoting a portion of your book.

Secondly, I am the publisher of Mr Waynes copyright work which we carefully vetted prior to publishing and have no affiliation, rights, or control of any shows, podcasts, or media comments given by Mr Wayne. Mr Wayne has never used or read allowed any portion of Dragon Legacy on air or anywhere else.

Hence, my company (Deep River Books LLC) has nothing to "cease and desist."

If you disagree regarding my position, Please document specific instances in which fair use of any copyright parts of Dragon Legacy has been violated in the Genesis 6 Conspiracy non-fiction copyright book, so we can further evaluate the portion of your allegations that are referenced in The Genesis 6 Conspiracy.

We are not liable or responsible for any podcast, show, or any other public discussion of de Vere's writings.

Kind Regards,

William Carmichael, CEO

Deep River Books LLC

My response

Dear Bill

I am writing as the rights holder and heir of the late Nicholas de Vere, author of *The Dragon Legacy* and related Dragon Court works.

I am contacting you regarding Gary Wayne's use of Nicholas de Vere's work, Laurence Gardner's related Grail/Ring Lord material, and the wider Dragon Court source-chain in *The Genesis 6 Conspiracy* and any associated editions, interviews, promotional material, podcast content, transcripts, articles, or derivative works.

I am not asking you to confirm whether Nicholas de Vere, Laurence Gardner, or Dragon Court material is used. I have already identified that information.

For context, this source-chain also predates Gary Wayne's later use of the material. *Realm of the Ring Lords* was first published in 1995, and *The Dragon Legacy* was published in 2004. I have personally been involved in this field for approximately 20 years, and my father's work extends back decades before that. Therefore, any suggestion that Gary Wayne has been working with the specific Dragon Court, Dragon Legacy, Dragon bloodline, Ring Lord, Scythian, Tuatha Dé Danann, Anjou/Vere, Melusine, and Royal Secret framework before Nicholas de Vere is not supported by the publication history I am aware of. If such a claim is being made, I require evidence of Gary Wayne's own pre-1995 published material demonstrating independent development of this specific framework before *Realm of the Ring Lords* and before Nicholas de Vere's Dragon Court body of work.

From my review of the Kindle edition/search results, "Vere" appears approximately 56 times, "de Vere" appears approximately 43 times, "Dragon Court" appears approximately 79 times, "Legacy" appears approximately 46 times, and "Gardner" appears approximately 456 times. I have also identified direct citations to Nicholas de Vere's *The Dragon Legacy*, including references to pages 1, 16, 32, 36–37, 42, 62, 66, 79, 101, 109, 115, 120, 121, and 221.

This is not a single citation, nor a minor passing reference. It would be inaccurate and dismissive to characterise it as such when the evidence shows repeated reliance throughout the work. The material appears across multiple sections, from the earlier chapters through to the later pages, including references in the 800s, 900s, and beyond. The scale and placement of these references demonstrate that Nicholas de Vere's work and the related Laurence Gardner / Dragon Court source-chain are not incidental. They appear to form part of the structure upon which Gary Wayne builds his argument.

The reliance begins early in the book and continues deep into the later sections. The screenshots I have reviewed show Nicholas de Vere / Vere / *The Dragon Legacy* / Dragon bloodline material appearing in the later part of the book, including around Kindle pages 856 and beyond, with further references and related material visible around pages 868, 871, 875, 879, 880, 882, 884, 895, 896, 899, 903, 908, 962, 1125, and 1126.

Those later screenshots include material relating to the Anjou bloodline, Merovingian, Plantagenet, Spencer, Mandeville and Jacobite lines, ancient bloodline claims, the "Ancient Royal Doctrine," Elvin kingship, the House of de Vere, the Priory of Sion, "Guardians of the Royal Secret," the "Secret of Secrets," Melusine, Plantanu, Imperial and Royal House material, and direct references to *The Dragon Legacy*.

They also include direct and associated references to *The Dragon Legacy* around pages 896, 899, and 908, including repeated entries such as "De Vere, *The Dragon Legacy*," "The Dragon Legacy, 66," "De Vere, *The Dragon Legacy*, 15–16," and further connected references to Gardner's *Realm of the Ring Lords* over 76 times which is actually my Dragon Legacy, *Grail Kings*, and *Lost Secrets*. This demonstrates that Nicholas de Vere's work and the related Gardner/de Vere Dragon Court source-chain are not confined to one chapter, one note, or one isolated citation. They continue throughout the book and into the later sections.

Gary Wayne also relies heavily on Laurence Gardner's works, including *Realm of the Ring Lords*, *Genesis of the Grail Kings*, *Bloodline of the Holy Grail*, and other related Grail and bloodline material. This is significant because Gardner's Grail, Ring Lord, and Dragon bloodline material is directly connected to the work of my father, Nicholas de Vere. My father was involved in that body of material and is acknowledged in Gardner's work. *Realm of the Ring Lords* is therefore not a remote or unrelated source, but part of the same Dragon Court, Ring Lord, Grail, and bloodline source-chain that leads directly into *The Dragon Legacy*.

Further review also shows that Nicholas de Vere's *The Dragon Legacy* is cited directly in sections dealing with the Anjou, Vere, Melusine, Elvin bloodlines, Dragon Queen material, Royal Secret material, Scythians, Tuatha Dé Danann, and associated Dragon bloodline claims. These are not incidental or unrelated references. They are central to the same framework through which Gary Wayne discusses the Royal Dragon Court, Dragon bloodlines, and related accusations or hostile interpretations.

The issue is not resolved by citation alone. Citation does not automatically grant permission to reproduce, closely paraphrase, substantially rely upon, or commercially build upon another author's protected expression, structure, terminology, argument, or distinctive body of research.

My concern is that Gary Wayne's work substantially relies upon Nicholas de Vere's Dragon Court material, including the Scythians, Royal Scythians, Ring Lords, Dragon Court, Transylvania, the Carpathian region, Tuatha Dé Danann, Dragon bloodlines, Anjou/Vere material, Melusine material, Elvin bloodline material, Royal Secret material, and related bloodline claims. This is not generic historical background. It is a distinctive framework associated with Nicholas de Vere and the Dragon Court works.

I am also concerned that this material has been used not merely as neutral source material, but as the basis for a hostile interpretive framework in which Nicholas de Vere's work, the Royal Dragon Court, and related bloodline material are publicly reframed through allegations of evil, satanic association, or religious fear-based interpretation. This gives rise not only to copyright and licensing concerns, but also to serious concerns of misrepresentation and reputational harm.

If the Laurence Gardner and Nicholas de Vere material, including *The Dragon Legacy*, *Realm of the Ring Lords*, *Genesis of the Grail Kings*, *Bloodline of the Holy Grail*, Grail, Ring Lord, Scythian, Dragon Court, Anjou/Vere, Melusine, Elvin bloodline, and Royal Secret material were removed or substantially reduced, I question how much of the relevant sections would remain, and what independent evidential basis would remain for Gary Wayne's arguments about the Royal Dragon Court, Dragon bloodlines, and alleged evil or satanic associations.

This is central to my concern: the material appears to be relied upon heavily throughout the book, from the earlier sections through to the later sections in the 800s, 900s, and beyond, while also being reframed in a manner that damages the original source, the author's legacy, and the living continuation of that work.

I therefore require a formal response to the following:

1. What formal written permission or licence was obtained from Nicholas de Vere, his estate, or the current rights holder for the use of this material?

2. On what legal basis does the publisher justify this level of reliance on Nicholas de Vere's material and the related Dragon Court/Gardner source-chain?

3. Does the publisher consider this use to be fair use, fair dealing, quotation, commentary, licensed use, or another legal category? Please provide the basis for that position.

4. If no formal permission or licence exists, what steps will be taken to remove, reduce, correct, or formally license the relevant material in current and future editions?

5. What proposal will be made regarding compensation for any unauthorised use, commercial reliance, or public authority-building from Nicholas de Vere's material?

6. What independent basis remains for the relevant arguments if the Laurence Gardner and Nicholas de Vere material, and the related Dragon Court/Grail/Ring Lord source-chain, is removed or substantially reduced?

My position is that where Nicholas de Vere's work and related Dragon Court material form a substantial foundation of Gary Wayne's argument, citation is not enough. The correct route is formal permission, licensing, correction, removal, and/or compensation where appropriate.

This matter is further aggravated by the fact that the material has not remained confined to print. It has been repeated and discussed publicly in podcasts, online posts, interviews, and other media, where audiences increasingly treat Gary Wayne as an authority on material that originates from Nicholas de Vere's Dragon Court works and related Dragon bloodline research.

For clarity, I am not objecting to lawful criticism, commentary, or independent historical research. I am objecting to the apparent substantial reliance on, repetition of, and public authority-building from Nicholas de Vere's distinctive published material without formal permission from the rights holder, especially where that material is then used to portray the Royal Dragon Court and associated bloodline material in a hostile or defamatory light.

There is also a practical difficulty in asking me to treat Gary Wayne's work as though it were wholly independent material. If I were to review the sections concerning the Royal Dragon Court, Dragon bloodlines, Scythians, Tuatha Dé Danann, Ring Lords, Anjou/Vere material, Melusine, and related claims, I would in many places be reviewing material derived from my own father's work, merely reframed through Gary Wayne's religious and biblical interpretation. At that point, the question becomes less whether I disagree with his conclusions and more whether he has built those conclusions by recycling earlier source material, including Nicholas de Vere and Laurence Gardner, while presenting himself publicly as the authority.

Please provide your formal response within 14 days, including your position on permission, licensing, correction, removal, and compensation.

I am preparing a side-by-side comparison of the relevant passages, citations, and Kindle search results and will provide this where necessary.

Yours sincerely,

Abbe De Vere

Rights holder and heir of Nicholas de Vere

Attached 15 Screenshots

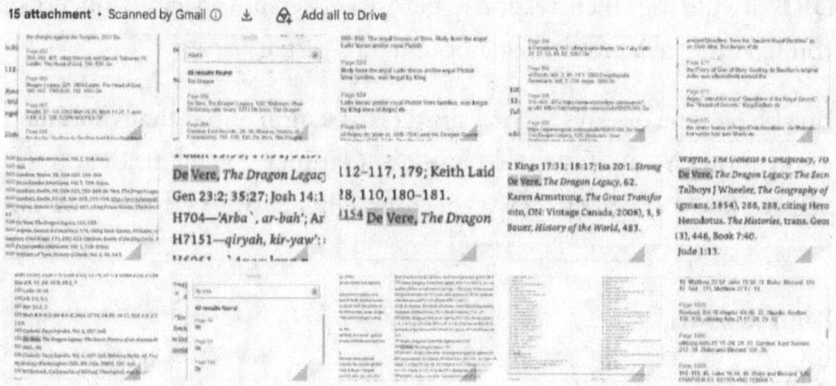

At This Point he realised that I come with receipts.

His Response

Dear Abbe,

Thank you for your quick reply. I have forwarded your email and the attachments to Mr. Wayne and also to our copyright specialist here at DRB. I will await their response before addressing specific concerns you have alleged and the legal boundaries of fair use.

But I have one question that I need clarification about that you failed to mention. You referenced Laurence Gardner several times and we need to know if you also own the copyrights to Mr. Gardner's writings. Please clarify.

Kind Regards,

William Carmichael

Deep River Books LLC

Sent from my iPhone

My Response

Hi William,

Thank you for your prompt reply.

To clarify, I am not claiming ownership of Laurence Gardner's entire body of work. However, I am claiming ownership and rights in Nicholas de Vere's work, contributions, manuscripts, Dragon Court material, and the specific Dragon bloodline framework that overlaps with certain Gardner titles because Laurence Gardner and my father worked closely together for many years.

This has been an issue within Dragon Court circles for a long time. Laurence Gardner and my father, Nicholas de Vere, were close friends and collaborators for over 20 years. My father's early material began as *From Transylvania to Tunbridge Wells*, and this material later developed into *The Dragon Legacy*. My position is that aspects of *Realm of the Ring Lords* and related Gardner material are directly connected to, and substantially overlap with, my father's Dragon Court/Ring Lord/Grail bloodline work.

It is well known within the Dragon Court community that after my father and Laurence Gardner fell out, there were disputes over attribution. Before matters proceeded further, proper attribution was agreed as part of their reconciliation. This is why Laurence Gardner is relevant to my complaint: not because I am claiming ownership of every word Gardner wrote, but because Gary Wayne's reliance on Gardner is also reliance on the same Dragon Court, Grail, Ring Lord, and bloodline source-chain that comes directly through Nicholas de Vere.

The Royal and Imperial Dragon Court was revived and reconstituted by my father in 1993. I also hold material from him referring to this, as well as an original manuscript from 1995 referring to the Royal Dragon

Court. This predates Gary Wayne's later published use of this material and is directly relevant to provenance.

My father was also connected to *Genesis of the Grail Kings*, and his involvement and acknowledgements within the Gardner/de Vere source-chain are part of the wider context. Laurence Gardner also acknowledged use of my father's work in connection with *Bloodline of the Holy Grail* and related material. By 2012 they had parted ways, and my father died in 2013. From that point, I took over the Royal Dragon Court, the books, and my father's work as part of my inheritance.

Over the last year I have had to deal with repeated misuse of this material, including more than 30 DMCA takedowns and a separate dispute with my former publisher. Multiple platforms have recognised me as the copyright owner and authority for Nicholas de Vere's work.

Therefore, the Gardner issue should not be treated as a distraction from my complaint. It is part of the provenance chain. Gary Wayne's book appears to rely heavily on both Laurence Gardner and Nicholas de Vere, but the relevant Gardner material itself overlaps with, acknowledges, and draws from the same Dragon Court material connected to my father.

My primary complaint remains that Gary Wayne has used, relied upon, and publicly reframed Nicholas de Vere's Dragon Court material without my consent, and in a manner I consider highly damaging. This is especially serious where he names or frames the Royal Dragon Court, Dragon bloodlines, and related material through language of evil, satanic association, and religious fear-based interpretation.

I have spent the last 13 years doing damage control around this material, correcting pseudo-historical claims, and separating my own evidence-based work from sensationalised or hostile interpretations. I am an author and researcher working to place my father's legacy and my own work within a serious academic and historical context. I do not accept Gary Wayne using this material as a platform for public authority, commercial gain, and hostile reframing without proper permission, licensing, correction, or compensation.

To be clear: my claim relates to Nicholas de Vere's work, Nicholas de Vere's contributions, the Dragon Court material, and the overlapping Gardner/de Vere source-chain where my father's work and acknowledgements are involved. I am not claiming blanket ownership of Laurence Gardner's entire catalogue.

I hope that clarifies the position.

Kind regards,
Abbe De Vere

Dear Bill,

To give further context regarding provenance, I am providing a Wayback Machine link showing historical Royal Dragon Court material as it appeared more than 20 years ago. I allow some archived websites to remain available because they demonstrate the history of our work, its terminology, and the framework already being used long before Gary Wayne's later publication.

This material is also set out in my father's own books, which I have now republished myself, including *The Dragon Legacy*, *The Dragon Cede*, *From Transylvania to Tunbridge Wells*, and related Royal Dragon Court material. Other historical writings, including *My Kingdom is Not of This World*, also support the same provenance.

In Nicholas de Vere's books, and in Laurence Gardner's related works, there are clear copyright notices stating that the work is not to be reproduced, copied, or used without permission. The material is not in the public domain. It remains protected by copyright, including under the Berne Convention framework and the relevant posthumous copyright term. The same applies to my own new work and to any editorial work, revisions, republications, and updated editions I have produced in relation to *The Dragon Legacy*, *The Dragon Cede*, and *From Transylvania to Tunbridge Wells*.

I hope you appreciate my position. I am not objecting to lawful citation, nor am I objecting to fair and properly attributed discussion. My concern is the scale, framing, and reliance on Nicholas de Vere's material and the related Dragon Court source-chain, particularly where that material is then used to portray the Royal Dragon Court, Dragon bloodlines, or associated families through hostile language of evil, satanic association, or religious fear-based interpretation.

The Royal Dragon Court is now in a new era under my stewardship. My work is evidence-based and focused on verified genealogy, provenance, historical correction, and responsible publication. I do not accept continual persecution, misrepresentation, or sensationalised reframing of this material, especially where it affects my father's legacy, my own work, and the public understanding of the Royal Dragon Court brand.

Many readers have also raised similar concerns in reviews of Gary Wayne's books, particularly regarding the level of reliance on earlier source material and the fear-based framing used throughout.

I am therefore asking that your copyright specialist consider not only isolated quotations, but the wider pattern of reliance, the documented provenance of the material, the historical relationship between Nicholas de Vere and Laurence Gardner's work, and the impact of Gary Wayne's treatment of that material.

Kind regards,
Abbe De Vere

My Kingdom is Not of This World,

(Just to help him along a little bit)

Email:<royaldragoncourt@gmail.com>

06/19/2026

Dear Ms. de Vere,

Thank you for your correspondence regarding The Genesis 6 Conspiracy Part II: How Understanding Prehistory and Giants Helps Define End-Time Prophecy.

We have carefully reviewed your concerns and have attempted a detailed re-examination of all references attributed to Nicholas de Vere within the manuscript. I have consulted with Gary Wayne and our editorial team regarding the specific passages and concepts at issue.

I have been a publisher of Christian literature, both non-fiction and fiction for over 40 years.

During that time, I have published over 400 different authors and approximately 600 separate titles. Because many books I have published take on various theological questions and both pro-Christian and anti-Christian suppositions, I have been a diligent student of copyright law and the nuances of fair use.

At the outset, it appears that your concerns encompass several distinct matters:

1. Attribution and provenance of ideas;
2. Disagreement with the characterization or interpretation of those ideas; and
3. Alleged copyright infringement.

These issues should be considered separately.

With respect to attribution and provenance, it is important to recognize that theories concerning Genesis 6, Nephilim traditions, bloodlines, giant clans, Grail traditions, and related subjects have been discussed, debated, expanded, and challenged by numerous authors and traditions over many centuries. While Nicholas de Vere and Laurence Gardner contributed their own interpretations and perspectives to these subjects, discussion of those topics is not limited to any single author or source.

More importantly, while copyright law generally protects an author's original expression of a concept, particularly if another author is attempting to claim those ideas are his/hers. That is obviously a form of plagiarism.

But copyright law generally does not protect the underlying ideas, theories, interpretations, historical claims, or theological positions themselves. Authors remain free to quote, discuss, analyse, critique, support, or reject such ideas, provided that protected expression is not improperly copied and is properly footnoted.

Reliance on those ideas, suppositions, and concepts is generally accepted use in the attempt to argue or refute them. For example, thousands of authors rely on the writings of Martin

Luther, thousands more rely on Charles Darwin. The same is true for dozens of more contemporary works where a basic premise or theory is challenged, such as Yuval Noah Harari.

Regarding your concerns about how certain theories are characterized within Gary Wayne's work, we respectfully note that theological, historical, and academic debate necessarily involves analysis and criticism of competing viewpoints. Disagreement with an author's conclusions or characterization of a theory is distinct from a copyright claim. The expression of opposing religious, historical, or scholarly viewpoints is a recognized and

protected part of public discourse and is generally supported under fair use.

With respect to copyright, our review indicates that references to Nicholas de Vere's work are limited in scope, are attributed to their source, and are used within a broader context of commentary, analysis, criticism, and comparison with other published works. Many references appear in footnotes or source citations, and the material is discussed as part of a larger examination of competing theories and interpretations. At present, we are not aware of any substantial reproduction of Nicholas de Vere's copyrighted expression within the work. Based upon our current review, we believe the cited material constitutes permissible scholarly reference, commentary, criticism, and fair-use treatment. However, we remain willing to consider any specific passages that you believe infringe copyright and would welcome identification of the exact text at issue.

Accordingly, if you contend that particular passages constitute copyright infringement, we respectfully request that you identify the specific pages, word for word quotations, or excerpts that you believe infringe upon your father's copyrighted work, together with the corresponding source material from which you believe the alleged infringement is derived. Upon receipt of that information, we will review the matter further and respond accordingly. We appreciate your concerns and your desire to protect your father's legacy and work. At the same time, we believe that scholarly and theological discussion of published ideas, including criticism and disagreement, remains an important and protected aspect of public discourse.

Sincerely,

William Carmichael, CEO & Publisher

Deep River Books LLC

My Response

Dear Mr Carmichael,

Thank you for your response regarding *The Genesis 6 Conspiracy Part II: How Understanding Prehistory and Giants Helps Define End-Time Prophecy.*

I note that although your letter is dated 19 June 2026, it was received by me on 22 June 2026. I reserve my position in relation to all timing, correspondence, and response periods.

I also note that you confirm you have reviewed my concerns, consulted with Gary Wayne and your editorial team, and conducted what you describe as a detailed re-examination of the references attributed to Nicholas de Vere within the manuscript.

My position remains clear.

Permission was never requested from me, nor has permission ever been granted by me, for Gary Wayne or Deep River Books to use Nicholas de Vere's protected work, distinctive theories, Dragon Court material, terminology, structure, provenance, or original intellectual framework in the manner in which it has been used.

I do not give permission now.

This is not simply a matter of whether a few isolated sentences have been copied word for word. Nor is it merely a disagreement over theology, interpretation, criticism, or the broad subject of Genesis 6. The issue is the scale, reliance, and structure of Gary Wayne's work in relation to the published works of Nicholas de Vere and Laurence Gardner.

If the material derived from Nicholas de Vere and Laurence Gardner is removed, what remains? In my view, what remains is largely an edited and reinterpreted Bible narrative. The distinctive framework, the Dragon Court material, the bloodline construction, the Grail and dragon lineage arguments, and the wider structure being discussed are not generic ideas floating freely in the public domain. They have a clear modern provenance.

The Royal Dragon Court was reconstituted in 1993 by my father, Nicholas de Vere. That provenance matters. It cannot simply be absorbed into another author's commercial work, repeatedly cited, relied upon, reframed, and then treated as though permission and provenance are irrelevant because the book sits within a broader theological argument.

You refer by example to authors relying on Martin Luther, Charles Darwin, and other widely discussed figures. That comparison is not appropriate in this context. Much of the material associated with Luther and Darwin is in the public domain. Nicholas de Vere died only thirteen years ago. His work is not in the public domain. His books, terminology, structures, and original written expression remain protected. The fact that an author is published does not make his work free for commercial reliance by another author.

Your letter states that copyright does not generally protect underlying ideas, theories, interpretations, historical claims, or theological positions. I understand that argument. However, your own letter also acknowledges that where another author attempts to claim another person's ideas as his or her own, that is "obviously a form of plagiarism." That statement is important, because my concern is not limited to direct copying. It includes the use of my father's distinctive body of work, his structures, his terminology, his provenance, and his intellectual framework without permission and without adequate recognition of the original source and rights-holder.

Citation alone does not equal permission.

There is no automatic rule by which a certain number of citations makes use lawful, fair, or acceptable. The issue is not simply how many times Nicholas de Vere or Laurence Gardner are cited. The issue is the extent of the reliance, the purpose of that reliance, the commercial nature of the publication, the amount and substantiality of the protected body of work being drawn upon, and whether the resulting work depends upon that protected material for its own structure and argument.

Whether Gary Wayne cites one title, two titles, or repeatedly relies upon *The Realm of the Ring Lords*, *The Grail*, *The Dragon Legacy*, or related Nicholas de Vere material, the basic point remains the same: I have not granted permission for the use, absorption, reliance upon, reframing, or commercial exploitation of that body of work.

Footnotes alone do not make extensive reliance fair.

Nor does hostile or defamatory characterisation amount to adequate recognition. Where Nicholas de Vere, his work, his family, his bloodline material, or the Royal Dragon Court are used as part of a framework that casts them as evil, satanic, corrupt, or spiritually dangerous, that is not neutral scholarly attribution. That is reputationally damaging characterisation attached to a protected body of work and to identifiable living descendants and associated parties.

This is particularly serious where Gary Wayne relies upon my father's work while simultaneously framing that same material in a derogatory and damaging manner. To use Nicholas de Vere's research as structural support for a commercial book, while presenting the Dragon Court, its bloodline material, or associated legacy in terms that are defamatory or prejudicial, is not acceptable.

Nor can this be separated from the promotional and commercial benefit gained by attaching Gary Wayne's work to Nicholas de Vere, the Royal Dragon Court, and the Dragon Court bloodline material. In practical terms, my father's name, legacy, and the Dragon Court material are being used as attention-drivers. They are being used to provoke interest, controversy, and audience engagement around Gary Wayne's work.

That is not neutral scholarship. That is commercial and reputational exploitation.

Where Gary Wayne appears on podcasts, interviews, or promotional platforms and uses Nicholas de Vere, the Dragon Court, or associated bloodline material as a point of controversy, attraction, or sensational framing, that amounts to click baiting and clout-chasing from a body of work he does not own and did not have permission to use in that manner.

If Gary Wayne's work did not rely upon Nicholas de Vere, Laurence Gardner, the Royal Dragon Court, the Dragon bloodline material, and the controversy attached to those names, it is reasonable to ask what audience interest would remain. The use of this material is not incidental. It is central to the reach, marketability, and controversy surrounding his work.

A publisher cannot take comfort merely in the fact that Nicholas de Vere is cited in places, when the issue is that the framework being used depends heavily upon the very authors whose work is being treated as available material for Gary Wayne's commercial construction.

I am not required to reduce this complaint to a passage-by-passage exercise when the issue is broader than individual quotations. The issue is the substantial reliance upon a protected body of work. The issue is that Nicholas de Vere's Dragon Court material and related framework are central to the architecture of the discussion. The repeated use of his work, and the reliance upon that work to build Gary Wayne's argument, cannot be dismissed as minor scholarly reference.

Your response attempts to separate attribution, interpretation, and copyright. I agree that they may be considered separately, but in this case they overlap. Where a distinctive protected body of work is repeatedly relied upon, where its provenance is not properly respected, where permission was never requested, where it is used commercially, and where the author and associated legacy are characterised in a damaging manner, this becomes a serious matter of rights, authorship, attribution, misuse, and reputational harm.

For the avoidance of doubt, I reserve all rights in relation to copyright, moral rights, attribution, provenance, misrepresentation, defamation, reputational harm, commercial use, and any further publication or distribution of material derived from Nicholas de Vere's work.

I do not grant permission for continued reliance upon my father's protected work beyond what is strictly lawful. I do not accept that the use complained of is resolved by broad references to fair use, public discourse, theological debate, or the fact that some citations appear in the text.

I therefore ask Deep River Books to confirm what practical steps it now intends to take regarding the continued publication, sale, correction, attribution, characterisation, promotion, and commercial use of material derived from Nicholas de Vere's work.

Yours sincerely,

Abbe de Vere
Literary heir and rights-holder for the works of Nicholas de Vere

His response note from an iPhone and him misspelling his business name

Dear Ms. de Vere,

Thank you for your response.

We note that your most recent correspondence continues to express concerns regarding reliance upon, characterization of, and commentary relating to Nicholas de Vere's work. However, despite our request, you have not identified the specific passages, quotations, excerpts, or portions of text that you contend constitute copyright infringement.

As stated previously, we have reviewed the references attributed to Nicholas de Vere within the manuscript and have not identified any passages that we presently believe constitute copyright infringement. If there are particular passages that you believe infringe upon a copyrighted work, we would appreciate your identifying the specific pages and text at issue, together with the corresponding source material from Nicholas de Vere's work that you believe has been improperly used.

Receipt of that information would assist us in evaluating your concerns more precisely and responding appropriately.

We remain willing to review any specific examples you wish to provide.

Sincerely,

Bill Carmichael

Derp River Books LLC

Sent from my iPhone

Dear Bill,

Thank you for your response.

I do not accept the suggestion that Gary Wayne's use of Nicholas de Vere's work can be reduced to one citation or dismissed as incidental.

I am currently preparing a structured review dossier, already over 166 pages, comparing Gary Wayne's work against the Nicholas de Vere / Dragon Publishing source-field, including The Dragon Legacy, The Dragon Cede, the House of Vere material, Royal Dragon Court material, interviews, archived online material, and associated public sources.

This review is not limited to isolated quotations. It examines shared narrative structure, framework reliance, citation chains, indirect reliance through Laurence Gardner, self-citation, source displacement, and repeated use of the same distinctive House of Vere / Dragon / Elven / Anunnaki / Grail / Templar / Anjou / Plantagenet bloodline architecture.

The central issue is this:

If Gary Wayne's work is not directed at, reliant upon, or commercially using the Nicholas de Vere / House of Vere framework, why does his book require whole chapters concerning the Elvin Houses of Vere, Anjou and Plantagenet, the King of Jerusalem title, and the Dragon Kingdom of Heaven?

The House of Vere is not a generic topic. It is my surname, my family field, my father's published framework, and the core of the Dragon Legacy / Royal Dragon Court material. Gary Wayne was free to make a broad Christian argument about evil, prophecy, Nephilim, fallen angels or world corruption. He did not need to identify and build chapters around my specific House, surname, bloodline and family framework unless that framework was central to the argument he was making.

This is not simply a question of how many times Nicholas de Vere is named in footnotes. A citation count does not address framework reliance, source displacement, self-citation laundering, or hostile recharacterisation.

The House of Vere material was not only present in my father's books. It was publicly associated with Nicholas de Vere before his death in 2013 through interviews, websites, Dragon Court material, Drakenberg material, archived webpages and other online sources. The specific combination of House of Vere, Dragon bloodline, Elven/Fairy descent, Anunnaki, Tuatha Dé Danann, Scythian/Sidhe ancestry, Grail/Ring Lords material, Templar/Sion structures, Anjou and Plantagenet genealogy is not a generic historical subject. It is a distinctive framework developed and circulated through Nicholas de Vere's work.

Where Gary Wayne relies on Laurence Gardner or cites his own earlier work, that does not answer the issue. Laurence Gardner was not a Vere. If Gardner's Ring Lords / Grail / Dragon bloodline material was itself drawn from, influenced by, or connected to Nicholas de Vere's earlier work, then citation to Gardner may still be citation into the Nicholas de Vere source-field. Likewise, Gary Wayne's self-citations do not make the material independent if his earlier book already relied on the same House of Vere / Dragon Legacy / Royal Dragon Court framework.

That is why I consider this a source-chain issue, not merely a footnote issue.

There is also a reputational issue. Gary Wayne does not appear to discuss my father's material neutrally. He places the House of Vere / Dragon Legacy / Royal Dragon Court field within an Antichrist, serpent-seed, demonic, Rephaim, beast-empire or occult-conspiracy narrative. In doing so, he commercially uses and negatively recharacterises a living family field and publishing estate that I now administer.

A further issue is his apparent treatment of Nicholas de Vere's wit, satire, humour and provocative self-mythologising as literal factual admission. Those who knew Nicholas de Vere understood that he frequently used irony, humour, theatrical language and satire. To strip that context away and treat it as proof of an Antichrist bloodline narrative creates a misleading and hostile impression.

My position is therefore clear: this is not one incidental citation. It is, in my opinion, substantial use of Nicholas de Vere's distinctive framework, commercially repackaged and negatively recharacterised.

A single citation does not cure substantial use. Nor does citation give permission to commercially exploit, reframe, or damage the reputation and market of the original work.

I am continuing to collate the chapter-by-chapter comparison and will provide further structured examples in due course.

For the avoidance of doubt, I reserve all rights in relation to Nicholas de Vere's literary estate, Dragon Publishing, The Dragon Legacy, The Dragon Cede, the Royal Dragon Court material, and associated intellectual property.

For the avoidance of doubt, no permission was requested from me, granted by me, or granted by Dragon Publishing for Gary Wayne to use, reproduce, commercially rely upon, reframe, or build upon Nicholas de Vere's House of Vere / Dragon Legacy / Royal Dragon Court framework in this manner.

The fact remains that citation is not permission. Even if Nicholas de Vere, Laurence Gardner, or related sources are cited, citation does not authorise substantial use, commercial exploitation, hostile recharacterisation, or damage to the market and reputation of the original work.

I also note that your previous email appears to misstate your own business name as "DERP RIVER" rather than "DEEP RIVER."

I mention this not as a minor criticism, but because it reinforces my concern that this matter is not being reviewed with the level of care required. If even the basic business name is misstated, it raises a reasonable concern that the underlying copyright, citation-chain, and source-field issues may also not have been examined properly.

Kind regards,

Abbe de Vere

Dragon Publishing

The Last Email I sent was on the 26th June 2026

SOVEREIGN GRAND DUCHY OF DRAKENBERG:

royaldragoncourt@gmail.com

Attachments

Fri 26 Jun, 00:38 (8 days ago)

to Bill

Subject: Representative Side-by-Side Review and Supporting Evidence

Dear Mr Carmichael,

Please find attached confirmation of my updated side-by-side review, together with a letter from me setting out my current position.

I have also attached photographs from Genesis of the Grail Kings, showing the acknowledgement page and the foreword written by my father, Prince Nicholas de Vere von Drakenberg. I have included these to show the provenance of the material, the acknowledged reliance upon Dragon Court archival material, and my father's direct involvement in the wider source-field now under discussion.

I do not wish to bombard you with pages and pages of evidence at this stage. My preference is to resolve this matter as peacefully and professionally as possible, as fellow authors, researchers, intellectuals, and publishers.

My aim is simply to protect my work, my father's work, and the inheritance I am legally and morally responsible for preserving. I am sure you will understand that, given the hard work you have put into building your own company and publishing platform.

I hope the enclosed material clarifies my position and assists you in reviewing the matter substantively.

Kind regards,

Abbe de Vere
Dragon Publishing
The Royal Dragon Court ®

The Letter

Dear Mr Carmichael,

Thank you for your reply requesting specific examples of the passages, quotations, excerpts, or portions of text forming the basis of my complaint.

I am not sending the full review manuscript at this stage. Instead, I enclose a concise evidence schedule dealing with one of the clearest examples: the chapter titled "The Elvin Houses of Vere, Anjou, and Plantagenet."

This chapter is not a passing reference to Nicholas de Vere. It is built around the House of Vere, Anjou, Plantagenet, Dragon / Elvin bloodline material, the Grail Code, the Tree of Life, the Dragon Dynasty, the Merovingian Bee, the Priory of Sion, the Templars, the King of Jerusalem title, and future Dragon / Elvin Antichrist claims.

My concern is therefore not merely that Nicholas de Vere is cited. A citation does not automatically make substantial use fair. The issue is the scale of reliance, the repeated use of distinctive terminology and framework, the source-chain displacement, and the hostile recharacterisation of Nicholas de Vere's Dragon Legacy / Dragon Cede / House of Vere material.

Your request assumes that the disputed material will exist as continuous passages capable of simple one-to-one comparison. That is not the pattern identified. The material has been fragmented, reordered and recombined from multiple locations across *The Dragon Legacy* and *The Dragon Cede*. I will therefore provide a thematic mosaic comparison showing Wayne's completed passage against the constituent De Vere passages, together with the intervening citations and any substantive alterations. A lack of one continuous matching paragraph does not establish independent authorship where the distinctive constituent framework, terminology and sequence of associations remain traceable to the source works.

The enclosed schedule identifies:

the relevant Gary Wayne extract;

the corresponding Nicholas de Vere / Dragon Publishing source-field;

the strongest examples of textual and structural overlap;

the citation issue, including repeated references to The Dragon Legacy;

and the reason I do not accept that this can be reduced to "one citation" or dismissed as ordinary fair use.

I reserve all rights in relation to Nicholas de Vere's literary estate, Dragon Publishing editions, associated copyright material, moral rights, trademarked Royal Dragon Court material, and any further legal or platform action.

This evidence schedule is sent without prejudice to my wider position and without waiving any rights.

Please confirm receipt and let me know whether you are now willing to review the matter substantively.

Yours sincerely,

Abbe de Vere
Dragon Publishing
The Royal Dragon Court ®

THE ELVIN HOUSES OF VERE, ANJOU, AND PLANTAGENET

so much so that de Bouillon was coronated with the "crown of fairy thorns" that represented Duke Godfrey's alleged Elvin bloodline from the Merovingians

Godfrey de Bouillon held Anjou bloodlines from the kings of Lorraine, via the Vere bloodline. The house of Vere had previously left Anjou and the Comite of Anjou circa AD 800. The house of Vere was one of the branches of the Angevin dynasties but was not the senior branch; it was a junior branch that extended out of the first of three houses of Anjou. The Vere coat of arms contained a field of red and gold symbolizing the phoenix, superimposed by a white star that symbolized ascending to the throne of the world. When supported by two dragons, the coat of arms becomes the official seal of the house. Red and gold colors accompanied the coat of arms of the Merovingians, Plantagenet, Spencer, Mandeville, and the Jacobite house of Scotland. Godfrey de Vere de Bouillon was further ennobled with royal bloodlines that descended from an ancient bloodline, from the "Ancient Royal Doctrine" as an Elvin king. The house of de Vere traces their royal ancestry back to the Merovingians and allegedly includes the Davidic bloodline scioned into the Tuatha De Danann royalty, the tribes of d' Anu, which in part is patronymic in the first syllable of the Anjou.

Rex Deus (kings of god) believe Benjamite bloodlines grafted into the Merovingian bloodlines, and that de Bouillon, Anjou, and de Payen of Lorraine claimed descent from via Dagobert. Merovingians also claimed Davidic bloodlines via intermarriage with Celtic grail dynasties of Wales, when Eurgen married the Merovingian Aminadab. The Merovingian kings in this heraldic tradition were the priestly and kingly bloodline descended from the Arya, Sidhe, and Scythian giants, the ancient grail bloodline that was later grafted into various Israelite bloodlines.

the pure form of grail is San Greal, meaning "royal bloodline," and to others, Sang Real, again meaning "royal blood." According to Rex Deus genealogist Laurence Gardner, the "Grail" always secretly represented the royal bloodline, the Messianic Sang Real of Judah, and not the chalice we are all familiar with. The Priory of Sion further insisted that Holy Grail and Arthurian tales encrypted the genealogy to the royal bloodline of Mary Magdalene and Jesus, descending through the Merovingian dynasty. Grail literature was patronized by Rex Deus houses and the Knights Templar, and that the Holy Grail, the Sangreal bloodline, housed the secrets to the Kings of God dynasty. The "Grail Code" observed by grail kings like the Knights of the Round Table, the Knights Templar, and the Elvin royals maintained a "behavioural manifestation" "devoted to a 'particular form of consciousness,'" a divine essence attuned to a specific organization working toward a common good and agenda. **This harmonious consciousness participation required a "Hive Mind—a collective consciousness—or at least a heightened capacity toward sensitivity and the anticipation of the needs of all within the genome.. .. Without the 'Hive Mind' (symbolized in the Dragon Dynasty by the Merovingian Bee,** t

he Phoenician 'House of the Gods' and the hexagonal figure of the Tree of Life of the Kabala) the Grail Code is a meaningless set of unattainable social aspirations." "The Grail Code" was applicable only to grail blood produced by a specific genome.

The ten end-time kings will have "one mind"/gno'-may, one cognition: to give their power and strength to the beast in the end times.

The badge of the bee was the heraldic imagery of the Merovingians. "Bees live as equal entities in hives under the rule of one Sovereign who is chosen and created from their number, by the administration of "Royal Jelly" (Dergflaith) by and from the body of the previous Queen. In this respect the clans of the Danann, the Elvin King Tribes of the Western-Aryans, once replicated in their social structure the organization of the hive. Furthermore, the hexagonal construction of the bee's incubation chamber, their place of origin or birth, is repeated in the hexagonal shape of the Kabalistic Tree of Life (the Planta-Genista, the family tree of Origen)."

Godfrey de Bouillon's original order was alternatively named the "Vere Order of Anjou," ennobled royal "Guardians of the Royal Secret," the "Secret of Secrets." King Baldwin de Vere de Bouillon, at his succession in AD 1100, established "the original 'Hierarchical Rule'" of the Templars.

Baldwin II's daughter Melisende married Fulk V the Count of Anjou, who fathered Geoffrey Plantagenet.

Baldwin de Bourg was Anjou, Plantagenet, and perhaps the latter's patriarch. The Plantagenets were regarded as the younger familial cousins to the second house of Anjou, and of Elvin pedigree. Matriarchally, the Plantagenets derived from two Anjou bloodlines, "Melusine daughter of King Elinos of Albany, and Melisende, the daughter of Baldwin de Bourg of Jerusalem." The Plantagenet mythos indicates their name derived from "Planta-Anu" and/or "planta-genista" meaning the "plant of generations," "the Tree of Life." The Plantagenets received ennobled bloodlines from the senior house of Anjou Elvin bloodlines, via Melusine; her senior heir was Maelo de Vere. The Plantagenet name descended from Melusine's younger sister Plantanu and a junior branch of the Imperial and Royal House of Vere. Baldwin II was crowned King of Jerusalem in his succession authorized by the Order of Sion's greater barons, through the "ancient law of hereditary succession" as Godfrey and Baldwin I's kin.

The future Dragon/Elvin Antichrist will likely claim the Jerusalem title "owed" as his right of inheritance," in the "Kingdom of Heaven on Earth" at the abomination. Oddly though, Count Eustace/William, Godfrey's second brother (in Lorraine at that time), was not elected King of Jerusalem as the first selection,

Godfrey de Bouillon held Anjou bloodlines from the kings of Lorraine, via the Vere bloodline. The house of Vere had previously left Anjou and the Comite of Anjou circa AD 800. The house of Vere was one of the branches of the Angevin dynasties but was not the senior branch; it was a junior branch that extended out of the first of three houses of Anjou. The Vere coat of arms contained a field of red and gold symbolizing the phoenix, superimposed by a white star that symbolized ascending to the throne of the world. When supported by two dragons, the coat of arms becomes the official seal of the house.

Red and gold colors accompanied the coat of arms of the Merovingians, Plantagenet, Spencer, Mandeville, and the Jacobite house of Scotland. Godfrey de Vere de Bouillon was further ennobled with royal bloodlines that descended from an ancient bloodline, from the "Ancient Royal Doctrine" as an Elvin king. The house of de Vere traces their royal ancestry back to the Merovingians and allegedly includes the Davidic bloodline scioned into the Tuatha De Danann royalty, the tribes of d' Anu,

De Vere, The Dragon Legacy, 3, 32. 3181 Page 3 Frontispeice *The Beast, the Dragon, the terrible monster, is the disguise of the beloved; the horror to be overcome itself is, or contains, the Reward. Beauty and the Beast must be conjoined. The old tag that a serpent becomes not a Dragon save by devouring another serpent, has an Alchemical sense:*

These are the two Dragons, male and female: they destroy one another, or one destroys the other and a new and mightier one is born, a fiery won- der: A Phoenix (traditionally depicted as having red and gold plumage), a leaping glory, a STAR of dream ascending to the throne of the world. This was the Transmutation, the Great Work of the hidden glory of perfection.*

—Arthur Machen, Fr.GD.
(Frater of the Hermetic Order of the Golden Dawn)

The mating of Ravens is the rhythmic inhalation and exhalation of the breath of Ravens, one by the other. And in this way are the children of Ravens fashioned. (The Raven is the Phoenix of the Elven Kings).

—Traditional country folklore (England)

* The red and gold field, traditionally symbolising the plumage of the Phoenix— super- imposed by the white Star—are the Arms of the Vere. Supported by two Dragons, they historically have become one of the Seals of the House. Red and gold are also the colours of other descendants of the Merovingian dynasty, including the Planagenets, the Mandevilles, the Spencers and the pre-Jacobite Royal House of Scotland.

Pg 32 The Dragon Legacy
This also means that The Holy Grail itself was Elven as was Jesus

him- self, complete with his Crown of Fairy Thorns, depicted as the headgear of Godfroi de Vere de Bouillon in the 12th century. Throughout the generations, ignorant outsiders have distorted the history of the ancient families and the ancient Royal doctrine.

Pg 15

The Imperial and Royal Dragon Court of the Dragon Sovereignty: Sarkany Rend 1408; Curia Regis et Ordo Draconis

The Imperial and Royal Dragon Court of the Dragon Sovereignty intends to continue to publish individual aspects of its history, along with references to the classical folklore and mythic customs of Europe and Asia which are directly linked to the Dragon tradition.

We trust that readers of this work will find the given details sufficient to cement the facts pertaining to the "Dragon" peoples, the Dragon Sovereignty and its Court.

As defined within the main body of the following text, the Imperial and Royal Dragon Court represented herein, legitimately recognised as the Sovereign Court of The Sovereign Dragon Nation by the relevant and appropriate Government of a European Member State, is a closed fraternity of individuals, representing those who trace their ancestry and affiliations back to the ancient Grail and Dragon families.

A Closed Fraternity

When the Imperial and Royal Dragon Court was reconstituted by King Sigismund in 1408 as the Societas Draconis, it was based upon an ancient bloodline tradition which Sigismund assumed that he had inherited from his presumed Egyptian and Scythian ancestors through the Pictish, Dragon Princess Maelasanu of Northumbria and the Ancient and Original Angevin Royal House of Vere of Anjou, the Imperial Dukes of Angiers.

This line had descended through the Tuatha de Danaan (the Dragon Kings of Anu) on the one hand, and the Egyptian Dragon Dynasty of Sobek on the other. The latter strain included the bloodline of the Davidic House of Judah who married into the descent of the Merovingian Kings of the Franks.

Human Vanities

Emperor Sigismund (as he was styled from 1410) was a son of the House of Luxembourg—dynasts who flagrantly altered their genealogy in order to be able to claim a fraudulent descent from this Dragon Dynasty of Maelasanu and Anjou. It is from this descent—from Maelasanu or Melusine—and upon her British, later Angiers-Angevin, Dragon Court, that Sigismund claimed the right to base Societas Draconis as a bloodline continuation of this ancient, prehistoric, anti-Christian, pre-Catholic, British Elven Institution.

One of the most famous members of Sigismund's misappropriated organisation was Vlad Basarab or Draculea, the son of Vlad Drakul. After Draculea's death, his son Michael wrote that his father proudly claimed a linear descent from the Priests of the Dragon Court of Queen Sobekh Nefru of Egypt, whose predecessor Amenhemet had built the Dragon Labyrinth of Fayyum—dedicated to Sobekh—which was later copied in Crete as the Labyrinth of the Minotaur.

Pg 112

De Vere, The Dragon Legacy,3,32, 15, 112, 120, 121. 3187 Ibid., 3, 16. 3188 Ibid., 3–4. 3189 Ibid., 32, 121. 3190 Ibid., 21, 340.

Laurence Gardner, Bloodline of the Holy Grail (Rockport, MA: Element Books Inc., 1996), 147, 164, 236. 3193 De Vere, The Dragon Legacy, 84. 3194

De Vere, The Dragon Legacy, 47–49. 3196

417–427; De Vere, The Dragon Legacy, 79.

De Vere, The Dragon Legacy, 79. 3207 De Vere, The Dragon Legacy, 270. 3208 Ibid., 79.

De Vere, The Dragon Legacy, 16, 120, 121. 3236 Ibid., 120. 3237 De Vere, The Dragon Legacy, 120. 3238 276–277;

The strongest evidence is not just the phrase "Dragon bloodline" by itself. It is the cluster: Dragon blood / Grail Code / Hive Mind / Merovingian Bee / Tree of Life / Vere of Anjou / Elvin bloodline / Dragon Court / Societas Draconis / Sobekh / Tuatha de Danaan. That combination is highly distinctive to Nicholas de Vere's framework.

Strongest similarity found

Gary Wayne writes about the Grail Code requiring:

"a Hive Mind—a collective consciousness—or at least a heightened capacity toward sensitivity and the anticipation of the needs of all within the genome…"

In *The Dragon Legacy*, Nicholas de Vere's text says the Grail Code required:

"a 'Hive Mind'—a collective consciousness—or at least a heightened capacity towards sensitivity and the anticipation of the needs of all within the genome…"

That is not just the same idea. That is substantially the same phrasing, structure, and terminology. Gary's extract then continues with the same surrounding symbolic package: Dragon Dynasty, Merovingian Bee, Phoenician House of the Gods, Tree of Life of the Kabala, Grail Code, genome.

Very strong near-direct overlap: the bee passage

Gary Wayne includes:

"Bees live as equal entities in hives under the rule of one Sovereign who is chosen and created from their number, by the administration of 'Royal Jelly' (Dergflaith)…"

The Dragon Legacy contains the same bee/hive passage, including Sovereign, Royal Jelly, Dergflaith, previous Queen, Danann/Danaan,

Elven King Tribes, and the hexagonal construction of the bee's incubation chamber. My text comparison found a 44-word near-exact matching sequence in this section, followed by another long match about the bee chamber and the Kabalistic Tree of Life.

That is the strongest examples.

Heraldry: red and gold, Phoenix, white star, two dragons

Gary writes that the Vere coat of arms contained:

"a field of red and gold symbolizing the phoenix, superimposed by a white star that symbolized ascending to the throne of the world. When supported by two dragons, the coat of arms becomes the official seal of the house."

The Dragon Legacy frontispiece has the same symbolic chain: red and gold field, Phoenix, white Star, ascending to the throne of the world, and supported by two Dragons as one of the seals of the House.

That is a clear distinctive expression/symbolic arrangement match, not just a generic dragon reference.

Vere of Anjou / Plantagenet structure

Gary's extract says the House of Vere had left Anjou circa AD 800, that Vere was a branch of the Angevin dynasties, and that the Plantagenets were a junior branch.

The Dragon Legacy has the same structure: the House of Vere of Anjou, Maelasanu/Melusine, Maelo de Vere, Anjou, Plantagenet junior branch, and the Veres leaving Anjou in 800 AD.

This is important because it is not merely "both books mention Anjou." It is the same genealogical architecture.

Dragon Court / Societas Draconis / Sigismund / Sobekh

Gary's passage uses the same constellation of material: Dragon Court, Societas Draconis, Sigismund, Vere/Anjou, Sobekh/Sobekh Nefru, Tuatha de Danaan, Dragon Dynasty, Davidic bloodline, Merovingian kings. In *The Dragon Legacy*, the Dragon Court section lays out Sigismund's Societas Draconis as being based on a presumed Egyptian and Scythian inheritance through Maelasanu, Vere of Anjou, Tuatha de Danaan, Sobek, and the Davidic/Merovingian strain.

That is a strong "framework borrowing" point.

"Dragon bloodline" specifically

You are right that "Dragon bloodline" is not just a throwaway phrase in this context. In *The Dragon Legacy*, "Dragon blood," "Dragon families," "Royal Dragon blood," "Dragon Dynasty," "Dragon Court," and "Grail bloodline" are part of Nicholas de Vere's central vocabulary and system. The explicitly frames de Vere's work around the Grail bloodline, Dragon tradition, Dragon blood, magical/genetic inheritance, and the Dragon Court.

Gary's extract then uses that same vocabulary and structure while placing it inside his own hostile Antichrist/Rex Deus framing. That supports your argument that he is not merely making a casual reference; he is building from the terminology and internal logic of the work.

My assessment

Three levels of similarity here:

1. Direct or near-direct textual overlap
The Grail Code / Hive Mind / Merovingian Bee / Tree of Life passages are the strongest. Some wording is extremely close.

2. Distinctive terminology and symbolic package
Dragon blood, Dragon Dynasty, Grail Code, Hive Mind, Merovingian Bee, Royal Jelly/Dergflaith, Phoenician House of the Gods, Tree of Life, Elven King Tribes.

3. Structural reliance
The same genealogical-historical framework appears: Vere of Anjou, Maelasanu/Melusine, Tuatha de Danaan, Sobekh, Davidic/Merovingian bloodline, Plantagenets as junior branch, Societas Draconis, Dragon Court.

So yes: based on the uploaded material, this is not just "he cited Nicholas de Vere." There are passages where Gary's wording and structure appear to track *The Dragon Legacy* closely enough that you can put them into a formal comparison schedule.

The first DMCA/evidence table should start with:

Issue	Gary Wayne extract	Nicholas de Vere source	Type
Grail Code / Hive Mind	Uses "Hive Mind—a collective consciousness…" and "needs of all within the genome"	Same wording and structure in *The Dragon Legacy*	Near-direct textual overlap
Bee / Royal Jelly / Dergflaith	Uses bees, Sovereign, Royal Jelly, previous Queen, Danann, Elvin King Tribes	Same passage in *The Dragon Legacy*	Near-direct textual overlap
Vere arms	Red/gold Phoenix, white star, throne of the world, two dragons	Same symbolic construction in frontispiece	Distinctive expression/symbolic arrangement

Issue	Gary Wayne extract	Nicholas de Vere source	Type
Vere-Anjou-Plantagenet	Vere left Anjou c.800, Plantagenets junior branch	Same genealogical structure	Structural reliance
Dragon Court/Societas Draconis	Sigismund, Maelasanu, Sobekh, Tuatha de Danaan, Vere of Anjou	Same framework in *The Dragon Legacy*	Framework borrowing

In the Gary extract, his footnotes repeatedly cite *The Dragon Legacy*, Gardner, Baigent/Leigh/Lincoln, Markale, William of Tyre, etc., but I have not yet seen him cite *The Dragon Cede* in the extract. His footnotes shown around this chapter cite *The Dragon Legacy* several times, but the search for "Dragon Cede" in the Gary document did not bring up a Gary citation to *The Dragon Cede*; it returned the *Dragon Cede* file itself instead.

So, the wording to use is:

"The chapter appears to contain material overlapping with *The Dragon Cede*, while the citations supplied in the extract point to *The Dragon Legacy* and other authors, not *The Dragon Cede*."

That is safer than saying absolutely "he never cited it" until we check the whole bibliography.

1. House of Vere as central imperial/royal dynasty

Gary's chapter is literally titled "The Elvin Houses of Vere, Anjou, and Plantagenet" and then builds a section around the House of Vere, Anjou, Elvin descent, Plantagenets, Merovingians, and Dragon bloodline material.

The Dragon Cede opens its main as "A Brief Outline of the Prehistoric Nascence of the Imperial and Royal House of Vere", and Nicholas states that the Veres are not merely a provincial Scottish family, but "the senior imperial and royal dynasty of Britain, Europe and the Middle-East," reached through genealogy, heraldry, genetics, mythology, symbolism, magic, occultism, folklore and etymology.

That is a major structural overlap: Gary's chapter is built around exactly the House of Vere / Anjou / Plantagenet framework that *The Dragon Cede* presents as Vere family material.

2. Melusine / Plantina / Anjou / Plantagenet

Gary writes that the Plantagenets derive from Anjou bloodlines, that the name connects to Planta-Anu / planta-genista / Tree of Life, and that the Plantagenet line descends from Melusine's younger sister Plantanu/Plantina and a junior branch of the Imperial and Royal House of Vere.

The Dragon Cede has the same material: Melusine, Plantina, Angiers/Anjou, the later Plantagenet name adopted in memory of Plantina, and the claim that the Veres descend from all three Melusines. It specifically says Melusine Vere I fled to Angiers and married Rainfroi de Vere, Duke of Angiers and Count of Anjou, and that Plantina's descendants later adopted the dynastic name Plantagenet.

That is not casual overlap. That is the same rare genealogical architecture.

3. Scythian / Danaan / fairy descendants

Gary's extract uses the Elvin/Fairy/Scythian/Danaan structure in connection with Vere, Anjou and Plantagenet. In *The Dragon Cede*, Nicholas states that he was the first in this field to establish the Danaan and their "fairy" descendants as historical figures, using cross-referencing, symbolism, etymology and genetic findings.

That matters because Gary is not just talking about "Vere" in a normal peerage sense. He is using the Vere + Scythian + Danaan + Fairy/Elvin + Dragon bloodline package.

4. Sobekh Nefru / Dragon Court / Egyptian Dragon bloodline

Gary's chapter uses the Dragon Court/Sobekh/Sobekh Nefru material in the same wider structure of Egyptian, Scythian, Davidic and Merovingian descent. In *The Dragon Cede*, Nicholas gives the Queen Sobekh Nefru / Dragon Court framework: Prince Ankh-fn-Khonsu first establishing the Dragon Court in the lineage, Sobekh Nefru re-establishing or ratifying it under Sobekh, and the Dragon legacy descending through Merytaten/Scota, Niall, Fenius Farsaidh, Scythia and the Danaan.

The genealogical tables in *The Dragon Cede* also set out Sobeknefru, the Dragon Kings and Queens of Sobekh, Kiya Tasherit, the House of David, Solomon, Sheba-Lilith, Jesus, Mary Magdalene, the Fisher Kings, Merovingian Sorcerer Kings and the Imperial and Royal House of Vere.

That gives you a strong "uncited *Dragon Cede* overlap" point, because *The Dragon Cede* is explicitly a genealogical book, while Gary's chapter is making genealogical claims about the House of Vere.

5. 16q24.3 / red-haired Anunnaki / Dragon Gods

The Dragon Cede has a distinctive section claiming the Veres inherited 16q24.3 genes through Merovingian and Angevin descent, tying this to red hair, Enki, Lilith, Sumerian/Anunnaki origins, Dragon Gods, and Central Europe/Transylvania.

Gary's provided chapter is less focused on the 16q24.3 gene phrase in the visible extract, but his "Elvin Houses of Vere, Anjou, and Plantagenet" chapter uses the same larger mythology: Elvin bloodlines, Scythian/Danaan, Merovingian, Davidic and Dragon dynastic inheritance. If another Gary chapter uses 16q24.3, red-haired Anunnaki, Enki/Lilith, or Transylvanian Dragon Gods without citing *The Dragon Cede*, that would be a very strong match.

Best preliminary finding

The strongest similarities to *The Dragon Cede* are:

Gary Wayne theme	*The Dragon Cede* match	Strength
Elvin House of Vere / Anjou / Plantagenet	*The Dragon Cede* frames the House of Vere as the senior imperial/royal dynasty with Angevin, Merovingian, mythic and genealogical roots	Strong structural overlap
Melusine / Plantina / Plantagenet	*The Dragon Cede* gives the Melusine-Plantina-Anjou-Plantagenet descent structure	Strong
Scythian / Danaan / Fairy descendants	*The Dragon Cede* states Nicholas established the Danaan/fairy descendants as historical figures through cross-disciplinary research	Strong
Sobekh Nefru / Dragon Court / Egyptian line	*The Dragon Cede* lays out Sobekh Nefru, Dragon Court, Scota, Niall, Danaan, House of David, Merovingians and Vere	Strong
House of Vere genealogy	*The Dragon Cede* is specifically "The Holy Grail Descent of the House of Vere" and contains the Vere genealogical chapters	Very strong contextual reliance

Gary's chapter appears to rely not only on *The Dragon Legacy*, but also on the distinctive genealogical structure and House of Vere material set out in *The Dragon Cede.* Yet the citations visible in the Gary extract refer to *The Dragon Legacy* and other sources, not *The Dragon Cede.*

The original source material has been scraped from a number of places, Firstly to use a comparison I will add this material here now.

Personal Reflection

If Gary Wayne's use of Nicholas de Vere's material is supposedly incidental, the obvious question is why an entire chapter appears under the title "The Elvin Houses of Vere, Anjou, and Plantagenet."

That title is not generic. It names the House of Vere and places it inside the exact Dragon/Elvin/Grail bloodline field associated with Nicholas de Vere's work.

If the material has nothing to do with Nicholas de Vere, there would be no need to include a chapter on the Elvin Houses of Vere, Anjou and Plantagenet. There would be no need to discuss the House of Vere, Dragon Dynasty, Grail Code, Tree of Life, Anjou, Plantagenet, Priory of Sion, Templars, King of Jerusalem title and future Dragon/Elvin Antichrist claims.

The inclusion of that chapter proves relevance. It shows that Gary Wayne understood the House of Vere / Dragon Legacy / Royal Dragon Court field was central to the argument he was making.

The publisher cannot have it both ways. They cannot say Nicholas de Vere was only cited once and therefore barely used, while the book contains an entire chapter built around his named family field and the distinctive Dragon/Elvin/Grail framework publicly associated with him.

This is not incidental citation. It is targeted use of a named source-field.

The question is simple:

If this had nothing to do with Nicholas de Vere, why is the House of Vere in the book at all?

Why has he cited Nicholas de Vere 17 times in one chapter?

And if the House of Vere is important enough to form the basis of a chapter, then the use cannot honestly be reduced to "one citation" or dismissed as fair use.

Core Rebuttal to "Only One Citation / Fair Use" Claim

The publisher's position that Gary Wayne "only cited Nicholas de Vere once" and that this therefore amounts to fair use is not supported by the structure of the chapter evidence.

The issue is not the number of footnotes alone. The issue is the extent to which Gary Wayne's argument relies on Nicholas de Vere's named source-field.

Chapter 66 is titled "The Elvin Houses of Vere, Anjou, and Plantagenet." It is not a passing reference. It is an entire chapter constructed around the House of Vere, Anjou, Plantagenet, Dragon/Elvin bloodline material, the Grail Code, Tree of Life, Dragon Dynasty, Merovingian Bee, Priory of Sion, Templars, King of Jerusalem title and future Dragon/Elvin Antichrist claims.

That is Nicholas de Vere's field.

A single citation does not transform substantial use into fair use. Nor does it excuse hostile recharacterisation. Citation is not permission. A work can be cited and still be misused, misrepresented, over-used, commercially exploited or reframed in a damaging way.

The repeated claim that Nicholas de Vere is only cited once ignores the reality that Gary Wayne repeatedly uses De Vere's distinctive architecture: House of Vere, Dragon bloodline, Elven kings, Anjou, Plantagenet, Tuatha Dé Danann, Scythian/Sidhe descent, Grail bloodline, Tree of Life, Dragon Dynasty, Ring Lords, divine-right kingship and Royal Dragon Court material.

This is not merely background research. It is the framework of the chapter.

The citation problem is made worse by Gary Wayne's repeated use of self-citation. Gary cites his own previous book, and that earlier book cites Laurence Gardner. Gardner's *Realm of the Ring Lords* is itself tied to Nicholas de Vere's earlier *From Transylvania to Tunbridge Wells*, later published as *The Dragon Legacy*. This creates a source-displacement chain:

Nicholas de Vere / Dragon Legacy source-field;
then Gardner / Realm of the Ring Lords;
then Gary Wayne's earlier book;
then Gary Wayne's later chapter citing himself.

This citation chain makes Nicholas de Vere's source-field appear more distant than it is.

The evidence therefore shows that the issue is not "one citation." The issue is substantial reliance on Nicholas de Vere's named work, named family field, and distinctive Dragon/Elvin/Grail bloodline framework.

Chapter 66 should be treated as direct use of Nicholas de Vere's work and identity-field, not incidental quotation.

The publisher's "fair use" claim is further weakened because Gary Wayne does not merely cite the material neutrally. He uses it within a hostile Antichrist framework. The House of Vere, Anjou and Plantagenet material is reframed as part of a future Dragon/Elvin Antichrist pedigree, King of Jerusalem claim and occult bloodline conspiracy.

That is reputationally harmful recharacterisation, not fair academic citation.

In summary:

Gary Wayne did not merely cite Nicholas de Vere once.
He built an entire chapter around Nicholas de Vere's named field.
The chapter directly targets the Elvin Houses of Vere, Anjou and Plantagenet.
It uses Dragon, Elvin, Grail, Tree of Life, Merovingian, Anjou, Templar and King of Jerusalem material.
It then reframes that material as Antichrist bloodline preparation.

The use is substantial, structured and hostile.
A single footnote cannot cure that

Chapter 67 Review – The Dragon Kingdom of Heaven

Gary Wayne builds "The Dragon Kingdom of Heaven" around Anjou, Vere, Plantagenet, Royal Scythians, Tuatha Dé Danann, Dragon/Fairy genes, Albi-Gens, divine-right kingship, King of Jerusalem claims, Sigismund, Lorraine and the Double Cross. This is the Dragon Legacy / Dragon Cede / House of Vere framework padded with outside citations and recast as Antichrist prophecy. It strongly rebuts the publisher's "one citation / fair use" claim because the use is structural, substantial and hostile, not incidental.

Overview of the issue

Chapter 67, titled "The Dragon Kingdom of Heaven," is a major framework chapter and should be treated as direct reliance, source displacement, hostile recharacterisation and evidential confirmation of the wider pattern.

This chapter does not merely discuss Anjou, medieval France, the Kingdom of Jerusalem, Fulk V, Baldwin, the Lusignans, Lorraine, Hungary, the Double Cross or Templar history. Gary Wayne uses those historical materials to construct a wider Dragon/Elvin royal-bloodline framework involving the House of Vere, Anjou, Plantagenet, Royal Scythians, Tuatha Dé Danann, Fairies, Shining Ones, Elvens, Lords of Anu, Dragon/Fairy genes, Albi-Gens, Rh-negative blood, divine-right kingship, King of Jerusalem title claims, Dragon kingdoms, the Cross of Lorraine, Sigismund, Dragon kingship and the eventual world-monarch / Antichrist structure.

This is not independent medieval history. It is the Dragon Legacy / Dragon Cede / House of Vere source-field being rebuilt inside Gary Wayne's hostile prophetic structure.

Why Chapter 67 matters, The bibliography is extensive with Ibids

Without having to copy every single paragraphs, to a person like myself who has grown up with this material all my life, I know what dads is work and what is not, The amount of citations show the truth, likewise with using the etymology framework.

The Angevin province was the source name accepted by its ruling French family, who established the dukes of Angiers and the first house of Anjou in the ninth century AD with Fulk I Anjou, circa 888–938. The royal houses of Vere, likely from the royal Latin Verus and/or royal Pictish Vere families, was begat by King Vere of Anjou de Vere (c. 659–704) and his Dragon Queen Melusine (685–714).

Rosicrucian esoteric theology was the furtive source for Nazi occultism, Nazi Aryanism, and Vril ideology, according to Baigent and Leigh. As such, the Anjou gentry was the Albigens from Albi/albus, Old French and Latin meaning white, shining one, bright, pale-skinned, fair, and hoar(y), whereby gens derives from Latin for race, tribe, and in royal circles, the "Elvin blood."

3256 Gardner, Realm, 58, 324–325, 355–364.

3258 Gardner, Realm, 58, 324–325, 355–364; De Vere, The Dragon Legacy, 12–127, 340. 3

259 Gardner, Realm, 55–58, 324–325, 355–364; http://www.houseofvere.com/ver.htm.

3261 De Vere, The Dragon Legacy, 115, 120.

Gardner, Realm of the Ring Lords, 3.

3266 De Vere, The Dragon Legacy, 1, 32, 109. 3267 Ibid., 36–37. 3268 Gardner, Grail Kings, 219.

3https://www.etymonline.com/search?q=albi; https://etymologeek.com/ron/albi/90876344; De Vere, The Dragon Legacy, 120; Websters: Hoar; Dictionary.com: hoary. 3273 De Vere, The Dragon Legacy, 120; Gardner, Realm, 315. #

3277 Gardner, Realm of the Ring Lords, 365. 3.

*550; Gardner, Bloodline of the Holy Grail, 129,

3319 Gardner, The Grail Kings, 313

3332 Gardner, Lost Secrets, 28–36; De Vere, The Dragon Legacy, 66. 3333 Gardner, The Shadow of Solomon, 113; De Vere, The Dragon Legacy, 79, 112.

3338 Gardner, Lost Secrets, 233.

Gardner and De Vere are cited more than 20 times.

Chapter 66 names the target field: "The Elvin Houses of Vere, Anjou, and Plantagenet."

Chapter 67 then expands that field into "The Dragon Kingdom of Heaven."

Together, these chapters show that Gary Wayne is not making a passing reference to Nicholas de Vere. He is building a multi-chapter argument around the same named family field, the same Dragon/Elvin/Grail bloodline architecture and the same royal genealogy structure associated with Nicholas de Vere's work.

This directly undermines the publisher's argument that Nicholas de Vere was only cited once and that the use was incidental or fair.

Gary Wayne's Chapter 67 framework

Gary Wayne builds Chapter 67 around:

Anjou;
Angers;
Fulk I Anjou;
King Vere of Anjou de Vere;
Dragon Queen Melusine;
House of Vere;
senior and junior Anjou branches;
Plantagenets;
Royal Scythians;
Fairies;
Shining Ones;
Elvens;
Tuatha Dé Danann;
Lords of Anu;
D'Anjou as born of Anu;
Gentry as fairy blood / Dragon bloodline;
Albi-Gens;
Dragon/Fairy gene;
Royal Scythian families;
Mitanni;
Horim;
Rh-negative blood;
Gene of Isis;
Vril;
Rosicrucian and Nazi Aryan theology;
Cathars and Albigensians;
Fulk V as King of Jerusalem;
Baldwin, Sibylla, Lusignan, Champagne, Brienne and Cyprus succession;
Anjou of Naples and Sicily;
Hungary, Lorraine and Hapsburg-Lorraine claims;
King of Jerusalem title claims;
Sigismund of Luxembourg;
Lusignan Dragon Kings of Draconis;
the Double Cross;
the Cross of Lorraine;

the Double Cross as Aryan kingship and Shining Ones symbolism;
the "Forgotten Ones";
and the world-monarch / United Kingdom structure.

This is not just a history of Anjou. It is Gary Wayne's hostile version of the Dragon Kingdom.

Direct overlap with Nicholas de Vere's field

The overlap with Nicholas de Vere is direct and substantial.

Nicholas de Vere's work and House of Vere material concern the House of Vere, Dragon blood, Royal Dragon Court, Anunnaki, Elven Kings, Ring Lords, Scythian descent, Tuatha Dé Danann, divine-right kingship, Anjou/Vere descent, Dragon queens and kings, and the Dragon lineage as a hereditary royal structure.

Gary Wayne's Chapter 67 uses the same architecture but recasts it as a future Antichrist / Dragon Kingdom of Heaven claim.

This is the central evidential point. Gary is not discussing detached public-domain history. He is using the same unusual cluster of claims, names, bloodlines, titles, symbols and mythic interpretations that define Nicholas de Vere's work.

The "scurried around for citations" problem

Chapter 67 appears to show Gary Wayne assembling a large citation net around a framework that is already recognisably Nicholas de Vere's.

He cites encyclopedia entries, William of Tyre, Catholic Encyclopedia, Gardner, Rex Deus material, Baigent and Leigh, Leadbeater, Mackey, Markale, Rabelais and other sources. Some of those sources may support individual historical details such as Fulk V, Baldwin, Jerusalem succession, Lorraine, Anjou or heraldic history.

However, those sources do not independently account for the complete Dragon/Elvin/Vere/Anjou/Scythian/Tuatha/Grail/King of Jerusalem framework.

The chapter's architecture is not created by those scattered citations. The citations appear to be used to support and decorate a framework already drawn from the Dragon Legacy / Dragon Cede / House of Vere field.

This should be recorded as source-padding or citation scaffolding.

Source displacement through Gardner

The Gardner issue remains central.

Gary Wayne repeatedly relies on Gardner's *Realm of the Ring Lords* and related Gardner books. However, Nicholas de Vere stated that Gardner based *Realm of the Ring Lords* largely on Nicholas's earlier online work, *From Transylvania to Tunbridge Wells*, later *The Dragon Legacy*.

Therefore, when Gary cites Gardner for Anjou, Dragon, Ring Lords, Elven, Tuatha Dé Danann, Scythian or Grail material, the citation may still be passing through Nicholas de Vere's source-field.

This is source displacement.

The chain remains:

Nicholas de Vere / Dragon Legacy / Dragon Cede / House of Vere source-field;
then Gardner / Realm of the Ring Lords;
then Gary Wayne's earlier book or later chapters;
then Gary Wayne's expanded hostile framework.

My genealogical work and Nicholas de Vere's work

This chapter also matters because the material is not only Nicholas de Vere's published field; it is part of my wider genealogical and family-research field.

I have been working for years on the House of Vere, Anjou, Plantagenet, Dragon Court, royal bloodline, Dragon Legacy and Dragon Cede material. Gary Wayne's chapter does not simply mention one historical family. It walks through the same genealogical terrain and then recasts it as Antichrist bloodline material.

That is why the publisher's "one citation" defence is inadequate.

The issue is not one sentence. The issue is a whole framework, developed over decades by Nicholas de Vere and carried forward through your own research.

Hostile recharacterisation

Gary Wayne's recharacterisation is hostile.

Nicholas de Vere's field presents Dragon blood, Dragon kingship, Anjou/Vere descent, Royal Scythian heritage, Tuatha Dé Danann, Elven kings, divine-right kingship and the Royal Dragon Court as a hereditary, sacred, royal and mythic tradition.

Gary Wayne recasts that field as:

Antichrist contenders;
Dragon Kingdom of Heaven;
fallen bloodline claims;
Vril and Nazi Aryan theology;
Rh-negative occult genetics;
world-monarch ambition;
King of Jerusalem usurpation;
beast empire preparation;
and a counterfeit Kingdom of Heaven.

That is not neutral citation. It is hostile inversion.

Relationship to Chapters 65 and 66

Chapter 67 should be read with Chapters 65 and 66.

Chapter 65 frames the King of Jerusalem title as an Antichrist claim.

Chapter 66 names the Elvin Houses of Vere, Anjou and Plantagenet.

Chapter 67 then expands Anjou/Vere/Plantagenet into the Dragon Kingdom of Heaven.

Together, the three chapters form a structured hostile argument:

King of Jerusalem title;
Elvin Houses of Vere, Anjou and Plantagenet;
Dragon Kingdom of Heaven.

This is a direct multi-chapter targeting of the Nicholas de Vere / House of Vere / Dragon Legacy field.

Rebuttal to "one citation / fair use"

The publisher's argument that Nicholas de Vere was only cited once and that this is fair use cannot stand against Chapter 67.

Even if a particular page contains only one visible citation to De Vere, the chapter's substance is drawn from the House of Vere / Dragon Legacy / Dragon Cede framework. Fair use is not determined by counting one footnote while ignoring the surrounding structure.

The relevant question is not simply "how many times was Nicholas cited?"

The relevant questions are:

How much of the framework is Nicholas de Vere's field?
How distinctive is the structure being used?
Is the use incidental or central?
Is it neutral or hostile?
Does the chapter use named House of Vere / Anjou / Dragon / Elvin material?
Does it commercially exploit and reframe the work?
Does it mislead readers into thinking the framework is Gary Wayne's own synthesis?

Chapter 67 answers those questions clearly.

The use is central, substantial, structured and hostile.

Preliminary assessment

Chapter 67 should be recorded as one of the strongest framework chapters.

It demonstrates that Gary Wayne is not merely quoting Nicholas de Vere. He is reconstructing the Dragon Legacy / Dragon Cede / House of Vere framework across multiple chapters and reframing it as Antichrist prophecy.

Chapter 67 should be marked as:

direct framework reliance;
source displacement through Gardner;
citation scaffolding;
substantial use of House of Vere material;
hostile recharacterisation;
and rebuttal evidence against the publisher's "one citation / fair use" claim.

In summary:

Gary Wayne builds Chapter 67 around Anjou, Vere, Plantagenet, Dragon/Fairy genes, Royal Scythians, Tuatha Dé Danann, Elvens, Shining Ones, Lords of Anu, Albi-Gens, King of Jerusalem claims and Dragon Kingdom language.
This is the same field developed by Nicholas de Vere and continued through the House of Vere / Dragon Court research.
Gary pads the framework with many citations, but the architecture remains Dragon Legacy / Dragon Cede.
He recasts the material as Antichrist bloodline preparation and a counterfeit Kingdom of Heaven.
This is not one citation. It is a whole chapter built from the named source-field.

Chapter 68 Review

THE NEW TEMPLARS

Royal Masonic orders, and the refugee Templar adepts begat with the establishment of Ordo Draconis in Hungary. The Dragon Court of Luxemburg, from which Sigismund king of Hungary descended from, donned the insignia of a dragon incurved into a circle around a red cross, which was the same emblem adopted by the Rosicrucian order. Sigismund inherited this legacy through the throne of Hungary in 1397, as a descendant of the Lusignan "Dragon Kings of Draconis," and through his Scythian and Pict ancestry via the Angevin Royal House, the Imperial Dukes of Angiers. The ancient Aboriginal bloodline descended thorough the "Dragon Kings of Anu," the Tuatha De Danann (Picts) from the "Egyptian Dragon Dynasty of Sobek," and the Anjou lineage-derived house of Merovingians. Accordingly In 1411, Sigismund was crowned Holy Roman Emperor, antichrist title in addition to the King of Jerusalem title. The Dragon Court was officially established in 1408 as the Ordo Draconis with twenty-three kin Rex Deus sovereigns and registered in Budapest. The Inner Court, the secret and senior Sarkany Rend, acted as the repository for ancient knowledge and secrets, which was likely the seeds for the Committee of Three Hundred order. "The family officers" of the Inner Court were/are Vere grandmasters of Britain and Europe, who venerate the Egyptian Ankh as the Albigensian Cross. Ordo Draconis was established to regain the thrones of Europe and to advance the Pursuits of Thoth.

3340 Gardner, Lost Secrets, 233.

3348 Gardner, Lost Secrets, 233. Left in as it's the same framework.

3355 Gardner, Realm of the Ring Lords, xvii, 242; De Vere, The Dragon Legacy, 16. 3356 Gardner, Grail Kings, 313;

3357 De Vere, The Dragon Legacy, 15. 3358 Ibid., 16.

3359 Gardner, Realm of the Ring Lords, xvii, 242 3360 Ibid.; De Vere, The Dragon Legacy, 15–16. 3361 Gardner, Grail Kings, 316. 3362 De Vere, The Dragon Legacy, 16–17. 3363 Gardner, Realm of the Ring Lords, 242.

Chapter Comparison Note — "The New Templars"

This chapter should be treated as a major comparison chapter.

Gary Wayne's chapter is not simply about the historical Knights Templar. It builds a larger structure in which the Templars, Priory of Sion, Rosicrucians, Royal Masonic orders, Ordo Draconis, Sigismund, the Dragon Court of Luxemburg, Lusignan Dragon Kings, Scythian and Pict ancestry, the Angevin Royal House, Imperial Dukes of Angiers, Tuatha Dé Danann, Egyptian Dragon Dynasty of Sobek, Merovingians, Vere grandmasters and the Albigensian Cross are all drawn into a single hostile end-times framework.

The chapter presents the Templar/Rosicrucian/Dragon Court structure as part of a Nephilim or Antichrist world-order system. This is a hostile recharacterisation of material that belongs to the Nicholas de Vere / Dragon Legacy / Dragon Cede / Royal Dragon Court source-field.

The chapter is especially important because Gary Wayne does not merely cite Nicholas de Vere once. In the footnotes attached to this section, he directly cites *The Dragon Legacy* several times, while also citing Laurence Gardner's *Realm of the Ring Lords* and *Grail Kings* around the same House of Vere / Dragon Court / Anu / Tuatha Dé Danann / Angiers / Sobek / Merovingian material.

This shows direct and indirect reliance.

The direct reliance is shown where Gary Wayne cites *The Dragon Legacy*.

The indirect reliance is shown where he cites Gardner's *Realm of the Ring Lords*, because Gardner's Ring Lords material is itself tied to Nicholas de Vere's earlier Dragon Legacy / From Transylvania to Tunbridge Wells source-field.

The chapter therefore strengthens the argument that Gary Wayne's use of Nicholas de Vere's work is structural, repeated and central to his book. It is not incidental, and it cannot be dismissed as one citation or fair dealing.

Key overlap

Nicholas de Vere / Dragon Publishing source-field:

Royal Dragon Court;
Societas Draconis / Ordo Draconis;
Sigismund;
Dragon Court inheritance;
House of Vere / Angiers / Anjou;
Melusine / Lusignan Dragon Kings;
Scythian and Pict ancestry;
Tuatha Dé Danann / Dragon Kings of Anu;
Egyptian Dragon Dynasty of Sobek;
Merovingian bloodline;
Albigensian / Grail / Templar material;
Vere grandmasters / Dragon officers.

Gary Wayne's chapter:

Templars;
Priory of Sion;
Rosicrucians;
Invisible College;
Royal Masonic orders;
Ordo Draconis;
Dragon Court of Luxemburg;

Sigismund;
Lusignan Dragon Kings of Draconis;
Scythian and Pict ancestry;
Angevin Royal House;
Imperial Dukes of Angiers;
Dragon Kings of Anu;
Tuatha Dé Danann;
Egyptian Dragon Dynasty of Sobek;
Anjou-derived Merovingians;
Vere grandmasters;
Albigensian Cross;
Antichrist / Nephilim world-order framing.

Evidential point

This chapter is not independent Christian commentary on the Templars. It is a hostile reconstruction of the Dragon Legacy / Royal Dragon Court framework using Nicholas de Vere's own material, Gardner's related material, and Gary Wayne's biblical-prophecy framing.

The result is commercial use of the House of Vere / Dragon Court source-field while presenting that field as part of a Nephilim, Antichrist, New Babylon and world-government conspiracy.

This is source displacement, structural reliance and hostile recharacterisation.

Chapter 69 The Thelemic Tree

Chapter 69 Comparison Note — "The Thelemic Tree"

Chapter 69 should be treated as a significant structural comparison chapter.

Gary Wayne does not merely discuss biblical trees, groves or idolatry. He builds a wider symbolic system in which the World Tree, Tree of Life, Dragon Tree, Family Tree, Genealogical Tree, Phylogenetic Tree, secret-society hierarchy, royal masonic orders, Ordo Draconis, Thelema, Babylon and the Holy Grail are drawn into one occult bloodline and Antichrist framework. You have to question how many times can the bible be written out, how many people wish to coin un under the mask of god?

The chapter is relevant because it uses tree symbolism not only as religious metaphor, but as genealogy, hierarchy and inherited spiritual power.

This overlaps with the Nicholas de Vere / Dragon Legacy / Dragon Cede source-field, where the Dragon bloodline, Grail, Tree of Life, sacred genealogy, royal descent, hidden transmission and esoteric Dragon symbolism are part of the same larger framework.

Gary Wayne's version is hostile. He reframes the tree/genealogy/Dragon/Grail field as a Thelemic, Nephilim, Rephaim, Hades-rooted, secret-society and Antichrist structure.

Key overlap

Nicholas de Vere / Dragon Publishing source-field:

Tree of Life symbolism;
Dragon bloodline;
Grail inheritance;
royal genealogy;
hidden lineage;
divine or semi-divine descent;
Dragon kingship;
esoteric transmission;
sacred bloodline symbolism;
Dragon / serpent / tree imagery.

Gary Wayne's Chapter 69:

World Tree;
Tree of Life;
Dragon Tree;
dragons as protectors of the World Tree;
Anunnaki tree rituals;
Nephilim and Rephaim immortality;
Family Tree / Genealogical Tree / Phylogenetic Tree;
secret-society hierarchy as an evergreen tree;
Thirteen European Families;
Council of Thirty-Three;
Committee of Three Hundred;
Rosicrucians;
Illuminati;
Freemasonry;
royal masonic branch orders;
Ordo Draconis;
Thelema;
Babylon;
Holy Grail;
Antichrist / Babylon framework.

Evidential point

This chapter strengthens the argument that Gary Wayne is not simply quoting isolated material. He is absorbing and reworking the symbolic architecture of the Dragon Legacy / Dragon Cede field.

The tree is used as a structure for genealogy, authority, secret transmission and spiritual inheritance. That is central to Nicholas de Vere's Dragon/Grail/bloodline framework.

Gary Wayne then converts that architecture into a hostile biblical-prophecy narrative involving Nephilim, Rephaim, Hades, secret societies, Babylon, Antichrist and world government.

This is relevant to the wider complaint because it shows:

structural reliance;
symbolic borrowing;
hostile recharacterisation;
genealogical reframing;
and continued use of Dragon/Grail/Tree of Life material within an Antichrist narrative.

This chapter should be linked back to the earlier "Mysterious Trees of Eden" chapter and to all chapters where Gary Wayne uses Dragon, Grail, Tree of Life, Ordo Draconis, Templar, Rosicrucian and royal bloodline material.

CHAPTER 70 THE JESUITS

"Chapter 70 does not merely discuss Jesuits. It extends the Dragon Legacy conflict between Church power, false kingship, Templar structures, hidden bloodlines and royal legitimacy into a hostile Jesuit/Hapsburg/New Babylon framework. This is a continuation of the same source-field, recoded through Gary Wayne's Antichrist narrative."

He takes several paragraphs

One might anticipate a royal bloodline and heraldry like the ennobled house of Stuart, which boasted the unification of Rex Deus bloodlines from the Merovingians, the Dalriada dynasties of Tara in Ireland, the Celtic Camelot dynasty of Wales, Norse bloodlines from Rollo via the de Bruce and Saint Claire houses, David and Saul's bloodlines, as well as alleged bloodlines from Jesus and Mary Magdalene via the Celtic and Merovingian dynasties. The Stuart bloodline, the heraldic "House of Unicorn," commingled with so many Rex Deus bloodlines that they were regarded as the most ennobled bloodline of their era.

The Templar Order at the adept level worshipped a head or a skull of a goat god named Baphomet, a fallen angel of Celtic and Galatian tradition (Scythian). Baphomet was "rendered as the

Head or Source of Wisdom," whom the Templars entitled agios ischyros Baphomet (Holy Strong Baphomet),

"Baphomet has Angel Wings (Swan feathers) and a torch between his horns. Its right arm is raised with the index finger extended. On the forearm is written the word Coagula. The finger points to the new moon. Its left arm points down and to the side and the index and little finger are extended in the form of the horns the goat.. .. On its forehead there is displayed a pentagram with the single point upper most. In the simpler form, the goat's head traces the figure of the inverted pentagram and thus it is to be understood that one pentagram equals the other. Therefore, if the single point pentagram represents the Goddess, then she and the goat are one, as is represented by the combining of male and female sexual attributes in one symbol. Such a thorough union of the two sexes negates the individuality of both. Its legs are the legs of Pan. Its head is the head of Khem, which conjoined to the serpent or Dragon's torso represents Leviathan. Entwined around the Phallus of Baphomet are the serpents of the type represented on the caduceus of Hermes. The Phallus as staff or Tree of Life is the Planta-genista in one sense, in being capped by an egg, is the symbol of potential which qualifies the image. Conclusion: Baphomet is a type of Chem-Zoroaster who is the Quinotaur associated with Meroveus.

Mithras was the god of Mithraism of Rome that originated in Zoroastrianism, the religion of the Indo-Aryans.

Dad's version: the Church and Church-backed establishment suppressed, distorted, mocked and displaced the older Dragon/Grail royal heritage. *The Dragon Legacy* explicitly says the Church and establishment attempted to eclipse the pure origins and sovereign status of the Royal House of Vere, and that authorities twisted or concealed truth to control information.

Gary's version: he takes that same conflict pattern and says these orders are not suppressing the Dragon line because they fear it; rather, they are part of a satanic/Nephilim/Antichrist New Babylon machine.

That is the inversion.

Chapter Comparison Note — "The Jesuits" / "Francis Borgia and the Montesa Order"

This chapter should be treated as a supporting structural chapter within the wider Gary Wayne comparison.

It is not as directly House-of-Vere centred as the chapters on the Elvin Houses of Vere, Anjou and Plantagenet, or The Dragon Kingdom of Heaven. However, it continues the same architecture: Templars, Rosicrucians, royal bloodlines, Church power, hidden orders, Dragon Court-adjacent structures, Hapsburgs, Borgia/Borja, Montesa, Vatican authority, banking, New World control and world-government prophecy.

Gary Wayne's chapter argues that the Jesuits were effectively a "New Templar" order inside the Roman Church. He links Ignatius of Loyola, Francis Borgia, the Montesa Order, Charles V, Hapsburg/Tras Tamara bloodlines, Aragon, the Order of the Golden Fleece, Vatican banking, Swiss banking, Rothschild banking, Black Nobility, Rosicrucian oversight and the New Babylon / Antichrist agenda.

The relevance to Nicholas de Vere's work is structural.

Nicholas de Vere's Dragon Legacy / Dragon Cede field already presents the Roman Church and Church-backed establishments as forces that suppressed, distorted or fraudulently displaced the older Dragon / Grail / royal bloodline tradition. Nicholas's work also lays out Societas Draconis, Sigismund, Luxembourg, Anjou, Melusine, the Dragon Court, Egyptian and Scythian inheritance, Templar connections, the Albigensian Cross, Inner Temple structure and Vere Grand Masters.

Gary Wayne takes that wider Dragon Court / Templar / Church / royal-bloodline conflict and extends it into a later Jesuit-Hapsburg-Borgia-Montesa framework.

The issue is therefore not that Nicholas de Vere wrote a Jesuit history, and Gary copied it word for word. The issue is that Gary Wayne appears to build a later-stage continuation of Nicholas de Vere's Church-versus-Dragon-bloodline framework and then recasts it as a hostile Antichrist / New Babylon / Nephilim world-order system.

Nicholas de Vere / Dragon Publishing source-field

Church-state suppression of Dragon royal heritage;
Roman Church distortion of older bloodline traditions;
Societas Draconis;
Sigismund von Luxembourg;
Luxembourg genealogy altered to claim Dragon descent;
Melusine / Maelasanu / Anjou;
Vere / Dragon Court inheritance;
Egyptian Dragon Court and Sobekh Nefru;
Scythian and Pict ancestry;
Grail succession;
red cross within a circle;
Albigensian Cross / Egyptian Ankh;
Inner Temple / Vere Grand Masters;
Templar connection;
anti-Christian, pre-Catholic Elven institution.

Gary Wayne's Jesuit / Hapsburg continuation

Jesuits as New Templars;
Ignatius of Loyola as knightly founder;
Borgia/Borja patronage;
Montesa Order as Templar continuation in Spain;
Charles V as Hapsburg/Tras Tamara universal monarch;
Aragon, Spain and New World authority;

Jesuits controlling education, records and colonial knowledge;
Vatican banking;
Swiss banking;
Rothschild banking;
Order of the Golden Fleece;
Bourbon/Hapsburg division;
Black Nobility;
Rosicrucian oversight;
New Babylon / Antichrist world-order framing.

Evidential point

This chapter shows Gary Wayne continuing the same pattern of hostile expansion.

He takes the already-established Dragon Legacy conflict between older Dragon/Grail royal inheritance and Roman Church-backed structures, then extends it into Jesuits, Hapsburgs, Borgia, Montesa, banking, New World control and New Babylon.

That matters because it shows that Gary's use of the Nicholas de Vere source-field is not confined to the explicit House of Vere chapters. The same architecture continues into later institutional history.

This should be recorded as:

structural reliance;
framework extension;
hostile recharacterisation;
Church-versus-Dragon-bloodline inversion;
and source-field continuation into Jesuit/Hapsburg material.

Appendix

Attached The Foreword and acknowledgement pages from The Genesis of The Grail King By Laurence Gardner who accepts that a lot of his research comes from Nicholas de Vere

The Foreword written by Nicholas de Vere

FOREWORD

In a genuine attempt to find answers to the problems and pressures of our modern age, many people are today seeking enlightenment from books which purport to convey the hidden mysteries of ancient wisdom. Unfortunately, there are numerous quasi-mystical and pseudo-magical offerings in this regard, and much of their dubious content stems from misconceptions of the root elements of the Draconian scientific tradition. This occurs because researchers, who might well study literature that is readily available in the public domain, do not have access to those archives wherein the original base material is held. They are, furthermore, not remotely connected to the ancient Dragon Court or to any of its related Grail families or institutions.

It pleases me, therefore, to convey to readers the fact that Laurence Gardner writes not as an uninitiated commentator, but as an extremely well-informed member of the time-honoured school upon which he so eloquently reports.

In *Genesis of the Grail Kings*, the author has imparted a good deal of ancient material from the archives of the Imperial and Royal Dragon Court, and has aligned this with a hitherto rarely published classical chronology of events in Old Testament times. The result is a work of scholarly integrity which advances a radically alternative view of history, challenging that which has for too long been foisted upon people by those following a predetermined course of vested interest.

The destiny of any individual depends upon whence they begin their journey and the path they elect, or are obliged, to travel. What pertains to individuals is also pertinent to society as a whole, and the conditions,

xv

culture and ultimate achievements of society are marked by the inherent perceptions of its origin and purpose. Such perceptions are generally the result of an authorized education programme, but when this teaching is at odds with the underlying truth, a dichotomy of interests will prevail and the society will have no attainable goal except that of disunity and ultimate demise.

In this work, Laurence Gardner paves the way for a restitution of our society's true history and for the rightful return of its cultural heritage to the front line of conscious awareness. In view of this, and in recognition of his erudite accomplishment in restoring the Messianic Dragon tradition to its position as the *fons et origo*, I commend this text to all who quest for the eternal Grail.

HRH Prince Nicholas de Vere KGC, KCD
Princeps Draconis, Sovereign Grand Master
and Magister Templi of Sarkany Rend
The Imperial and Royal Dragon Court and Order

Acknowledgements

For their invaluable assistance in the compilation of this work, I am indebted to the good offices of the Imperial and Royal Dragon Court and Order (Sarkany Rend 1408), Curia Regis et Ordo Draconis; the President of the European Council of Princes, and the directors of Mediaquest International.

My particular gratitude is due to HRH Prince Nicholas de Vere von Drakenberg, and to HRH Prince Michael of Albany, for affording me privileged access to their respective household archives. I am also thankful to my wife, Angela, and son, James, for their enduring tolerance of my time-consuming quest.

Grateful thanks also to Simon Trewin, Susy Behr, Chi-ann Rajah, and all at Sheil Land Associates, together with Broo Doherty, Simon Taylor, Katrina Whone, indexer Valerie Elliston, copy-editor Brenda Updegraff, and those others at Bantam Press who have seen this book through to its publication.

To those many friends and colleagues who have directly aided this project I similarly offer my appreciation, while acknowledgements are individually due to those whose inspired research has been of considerable assistance. In this regard, and for their pioneering scholarship in variously related fields of contemporary study, I am greatly obliged to Chevalier David Wood, Baron Richard von Hymir de Dufton, Chevalier Yuri Stoyanov, and Herbert Kessler.

For their generous support of this undertaking, my special thanks to JZ Knight and all at Ramtha's School of Enlightenment; to Christina Zohs of *The Golden Thread*, and to Duncan Roads, Ruth Parnell and

Mr Carmichael has not responded to my letter.

Notice, Continued Sale, and Absence of Good Faith

A further issue arises from the response to my correspondence. Once a publisher has been placed on notice that a rights holder objects to the use of protected material, the matter can no longer be treated as though the publisher was unaware of the dispute.

In this case, my emails were not casual complaints. They identified a serious copyright and source-field concern involving Nicholas de Vere's work, the Dragon Publishing editions, the House of Vere material, and the Royal Dragon Court framework. The publisher was asked to review the position and was supplied with the basis of my complaint. The publisher then requested specific passages, quotations, excerpts, or portions of text for further review.

That request is significant. It shows that the publisher was aware that a substantive rights complaint had been raised and that specific comparison evidence was being prepared.

If, after receiving notice of the complaint and requesting the evidence, the publisher continues to permit the books to be sold without suspension, restriction, review, takedown, correction, or any meaningful interim safeguard, that conduct cannot easily be characterised as good faith. At that stage, continued sale is not passive. It is continued commercial distribution after notice.

This matters because a publisher cannot reasonably say that it did not know there was a dispute while simultaneously choosing to keep the disputed works available for sale. Nor can it place the burden entirely on the rights holder, request a detailed evidential review, and continue profiting from the publication while that review is being prepared.

The issue is not merely whether the publisher ultimately agrees with my complaint. The issue is whether it acted responsibly once the complaint had been raised. A reasonable response would have been to pause, review, investigate the passages, assess the citation chains, and consider temporary removal or suspension while the matter was examined.

Where the disputed material continues to be commercially sold after notice, the position becomes more serious. It may support an argument that the publisher had knowledge of the claim, chose not to take protective action, and allowed the continued sale of the disputed work despite being aware that the rights holder had made a reasonable and evidence-based objection.

That is not good-will engagement. It is avoidance of meaningful action while the commercial benefit of the disputed publication continues.

For that reason, this review records not only the alleged textual and structural use of Nicholas de Vere's material, but also the publisher's conduct after notice. The correspondence shows that they were informed of the complaint, asked for specific evidence, and were given the opportunity to investigate. If the books remained on sale during that period, that continued sale should be treated as part of the factual record.

It is reasonable for me to comment on the publisher's handling of this matter. A whole chapter is dedicated to my family surname, the House of Vere, and to the bloodline framework associated with my father's published work. That chapter contains repeated citations to Nicholas de Vere and *The Dragon Legacy*, despite the publisher initially suggesting that the matter amounted to only one citation in the whole book.

That discrepancy matters. It suggests either that the book had not been properly reviewed before my concerns were minimised, or that the extent of the reliance was not being meaningfully addressed. Neither position reflects well on the publisher's handling of a serious rights complaint.

After going through the material myself, chapter by chapter, I can see why no one wished to do the job. It is not light reading. Even Lucifer might have considered early retirement before reaching the end of it. Nevertheless, humour aside, the point remains serious: the publisher's response showed a lack of care, a lack of accountability, and an apparent reluctance to engage properly with the evidence once the matter had been raised.

This is not hostility. It is fair comment. I am entitled to use humour when describing the burden of reviewing material that concerns my father's work, my family surname, and a source-field I now administer. The underlying criticism remains factual: the use was greater than initially represented, the citations were more extensive than suggested, and the continued sale of the books after notice raises a legitimate question about good faith.

Case-Law Authorities Relevant to Fair Dealing, Fair Use, Substantial Taking, and Critical Review

1. Hubbard v Vosper [1972] 2 QB 84 — fair dealing for criticism and review

In *Hubbard v Vosper*, the Court of Appeal considered whether extracts from L. Ron Hubbard's Scientology writings could be reproduced in a critical book. The court held that the defendant's use could fall within fair dealing for the purposes of criticism or review.

Lord Denning MR stated that it is impossible to define "fair dealing" by a rigid formula. The court must consider the facts of the particular case, including the number and extent of the quotations, the use made of them, and the proportions involved. A taking which might be unfair in one context may be fair in another if it is genuinely used for criticism or review.

This case is relevant because the present work is not intended to reproduce Gary Wayne's book as a substitute reading copy. It is a structured review and evidential comparison. Extracts are included where necessary to demonstrate textual similarity, citation-chain reliance, source displacement, framework borrowing, hostile recharacterisation, and the use of Nicholas de Vere / Dragon Publishing material.

The principle drawn from *Hubbard v Vosper* is that quotation for criticism and review may be lawful where the dealing is fair, properly acknowledged, and genuinely tied to the critical purpose. The case also supports the position that fairness depends on the surrounding use, not on a fixed word count or percentage.

This authority supports my right to quote relevant extracts for the purpose of criticism, review, and evidential comparison, provided the quotations are no more than necessary for the point being made.

2. Designers Guild Ltd v Russell Williams (Textiles) Ltd [2000] UKHL 58 — substantial part is qualitative, not merely quantitative

In *Designers Guild Ltd v Russell Williams*, the House of Lords considered whether one fabric design infringed another. The issue was not simply whether every detail had been copied, but whether the defendant had copied a substantial part of the claimant's original work.

The House of Lords confirmed that "substantial part" is not judged by quantity alone. The court must consider the quality and importance of what has been taken. A defendant may infringe copyright by taking the author's distinctive selection, arrangement, design, structure, or combination of elements, even if individual elements could be found elsewhere.

This principle is important to the present review because the dispute is not only about isolated copied sentences. It is also about the alleged taking of a distinctive source-field: the House of Vere, Dragon Court, Grail, Elven/Fairy, Anjou, Plantagenet, Melusine, Scythian, Danaan, Baphomet, Khem, Leviathan, and related Nicholas de Vere framework.

The case supports the argument that protected expression may lie in the original arrangement, combination, and cumulative structure of material. A work may infringe where it takes the heart, architecture, or distinctive pattern of another work, even where the defendant attempts to break that taking into smaller fragments.

This authority supports the argument that the issue is not merely how many words Gary Wayne copied, but whether he took a substantial and distinctive part of Nicholas de Vere's intellectual architecture, terminology, symbolic arrangement, and source-field.

3. Ashdown v Telegraph Group Ltd [2001] EWCA Civ 1142 — fair dealing, public interest, and copyright limits

In *Ashdown v Telegraph Group Ltd*, the Court of Appeal considered the unauthorised publication of confidential political meeting notes. The newspaper argued, among other things, fair dealing and public interest.

The court recognised the importance of freedom of expression but also held that copyright remains a real property right and cannot be ignored merely because the subject matter is politically or publicly interesting. Public interest and freedom of expression may be relevant, but they do not automatically override copyright.

This case is useful because it shows the balance between public debate and copyright protection. A person may discuss, criticise, or report on a matter, but that does not automatically entitle them to reproduce protected material beyond what is fair and necessary.

For this review, the case cuts both ways. It confirms that my use of extracts should remain limited, purposeful, acknowledged, and tied to criticism and review. It also supports the broader principle that another writer cannot simply rely on the importance or controversial nature of a subject as a justification for taking protected material.

This authority supports a careful balance: my review uses extracts for criticism and evidence, while the complaint concerns whether Gary Wayne's use went beyond fair quotation into substantial source-field reliance and hostile recharacterisation.

4. Harper & Row Publishers Inc v Nation Enterprises, 471 U.S. 539 (1985) — taking the "heart" of a work may defeat fair use

In *Harper & Row v Nation Enterprises*, *The Nation* magazine published extracts from President Gerald Ford's unpublished memoir before authorised publication. Although the amount used was not the whole memoir, the United States Supreme Court held that the use was not fair.

A major factor was that the magazine had taken the "heart" of the work and damaged the copyright owner's market for authorised publication. The case is often cited for the principle that even a relatively small taking can be unfair where it captures the most important, valuable, or expressive part of the original work.

This is relevant because copyright analysis is not purely numerical. If a later author takes the central framework, distinctive symbolic chain, or key original material from an earlier author, the fact that the whole book was not copied does not automatically make the use fair.

This authority supports the argument that taking the most distinctive and valuable part of Nicholas de Vere's work — the Dragon/Grail/Vere source-field and its specialised terminology and structure — may be substantial even if the whole book was not copied.

5. Salinger v Random House, 811 F.2d 90 (2d Cir. 1987) — close paraphrase and unpublished material

In *Salinger v Random House*, a biographer used and closely paraphrased unpublished letters written by J.D. Salinger. The court held that the use was not fair. The fact that the letters could be read in a library did not mean they could be freely reproduced or paraphrased in a published biography.

The court was concerned that the letters formed the backbone of the biography and that the biographer had taken protected expression, not merely facts. The case is useful because it shows that infringement can occur through close paraphrase as well as verbatim copying.

This case is relevant where a writer uses another author's protected expression, organisation, structure, or distinctive phrasing, even if some wording has been altered. It also supports the point that public access to material does not make it public domain.

This authority supports the argument that if Nicholas de Vere's material forms the backbone of another author's chapter or argument, the issue is not cured simply because the material was visible online, available in a book, or partially paraphrased.

6. Warner Bros Entertainment Inc v RDR Books, 575 F.Supp.2d 513 (S.D.N.Y. 2008) — reference works and excessive verbatim use

In *Warner Bros v RDR Books*, the publisher of the proposed *Harry Potter Lexicon* argued that its reference work was protected by fair use. The court accepted that the lexicon had some transformative purpose because it organised information from the Harry Potter books into reference form. However, the court held that the use was not fair because it copied too much protected expression from J.K. Rowling's works.

The case is important because it shows that a work can be partly analytical, scholarly, or reference-based and still infringe if it relies too heavily on the protected expression of the original author.

The court treated extensive verbatim use as a serious factor against fair use. The fact that the new work had a different format did not justify taking more than necessary from the original works.

This authority supports the argument that citation, commentary, or reference-style organisation does not automatically make extensive borrowing fair. If Gary Wayne copied distinctive passages or reproduced Nicholas de Vere's specialised framework in a new form, the use may still be infringing.

7. Twin Peaks Productions Inc v Publications International Ltd, 996 F.2d 1366 (2d Cir. 1993) — unauthorised companion works

In *Twin Peaks v Publications International*, the defendant published an unauthorised guide to the television series *Twin Peaks*. The book contained direct quotations, paraphrases, plot summaries, character descriptions, and detailed material from the programme.

The court held that the use was not fair. The amount taken was substantial, and the book affected the copyright owner's potential market for authorised derivative or companion works.

This case is relevant because it shows that a book cannot simply repackage another protected world, structure, storyline, setting, terminology, or distinctive field and claim that it is merely commentary or reference. Where the new work substitutes for or occupies the market for an authorised companion or derivative work, fair use becomes much weaker.

This authority supports the argument that unauthorised use of a distinctive created source-field can interfere with the rights holder's ability to publish, control, or authorise their own companion works, reviews, explanations, and source-field materials.

8. Castle Rock Entertainment Inc v Carol Publishing Group, 150 F.3d 132 (2d Cir. 1998) — derivative-market harm and protected fictional/source worlds

In *Castle Rock v Carol Publishing*, the defendant published a trivia book based on the television series *Seinfeld*. The book drew heavily on the series' events, characters, dialogue, and distinctive details. The court held that the work was not protected by fair use.

The case is useful because the trivia book did not reproduce whole episodes, but it still appropriated protected expressive material from the series. The court was particularly concerned with the copyright owner's right to control derivative markets, including authorised trivia, guides, and companion publications.

This case supports the wider principle that a person cannot build a commercial work from another author's protected universe, terminology, structure, and distinctive material merely because the new work rearranges that material into questions, commentary, or another format.

: This authority supports the argument that Gary Wayne's alleged use of the Dragon/Grail/Vere source-field may affect Dragon Publishing's right to control authorised explanatory, companion, review, and derivative works concerning Nicholas de Vere's material.

9. Religious Technology Centre v Lerma, 40 U.S.P.Q.2d 1569 (E.D. Va. 1996) — fair use is not a licence to reproduce whole works

In *Religious Technology Centre v Lerma*, individuals posted entire Scientology publications online without permission. The court held that this was not fair use.

The key principle is straightforward: fair use may permit limited quotation or excerpting in proper circumstances, but it does not normally permit wholesale reproduction of protected works.

This case is useful in two ways. First, it supports my decision not to reproduce Gary Wayne's whole chapters, but only relevant extracts for criticism and comparison. Secondly, it supports the argument that another author cannot reproduce or build upon substantial protected material and then rely on fair use as a blanket excuse.

: This authority supports the distinction between limited evidential quotation and wholesale reproduction. My review is structured around selected extracts and analysis, not republication of Gary Wayne's book.

10. Hustler Magazine Inc v Moral Majority Inc, 606 F.Supp. 1526 (C.D. Cal. 1985) — copying for direct response and criticism

In *Hustler Magazine v Moral Majority*, Reverend Jerry Falwell copied and distributed a page from *Hustler* magazine that had attacked him. The court found the use to be fair.

The context was important. The copied page was being used as part of a response to the attack, and the copying did not damage the market for the original magazine. The use was not designed to replace the original publication, but to show supporters what had been said and to respond to it.

This case is useful for a review or rebuttal work because it recognises that a person may need to reproduce the specific material being criticised in order to make the criticism intelligible.

: This authority supports the limited reproduction of Gary Wayne extracts where those extracts are necessary to show what was written, how Nicholas de Vere's material was used, and why the use is being challenged.

11. Wright v Warner Books Inc, 953 F.2d 731 (2d Cir. 1991) — limited quotation for biography and information

In *Wright v Warner Books*, a biographer quoted from unpublished letters and journals of Richard Wright. The court held the use to be fair, noting that only a very small portion of the total material had been used and that the purpose was informational.

This case is useful because it shows that quotation can be fair when it is selective, proportionate, and used for a genuine critical, biographical, historical, or informational purpose.

The case also demonstrates the importance of restraint. The more limited and purposeful the quotations are, the stronger the fair-use or fair-dealing position becomes.

: This authority supports the method used in this review: specific extracts are used to evidence the comparison, while the analysis is carried in my own words.

12. Swatch Group Management Services Ltd v Bloomberg LP, 742 F.3d 17 (2d Cir. 2014) — publication of a whole work may be fair only where necessary for the purpose

In *Swatch v Bloomberg*, Bloomberg published a recording and transcript of an earnings call by Swatch. The Second Circuit held that the use was fair, partly because the call contained newsworthy financial information and publication served a reporting purpose.

The case is useful because it shows that, in exceptional circumstances, even the use of an entire work may be fair where the purpose genuinely requires it and there is no meaningful market harm. However, it should not be treated as a general permission to reproduce whole works. The justification depends on necessity, purpose, and market effect.

: This authority supports the principle of necessity: where an extract is needed to prove the point, quotation may be justified. However, this review still avoids reproducing whole chapters where shorter extracts can prove the same issue.

13. Equals Three LLC v Jukin Media Inc, 14-09041 (C.D. Cal. 2015) — commentary may justify necessary use of source material

In *Equals Three v Jukin Media*, a humour and commentary programme used viral video clips and commented on them. The court held that most of the uses were fair because the defendant added jokes, commentary, and new meaning, and used no more of the videos than necessary for that commentary.

This case is useful because it supports the idea that a reviewer may use parts of the work under review where the use is tied directly to criticism, analysis, or commentary. The copied material must serve the new purpose; it must not simply be reposted for its own sake.

This authority supports the use of Gary Wayne extracts where they are immediately followed by analysis showing textual similarity, source reliance, citation displacement, or hostile recharacterisation.[12]

For the legal basis of limited quotation, criticism, review, and evidential comparison, see Copyright, Designs and Patents Act 1988, s.30, which provides for fair dealing for criticism, review, quotation, and news reporting where the work has been made available to the public and sufficient acknowledgement is given; Berne Convention for the Protection of Literary and Artistic Works, Article 10, which permits quotations from works lawfully made available to the public where compatible with fair practice and not exceeding the extent justified by the purpose; and 17 U.S.C. §107, which sets out the U.S. fair use factors, including purpose and character of use, nature of the work, amount used, and effect upon the potential market. See also *Hubbard v Vosper* [1972] 2 QB 84; *Ashdown v Telegraph Group Ltd* [2001] EWCA Civ 1142; and *Harper & Row Publishers Inc v Nation Enterprises* 471 U.S. 539 (1985).

---

[12] Summaries of Fair Use Cases - Copyright Overview by Rich Stim - Stanford Copyright and Fair Use Centre

DMCA Takedown Notice

You can use this takedown notice on Amazon, Google and other platform where your intellectual property is being exploited without your permission.

To: [Platform / Website / Hosting Provider / Designated DMCA Agent]
Email: [Insert email address]
Date: [Insert date]

Subject: DMCA Takedown Notice — Unauthorised Use of Copyrighted Material Belonging to Abbe de Vere / Dragon Publishing / Nicholas de Vere Literary Estate

Dear Copyright Agent,

I am the copyright owner, authorised representative, legal heir, and administrator of the relevant works connected to Nicholas de Vere's literary estate, Dragon Publishing, and the Royal Dragon Court material.

This notice concerns unauthorised use of copyrighted material belonging to, administered by, or controlled by me, including but not limited to material from:

The Dragon Legacy by Nicholas de Vere;
The Dragon Cede by Nicholas de Vere and Michael Hunter;
Royal Dragon Court material;
House of Vere material;
Dragon Publishing editions, s, editorial matter, artwork, titles, emblems, logos, and associated written content.

The infringing material appears at the following location or locations:

[Insert URL 1]
[Insert URL 2]
[Insert URL 3]

The original copyrighted work can be identified as follows:

[Insert title of original work]
[Insert author]
[Insert publication details, website, archive link, ISBN, or other identifying information]
[Insert relevant page numbers, chapter titles, screenshots, or comparison notes if available]

The unauthorised material includes one or more of the following:

copied text;
close paraphrase;
unauthorised reproduction;
unauthorised use of titles;
unauthorised use of logos, emblems, artwork, or branding;
use of protected Dragon Publishing / Royal Dragon Court material;
use of material from Nicholas de Vere's works without permission;
use of my work or my father's work in a way that creates false association, passing off, or misleading brand connection.

I have not authorised this use. Permission has not been granted. The material is not being used with my consent.

I have a good faith belief that the use of the copyrighted material described above is not authorised by the copyright owner, the copyright owner's agent, or the law.

I request that you remove or disable access to the infringing material immediately.

I also request that you confirm in writing when the material has been removed or disabled.

My contact details are:

Name:
Publisher / Rights Holder: Dragon Publishing
Email: [Insert email address]

Address: [Insert address if required by the platform]
Telephone: [Insert telephone number if required by the platform]

I declare, under penalty of perjury, that the information in this notice is accurate and that I am the copyright owner or authorised to act on behalf of the copyright owner.

Signed,

Cease and Desist

The Final Take Down

As we draw to the end of this book, I add my last update to what has been happening to me while I have taken this on, This is my final straw, and message to anyone who thinks that they can take advantage of my work.

It the last few days I have sent a side-by-side comparison to Deep River books, I started this process on the 12th with my realising the extent on the 10th, I insisted on giving 14 days' notice before I would commence acting, That was fair warning for them to remove my content, respond adequately to my copyright enforcement.

Even though the Publisher did not take me seriously, I hoped that the screenshots would have prompted him to act accordingly, Which coming back and saying it was fair use, clearly was not the right steps a professional publisher she take.

We are on the 29th now which exceeds that notice period so today, What I assume is that The Publisher will do nothing, he will not take accountability, and he will continue to try to sell the books,

I took further steps in making formal notice to Amazon, which I will have to go through Barnes and noble and other platforms, In the hope that cutting off the money or gravy train as my father would call it, will prompt them to act. I have also sent out copyright infringements to Doc Brown on his You Tube channel and spoke with him personally to tell him that although he has bought my other books he is not permitted to publish in any format my material, I have since been notified that he had taken it upon himself to do a series on Instagram posts concerning the Royal Dragon Court saying we drink blood, Whilst dressed as a vampire, This proves to me that these sorts of people are mainly performing false prophets. Which is ridiculous behaviour, This is coming from an apparent christian preacher who mainly posts videos about the bible.

I have made several misinformation reports about other channels that Gary Wayne has appeared on, but with over 400 it will be a task that I am not willing to put any more energy into, If I cut off the book, then people have nothing to speak about.. The video infringement notice will come up with my name instead of the content.

This book was only supposed to be a few pages of showing what this man had done, before I knew it, it had turned into 166 pages in 3 days, as the information kept pouring in with the content in Gary Waynes books and the You Tube videos, I realised that I had started to create one of the best case law evidence based manuscripts that would actually assist other either doing copyright law at university or facing their own issues and not knowing how to manage such a huge and daunting task.

I have been very emotional, especially today, Not just because of the endless nights, I have been up until 2 or 3am collect this evidence and writing, being drained from ADHD hyperfocus and inspiration, but also how much I am proud of the legacy my father left behind for me and what I have turned it into.

We are a global family of historians some novices and some very highly intelligent people who enjoy the journey and community within our genealogy group, We love history and learning, Last night I had a fan ask me questions about her genealogy and due to our shared interest I don not say, well this is a paid service, I spent time speaking to her and getting to know her, as I was about to go to bed, I got inspired and ended up messaging her with the links she was not aware of before, the links that would show her that she is related to Scottish ancestry and royalty, and this is what I bring, Love to all if not most that treat me and my community with respect, A safe space for our personal journey and growth, a grounded sense of humanity that does not take advantage, which is why this sort of behaviour from others that have treated me this way bewilders me to why they would attempt to ruin it for the new comers.

I learned 8 years ago not to be anyone's victim and that is why I did the law degree in the first place, Never to allow anyone to posture over me or think that I am an easy target, I have set this boundary and now the precedent for what happens if people attempt to take me on, It's not about money.

It's about pride and dignity and putting the record straight.

Bibliography

Note on Sources and Citation Chain

This review concerns material administered by Abbe de Vere / Dragon Publishing, including works by Nicholas de Vere, *The Dragon Legacy*, *The Dragon Cede*, *The House of Vere*, and works co-authored by Nicholas de Vere and Laurence Gardner. As this review is written from the position of the rights holder, editor, publisher, and literary representative of the Nicholas de Vere / Dragon Publishing material, a full external bibliography is not required for the works owned, edited, or administered within this source-field.

However, Gary Wayne's method requires citation-chain identification, because his work repeatedly routes Nicholas de Vere / Dragon Publishing material through Gary Wayne's own books, Laurence Gardner's work, and related Grail / Ring Lords / Dragon bloodline material.

The relevant chain may be recorded as follows:

Abbe de Vere, review and commentary on Gary Wayne, *The Genesis 6 Conspiracy II*; citing Gary Wayne's use of Laurence Gardner, *Realm of the Ring Lords*; Nicholas de Vere, *The Dragon Legacy*; Nicholas de Vere, *The Dragon Cede*; Abbe de Vere, *From Transylvania to Tunbridge Wells*; and Laurence Gardner, *Genesis of the Grail Kings*, with foreword and/or contribution by Nicholas de Vere.

Updated Chicago-Style Bibliographic Form

De Vere, Abbe. *Cease and Desist: An Unwanted Companion*. Dragon Publishing, 2026.

De Vere, Abbe. *From Transylvania to Tunbridge Wells.* Dragon Publishing, 2000, 2025

De Vere, Nicholas. *The Dragon Cede.* The Book Tree 2006, 2012 Edited and/or published by Abbe de Vere. Dragon Publishing, 2026

De Vere, Nicholas. *The Dragon Legacy.* The Book Tree. 2004 Edited and/or published by Abbe de Vere. Dragon Publishing, 2026

Gardner, Laurence. *Genesis of the Grail Kings: The Explosive Story of Genetic Cloning and the Ancient Bloodline of Jesus.* Foreword and/or contribution by Nicholas de Vere. London: Bantam Press, 1999.

Gardner, Laurence. *Realm of the Ring Lords: The Myth and Magic of the Grail Quest.* London: Element, 1995, 2000.

Wayne, Gary. *The Genesis 6 Conspiracy II.* Deep River Books: 2023.

Chicago-Style Footnotes

1. Abbe de Vere, *Cease and Desist: An Unwanted Companion* (Dragon Publishing, 2026),

2. Gary Wayne, *The Genesis 6 Conspiracy II* Copyright © 2023 by Gary Wayne Published by Deep River Books Sisters, Oregon www.deepriverbooks.com All rights reserved. No part of this book may be reproduced or transmitted in any form or by any means, electronic or mechanical, including photocopying and recording, or by any information storage and retrieval system, without permission in writing from the publisher. (but apparently its ok for them to do it)

3. Laurence Gardner, *Realm of the Ring Lords: The Myth and Magic of the Grail Quest* (London: Element, 2000), whole book

4. Nicholas de Vere, *The Dragon Legacy*, ed. and/or pub. Abbe de Vere (Dragon Publishing, [2004, 2026], whole book

5. Nicholas de Vere, *The Dragon Cede*, ed. and/or pub. Abbe de Vere (Dragon Publishing, [2006, 2012, 2026], whole book

6. Abbe de Vere, *From Transylvania to Tunbridge Wells* (Dragon Publishing, [2026] whole book

7. Laurence Gardner, *Genesis of the Grail Kings: The Explosive Story of Genetic Cloning and the Ancient Bloodline of Jesus*, foreword and/or contribution by Nicholas de Vere (London: Bantam Press, 1999).

8. Copyright protection for original literary works arises under the Copyright, Designs and Patents Act 1988, including ss.1, 3, 16 and 17, which recognise copyright in literary works and the restricted acts of copying, issuing copies, communicating the work to the public, and reproduction. Limited quotation for criticism, review, and quotation is addressed under s.30 of the same Act. International protection is also recognised under the Berne Convention for the Protection of Literary and Artistic Works, including Article 5, which provides protection without formalities, and Article 10, which permits quotation only where compatible with fair practice and justified by purpose. See Copyright, Designs and Patents Act 1988, ss.1, 3, 16, 17 and 30; Berne Convention for the Protection of Literary and Artistic Works, Arts. 5 and 10.

9. Copyright, Designs and Patents Act 1988

10. https://www.gov.uk/guidance/protecting-your-copyright-abroad

11. Summaries of Fair Use Cases - Copyright Overview by Rich Stim - Stanford Copyright and Fair Use Centre

SEE BIBLIOGRAPHY FOR FULL CITATION: NICHOLAS DE VERE AMENDMENTS

Cleaned, ordered and de-duplicated source list.

1. VERE AND COLLISON PRIMARY GENEALOGICAL SOURCES
2. Classical Sources
3. Sumerian Anunnaki King Lists – Library of Nineveh, northern Iraq, and the Library of King Nebuchadnezzar of Babylon.
4. Egyptian Kings Lists, by Dr. David Rohl.
5. Egyptian Hyksos King Lists by the dynastic priest and historian Manetho of Egypt.
6. Scythian Mittani King Lists for Syria, researched and collated for the House of Vere by Sir Laurence Gardner.
7. Scythian martial custom and practice, Herodotus, c. 400 BC.
8. Scythian Pictish King Lists for Scotland and France, researched and collated for the House of Vere by Sir Laurence Gardner.
9. Historia Britonum, Nennius, c. 800 AD.
10. Medieval Scottish Manuscripts
11. Bain I, 174.
12. Panmure II, 126.
13. Colne Priory MSS.
14. Kelso Abbey MSS.
15. Paisley Abbey MSS.
16. Arbroath Abbey MSS.
17. Charter "De Decimus Episcopatus," 1100 AD, Moray.
18. Medieval and Post-Reformation Sources
19. Family Archives of the House of Vere of Oxford, Lanark, Fermanagh and Clare.
20. Collison Royal Genealogies, House of Vere, Co. Clare, Ireland.
21. The Plantagenet Chronicles, Thomas de Loche (1130) and Jean de Mortimer (1164–1173).
22. Transcript of the trial of Major Thomas Weir, Edinburgh, 10 April 1670, House of Vere.
23. Sir Randolph Crew's summary – House of Lords Archives.
24. Roll of Arms of the Lord Lyon King of Arms of Scotland, Lyon Court, Edinburgh, Scotland.

25. Arden, St. George and Glover Rolls of Arms, College of Arms, London, England.

26. Victorian Government Documents
27. Parish Records and Census Returns for County Tyrone – Public Records Office, Belfast, Northern Ireland.
28. Griffith's Valuations for Tyrone – Public Records Office, Belfast, Northern Ireland.
29. Parish Tithe Records for County Tyrone – Public Records Office, Belfast, Northern Ireland.

30. Post-Great War Government Documents
31. Parish Records and Census Returns for Wigtonshire – Scottish Records Office, New Register House, Edinburgh, Scotland.

32. Post-Second World War Government Documents
33. Registry for Births, Marriages and Deaths for Cumbria, Kent, East Sussex, Hertfordshire and West Sussex – St. Catharine's House Records, Preston, Lancashire, England.

34. Official Government Documentary Proofs of Identity and Title
35. British Government Home Office Identity and Passport Agency.
36. Government Register of Electors for West Sussex and Carmarthenshire up to 2009.
37. Department for Work and Pensions, National Insurance Identity Division.
38. Department of Transport, Licensing and Identity Agency.
39. European Union Health Services Department, Medical Identity Card Division.
40. Republic of Ireland Financial Services Department, Identity Card Division.
41. Department of Genetics and Hematology, London University, U.K.
42. Home Office Policy Review Committee, Whitehall, London, England.

43. SECONDARY SOURCES FOR GENEALOGIES
44. Histories of England – Baron Thomas Babington Macaulay, Lord Macaulay of Rothley Temple (1800–1859). Politician and historian. Educated at Trinity College, Cambridge, he became one of the acknowledged intellectual pundits of his age. He entered the Supreme Council for India in 1834, where his famous Minutes on Law and Education had a decisive influence on the development of the sub-continent. He was Secretary-at-War, 1839–1841, and went on to write his acclaimed, best-selling Histories of England between 1849 and 1855. "He used a wide range of manuscript sources with great skill, and modern historians neglect his reconstruction of events at their peril": Margaret Drabble CBE, Morley College.
45. The Dictionary of National Biography – designed and published by George Smith (1824–1901). The Dictionary was first published in 1882 with Sir Leslie Stephen (1832–1904) as editor. The DNB in its original form included biographies of national notabilities from the earliest time to 1900. The work continued through decennial supplements. Stephen was succeeded as editor by Sir Sydney Lee, and their names appear jointly on the title pages of volumes XXII to XXVI (1890). In 1917 the Dictionary was transferred to Oxford University.
46. Myths of the Middle Ages – Reverend Father Sabine Baring-Gould, Lord of Lew Trenchard, Devon (1834–1924). Baring-Gould travelled the Continent extensively and was educated at Clare College, Cambridge. An antiquarian and folklorist, Baring-Gould was a prolific writer and the author of numerous works including Mehalah, which Swinburne compared to Wuthering Heights.
47. Burke's Peerage – properly A Genealogical and Heraldic History of the Peerage and Baronetage of the United Kingdom, first compiled by John Burke in 1826 and published annually after 1947.
48. Burke's Irish Landed Gentry – published 1897.

49. The Itinerary – Reverend John Leland (1503–1552). "The earliest of modern antiquaries," Leland was educated at St. Paul's School and Christ's College, Cambridge. He studied in Paris, took holy orders, and by 1530 was involved with the Royal Libraries. From 1533 he received a commission from King Henry VIII to search the monastic and collegiate libraries for old authors. He made a tour through England between 1535 and 1543, intending his research to form the basis of an opus magna on the Histories and Antiquities of the Nation. His notes were first published at Oxford University by the historian Thomas Hearne (1678–1735) as The Itinerary in nine volumes in 1710–1712. Lucy Toulmin Smith produced an edition of The Itinerary in 1906–1910, noting that the descent of Vere was included as an extract from Folio 42 of the original work, formerly preserved in Stow's original collection.
50. Stow MSS – John Stow (1525–1605). A collection of manuscripts first collated in 1564. Stow transcribed manuscripts and was the first person to compose historical works based on a systematic study of Public Records. He assisted Parker with editing historical texts, and his chief publications were The Workes of Geoffrey Chaucer (1561), Summary of English Chronicles (1565), The Chronicles of England (1580), and A Survey of London. An edition of the collection was published by Strype in 1720, and the fullest edition of the original work was C. L. Kingsford's, published in 1908.
51. Complete Peerage of England, Scotland, Ireland, Great Britain and the United Kingdom, Extant, Extinct or Dormant – George Edward Cokayne MA, born in Russell Square, London in 1825, son of Dr. William Adams LLD and The Hon. Mary Anne Cokayne, niece and co-heiress of Borlase, 6th Viscount Cullen. Complying with his mother's wishes, Cokayne changed his name by royal license on 15 August 1873. Cokayne was educated at Exeter College, Oxford; Barrister, Lincoln's Inn

(1853); Rouge Dragon Pursuivant-of-Arms (1859–1870); Lancaster Herald (1870–1882); Norroy King-of-Arms (1882–1894); Clarenceux King of Arms from 1894. His Complete Peerage of the United Kingdom in eight volumes was compiled between 1887 and 1898 and published by George Bell. Holding Library: Trinity College Dublin.

52. Royal Genealogies; or The Genealogical Tables of Emperors, Kings and Princes from Adam to These Times – Dr. James Anderson DD, MA (1680–1739). Anderson was born and educated in Aberdeen. He was appointed Presbyterian Minister for Swallow Street and Lisle Street, Leicester Fields, London, between 1710 and 1734. Described as "a learned man," Anderson, who was a Freemason, was assigned the task in 1721 of compiling an authoritative digest of the Constitutions of the fraternity (see Entick's edition of 1747, p. 194 et seq.). As Grand Warden of the Grand Lodge in London, he presented his work to the Order in 1723. It appeared in numerous subsequent editions and has long been recognised by English Freemasons as the standard code on its subject. Editions were translated into German and appeared in America in 1855 as facsimiles of the earlier English version. The work by which Anderson is chiefly remembered, Royal Genealogies, was first published in two volumes in London in 1732. Anderson based this work on the earlier Genealogische Tabellen of Johann Hübner. The later tables of the Genealogies were considered by Sir Leslie Stephen in the Dictionary of National Biography "to be of use" in relation to the genealogies of continental dynasties and houses. Royal Genealogies: Holding Library, Cambridge University.

53. Genealogische Tabellen – Johann Hübner. Properly: Der Genealogische Tabellen zur erlauterung der politische historie vom anfange biss auf diesen tag continuiret, published in one volume, Leipzig, 1719. Holding Library: Glasgow.

54. The Collections – Sir James Dalrymple. Collections concerning the Scottish History, preceeding the death of King David the First, in the year 1153. Wherein the sovereignty of the crown and independency of the church are cleared; and account given of the antiquity and purity of the Scottish British church, and the novelty of popery in this kingdom. With an appendix containing copies of charters of foundation of some churches; with genealogical accounts of the donors and witnesses. First published in Edinburgh in 1705 by the heirs and successors of Andrew Anderson; sold by John Vallange and Mrs. Ogstoun. Holding Library: Durham.
55. The Surnames of Scotland: Their Origin, Meaning, and History – Dr. George Fraser Black. Published in New York in 1946: The New York Public Library. Holding Libraries: Cambridge, Edinburgh, Leeds, Liverpool, Nottingham, SAS, Sheffield.
56. The Scottish Hazard – Beryl Platts. British Library.
57. The Bloodline of the Holy Grail – Sir Laurence Gardner. Element Books, 1997.
58. Genesis of the Grail Kings – Sir Laurence Gardner. Bantam Press, 1999.
59. The True Elves of Europe – essay by Leonid Korablev.
60. God of the Witches – Professor Margaret Murray. Rider & Co.
61. The Witch-Cult in Western Europe – Professor Margaret Murray. Rider & Co.
62. The Veres of Hedingham Castle – Verily Anderson.
63. The Madness of Kings – Professor Vivian Green.
64. Lady Pembrokeshire's Genealogies – Reference Section, City of Brighton Library.
65. Jesus: Last of the Pharaohs – Ralph Ellis. The Egyptian descent of Jesus Christ.
66. The Secret Gospel of Mark – Professor Morton Smith.
67. Christine Bonnet, Lusignan.
68. Professor Vivien Greene / Vivian Green, citations within text, The Dragon Cede, Nicholas de Vere.

69. Nicholas de Vere, The House of Vere: References.
70. Nicholas de Vere, The Duchy of Angiers.
71. Nicholas de Vere, Vere of Blackwood.
72. Nicholas de Vere, The Dragon Cede, published by The Book Tree.
73. ADDITIONAL FOOTNOTES AND HOUSE OF VERE REFERENCE NOTES
74. **For certain information regarding the House of Vere and footnotes within Nicholas de Vere's other PDFs, please see:** Footnotes for Nicholas de Vere House of Vere papers. For all other footnotes, refer to The Dragon Legacy and The Dragon Cede. Other footnotes and citations have been provided within the book on each page where required.
75. (a) Item in comite Alberico Alberici comitis de Ver filio, simile naturae miraculum vidimus. Cum enim pater ejusdem, matre jam Praegnante, filia scilicet Henrici de Essexia, ob ignominiosum patris eventum jam ad divortium modis omni elaborasset, partu prodeunte; quem pater in oculo casuali laesione sustinuit, eadem parte defectus in filio parentavit. Giraldus Cambrensis, op. cit., p. 132. Albericus Comes Oxeneford. "His testibus Alberico filio meo et Herede et Roberto Henrico Filiis meis." Colne Cart., no. 42.
76. (b) There is no proof that his parents did not cohabit between 1163 and 1172; for his mother's age, cf. p. 206, note "e."
77. (c) "His Testibus Alberico filio meo Radulpho de Ver. Radulpho magistro Alberici." Colne Cart., no. 38; cf. idem, no. 45. That Aubrey had a master proves that he was a boy at the time.
78. (1) His affiliation is proved by his attestations to four of his father's charters at Colne, e.g. "His testibus Albrico filio meo et Roberto fratre ejus." Colne Q, no. 46. He has always been described as the second son, but in the three charters for Colne

Priory which are witnessed both by Robert and by his brother Ralph, his name precedes Robert's. Idem, nos. 36, 41, 85.

79. (a) On the assumption that Robert was the third son; after 1172 if his parents did not resume cohabitation before 1171. He seems to have been with his brother Aubrey in Normandy in August 1197. Landon, op. cit., pp. 120–121. See Source Profile.

NOTICE, DISCLAIMER, AND RESERVATION OF RIGHTS

This work, *Cease and Desist: An Unwanted Companion*, is an independent intellectual, genealogical, and anthropological critique. All analysis, reviews, and evaluations of contemporary authors, podcasters, and public theories, including but not limited to the published works of Gary Wayne, are presented under the principles of fair dealing, fair use, fair comment, criticism, review, quotation, scholarly reference, and academic cross-examination.

The contents of this book are intended for educational, evidential, legal, scholarly, and research purposes. The Author assumes no liability for the misinterpretation, distortion, or hostile misuse of this data by readers, critics, commentators, or third parties operating outside verified scientific, genealogical, historical, or legal frameworks.

Copyright Acknowledgements

Every reasonable effort has been made to identify and acknowledge the copyright holders of quoted material, cited material, images, extracts, and referenced works. Ancient and pre-1900 sources are treated as public-domain material where applicable. Modern extracts are reproduced only where necessary for fair dealing, fair use, quotation, criticism, review, scholarly reference, evidential comparison, provenance analysis, and formal response.

This work has been prepared by Abbe de Vere, rights holder, editor, publisher, and literary representative of the Nicholas de Vere / Dragon Publishing material under review. The purpose of this book is to examine and critique the use, treatment, representation, citation-chain reliance, and public recharacterisation of material connected to my owned and administered works, including *The Dragon Legacy*, *The Dragon Cede*, the House of Vere material, and the wider Royal Dragon Court / Dragon Publishing source-field.

Any third-party extracts are included only to the extent necessary to demonstrate citation-chain reliance, textual similarity, framework use, source-field dependency, hostile recharacterisation, reputational harm, evidential context, or other matters relevant to this review. If any unintentional omission, typographical error, or attribution issue has occurred, rights holders are invited to contact Dragon Publishing so that appropriate acknowledgement, correction, or review can be considered for future editions.

This book has been prepared in response to correspondence from the publisher requesting specific examples of the passages, quotations,

www.ingramcontent.com/pod-product-compliance
Lightning Source LLC
LaVergne TN
LVHW041206061126
851857LV00018B/1953
* 9 7 8 1 9 1 8 5 8 8 9 8 9 *